Lecture Notes of the Institute for Computer Sciences, Social Informatics and Telecommunications Engineering 497

The LNICST series publishes ICST's conferences, symposia and workshops.

LNICST reports state-of-the-art results in areas related to the scope of the Institute. The type of material published includes

- Proceedings (published in time for the respective event)
- Other edited monographs (such as project reports or invited volumes)

LNICST topics span the following areas:

- General Computer Science
- E-Economy
- E-Medicine
- Knowledge Management
- Multimedia
- Operations, Management and Policy
- Social Informatics
- Systems

Der-Jiunn Deng · Han-Chieh Chao ·
Jyh-Cheng Chen
Editors

Smart Grid and Internet of Things

6th EAI International Conference, SGIoT 2022
TaiChung, Taiwan, November 19–20, 2022
Proceedings

 Springer

Editors
Der-Jiunn Deng
National Changhua University of Education
Changhua City, Taiwan

Han-Chieh Chao
National Dong Hwa University
Hualien City, Taiwan

Jyh-Cheng Chen
National Yang Ming Chiao Tung University
Hsinchu, Taiwan

ISSN 1867-8211 ISSN 1867-822X (electronic)
Lecture Notes of the Institute for Computer Sciences, Social Informatics
and Telecommunications Engineering
ISBN 978-3-031-31274-8 ISBN 978-3-031-31275-5 (eBook)
https://doi.org/10.1007/978-3-031-31275-5

This Springer imprint is published by the registered company Springer Nature Switzerland AG
The registered company address is: Gewerbestrasse 11, 6330 Cham, Switzerland

Preface

We are delighted to introduce the proceedings of the 6th edition of the European Alliance for Innovation (EAI) International Conference on Smart Grid and Internet of Things (SGIoT 2022). This year, it took place at the Windsor Hotel, Taichung, Taiwan during November 19–20, 2022. This conference provides an opportunity to connect with researchers, developers, and practitioners from around the world to discuss recent findings in the area of the emerging Smart Grid and Internet of Things. The technical program of SGIoT 2022 consisted of 33 full papers in oral presentation sessions at the main conference tracks.

These technical papers cover a broad range of topics in wireless sensors, vehicular ad hoc networks, security, deep learning, and big data. Aside from the high-quality technical paper presentations, the technical program also featured a keynote speech. The keynote speech was entitled "Cross-Disciplinary Application of AIoT," by Han-Chieh Chao, from National Dong Hwa University, Taiwan. Prof. Chao currently serves as president of National Dong Hwa University, Taiwan and has also been the Director of the Computer Center for the Ministry of Education, Taiwan from September 2008 to July 2010. He has authored or co-authored 4 books and has published about 400 refereed professional research papers. He serves as the Editor-in-Chief for the Institution of Engineering and Technology Networks, the Journal of Internet Technology, the International Journal of Internet Protocol Technology, and the International Journal of Ad Hoc and Ubiquitous Computing. He is a Fellow of IET (IEE) and a Chartered Fellow of the British Computer Society. Professor. Chao has been ranked as one of the top 10 Computer Scientists in Taiwan for 2020 by Guide2Research.

Coordination with the steering chair, Imrich Chlamtac was essential for the success of the conference. We sincerely appreciate his constant support and guidance. It was also a great pleasure to work with such an excellent organizing committee team for their hard work in organizing and supporting the conference. In particular, the Technical Program Committee, led by our Chairs Der-Jiunn Deng, Han-Chieh Chao, and Jyh-Cheng Chen completed the peer-review process of technical papers and made a high-quality technical program. We are also grateful to Conference Manager, Veronika Kissova, for her support and to all the authors who submitted their papers to the SGIoT 2022 conference.

We strongly believe that the SGIoT conference provides a good forum for all researchers, developers and practitioners to discuss all science and technology aspects that are relevant to smart grids and Internet of Things. We also expect that the future SGIoT conferences will be as successful and stimulating, as indicated by the contributions presented in this volume.

Der-Jiunn Deng
Han-Chieh Chao
Jyh-Cheng Chen

Organization

Steering Committee

Imrich Chlamtac — Bruno Kessler Professor, University of Trento, Italy

Al-Sakib Khan Pathan — Independent University, Bangladesh

Der-Jiunn Deng — National Changhua University of Education, Taiwan

Organizing Committee

Honorary Chair

Pao-Tao Chen — Overseas Chinese University, Taiwan

General Chairs

Der-Jiunn Deng — National Changhua University of Education, Taiwan

Han-Chieh Chao — National Dong Hwa University, Taiwan

Jyh-Cheng Chen — National Yang Ming Chiao Tung University, Taiwan

TPC Chair and Co-chairs

Chun-Cheng Lin — National Yang Ming Chiao Tung University, Taiwan

Lun-Ping Hung — National Taipei University of Nursing and Health Sciences

Chien-Liang Chen — Overseas Chinese University, Taiwan

Sponsorship and Exhibit Chair

Hui Hsin Chin — Overseas Chinese University, Taiwan

Local Chair

Rung-Shiang Cheng   Overseas Chinese University, Taiwan

Workshops Chair

Jun-Li Lu   University of Tsukuba, Japan

Publicity & Social Media Chair

Hsiang-Yun Wu   TU Wien Informatics , Austria

Publications Chair

Yu-Liang Liu   Overseas Chinese University, Taiwan

Web Chair

Chien-Liang Chen   Overseas Chinese University, Taiwan

Technical Program Committee

Chun-Cheng Lin	National Yang Ming Chiao Tung University
Rung-Shiang Cheng	Overseas Chinese University
Yu-Liang Liu	Overseas Chinese University
Chang Li Wei	Overseas Chinese University
Hung-Chang Chan	Overseas Chinese University
Hui Hsin Chin	Overseas Chinese University
Jen-En Huang	Overseas Chinese University
Chao-Tung Yang	Tunghai University
Hai-Yan Kang	Beijing Information Science and Technology University
Lun-Ping Hung	National Taipei University of Nursing and Health Sciences
Chia-Ling Ho	National Taipei University of Nursing and Health Sciences
Fang-Chang Kuo	National Ilan University

Shun-Chieh Chang	Department of Business Administration, Shih Hsin University
Chih-Kun Ke	National Taichung University of Science and Technology
Mei-Yu Wu	National Taichung University of Science and Technology
Mao Yang	School of Electronics and Information, Northwestern Polytechnical University
Chih-Peng Li	National Sun Yat-Sen University
Xie Shen	Jimei University
Ching-Sheng Wang	Aletheia University
Ding-Jung Chiang	Taipei Chengshih University of Science and Technology
Aravind Kailas	University Of North Carolina Charlotte in Charlotte
Chih-Cheng Tseng	National Ilan University
Chih-Lin Hu	National Central University
Chih-Lun Chou	Ming Chuan University
Chih-Yang Kao	Ming Chuan University
Fangyuan Chi	University of British Columbia
Haw-Yun Shin	National Taiwan Ocean University
Ilsun You	Soonchunhyang University

Contents

Protocol, Algorithm, Services and Applications

IoT, Communication Security, Data Mining or Big Data

Research on Information Platform of University Performance Appraisal Based on Big Data Collection Based on Internet of Things Technology

Shuo Huang[✉]

Capital University of Economics and Business, 121 Zhangjia Road, Huaxiang, Fengtai District, Beijing, China
13581977822@163.com

Abstract. In recent years, with the continuous advancement of the information construction process, the construction of a college information platform based on the smart campus has attracted people's attention. At the same time, the rapid expansion of the demand for university resources also brings people's vision to the performance of higher education. Big data collection based on Internet of Things technology is widely adopted by high-tech enterprises and applied to information platforms. Besides, it also provides new ideas for colleges and universities education development and talent training. This paper puts forward the idea of using big data collection based on Internet of Things technology to build an information platform for university performance assessment. Therefore, encourage teachers to increase their enthusiasm for scientific research, drive the continuous growth of university employees, and provide technical support for the realization of a more scientific and effective performance management mode. To promote the sustainable development of college education and teachers.

Keywords: Internet of Things · big data · performance appraisal · colleges and universities · information platform

1 Introduction

Most of the year 2022 has passed. The Research on China's Digital Human Resources Report pointed out that under the background of the normalized epidemic situation, the flow of human resources is severely limited and the available human resources are insufficient. Therefore, throughout the country, the enterprise management tool HR Software as a Service (SaaS) industry is developing rapidly [1].

At the same time, the staff structure of colleges and universities is changing. In recent years, Generation Z and Millennials have started to work in colleges and universities. Their career preferences and work patterns are different from those of older employees. Colleges and universities need to find new ways to improve employee engagement.

© ICST Institute for Computer Sciences, Social Informatics and Telecommunications Engineering 2023
Published by Springer Nature Switzerland AG 2023. All Rights Reserved
D.-J. Deng et al. (Eds.): SGIoT 2022, LNICST 497, pp. 3–19, 2023.
https://doi.org/10.1007/978-3-031-31275-5_1

Therefore, in addition to enterprises and other social institutions, universities and other traditional institutions have an urgent need for digital human resources services.

This paper aims to create a performance management assessment platform based on the SaaS system design concept combined with big data and Internet of Things technology to meet the performance indicators and university performance [2]. On the other hand, overlay other information systems of colleges and universities to improve the efficiency of daily tasks such as school teaching. Finally, more vitality will be injected into colleges and universities to enhance cohesion.

2 Text

2.1 Demand Analysis

Before the design of the performance appraisal system, this paper first analyzes the needs of its customers.

We know that this system is for all staff in colleges and universities, so I will analyze customer needs from three levels, namely, college leaders, college teachers, and staff in the Personnel Department.

University leaders: can manage the information of all teachers at different levels, which is easy to find and manage. You have permission to view the performance appraisal progress interface for strategic planning. College teachers: can protect personal privacy. A timely reminder of performance appraisal time and requirements.

The staff of the HR Department: able to make absolute analysis and form HR grades. Performance objective: maximize the satisfaction of employers, strengthen the scientific research level of universities, and ensure the teaching quality of universities [3].

Big data technology refers to the large amount of data that cannot be analyzed and processed by mainstream software within a reasonable time. However, this is not only about a large amount of data, but also includes the process of effective professional processing under this huge amount of data to realize the value-added process of data [3]. In the process of specialized processing of large amounts of data, it also means that instead of using software analysis in the traditional sense, we are using a more innovative way - using cloud computing distributed processing, distributed database and cloud storage, virtualization technology, which can not only speed up computing but also reduce costs. Cloud computing technology is a new type of computer network technology and a landmark product of the continuous development of the information age [4]. The emergence of cloud computing has opened a new chapter for human development, which means that we have entered the era of big data. The essence of cloud computing is to integrate low-cost computing systems into a computing system with strong computing power through the network, because big data technology can process a large number of complex data [5], we can use structured data, semi-structured data, and even unstructured data collected about college teachers, to improve the quantitative accuracy and effectiveness of college teachers.

The Internet of Things refers to the collection of real object information in real-time through information sensors, global positioning systems, infrared sensors, and other equipment, and then the transmission of this information to the Internet to achieve the connection between things and people, so that any entity in life can be connected to the Internet, to achieve integrated intelligent management [6].

As the implementation of the Internet of Things will generate a large amount of data, in the process of analyzing a large amount of data, big data technology is required to provide support, and the two complement each other. The IoT system is divided into three layers, namely the perception layer, the network layer, and the application layer. The perception layer of the Internet of Things is responsible for using devices to perceive and detect the situation of entities in various dimensions [7]. The network layer is responsible for acquiring and transmitting the information observed by devices in the perception layer. The application layer is responsible for the connection between the Internet of Things and users. The specific support of big data technology for the Internet of Things is mainly reflected in the perception layer and the network layer.

System design principles: Before designing the system, the following principles should be met. Systematicity: ensure the consistency and integrity of the system. Flexibility; The system can flexibly adapt to the external environment, and various parameters can be transferred to each other to meet the changing performance appraisal needs [8]. Flexible integration with other systems. Ease of operation: considering the future development of computer technology and the user, the system shall be designed with a modular structure. The independence of modules is strong, and the increase, decrease or modification of modules has little impact on the whole system, which is convenient for the improvement and expansion of the system so that the system is in the process of continuous improvement and is conducive to the expansion and improvement of the system. Reliability: The system should have the ability to resist external interference and strong self-recovery ability. The system shall ensure the accuracy and reliability of data. Advanced and mature technology is adopted, which conforms to the specification. Economy: Based on meeting system requirements, minimize system overhead.

2.2 Assessment Process

Performance plan: including annual performance target, monthly performance target, performance target of each department, and individual performance target. Next, I will discuss the annual performance target and individual performance target in detail.

Annual performance target:

The purpose of setting up an efficient, fair, and reasonable annual performance target is to improve the school running level, improve the office efficiency and make the university famous. The design performance objectives need to meet the 'SMART' principle [9].

S (Strategic): performance objectives should be consistent with the organizational strategy. The performance target comes from the organizational strategy at first and must be subordinated to the organizational strategy at the same time.

M (measurable): Determine the number and time of performance objectives. Whether and to what extent the performance objectives are achieved must-have criteria and measurement methods that can be accurately determined, easy to measure, and not easily disputed.

Acceptable: Challenging and motivating. The setting of performance objectives should be aggressive, with growth breakthroughs, and reflect the competitive consciousness of surpassing rivals and self, which is an inevitable requirement of modern commercial society.

R (realistic) Realistic and feasible: the goal should not be set too high. It should be modest or it will lead to confusion. At the same time, it should also be challenging to improve the ability level of colleges and universities [10]. Finally, 10% of the people feel pressured, 10% of the people can play more potential to over fulfill the task, and the remaining 80% of the people can complete the task after hard work.

T (timetable) Time-limited: defines the time range of different goals.

Individual performance objectives:

The overall performance appraisal scheme covers managers and faculty groups but will focus on faculty performance appraisal. The system will focus on the characteristics of college teaching, ensure that the scientific research task will not be too heavy to affect the teaching task, and appropriately reduce the burden of college teachers when implementing the personal performance goals of college teachers. The number of scientific research papers is more important than the number.

At the same time, we should pay attention to the construction of teachers' values, and strive to create an example of teachers who are active, enterprising, dedicated, and diligent. For examiners, testing teachers' values is a long-term task, which needs to be implemented in daily life, to ensure that teachers can fully implement the profound connotation of core values.

Establish perfect performance appraisal standards.

Summarize and manage human resource information through big data technology, collect users' evaluation of the performance platform in real-time, and technicians regularly form feedback on the evaluation to repair system loopholes.

The assessment criteria embody several principles:

Transparency principle: everyone can find the appraisal criteria, appraisal process, and appraisal time on the platform. Objective principle: use a big data system to input data throughout the process to prevent omission. Conduct pre-examination training for examiners to improve relevant professional qualifications. Statistics shall be timely and accurate. Communication principle: use sensing technology to strengthen the connection between examiners and examinees. The principle of comprehensiveness: teachers work hard.

First, the school needs to set performance appraisal indicators:

Definition of relevant concepts:

KPI: a key result indicator that can be expressed by quota or ratio. At present, KPI is also widely used in the performance appraisal of colleges and universities, which can guide college teachers to complete teaching and research tasks with high quality and perfect teaching objectives. However, as a result-oriented indicator, KPI will guide teachers to focus on short-term results too much and ignore long-term changes and processes. Therefore, we will combine gs indicators with KPI indicators for comprehensive consideration.

GS: a phased indicator that is difficult to quantify. It refers to the completion of major work that is relatively long-term and has no direct control over the operating results.

The performance appraisal should focus on the process of self-examination of employees. Teachers should position their level in colleges, departments, and schools through horizontal comparison of teaching quality and self-evaluation of the quantity and quality of scientific research achievements. Teachers can judge whether they have made progress in all aspects, what is room for improvement, and simply judge the recent work status by viewing the longitudinal comparison of previous years' performance. In addition, employees need to listen to others' opinions to improve themselves. In the KPI and gs indicators of performance appraisal, there will be leaders' evaluation, colleagues' evaluation, parents' evaluation, students' evaluation of teaching, and other sectors. The experience of the latter two mainly reflects teachers' education level and ethics, which has high reference value.

The indicators are set by the 80/20 principle, adhering to the concept of "fewer but better" in terms of quantity, which is convenient for college employees to focus on their work and improve their work concentration within a certain period.

The establishment process of KPI and gs indicators is very complicated, but each step is indispensable. Therefore, good communication and discussion must be conducted before the establishment. All people involved in the assessment should participate in the meeting to modify the performance assessment rules.

In performance appraisal, weight setting is often very important, and reasonable weight setting can strengthen the rationality and fairness of performance appraisal. Therefore, for the in-service employees in different departments of colleges and universities, KPI indicators and gs indicators have different weights, which also have many considerations. The following three parts of the school are randomly selected for illustration:

Financial Management Department: KPI index accounts for 50%, gs index accounts for 50%. The members of the Financial Management Department will judge the performance level through the utilization rate of financial expenditure in the school, so the KPI accounts for a large proportion.

Top management: KPI index accounts for 80%, gs index accounts for 20%. For senior leaders, the purpose of performance appraisal is to assess their management philosophy and management level. The management level is mainly measured by quantitative indicators such as the completion of subordinate tasks, the quality change of students in a certain period measured by authority, and the performance report of each department in the university. Therefore, the KPI index accounts for a large proportion.

College teachers: KPI index accounts for 20%, gs index accounts for 80%. Only after strict layer upon layer screening can college teachers successfully enter the post. So they have strong professional ethics and a sense of responsibility and can meet the teaching workload on time. Similarly, most of their KPI indicators are difficult to open the gap. On the other hand, the reference significance of qualitative indicators is extraordinary. From the evaluation of others, we can observe the teacher's teaching level, performance ability, personal accomplishment, and other aspects. It is a very good assessment method, so it accounts for a large proportion.

Formation and determination of scoring principles for assessment results:

Set goals, and give a total score of five points. Three points will be given if the task is just completed. Then add up according to a certain model, and five points will be considered excellent.

Personal performance rating: I take work performance (KCL) and comprehensive quality (KPI+GS) as the horizontal axis and vertical axis of the coordinate system respectively to form a rating classification, as shown in Fig. 1 below:

Performance plan: including annual performance target, monthly performance target, performance target of each department, and individual performance target. Next, I will discuss the annual performance target and individual performance target in detail.

Annual performance target:

The purpose of setting up an efficient, fair, and reasonable annual performance target is to improve the school running level, improve the office efficiency and make the university famous. The design performance objectives need to meet the 'SMART' principle.

S (Strategic): performance objectives should be consistent with the organizational strategy. The performance target comes from the organizational strategy at first and must be subordinated to the organizational strategy at the same time.

M (measurable): Determine the number and time of performance objectives. Whether and to what extent the performance objectives are achieved must-have criteria and measurement methods that can be accurately determined, easy to measure, and not easily disputed.

Acceptable: Challenging and motivating. The setting of performance objectives should be aggressive, with growth breakthroughs, and reflect the competitive consciousness of surpassing rivals and self, which is an inevitable requirement of modern commercial society.

R (realistic) Realistic and feasible: the goal should not be set too high. It should be modest or it will lead to confusion. At the same time, it should also be challenging to improve the ability level of colleges and universities. Finally, 10% of the people feel pressured, 10% of the people can play more potential to overfulfil the task, and the remaining 80% of the people can complete the task after hard work.

T (timetable) Time-limited: defines the time range of different goals.

Individual performance objectives:

The overall performance appraisal scheme covers managers and faculty groups but will focus on faculty performance appraisal. The system will focus on the characteristics of college teaching, ensure that the scientific research task will not be too heavy to affect the teaching task, and appropriately reduce the burden of college teachers when implementing the personal performance goals of college teachers. The number of scientific research papers is more important than the number.

At the same time, we should pay attention to the construction of teachers' values, and strive to create an example of teachers who are active, enterprising, dedicated, and diligent. For examiners, testing teachers' values is a long-term task, which needs to be implemented in daily life, to ensure that teachers can fully implement the profound connotation of core values.

Establish perfect performance appraisal standards.

Summarize and manage human resource information through big data technology, collect users' evaluation of the performance platform in real-time, and technicians regularly form feedback on the evaluation to repair system loopholes.

The assessment criteria embody several principles:

Transparency principle: everyone can find the appraisal criteria, appraisal process, and appraisal time on the platform. Objective principle: use a big data system to input data throughout the process to prevent omission. Conduct pre-examination training for examiners to improve relevant professional qualifications. Statistics shall be timely and accurate. Communication principle: use sensing technology to strengthen the connection between examiners and examinees. The principle of comprehensiveness: teachers work hard, 2.2.2 Assessment operation.

First, the school needs to set performance appraisal indicators:

Definition of relevant concepts:

KPI: a key result indicator that can be expressed by quota or ratio. At present, KPI is also widely used in the performance appraisal of colleges and universities, which can guide college teachers to complete teaching and research tasks with high quality and perfect teaching objectives. However, as a result-oriented indicator, KPI will guide teachers to focus on short-term results too much and ignore long-term changes and processes. Therefore, we will combine gs indicators with KPI indicators for comprehensive consideration.

GS: a phased indicator that is difficult to quantify. It refers to the completion of major work that is relatively long-term and has no direct control over the operating results.

The performance appraisal should focus on the process of self-examination of employees. Teachers should position their level in colleges, departments, and schools through horizontal comparison of teaching quality and self-evaluation of the quantity and quality of scientific research achievements. Teachers can judge whether they have made progress in all aspects, what is room for improvement, and simply judge the recent work status by viewing the longitudinal comparison of previous years' performance. In addition, employees need to listen to others' opinions to improve themselves. In the KPI and gs indicators of performance appraisal, there will be leaders' evaluation, colleagues' evaluation, parents' evaluation, students' evaluation of teaching, and other sectors. The experience of the latter two mainly reflects teachers' education level and ethics, which has high reference value.

The indicators are set by the 80/20 principle, adhering to the concept of "fewer but better" in terms of quantity, which is convenient for college employees to focus on their work and improve their work concentration within a certain period.

The establishment process of KPI and gs indicators is very complicated, but each step is indispensable. Therefore, good communication and discussion must be conducted before the establishment. All people involved in the assessment should participate in the meeting to modify the performance assessment rules.

In performance appraisal, weight setting is often very important, and reasonable weight setting can strengthen the rationality and fairness of performance appraisal. Therefore, for the in-service employees in different departments of colleges and universities, KPI indicators and gs indicators have different weights, which also have many considerations. The following three parts of the school are randomly selected for illustration:

Financial Management Department: KPI index accounts for 50%, gs index accounts for 50%. The members of the Financial Management Department will judge the performance level through the utilization rate of financial expenditure in the school, so the KPI accounts for a large proportion.

Top management: KPI index accounts for 80%, gs index accounts for 20%. For senior leaders, the purpose of performance appraisal is to assess their management philosophy and management level. The management level is mainly measured by quantitative indicators such as the completion of subordinate tasks, the quality change of students in a certain period measured by authority, and the performance report of each department in the university. Therefore, the KPI index accounts for a large proportion.

College teachers: KPI index accounts for 20%, gs index accounts for 80%. Only after strict layer upon layer screening can college teachers successfully enter the post. So they have strong professional ethics and a sense of responsibility and can meet the teaching workload on time. Similarly, most of their KPI indicators are difficult to open the gap. On the other hand, the reference significance of qualitative indicators is extraordinary. From the evaluation of others, we can observe the teacher's teaching level, performance ability, personal accomplishment, and other aspects. It is a very good assessment method, so it accounts for a large proportion.

Formation and determination of scoring principles for assessment results:

Set goals, and give a total score of five points. Three points will be given if the task is just completed. Then add up according to a certain model, and five points will be considered excellent [11].

Personal performance rating: I take work performance (KCL) and comprehensive quality (KPI+GS) as the horizontal axis and vertical axis of the coordinate system respectively to form a rating classification, as shown in Fig. 1 below [12]:

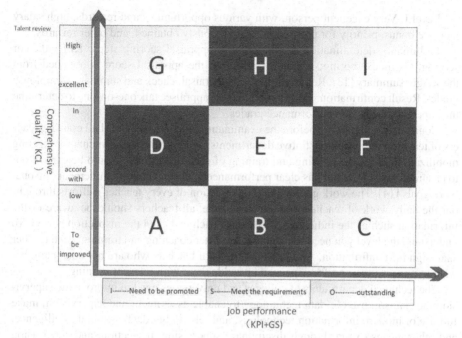

Fig. 1. .

Level A: The losers at this level will face job transfer or immediate elimination.

Level B: For those with problems, stop all opportunities and rewards, strictly require the ability and quality, participate in training, enter the observation period of performance, consider how to deal with the next step, and consider salary reduction.

Level C: The promotion opportunity will be suspended for those with deficiencies. They will be given a year's opportunity to improve their ability and quality, and require staff to participate in training and learning.

Level D: Those with problems should stop all opportunities and rewards, be strict in performance, participate in training and learning, enter the observation period, consider how to deal with the next step, and consider salary reduction.

Level E: Those who perform fairly well should carefully consider salary reduction and promotion, put forward performance requirements, and conduct training to improve their ability, but do not let them hinder the development of talented employees in the department.

Grade F: excellent, reward: more salary increase, encourage: continue to improve quality, opportunity: have the conditions for the promotion.

Grade G: The promotion opportunity will be suspended for those with deficiencies. They will be given a year's opportunity to improve their ability and quality, and require staff to participate in training and learning.

Level H: excellent, reward: more salary increase, encourage: continue to improve quality, opportunity: have the conditions for the promotion.

Level I: Very excellent person, with various opportunities and rewards, high salary increase bonus, priority for promotion if continuously obtained, and other rewards.

Preliminary determination of performance appraisal scoring steps: KPI indicator scoring; Gs index scoring; Absolute Appraisal: the appraisal score is obtained from the weight summary [13]; Relative appraisal: appraisal: check and summarize employee grades; Result confirmation: the appraiser and the appraisee talk one-on-one to determine the appraisal results and performance grades.

Counseling and training before the examination: First, the school shall convene leaders of teaching units, administrative departments, and logistics departments for meeting mobilization. Next, the tutoring and training of each department should be carried out to ensure that each teacher has clear performance goals and how to implement personal work goals [14]. The work goal will be the direction of every teacher's efforts throughout the daily work of teachers. At the same time, all teachers should be aware of the information such as the indicators, the time of each task, and the inspection period. To understand the level you need to reach finally. After coaching and training, each teacher shall sign for confirmation. And meet the needs of teachers who are not competent but want to improve their performance, and provide them with relevant training.

The technical departments of colleges and universities need to improve the supervision mechanism, use big data technology to enable assessment and supervision, make full use of modern information technology, and rely on big data, artificial intelligence, and other means to run through disciplinary supervision, inspection, and supervision [15]. And we should improve the rules and regulations to prevent loopholes in the system. The above two nights can guarantee the accuracy of the assessment to the highest extent.

This system can collect attendance information, reward and punishment records, and other information across platforms. Ensure the accuracy of collected information and the continuous automatic collection of long-term information. Tables and various statistical charts can be automatically formed, and a brief analysis report can be formed through big data analysis for the reference of the HR Department.

The formation of assessment results will adopt the mode of "human-computer integration", that is, artificial intelligence replaces some of the examiner's functions, which can effectively avoid unfair and objective assessment results caused by the subjective impression and personal style of the examiner.

The confirmation of appraisal results mainly involves the following processes. The assessment results will be publicized by each department on a unified date. If teachers have objections and need to report them, they will review the parts with objections and re-identify them. After all the assessment results are confirmed, they will be reported to the school for approval and archiving.

The ultimate purpose of any performance appraisal is not only for testing but also for the ultimate development of college teachers and colleges. Therefore, after the confirmation of appraisal results, performance results must be analyzed and fed back [16]. Excellent performance results analysis and feedback can not only increase the enthusiasm of teachers but also help employees improve their performance. The analysis of performance results should reflect the vision and requirements of schools, students, and other groups for teachers. It should also indicate the objectives of the school managers for the next stage of performance and the detailed plans made for this purpose. The system will use information technology to analyze the data of the assessment results and assist in decision-making.

Convening performance analysis meeting: anonymous questionnaire survey was issued to college teachers to evaluate and suggest a performance appraisal. Relevant personnel absorbed opinions and formed a report, which was submitted together with the performance appraisal analysis report at the meeting [17]. On the other hand, the leader in charge should have strong communication ability, be able to actively communicate, and consciously collect opinions. At the meeting, all members of the meeting focused on discussing and correcting problems in the performance appraisal body and appraisal process. And discuss the performance objectives and work tasks of each department in the next stage.

Link with salary: salary is often the most concerned issue of every employee [18]. The performance results will be linked to the salary payment. The performance appraisal team and relevant appraisers can adhere to the principle of fairness and justice to pay teachers. The appraisal team takes the performance salary as the bonus part of its performance appraisal salary allocation.

Learning and training: After the confirmation of the performance appraisal results, teachers with poor performance levels need to participate in the performance improvement training organized by the school. Teachers with ordinary performance who wish to learn can also apply for training [19]. When there are limited learning exchange opportunities and training (provincial training and national training), teachers with excellent performance are preferred.

Professional title employment: the role of performance appraisal: the school will adjust the professional title employment and salary grade according to the performance level. The school will focus on training teachers with excellent performance appraisal results and give them extra points for their professional titles. When there are vacancies in school management posts, these teachers will be considered first. The following is part of the role of performance appraisal: to understand the ability level, strengths, and weaknesses of employees. This is conducive to the follow-up training of employees, personnel transfer, and other activities. In the training, it can make up for the lack of employees' working ability and improve their working quality [20].

At the same time, performance appraisal is also an effective means to motivate employees. It can create a benign competitive environment and improve teachers' motivation. Finally, the rational use of performance levers can realize the sustainable development of vocational education and help the strategy of rejuvenating the country through science and education.

2.3 Database Design

First, the feasibility of the system is analyzed.

Economic feasibility: The school is in good financial condition and able to bear the cost of system purchase and later maintenance [21]. Operational feasibility: the platform is divided into foreground operation and background operation. The front desk uses photoshop and other software to design beautiful web pages for users. It can be used in Windows systems for easy downloading. The system page is simple, the font size is adjustable, and the presbyopia users can also read it smoothly. It is easy to operate, and older teachers who are not good at using electronic devices can quickly learn and put them into use.

Technical feasibility: it is necessary to determine the development of the system through the analysis of economic, social, technical, and other aspects.

Analyze the user activities of university performance appraisal and form a business flow chart as shown in Fig. 2 below [22].

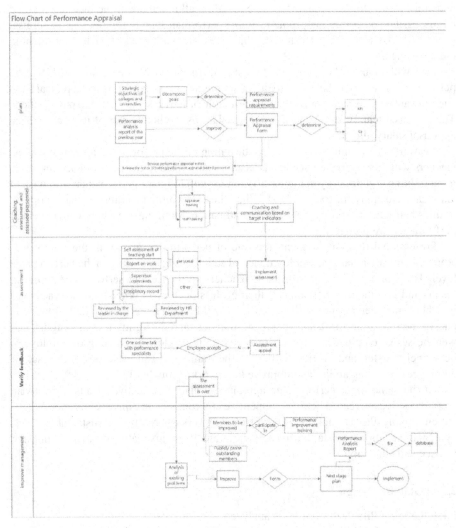

Fig. 2. .

Conceptual model: form ER diagram (entity contact method), as shown in Fig. 3, 4, 5 and 6 below:

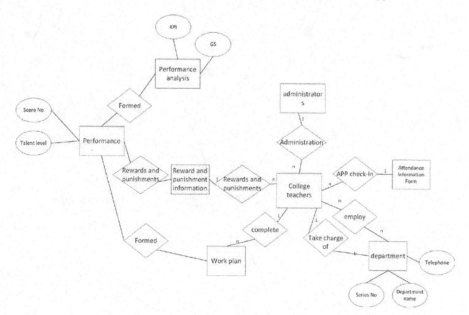

Fig. 3. .

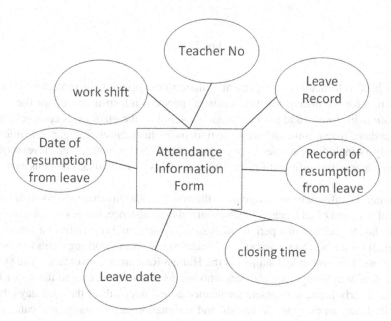

Fig. 4. .

The main functions of establishing a university teacher performance management database are:

Local ER - Teacher's basic
information

Fig. 5. .

Teachers' information management: adhere to the principle of protecting personal information for the management of teachers' personal information, reduce the risk of information disclosure, and the information entered on the platform is comprehensive, can be updated in real-time, and is easy to find. Individuals can click to generate information analysis, including the queries of previous years' performance, multi-level retrieval of a large amount of information, statistical analysis of individual compensation, etc. [23].

Attendance information management: the system will summarize and count the attendance information of all teachers, such as attendance, absence, leave, overtime date and working hours, etc. within a period, analyze the system, and finally form a report. It is convenient for the human resources department to master the working status of teachers in real-time. The assessment subject is the Human Resources Department. The system collects data and downgrades teachers who ask for more leave, exceed the upper limit of late and early leave, and whose attendance is less than half of the total days due to maternity leave, an entry in the month, and resignation in the month, and cancels the performance bonus of the month. Reward and punishment information management: this system will focus on building a more perfect reward and punishment mechanism. Teachers can add, delete, cancel and view reward information individually or in batches on the platform. The administrator has the right to review the reward and punishment information [24].

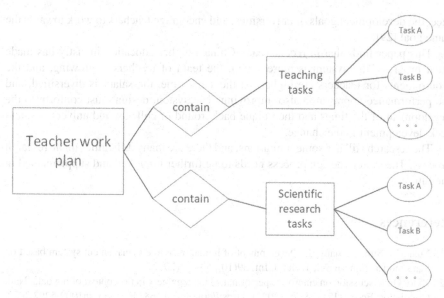

Fig. 6. .

A performance appraisal system based on the saas mode has been established [25]. Different users (different universities) can only open the browser to assess, view, manage and analyze the performance of hundreds of people [26]. This is a public platform, which can be personalized for different universities to meet different needs [27]. At the same time, each user will not be aware of the existence of other users. The prototype analysis method is used to pay more attention to the details of each module of the user interface, adapt to the needs of users in continuous improvement, and strive to give users a more comfortable experience. The system adopts the development method of separating the front end from the back end. The back end provides data to the front end, and the front end is responsible for HTML rendering and user interaction. Both parties standardize the interface content in the form of documents [28].

The front end uses Vue with node. of as the core Js front-end technology ecological architecture. The back-end uses spring boot+spring cloud+spring mvc+spring data. The front and rear ends use API documents to connect. After the front and rear ends are built, the front and rear ends are jointly tested.

Design Oracle or MySQL databases to support more tenants.

3   Conclusion

With the further development of higher education in the new era, the competition among universities across the country is becoming increasingly fierce. The importance of performance appraisal as a means to enhance the core competitiveness of universities is self-evident. At this time, build a high-tech performance appraisal information management system to optimize the overall performance appraisal. High-quality performance appraisal can better adapt to the concept of running a university in the new era, better meet the development goals of universities, and encourage teachers to work towards the same goal [29].

This paper finds that in recent years, China's higher education industry has made great progress, the system is more sound, the team of teachers is growing, and the requirements for teachers are higher. At the same time, the salary is diversified, and the performance appraisal is also improving. The system design must conform to the development of the times and the unique background of colleges and universities, and seek development in the change.

The research still has some limitations, and there are many difficulties in the research process. The system design process needs to be further improved and supplemented in the future.

References

1. Yuan, X., Sun, Y., Jiang, J.: Development of human resource management system based on SaaS model. Jiangsu Sci. Technol. Inf. **39**(10), 60–64 (2022)
2. Xiao, Q.: Discussion on enterprise performance management in the context of big data. Natl. Circulation Econ. (12), 75–78 (2022). https://doi.org/10.16834/j.cnki.issn1009-5292.2022.12.012
3. Li, W.: Do you still have privacy in the age of big data. Theory Guide (07), 9 (2013)
4. Zhang, M.: Research on the application of cloud computing technology in computer data processing. Inf. Comput. (Theory Ed.) **32**(06), 16–18 (2020)
5. Shao, Y.: Innovation analysis of enterprise human resource performance management in the age of big data. Financ. Econ. Circles (26), 197–198 (2021). https://doi.org/10.19887/j.cnki.cn11-4098/f.2021.26.098
6. Wu, Z., Ru, W., Wan, H., Wang, Y., Guo, X., Liu, F.: Based on the innovation practice of "Internet+" human resource management. In: Outstanding Achievements of China's Enterprise Reform and Development 2021 (the Fifth Session), vol. 1, pp. 442–451 (2021). https://doi.org/10.26914/c.cnkihy.2021.069927
7. Liu, X.: System design and implementation of university performance appraisal. J. Tianjin Univ. Technol. **38**(02), 52–57 (2022)
8. Xia, D.: University budget performance target management mechanism based on SMART principle – taking F University as an example. Bus. Account. (16), 68–71 (2021)
9. Wang, Q.: Thoughts on innovative application of OKR performance management model in the age of big data. Shanghai Chem. Ind. **46**(04), 54–56 (2021). https://doi.org/10.16759/j.cnki.issn.1004-017x.2021.04.017
10. Sun, T., Zheng, Q., Wang, W., Su, Z., Cai, X.: The construction of university teachers' performance appraisal system under the BSC+KPI vision – based on the application of the Delphi method and the analytic hierarchy process. China Univ. Sci. Technol. (06), 21–26 (2020). https://doi.org/10.16209/j.cnki.cust.2020.06.005
11. Lu, L., Zhang, M.: Design and implementation of performance appraisal system platform based on key performance indicators (KPIs). Measur. Test Technol. **49**(03), 99–101 (2022). https://doi.org/10.15988/j.cnki.1004-6941.2022.3.028
12. Wei, X.: Construction of college accounting performance evaluation system based on KPI AHP model. Financ. Account. Learn. (35), 125–126 (2020)
13. Shao, X.: Research on the Optimization of Teacher Performance Appraisal System of J College. Harbin Engineering University (2019). https://doi.org/10.27060/d.cnki.ghbcu.2019.000821

14. Chen, J.: Optimizing human resource management of public institutions in the network economy. In: Proceedings of the Social Development Forum (Guiyang Forum) (II). [Publisher unknown], pp. 346–348 (2022). https://doi.org/10.26914/c.cnkihy.2022.018739

15. Zhang, A.: Research on the performance evaluation of private colleges under the balanced scorecard – a college as an example. Friends Account. (22), 140–145 (2018)

16. Li, J.: Strategic performance assessment model and process analysis. SME Manag. Technol. (Mid term) (11), 174–176 (2021)

17. Meng, Y.: Problems and countermeasures in the current performance wage management of colleges and Universities in China. Contemp. Educ. Forum (03), 80–85 (2018). https://doi.org/10.13694/j.cnki.ddjylt.2018.03.010

18. Ge, F.: Research on Performance Appraisal System Based on Process. Shandong University (2006)

19. Li, J.: Big data's exploration in the management of university administrators. J. Liaoning Univ. Sci. Technol. **19**(04), 38–40 (2017)

20. Zhang, Y.: Reform path of human resources management informatization in public institutions. Hum. Resour. Dev. (04), 43–44 (2022). https://doi.org/10.19424/j.cnki.41-1372/d.2022.04.021

21. Zhang, Y.: Research and Development of Task based Team Performance Appraisal System. Jilin University (2012)

22. Ding, H.: Design and Implementation of Performance Appraisal System for Middle level Managers in Enterprises. Shandong University (2014)

23. Wang, Z.: 5G challenge and innovation of human resource management in the era of internet big data. Mod. Trade Ind. **42**(29), 65–66 (2021). https://doi.org/10.19311/j.cnki.1672-3198.2021.29.032

24. Wu, H.: Process and system construction of human resource performance appraisal in colleges and universities. J. Tianjin Manag. Coll. (01), 47–48 (2011)

25. Yang, D.: Research on the interactive mechanism of local university teachers' performance evaluation. Heilongjiang High. Educ. Res. **39**(02), 7–11 (2021). https://doi.org/10.19903/j.cnki.cn23-1074/g.2021.02.002

26. Qi, X.: SaaS+AI, make human resources simple – talk to Wu Xuening, CTO of Jinyou.com. Hum. Resour. (23), 14–21 (2021)

27. Cai, X.: Reasonably use performance leverage to release the potential of teacher resources. Economist (06), 219–220+238 (2019)

28. Huang, L.: On the application of SAP-HR in the informatization of human resources in colleges and universities. J. Mianyang Normal Univ. **29**(06), 139–142 (2010). https://doi.org/10.16276/j.cnki.cn51-1670/g.2010.06.030

29. Zhao, Z.: Basic principles of human resources work in colleges and universities under the background of "Double first-class". Mod. Mark. (Inf. Ed.) (02), 203 (2020)

The Impact of Disposal Effects Generated by Internet of Things Technology on Quantitative Investment

Qiong Wang[✉]

Beijing International Studies University, No.1 Nanli Community, Dingfu Town, Chaoyang District, Beijing, China
wqkerry@163.com

Abstract. At present, quantitative investment is still in the early stage of development in China, and most of them focus on traditional financial mathematical models. However, the development of Internet of things technology enables people to quickly obtain various industry data and financial data, leading to irrational investment in real life. The development of Internet of things technology has led to an important concept in behavioral finance, that is, investors tend to hold stocks with losses and sell stocks with profits, which may cause further losses to investors. Therefore, in order to make quantitative investment more effective to achieve the goal of stable returns, we should apply the conditions of irrational people to quantitative investment. This paper will mainly discuss the application of allocation effect in behavioral finance in quantitative investment. It is helpful to the development of China's quantitative investment theory and practice, and has certain reference significance for many Chinese individual investors to understand their investment behavior.

Keywords: Quantitative investment · Internet of things technology · disposal effects · behavioral finance

1 Introduction

1.1 Background and Needs

Although the traditional financial theory has a rigorous and complete logical deduction, but many of the assumptions are inconsistent with the real finance, so that there are many "visions" in the real market that cannot be explained, just like the disposal effect to be discussed in this article, the disposal effect is that investors have the tendency to hold loss-making stocks and sell profitable stocks, which may cause further losses to investors, and the reason should be that investors violate the assumption of rational people in traditional finance. According to past studies, because the rationality of retail investors is weaker than that of professional financial institutions, the disposal effect of retail investors will be more obvious, and because China's stock investment market is in

D.-J. Deng et al. (Eds.): SGIoT 2022, LNICST 497, pp. 20–27, 2023.
https://doi.org/10.1007/978-3-031-31275-5_2

the initial stage of development, the proportion of retail investors is large, up to 80%, then the disposal effect will be more obvious in China, the degree of impact on China's stock market is larger, and at the same time there is a certain impact on the fund market, so we should fully understand the disposal effect, so that investors understand the irrational side of their investment. In turn, we will understand the pricing mechanism with China's characteristics, so that investors can achieve profitability to the greatest extent, and at the same time contribute to the healthy development of the financial system [1].

The Internet of Things refers to the use of infrared sensors, information sensors, radio frequency identification technology, laser scanners, global positioning systems and other equipment, the state of the observation object is re-connected to the Internet, breaking the traditional connection between people and people, realizing the connection between things and people, things and things, and realizing the interconnection of people and machines and items at any time, any place, so that we can achieve intelligent monitoring and management. The Internet of Things is composed of a perception layer, a network layer, and an application layer [2].

At present, the Internet of Things in China has achieved deep integration with multiple industries, such as the integration of the Internet of Things and finance, the integration of the Internet of Things and finance will change the traditional sense of the financial model, Internet of Things finance refers to the financial services and innovation for all The Internet of Things, which extends the object of financial services from "people" to "things", which can be widely used in many fields to promote the automation and intelligence of financial services, and then promote the innovation and change of the financial industry [3]. Internet of Things finance enables the integrated management of information flow, capital flow and logistics.

1.2 Literature Roundup

The interpretation of the disposal effect in previous studies can be divided into two categories, one is from the perspective of traditional finance, and the other is from the perspective of behavioral finance.

The explanations of the disposal effect in traditional finance mainly include price reversal phenomenon, investment rebalancing theory and informed trading theory [4]. The price reversal phenomenon refers to a slight decrease in the price after the price rises, so the investor will sell the stock shortly after the profit will make the investor the most profitable, but empirical analysis in real life shows that most stocks do not have a price reversal effect in the subsequent performance, so this explanation does not hold. Investment rebalancing theory refers to the investor's own requirements for the weight of each stock in the portfolio, when the price of a stock in the portfolio rises, the weight of the stock on behalf of the stock also rises, then the investor sells the profitable stock, so that the stock weight returns to the previous level of the behavior can also be explained, that is, the disposal effect can be explained, but this theory also means that the investor has to take the funds from the sale of profitable stocks to buy loss-making stocks, and then in the case of maintaining the scale of investment, To maintain portfolio weights, however, under empirical analysis, investors do not buy loss-making stocks, so this explanation does not hold. Informed trading theory means that investors have insider information, and insider information shows that the price of a loss-making stock will rise or the price of a profitable stock will fall, so the disposal effect phenomenon of investors selling profitable stocks or holding loss-making stocks can be reasonably explained, but empirical analysis shows that the average return of profitable stocks sold is higher than the average return of loss-making stocks held, so this explanation is not valid. In general, the traditional financial interpretation of the disposal effect has been falsified in subsequent studies, but their existence brings us closer to the essence of the problem step by step [5].

The explanation of disposition effect in behavioral finance mainly includes prospect theory, psychological account, mean value regression and other theories. The value curve of prospect theory has three characteristics. The first point is that the utility of investors does not come from the profits or losses of relative absolute points, but for relative points, that is, the expected returns in the minds of investors. The second point is that the utility is not linear, and it has the effect of diminishing marginal value, that is, when the relative point is profitable, the utility curve is a convex function, that is, the more profits for the relative point, the less positive value feedback corresponding to unit profits, When there is a loss for the relative point, the utility curve is a concave function, that is, the more the loss for the relative point, the less the negative value feedback corresponding to the unit loss. The third point has asymmetry. When the amount of loss and profit is the same, the negative value feedback obtained by the loss is greater than the positive value feedback obtained by the profit. Therefore, investors are more willing to hold loss stocks and sell profit stocks, which explains the disposal effect [6].

The psychological account theory refers to that investors set up an account for each stock in their mind, and each account has a psychology of at least not losing money. Selling losing stocks means closing their account in their mind, which represents a permanent loss of a psychological account. Therefore, in order to avoid this phenomenon, investors will continue to hold losing stocks to keep the floating loss of the psychological account from becoming a real loss, the same is true for selling profitable stocks, that is, determining a psychological account and closing it after making profits, which greatly satisfies the psychology of investors and explains the disposal effect.

The mean value regression theory means that investors believe that stock prices will return to the mean value, that is, stocks with rising prices will fall back, and stocks with falling prices will rebound, so holding stocks with losses and buying stocks with profits can be reasonably explained. However, this theory also means that since investors believe that stock prices with losses will return to their higher mean values, investors will have two corresponding behaviors, one is to hold loss stocks and the other is to buy loss stocks. However, in previous empirical studies, it has been shown that investors will not buy loss stocks, so this theory cannot explain the disposal effect.

This paper first theoretically explains how to use the perspective of learned helplessness to explain the resolution effect and the impact of Internet of things technology on the resolution effect, secondly uses experiments to verify the relationship between learned helplessness and the resolution effect, and finally explains the impact of the resolution effect on the financial market and the methods to deal with the disposal effect.

2   Theoretical Explanation

The theoretical explanation can be divided into two steps. The first step demonstrates that the disposition effect is a market anomaly. We theoretically analyze whether there is learned helplessness in the market, which means that an individual will become helpless after repeated setbacks. If there is, we will carry out the second step to demonstrate whether the result of learned helplessness has a disposition effect. If there is a disposition effect, we can use the learned helplessness theory to explain the disposition effect, that is to achieve the goal of this paper. In the first step of the demonstration, the basis for this paper to determine whether there is learned helplessness is whether there is a reason for learned helplessness in the market. In the second step of the demonstration, according to the stock market scenario corresponding to the reason for learned helplessness, it is theoretically analyzed whether there is a disposal effect. The causes of learned helplessness are widely accepted as behavioral cybernetics, attribution theory, goal theory, self-esteem protection theory and so on [7]. Behavioral cybernetics, that is, thinking that if you can't control the occurrence of failure, you will feel helpless. At this time, helplessness is not caused by the result of failure, but by thinking that you can't control the process of failure, so you will treat the things you will face in the future with this helpless mentality. Learned helplessness in behavioral cybernetics includes three elements: uncontrollable environment and concomitant cognition, that is, thinking that no action can control the outcome of failure and giving up reaction, that is, adopting such a helpless attitude towards the future. Then, corresponding to our stock market, the unpredictable stock market can correspond to an uncontrollable environment. In the stock market, every investor acts as a passive receiver of the price and at this moment, investors do not know whether the stock will be in a loss state at the next moment. This corresponds to the concomitant cognition, that is, there is an element of learned helplessness in behavioral cybernetics in the stock market, and there is a phenomenon of learned helplessness, Investors will give up, that is, they will make the current decision with a passive and helpless attitude, that is, they will hold the losing stocks and sell the profitable stocks, that is, they will have a disposal effect.

Attribution theory, that is, for the explanation of failure events, attribution can be roughly divided into three factors. The first is inward attribution and outward attribution. If an individual attributes the failure to himself, he will lose self-esteem to a certain extent, and then will have learned helplessness. If the failure is attributed to the outside world, then there is a small probability of learned helplessness. The second is whether the failure is stable, that is, whether the failure is stable or unstable, that is, failure occurs only by accident. If the attribution is stable, it will lead to learned helplessness. The third common or specific factor, if the attribution is universal, will lead to learned helplessness [8]. Generally speaking, if it is attributed to internal, stable and universal, it will produce learned helplessness. Corresponding to the real stock market, the attribution of investors cannot be generalized, but according to the data of 2021, the per capita loss of retail investors is as high as 100000 yuan, which shows the stability and universality of investment failure, so we can think that retail investors will also attribute stability and universality. Institutional investors have more financial knowledge reserves than retail investors, and can often achieve profits, so they do not have the conditions for stable and universal attribution, As for whether the attribution is internal or not, I think it depends more on personality, so whether retail investors or institutional investors are not easy to compare in this point, from the perspective of stability and general theory of the latter two aspects of attribution, the learned helplessness of institutional investors should be weaker than that of retail investors. In the stock market, investors have learned helplessness due to attribution. If they think that their losses are due to their own ability problems, that losses are normal, and that most investors and themselves are losses, they will have a helpless mentality, and then give up "resistance", continue to hold losing stocks and sell profitable stocks, that is, the disposal effect will occur.

Goal theory, that is, people with the same ability have different reactions when facing multiple failures, one is learned helplessness, and the other is autonomy. The former pays more attention to performance goals and pays more attention to self evaluation than to ability improvement, so as to avoid failure as much as possible. The latter pays more attention to learning goals and pays more attention to ability improvement than to self evaluation, so as to face failure with a positive attitude. Corresponding to the stock market, it refers to the former, which pays more attention to performance, that is, whether the stock really brings me more profits than the ability gains brought me by the stock loss. In fact, the former does exist in a large range in the stock market. Investors want to realize real gains through the stock market, so there is a phenomenon of learned helplessness. They face losses with a negative attitude, the disposal effect occurs when the profit-making stocks are sold and the loss making stocks are held.

Self esteem protection mode, that is, people have expectations. If the results in reality are different from expectations for many times, they think that they have insufficient ability, and people will feel that their self-esteem decreases. Out of the maintenance of self-esteem, they will reduce their efforts, so it is reasonable to attribute the next failure to their insufficient efforts, not their insufficient ability, that is, self handicapping. Corresponding to the stock market, when investors receive the result of stock loss which is inconsistent with their expected profits, they will give up their efforts, self hinder, sell profitable stocks and hold loss stocks, and then protect self-esteem. In this process, there is a disposal effect.

From the above analysis, it can be seen that learned helplessness can theoretically explain the disposal effect, which can be embodied in that the more consecutive losses investors experience, the more helplessness they will give up and continue to hold loss stocks, resulting in disposal effect, which will further aggravate losses. The research in this paper is beneficial for understanding investor behavior and establishing quantitative investment models. Since retail investors account for a relatively high proportion and the degree of retail investors' disposal effect is greater, there are often "anomalies" in China's financial market. Understanding the disposal effect in behavioral finance will help us understand and make use of China's characteristic financial market. At present, most of the quantitative investment includes the disposal effect factor through CGO, which is not profitable, this indicator is formed based on the explanation of the prospect theory for the disposal effect. In this paper, explaining the disposal effect with learned helplessness will improve the algorithm of CGO, so that the disposal effect can be better quantified into the model, thus making the quantitative model more effective.

With the development of Internet of things technology, its impact on the disposal effect is becoming more and more profound, which can be divided into two reasons.

The first reason is that herding refers to that investors have a herd mentality in the market and will tend to the decisions made by most investors. Sometimes investors will give up their correct decisions and make wrong decisions after they have mastered the correct information. In the stock market, the proportion of retail investors is as high as 80%. Because of their poor professionalism and sensibility, retail investors are more prone to herd behavior, that is, herd behavior. The basis of herd behavior is the process of information transmission among investors. The development of Internet of things technology makes the transmission speed of information faster, which not only expands the scope of influence of herd behavior, but also enhances the degree of herd behavior. Herding is a transmission of irrational behavior. As a typical irrational behavior in behavioral finance, herding will enhance the degree of disposition effect, and Internet of things technology will enhance the intensity of herding. Therefore, in general, Internet of things technology will enhance the intensity of disposition effect [9].

The second reason is that Internet of things technology will speed up the transmission of information on the one hand and increase the breadth of information on the other. However, the broadening of information caliber cannot fully guarantee the accuracy of information. Generally, investors acquiesce that the information they get is accurate, so investors will have confidence because they think they have more information. Overconfidence means that investors overestimate their trading ability and information, resulting in irrational transactions, and overconfidence will enhance the degree of disposal effect [10], so in general, Internet of things technology will make investors overconfident, thus enhancing the degree of disposal effect.

3 Correlation Verification

Learned helplessness, that is, the more times you fail, the more helpless you will be and then give up. This paper takes the turnover rate and consecutive loss weeks of the CSI 300 index in 2021 as the research variables. The CSI 300 index covers a wide range of stocks in circulation in most markets. It is more representative and can accurately reflect the real situation of the whole market [11]. The turnover rate reflects the circulation degree of stocks in the corresponding market for a certain period of time. A high turnover rate indicates a high degree of stock activity and a large number of people selling stocks. Comparing the turnover rate of stocks with consecutive losses for different weeks, if the more consecutive losses, the lower the turnover rate of stocks, it indicates that the unilateral disposal effect and the degree of learned helplessness become larger, and the two are in a positive relationship, which further indicates that learned helplessness is related to the disposal effect [12] (Fig. 1).

The data of CSI 300 constituent stocks in 2021 is taken for the experiment. Due to the large amount of data, the experimental observation interval is in weeks. The scatter chart shows that when the number of consecutive loss weeks is within the range of 1–6, the disposal effect is not obvious. However, when the number of loss weeks is greater than 6, the weekly turnover rate is gradually decreasing with the increase of the number of loss weeks, that is, the number of transactions is getting less and less, indicating that people's willingness to trade is declining after continuous loss, That is, the degree of learned helplessness increases, while the degree of disposal effect also

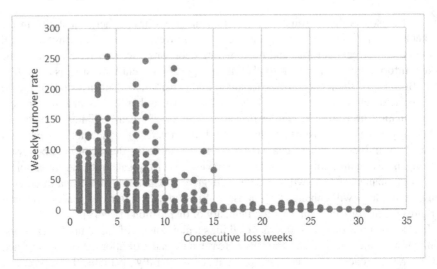

Fig. 1. The relationship between weekly turnover rate and consecutive loss weeks

increases [13]. Thus, under the condition of a certain number of consecutive loss weeks, learned helplessness can be used to explain the disposal effect.

4 Impact of Disposal Effect and Countermeasures

Disposal effect, that is, holding loss stocks and selling profit stocks, will make the vibration amplitude of the stock market smaller and maintain financial stability to a certain extent. However, relatively speaking, this phenomenon also delays the speed of information entering the pricing, reduces the efficiency of the financial market and reduces the return rate of investors. At the same time, this effect will also play a role in the fund market and produce "anomalies". When the fund loses money, people are unwilling to sell the fund. When the fund gains, people will sell the fund instead. For fund managers, sometimes they even deliberately lose money for the sake of fund size, there is no doubt that this way will damage the healthy development of finance [14, 15].

In order to mitigate the negative impact of the disposal effect on us, there are generally two aspects. The first aspect is that in terms of the way we participate in the financial market, we can participate in the financial market activities in the form of quantitative transactions to avoid the emotional part of our human nature and the disposal effect to the maximum extent, so as to maximize personal income and promote the healthy development of the entire financial system [16].

The second aspect is from the personal perspective. First of all, we should have our own judgment and try our best to avoid the phenomenon of following the crowd. Because there are many retail investors in China's stock market, it is often impossible to earn money to follow a large number of unprofessional retail investors. Therefore, although we have quickly obtained the information of many investors through the Internet of things technology, we should not blindly follow [17]. Secondly, the development of Internet of things technology makes a large number of unfiltered information fill our eyes. We can't blindly believe in data, but have our own judgment. Finally, we should have a correct understanding of the market and ourselves. The market is unpredictable, and it is normal to make profits and losses. Making profits in the market does not mean that one's personal ability is outstanding, and losing money does not mean that one's ability is insufficient. We should participate in the market calmly, neither overconfidence nor inferiority complex. Only by making rational decisions can we become the real winner in the market [5].

References

1. Lu, R., Li, J., Chen, S.: Portraits of investors' selling behavior in China's Stock market: advances in disposition effect. Manage. World (2022). issue 3
2. Haonan, L., Xu, Z.: Is the disposition effect related to overconfidence? Evidence from a social trading platform. Shanghai Manage. Sci. 43(6)
3. Cai, F., Li, Q., Li, Y.: Analysis of the current situation of Internet of things technology development. Inf. Syst. Eng. (01), 25–26 (2021)
4. Nie, Y.: Research on key technology and application of Internet of things. Comput. Prod. Circ. (09), 142 (2020)
5. Lu, M., Weng, T.: The past, present and future of China's Internet of things finance. Enterp. Res. (10), 21–25 (2017)
6. He, L.: Causes and theoretical research of disposition effect in behavioral finance. Mod. Mark. (Business Edition), (04), 205–206 (2020)
7. Chen, C.: Analysis of investment strategy based on disposal effect. Modern Bus (12), 66–692021). https://doi.org/10.14097/j.cnki.5392/2021.12.021
8. Lu, R.: Selling behavior deviation: profit or loss. Modern Commercial Bank, (04), 125–126 (2021)
9. Wen, Q.: The Relationship between Secondary Vocational School Students' Achievement Goal Orientation, Academic Self-efficacy and Learned Helplessness. Qinghai Normal University (2014)
10. Li, X.: Empirical research on the mystery of China's stock market volatility based on the perspective of disposition effect. Shanghai Academy of Social Sciences (2021)
11. Wang, L.: Research on investor disposition effect: a literature review. Hebei Finan. (05), 28–32 (2021). https://doi.org/10.14049/j.cnki.hbjr.2021.05.007
12. Wu, J., Wang, C., C, Zilin., Jie, M.G.: A Study of Disposition Effect among China's Individual Investors: the Perspective of Irrational Beliefs [J]. Financial research, 2020 (02): 147–166
13. Gao, S.: Research on the influence of fund manager reputation on disposition effect and fund performance. Zhongnan University of economics and law (2019)
14. Yu, X.: On the causes and Countermeasures of disposition effect in China's securities market. China Bus. Rev (07), 57–58 (2019). https://doi.org/10.19699/j.cnki.issn2096-0298.2019.07.057
15. Hu, G., W, Yiduo.: Analysis on the harm of disposal effect to individual investors and countermeasures. Times Finan. (09), 234–235 (2019)
16. Zhang, Y..: Research on the disposition effect and its influence factors of institutional investors in china. Chongqing University of technology (2019)
17. Qian, L.: Empirical research on the disposal effect of A-share market. Tax Payment, **12**(30), 182–184 (2018)

A Survey on IoT Modules: Architecture, Key Technologies and Future Directions

Yifan Gao[✉] and Rong Chai

School of Communications and Information Engineering, Chongqing University of Posts
and Telecommunications, Chongqing 400065, People's Republic of China
gyf20151210@163.com

Abstract. The Internet of things (IoT) is a promising technology which offers
the seamless connectivity of the global world via heterogeneous smart terminals.
As the core component of IoT intelligent terminals, IoT modules integrate various
electronic devices such as baseband chips, radio frequency modules and positioning modules, etc., and form single devices which can be embedded into different
types of IoT terminals. In this paper, we present a survey on IoT modules. The
architecture and the components of the IoT modules are briefly introduced. Then,
the classification of IoT modules is discussed, which mainly includes cellular
communication modules and non-cellular communication modules. One of the
most widely used cellular communication modules, i.e., narrow-band IoT (NB-
IoT) module, is further introduced and the characteristics of the module are exam-
ined in detail. In addition, the design and manufacturing process of IoT modules
is summarized and the key technologies are discussed. Finally, the future research
and development directions of IoT modules are specified.

Keywords: Internet of Things · IoT modules · NB-IoT architecture

1 Introduction

In recent years, the Internet of things (IoT) has received considerable attention and IoT
technologies and applications have experienced rapid development. It is expected that
the number of connected IoT devices will reach 41.6 billion by 2025 [1]. In order to
reduce production cost, simplify software development procedure and reduce product
release cycle time, terminal manufactures seek to exploit module-based technique and
develop various IoT related devices based on IoT modules [2–5].

In IoT modules, various electronic components including baseband chips, radio frequency (RF) modules and positioning modules, etc., are integrated into unified devices
which can then be embedded into different types of IoT terminals. By using IoT modules, the design and manufacturing process of IoT terminals can be simplified [6].
As one of the key components of IoT devices, the performance and characteristics of
IoT modules play an important role in determining the cost and performance of the
terminals.

In this paper, a survey on IoT modules is presented. We first introduce the architecture and components of IoT modules, then, discuss the classification of IoT modules

© ICST Institute for Computer Sciences, Social Informatics and Telecommunications Engineering 2023
Published by Springer Nature Switzerland AG 2023. All Rights Reserved
D.-J. Deng et al. (Eds.): SGIoT 2022, LNICST 497, pp. 28–39, 2023.
https://doi.org/10.1007/978-3-031-31275-5_3

and elaborate the characteristics of narrow-band IoT (NB-IoT) modules. The design process and key technologies of IoT modules are further summarized. Finally, the future research and development directions of IoT modules are specified.

2   Functional Architecture of IoT Modules

This section discusses the general functional architecture of IoT modules. As shown in Fig. 1, the functional architecture of an IoT module mainly consists of baseband chip, RF module, global navigation satellite system (GNSS) module, memory chip, power management module and peripheral interface, etc. The detail descriptions of the components contained in the module architecture will be discussed as below.

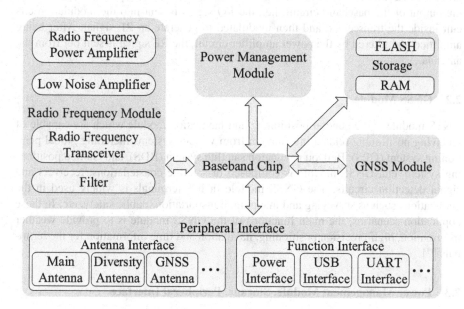

Fig. 1. General architecture of IoT modules.

The baseband chip in IoT modules is mainly responsible for processing baseband signals and protocols. The specific functions may include baseband codec, timing control, digital system control, RF control, power saving control and man-machine interface control, etc. According to the underline chip design technology, baseband chips can be divided into analog baseband chips and digital baseband chips, where analog baseband chips mainly process analog signals, such as audio signals, whereas digital baseband chips deal with digital signals, such as ARM core, digital input/output (I/O), etc.

2.1 RF Module

As the transmitters and receivers of IoT modules, RF modules are mainly responsible for sending and receiving the RF signals of IoT terminals. In order to process RF signals properly, certain signal processing operations including frequency synthesis, power amplification and signal filtering are commonly conducted. To implement the functions of RF signal processing, an RF module is composed of an RF transceiver, a power amplifier, a low noise amplifier and a filter, etc.

The receiving process of RF modules is briefly described as follows: An RF signal is received at the RF transceiver, and then processed by a low noise amplifier. The amplified signal is input into a mixer circuit to obtain the baseband in-phase/quadrature (I/Q) signal, which is sent into the baseband chip for further processing. The transmission process of RF modules is of the reverse order as that of receiving process. Specifically, the output of the baseband circuit, i.e., the I/Q signal is sent into the modulation circuit inside the transceiver, and then modulated to generate an RF signal. After being amplified and filtered by the power amplifier circuit, the RF signal is sent out from the antenna.

2.2 GNSS Module

GNSS module is the general positioning and navigation module which are capable of receiving positioning related information from various systems including global positioning system (GPS), BeiDou navigation satellite system (BDS), and Galileo positioning system, etc. GNSS module is composed of satellite constellations, receivers and signal detection circuits. The GNSS module in IoT terminals is widely used in the applications such as surveying and mapping, transportation, public safety, etc. In these application scenarios, the main functions of the GNSS module is to provide weather information, high-precision positioning, navigation and time information for the terminals [7].

2.3 Power Management Module, Storage, Peripheral Interface

The power management module in IoT terminals is mainly responsible for providing stable and reliable power supply for terminals. Its main functions include on/off control, voltage control, power supply and detection, and terminal charging control, etc. In addition, some specific power management operations can be applied so as to reduce the energy consumption of the IoT terminals during working and idle hours and prolong the service time of the terminals in battery power supply mode.

The storage unit in IoT terminals is mainly designed for storing data and information, including system and software parameters of wireless communication modules and the data generated by terminals. The storage units are divided into external flash memory and random access memory (RAM), where the flash memory is used to store system parameters, program codes and important data, and RAM is utilized to cache the temporary data when the terminals are operating.

According to various requirements and functions of IoT terminals, different peripheral interface units should be designed. The major peripheral interfaces include antenna interfaces and functional interfaces, where the antenna interfaces are in general composed of main antenna, diversity antenna, GNSS antenna, Bluetooth antenna and wireless fidelity (Wi-Fi) antenna, etc., and the functional interface provides the input and output of various signals for the IoT terminals, which can be power supply, universal serial bus (USB) flash disk, universal subscriber identity module (USIM), universal asynchronous receiver-transmitter (UART), security digital (SD) card, analog or digital audio, and general-purpose I/O (GPIO) interface, etc.

3 Classification of IoT Modules

According to the utilized wireless communication technologies, IoT modules can be categorized into two types, i.e., cellular modules and non-cellular modules, among which cellular modules are further divided into 2G modules, 3G modules, long-term evolution-category 1 (LTE-Cat1) modules, 5G modules, narrowband-IoT (NB-IoT) modules and enhanced machine-type communication (e-MTC) modules, and non-cellular communication modules can be divided into Wi-Fi modules, Bluetooth modules, ZigBee modules, long range (LoRa) and Sigfox modules.

With the global spread of 4G and the rapid development of 5G related technologies, as well as the gradual exit of 2G, 3G cellular applications, the migration of IoT services from 2G, 3G to 4G and 5G cellular systems has become an important trend. Consequently, an integrated system architecture consisting of NB-IoT, LTE-Cat1, 4G and 5G is expected to offer efficient and diverse support to IoT applications in a cooperative manner. Specifically, NB-IoT technology is mainly used for low-rate scenarios, and LTE-Cat1 is expected to become the long-term IoT standard which meets the requirement of medium-speed IoT applications. Benefited from the advanced performance, 5G technology will be employed to the IoT application scenarios which require high speed, low delay and high reliability.

It is apparent that various IoT modules and technologies are of highly different characteristics and offer diverse service performance. In Table 1, we summarize the characteristics, performance, cost and application scenarios of existing IoT modules. In practical applications, corresponding IoT modules can be chosen by jointly considering the related metrics.

4 NB-IoT Technology and Modules

Compared with LTE-Cat1 and 5G modules, NB-IoT modules have been widely used and received considerable attention in recent years [8,9]. This section presents an overview of NB-IoT technology and modules.

4.1 An Overview of NB-IoT Technology

NB-IoT technology was introduced in 3GPP Rel-13 as one of the cellular IoT (CIoT) technologies for low power wide area network (LPWAN) applications [10,11]. Evolved from LTE-Cat1, NB-IoT allows operators to offer service support to massive IoT

Table 1. Summary of IoT modules and technologies

Access technology		Band	Range	Peak Rate	Module cost	Application scenarios
Cellular	5G	450–6000 MHz, 24250–52600 MHz	–	2.1 Gbps	1000–3000 RMB	Cellular vehicle-to-everything, digital billboard, wise information technology of med
	LTE-Cat1	1.88–1.9 GHz, 2.32–2.37 GHz, 2.575–2.635 GHz	–	10 Mbps	100–150 RMB	Wearable device, intelligent security, smart agriculture, logistics tracking
	3G	1.88–1.9 GHz, 2.01–2.025 GHz	–	42 Mbps	100–150 RMB	POS, wearable device, smart home
	eMTC	1.88–1.9 GHz, 2.32–2.37 GHz, 2.575–2.635 GHz	–	1 Mbps	100–150 RMB	Wearable device, vehicle management, electronic billboard
	NB-IoT	1.88–1.9 GHz, 2.32–2.37 GHz, 2.575–2.635 GHz	–	≤100 Kbps	60–80 RMB	Smart meter reading, smart grid monitoring, smart parking
	GSM	890–915 MHz, 935–960 MHz, 1.71–1.784 GHz, 1.805–1.879G MHz	–	100–300 Kbps	≤20 RMB	SMS message, voice calls
Non-cellular	LoRa	868 MHz, 915 MHz	15 km	50 kbps	2 RMB	Smart street lamp, smart home
	Sigfox	915–928 MHz	20 km	100 bps	1 RMB	Mining industry, tunneling
	ZigBee	868 MHz, 915 MHz, 2.4 GHz	≤1 km	250 Kbps	1 RMB	Smart street lamp, smart factory
	Wi-Fi	2.4 GHz, 5 GHz	100 m	54 Mps	5–50 RMB	Smart home, remote video transmission, home gateway
	Bluetooth	2.4 GHz	50 m	2 Mbps	5–50 RMB	Wise information technology of med, wearable device, smart home

devices by utilizing existing network technology and part of available spectrum. Since the spectrum bandwidth assigned for NB-IoT technology is relatively narrow, which is equal to 180KHz, the technology is named as narrow-band IoT technology. To implement NB-IoT technology in cellular networks, various modes can be applied, including in-band, guard band or independent carrier.

Compared with the short distance communication technologies such as Bluetooth and ZigBee, etc., NB-IoT technology offers wide coverage, massive connection and low power consumption, which will be discussed briefly as follows.

Wide Coverage. In practical applications, NB-IoT is usually deployed in the frequency region less than 1 GHz. Since the utilized spectrum in NB-IoT is relatively low, especially compared to other wireless transmission technologies, such as 5G, LTE and WiFi, better signal transmission performance can be obtained, resulting in wider coverage area. It has been demonstrated that NB-IoT technology is expected to achieve an extended coverage of 20dB compared to commercially available legacy GPRS devices.

Massive Connection. In general NB-IoT applications, users may not transmit or receive data packets frequently. Indeed, the 3GPP NB-IoT service model assumes that the average number that users access the network is 0.467 per hour, which is relatively low. In addition, the size of the transmitted packets in NB-IoT applications is relatively small, resulting in short access and transmission time. In order to reduce the signaling overhead of NB-IoT, some signaling procedures, e.g., control side and the user side optimization, are simplified compared to LTE technology. Therefore, the connection capacity of NB-IoT network is enhanced significantly. According to 3GPP TR45.820, NB-IoT is capable of supporting 50,000 connections per sector.

Low Power Consumption. In order to save the power consumption of NB-IoT modules and terminals, various power saving technologies are utilized. For instance, power saving mode (PSM) and extended discontinues reception (eDRX) are both applied to greatly extend the battery life of NB-IoT terminals.

4.2 NB-IoT Modules

Designed based on NB-IoT technology, NB-IoT modules offer some desirable features, as discussed in detail in this subsection.

Low Complexity. Compared to LTE modules, NB-IoT modules mainly support frequency division duplexing (FDD) half-duplex mode, i.e., the modules does not need to deal with sending and receiving simultaneously, hence, the complexity is reduced greatly. In contrast to LTE modules which mainly use multiple antennas, NB-IoT modules in general support single antenna, thus reducing the complexity required for RF processing. Moreover, the lower rate requirements and low bandwidth of NB-IoT applications lead to simplified chip processing. As a result, the complexity of NB-IoT modules is significantly lower than that of LTE modules.

Low Cost. NB-IoT modules are usually operate in low data rate, low power consumption and small bandwidth environment. For low data rate communications, no large caching space is required, hence, the size and cost of the modules decrease accordingly. Benefited from low power consumption and small bandwidth applications, the requirements on RF circuits and signal processing algorithms can be reduced, leading to low module cost. Furthermore, operating in half-duplex mode, applying single antenna and sharing spectrum with LTE technology also result in low cost required to design and produce NB-IoT modules.

Diverse Interfaces. To meet the product development needs of different users, NB-IoT modules provide a wealth of external interfaces, such as antenna interface, subscriber identification module (SIM) card interface, universal asynchronous receiver-transmitter (UART) interface, etc. NB-IoT modules can also support multiple network protocol stacks, such as transmission control protocol/Internet protocol (TCP/IP), user datagram protocol (UDP), constrained application protocol (CoAP), message queuing telemetry transport (MQTT), etc.

Multi-Band Operation. As the frequency bands utilized by different IoT terminals may be different, in order to meet the transmission requirements of multiple frequency bands, NB-IoT modules are capable of operating in multiple frequency bands, thus supporting the application demand of terminals in various frequency bands.

Broad Applications. NB-IoT has a wide range of application scenarios, including environment monitoring, smart home, smart power grid monitoring, smart agriculture, intelligent remote meter reading, etc., [9]. Figure 2 shows several application examples of NB-IoT modules.

Fig. 2. Application samples of NB-IoT modules.

5   Design and Manufacturing Process and Key Technologies of IoT Modules

To design and manufacture IoT modules, various procedures are required. This section introduces the process of designing and producing IoT modules, and then discusses several key technologies.

5.1   Design and Manufacturing Process of IoT Modules

The process of designing and producing IoT modules mainly involves chip selection, schematic diagram design, printed circuit board (PCB) drawing, module debugging and testing, etc. This section discusses the steps of the process briefly.

Chip Selection. Selecting suitable IoT chips is the first and important step in designing and producing IoT modules. The characteristics including transmission performance, power consumption and available interfaces should be jointly considered when selecting chips. Furthermore, the cost, stability and reliable supply of the chips are key factors for commercial use, and thus should also be taken into account.

Schematic Diagram Design. Based on the selected chips, the schematic diagram of the IoT module can be designed. During this process, the stability of module structure, electromagnetic compatibility and the difficulty of large-scale manufacture should be considered.

In order to ensure that the modules work coordinately and effectively in various electromagnetic environments, electromagnetic compatibility issue should be addressed. In particular, the modules should be able to suppress various types of external interferences effectively. The difficulty of large-scale manufacture should also be considered ed in designing schematic diagram. Apparently, the desired schematic diagrams are expected to lead to relatively high process yield and facilitate large-scale production.

PCB Drawing. Once the design of a schematic diagram is completed, we may start drawing the PCB accordingly. During PCB board drawing phase, the issues such as RF requirement, stability, structure, aesthetic degree of the PCB board should be considered collectively. The general process of drawing a PCB board mainly consists of the following steps, i.e., component parameters create, schematic diagram input, parameter setting, PCB layout, PCB wiring, design verification, and computer aided manufacturing (CAM) file output. In the above design process, PCB layout and wiring are important steps as the quality of PCB layout and wiring may affect the performance of the whole module and terminal significantly.

Module Debugging. To debug IoT modules, both hardware circuits and software need to be debugged. For hardware debugging, RF circuit debug is of particular importance. Since RF circuits are responsible for transmitting and receiving RF signals, the transmission parameters including transmit power and phase errors, etc., and the receive performance such as sensitivity and reception level should be debugged.In addition, certain circuit function debugging may also be conducted according to the requirements of IoT modules.Software debugging is also performed so as to ensure that the software embedded in IoT modules can operate properly.

Module Testing. In order to guarantee that the designed IoT modules can achieve the required functions and performance metrics, module testing is mandatory which involves a series of measurement, judgment, adjustment and re-measurement processes [12]. In general, module testing includes functional testing, performance test, stability test, aging test and certification test, etc.

5.2 Key Technologies

The key technologies of designing and manufacturing IoT modules consist of packaging technology, power consumption control technology and the consistency in hardware interface and software design, etc. This section discusses the key technologies in detail.

Module Packaging Technology. The module packaging technology is a particular circuit integration technology which is utilized to implement the secondary development of the chips and achieve high-density integration of the chips and circuits in the module. There are mainly three packaging modes commonly used for IoT modules, i.e., land grid array (LGA) packaging [13], leadless chip carriers (LCC) packaging [14] and M.2 packaging [15].

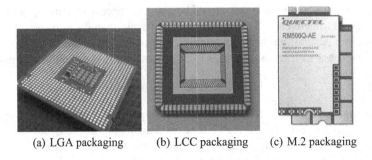

(a) LGA packaging   (b) LCC packaging   (c) M.2 packaging

Fig. 3. Samples of IoT module packaging.

Using LGA packaging technique, all the contacts are located on the PCB of IoT modules, and therefore the backside of the module looks like a grid. Figure 3(a) shows a sample of IoT module using LGA packaging.

The LCC packaging employs no-pin and patch packaging technique. An IoT module using LCC packaging technology is encapsulated by a patch, and all the pins are curved inwardly at the edge òf the module so as to reduce module volume. Compared to LGA packaging technology, the debug and weld process of the modules using LCC packaging technique is relatively difficult. Figure 3(b) plots a sample of LCC packaging module.

The M.2 packaging modules are packaged in accordance with the M.2 interface specification. The M.2 interface, also known as the next generation form factor (NGFF), is a new interface scheme launched by Intel Corp., which specifies a variety of interface types and dimensional specifications. An IoT module using M.2 packaging technology offers the advantages of fast transmission speed, small module size, and strong compatibility, etc., and are widely used in IoT application scenarios [15]. Figure 3(c) plots an example of M.2 packaging module.

Power Consumption Control Technology. In order to achieve low power consumption, IoT modules adopt PSM and eDRX power-saving technologies which reduce the power consumption of modules through increasing sleep time [16]. For an IoT module in PSM state, its transceiver is turned off and the access layer related functions are disabled, therefore, the power consumption resulted from signal transmission, receiving and processing is reduced significantly. By applying eDRX technology, IoT modules stay longer time in sleep state instead of sensing paging channel. Since the power consumption of the modules in sleep state is much lower than that in other states, power saving can be achieved [17].

Interface Consistency. To design a general IoT module, which can be applied to diverse IoT application scenarios, the requirement of various applications, the size, packaging mode and pin layout of the module and the cost issue should be considered comprehensively. In particular, through subdividing the interfaces according to

IoT industries, and defining specific power supply interface, module control and status interface, etc., different types of IoT modules and terminals can be designed and manufactured, and the terminal cost and research and development (R&D) cycle can be reduced as well.

In order to ensure the ease of use of IoT modules and the smooth interaction between IoT modules and the cloud and business platforms, it is necessary to conduct comprehensive software planning and design, and stress the consistency and compatibility of software interfaces. In particular, the basic attention (AT) command set interface of IoT modules should be of satisfactory consistency and compatibility so as to meet the basic needs of the IoT applications. Furthermore, to enable the efficient connection between IoT modules and the cloud and business platforms, the suitable software operating system should be chosen and the communication software development kit (SDK) interface should be designed.

6 Future Development Directions of IoT Modules

This section summarizes several important future development directions of IoT modules.

6.1 Miniaturization, High Integration and Standardization

With the explosive growth of IoT connections, wearable application scenarios such as smart bracelets have become one of the important scenarios of IoT applications. Such scenarios require portable, lightweight and miniaturized IoT modules. To design and manufacture miniaturized IoT modules, highly integrated chips can be employed. In addition, advanced manufacturing process can be applied to further reduce the size of IoT modules, in particular, 7 nm or even 5 nm manufacturing process has been adopted recently in making miniaturized IoT modules.

Aiming to facilitate the design and manufacturing of IoT terminals and boost the development of IoT applications, the standardization of IoT modules has become an important development trend. The standardization of IoT modules involves various aspects, e.g., the standard size of IoT modules, standardized hardware interfaces, standardization in pin positions and functions, and the support of pin-to-pin backwards compatibility, etc. By leveraging standardized IoT modules, the difficulties in developing IoT terminals and replacing new modules can be alleviated, and the cost of IoT terminals can be reduced as well.

6.2 eSIM Technology-Based IoT Modules

At present, pluggable SIM cards are commonly used in mobile communication systems and IoT applications. However, the rapid development of IoT services puts forward higher requirements on smart cards. For instance, certain harsh application environments require the SIM cards to have specific physical and electrical characteristics, such as high environmental temperature and humidity, etc. In some IoT applications, frequent reading and writing operations may occur, which pose requirement to the service life and reliability of the SIM cards. To enable remote access of IoT modules, the SIM cards should support remote configuration, remote activation, and user identity change over the air.

To meet the rising requirements of IoT applications, embedded SIM (eSIM) card technology has emerged in recent years. The eSIM cards are implemented by integrating a physical chip, much smaller than the SIM cards, into IoT modules. The eSIM cards offer many advantages, e.g., high temperature resistance, shock resistance, and super anti-interference ability, which are more suitable for use in future IoT applications. In addition, by applying software control and intelligent technology, eSIM card can achieve remote control and management conveniently.

7   Conclusion

The IoT module is a carrier of the IoT terminal to access the network, which is an important part of the end-to-end solution. This paper first provided a brief introduction to the IoT module, and then analyzed the architecture of the IoT module and briefly analyzed the function of each part. Then the modules have been divided into cellular communication modules and non-cellular communication modules according to the different communication modes,and NB-IoT module has been specifically introduced. The approximate design process of the IoT module was described below, and three key technologies existing-packaging technology, power consumption control technology and consistency of hardware interface and software design were introduced. Finally, based on the above analysis, the future development direction of the networking module technology have been expressed.

References

1. GlobalDots: 41.6 billion IoT devices will be generating 79.4 zettabytes of data in 2025. https://www.globaldots.com/blog/41-6-billion-iot-devices-will-be-generating-79-4-zettabytes-of-data-in-2025. Accessed 22 July 2021
2. Pleshkova, K.S., Panchev, K., Bekyarski, A.: Developing a functional scheme of an IoT based module to an acoustic sensor network. In: 2021 International Conference on High Technology for Sustainable Development (HiTech), pp. 01–04 (2021)
3. Niculescu, A.M., Pavel, D.M., Dumitraşcu, A., et al.: IoT module for air quality measurement. In: 2021 IEEE 27th International Symposium for Design and Technology in Electronic Packaging (SIITME), pp. 342–345 (2021)
4. Saji, M., Sridhar, M., Rajasekaran, A., Kumar, R.A., Suyampulingam, A., Krishna Prakash, N.: IoT-based intelligent healthcare module. In: Suresh, P., Saravanakumar, U., Hussein Al Salameh, M.S. (eds.) Advances in Smart System Technologies. AISC, vol. 1163, pp. 765–774. Springer, Singapore (2021). https://doi.org/10.1007/978-981-15-5029-4_66
5. Sruthy, S., George, S.N.: WiFi enabled home security surveillance system using raspberry Pi and IoT module. In: 2017 IEEE International Conference on Signal Processing, Informatics, Communication and Energy Systems (SPICES), pp. 1–6 (2017)
6. Swamy, S.N., Kota, S.R.: An empirical study on system level aspects of internet of things (IoT). IEEE Access **8**, 188082–188134 (2020)

7. Bernhard, H.W., Herbert, L., Elmar, W.: GNSS-Global Navigation Satellite Systems: GPS, GLONASS, Galileo, and More. Springer, Vienna (2007). https://doi.org/10.1007/978-3-211-73017-1

8. Chen, J., Hu, K., Wang, Q., et al.: Narrowband internet of things: implementations and applications. IEEE Internet Things J. **4**(6), 2309–2314 (2017)

9. Lin, Y., Tseng, H., Lin, Y., Chen, L.: NB-IoT talk: a service platform for fast development of NB-IoT applications. IEEE Internet Things J. **6**, 928–939 (2019)

10. 3GPP. TR45.850 Technical specification group GSM/EDGE radio access network, Rel. 13, v13.1.10 (2015)

11. 3GPP. TR45.820 Cellular system support for ultralow complexity and low throughput IoT (CIoT), Rel. 13, v13.1.0 (2015)

12. Hayashi, V.T., Ribeiro, C.M.N., Filho, A.Q., et al.: Improving IoT module testability with test-driven development and machine learning. In: 2021 8th International Conference on Future Internet of Things and Cloud (FiCloud), pp. 406–412 (2021)

13. Liu, W., Pecht, M.G.: IC Component Sockets, 1st edn. Wiley, Hoboken, NJ, USA (2004)

14. Engelmaier, W.: Fatigue life of leadless chip carrier solder joints during power cycling. IEEE Trans. Compon. Hybrids Manuf. Technol. **6**, 232–237 (1983)

15. Jn, R., Fodor, A.: Cooling techniques for M.2 to PCI(e) adapters. In: Proceedings of the 26th International Symposium for Design and Technology in Electronic Packaging, pp. 382–385 (2020)

16. Yeoh, Y., Man, A.B., Ashraf, Q.M., et al.: Experimental assessment of battery lifetime for commercial off-the-shelf NB-IoT module. In: 2018 20th International Conference on Advanced Communication Technology (ICACT), pp. 1–5 (2018)

17. Elhaddad, A., Bruckmeyer, H., Hertlein, M., et al.: Energy consumption evaluation of cellular narrowband internet of things (NB-IoT) modules. In: 2020 IEEE 6th World Forum on Internet of Things (WF-IoT), pp. 1–5 (2020)

The Calibration of Inspection Data on Juvenile Theft Cases in 5G Context and IOT Age

Cheng-yong Liu[1], Zhi-xin Wang[2], Hui-lin Liang[3], and Xiu-Wen Ye[3(✉)]

[1] College of Marine Culture and Law, Jimei University, Xiamen 361021, Fujian, China
cy.liu@jmu.edu.cn
[2] Higher School of Economics and Management, Far Eastern Federal University, Vladivostok, Russia
[3] Yulin Normal University, Guangxi, China
yeh@ylu.edu.cn

Abstract. In the context of 5g and IOT age, big data has many functions, and the core function of legal big data is to make predictions. However, there is a problem of data transmission errors, and all erroneous data signals cannot be ruled out. This article mainly takes juvenile theft cases as the starting point, and discusses the role of big data in the statistics of legal cases and the possibility of data transmission errors that may occur, and in the context of big data, for juvenile theft. Recidivism rates were studied and practical recommendations were made. Unlike other articles, this article integrates the Internet of Things into judicial issues, aiming to better serve the law through technology.

Keywords: 5G · juvenile theft · IOT

1 Foreword

In the context of 5G, data transmission has low latency, and data transmission is mostly transmitted by serial digital signals. During the transmission process, it is unavoidable that there will be digital changes resulting in signal data errors, so data verification will be performed during serial transmission, it does not necessarily rule out all erroneous data signals, there will be data transmission errors, especially when important data is transmitted, the confidentiality of accuracy is particularly important, so it is a problem that needs to be solved.

In terms of how to correct the inspection data for juvenile theft cases, the China Judicial Big Data Research Institute relies on the judicial trial information resources gathered by the people's court's big data management and service platform to review the trial situation and future progress of cases involving the protection of minors' rights and interests in recent years. The situation of adult crime cases was analyzed and relevant data were released, aiming to provide reference for strengthening the protection of the rights and interests of minors and the prevention of juvenile crime.

In other countries, taking the United States as an example, according to the National Center for Juvenile Justice, the categories of crimes that juvenile courts deal with the

D.-J. Deng et al. (Eds.): SGIoT 2022, LNICST 497, pp. 40–47, 2023.
https://doi.org/10.1007/978-3-031-31275-5_4

longest include: simple assault, drug law violations, theft, obstruction of justice, and disorderly conduct. Based on these data, the United States has developed a set of evidence-based practices, an example of which is the early detection program, which can detect juvenile offenders according to this early detection program, and based on the answers from the database with the corresponding, which may lead to higher risk factors for delinquency among juveniles, compared with interventions based on data that have been evaluated and shown to be effective in reducing or preventing crime.

However, there are still some deficiencies in the technology at this stage. For example, in the process of uploading data, there may still be transmission problems due to force majeure factors, resulting in uploading wrong data. How to reduce the data error during the transmission process? How to improve the efficiency and accuracy of data correction? Taking the data transmission correction of juvenile theft cases as the breakthrough point, this paper discusses how to correct the erroneous data in the transmission process more accurately and efficiently, and also studies how to scientifically and effectively prevent the occurrence of juvenile theft cases.

2   Literature Review of Data Correction

"Traditional statistical analysis methods cannot properly handle the relationship between latent variables, while structural equation models can handle both latent variables and explicit indicators" (Qin Zhengqiang, 2017). There are huge loopholes in traditional data statistics, which requires data correction to avoid data errors. "Through the processing and selection of the input data of the neural network, the accuracy of the online application of the neural network method is improved, and the "residual pollution" that occurs during data inspection is avoided, so that the bad values in the measurement data can be correctly detected and located. At the same time, it can correctly reconstruct and estimate bad data" (Si Fengqi, 2002). The bad data self-correction scheme of AANN solves the estimation of bad data temporarily after it is proposed, but there are still some loopholes in the inspection of wrong data. "On the basis of order statistics, a new test statistic is constructed. Using the distribution properties of order statistics, its exact distribution and related properties are deduced, and compared with Dixon-type test statistics" (Zhang Huijuan, 2012). After the abnormal data is tested, how to verify and modify the detected data becomes the next problem to be solved. "Correct data is the key to ensure the accuracy of state estimation results, and the existence of bad data will greatly reduce the credibility of the estimation results" (Li Shan, 2021) In big data statistics, correct data is to ensure the correctness of data statistics The key condition is that the occurrence of wrong and bad data will have a great impact on the correctness of data statistics. "Since the second half of the 20th century, with the continuous popularization of computers, the digital communication method not only improves the communication speed between police officers, but also realizes the transmission of large amounts of data between police officers in the same area. This breakthrough The achievements have also promoted the progress of other technologies based on massive data, such as real-time imaging, biostatistics, database search, and global positioning systems." (Le Bei, Zhong Xin, 2013) Data collection has become a key in modern times. The detection and correction of erroneous data has also become an important technology. "Before the new data is officially released and used, it needs to be verified to check the correctness, reliability and consistency of the new data set with other data sets." (Zhou Zihan, 2021) For data phones, correct and Error-free data is a key factor in performing analysis and giving correct results, and it is critical for the verification and correction of new data. "Missing data in surveys can cause estimators to be biased. There are some simple and easy ways to adjust the data, which, if used properly, can reduce estimator biases caused by missing data" (Jin Yongjin, 2001) In the statistical process of data, the erroneous data that occurs will affect the accuracy of the situation prediction.

3 Data Correction Issues in Juvenile Theft Cases

3.1 Data Statistics Delay

There is a delay in data statistics in Guangxi. Because the region is relatively underdeveloped, the villages and counties are scattered, the data input is not careful, and the communication and coordination are not timely, which brings certain difficulties to the data collection and causes the delay of the data collection. It is difficult to update the data at the first time, which brings certain difficulties to some tasks. In less developed areas, after a minor theft occurs, the victim may not dare to report the crime due to small losses, fear of trouble and other factors. On the other hand, the victims may not be able to provide detailed case information even if they report the case. For example, in a juvenile theft case that occurred in 2012, two juvenile offenders stole four mobile phones on a crowded pedestrian street and a farmers market. The victim It is impossible to find the trace of the suspect in the dense flow of people, which makes the case difficult to find. At the same time, due to the strong anti-reconnaissance ability of the criminal suspect, there is no valuable trace evidence at the scene, resulting in the case not being valid. It has been proved that the frequent occurrence of cases and the absence of valuable traces of physical evidence at the scene have made the prosecution rate and severe penalty rate low, making it difficult to obtain similar cases in the future due to the lack of network information infrastructure. Effective data support.

At the same time, there will also be exceptions caused by network connection terminals in advanced data protocols and network construction problems, and the disconnection of data during the transmission process may lead to the loss of data in transmission and statistical errors. For example, in the process of data transmission, when the data that needs to be transmitted is converted into binary, there are continuous and sudden errors, which will cause when the receiver receives this data, there is no problem with the verification method. An error occurred in the binary number, causing the receiver to misinterpret the data. And the emergence of failure data, which is a key component of predictive algorithms used to identify warning signs and trigger timely maintenance. Failure data may not exist if maintenance is performed frequently and never fails, or if the system is at a safety-critical level.

3.2 Data Security

My country pays more attention to the protection of the privacy of juvenile offenders in juvenile cases, but in less developed areas, due to the relatively insufficient infrastructure of network information, the transmission of these private information that needs to be protected may be in the process of transmission. Incorrect data and data errors due to force majeure during data transmission. It is also possible that in the process of data transmission, it will be maliciously attacked by middlemen, thereby stealing, intercepting, forging, and tampering with the data in transit, posing a further threat to the security of judicial data. According to Verizon's statistics on data breaches, nearly 50% of the main reasons for data breaches are due to hacker attacks, and malware hidden in computers also accounts for 50% of data breaches. 30%, and the rest due to improper configuration of technicians or operators, social engineering attacks, privilege abuse, and physical attacks (Fig. 1).

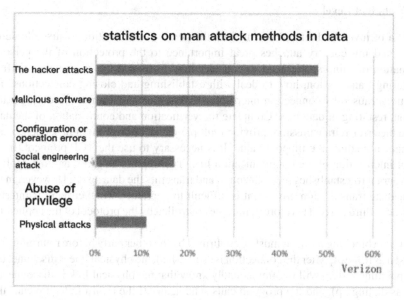

Fig. 1. Main attack methods in data breaches Source: Verizon

3.3 Data Analysis

Today's policy on juvenile offenders is relatively loose, taking into account their young physical and psychological age, so the implementation of arrest or non-arrest will not be arrested, and the prosecution may not be prosecuted. Said, it just increased its wrong understanding, that the crime is not a serious problem, and will commit the crime again. On the one hand, juvenile offenders have a fluke because the punishment they receive is not severe; In such cases, re-offending will occur.

In the process of punishing juvenile delinquents, due to the inconsistency of judicial databases in various places, some law enforcement officers could not find similar punishment cases. Reference and basis. With a unified database, when faced with similar cases, law enforcement officers can make corresponding punishments based on past law enforcement experience, so that a group of juvenile offenders who are subjectively malignant and difficult to correct feel the law Majesty, reducing the likelihood of them breaking the law again.

4 Data Correction Solutions for Juvenile Theft Cases

Technological innovations are carried out on the confidentiality and accuracy of data transmission to ensure that the data is transmitted to the corresponding database accurately and quickly.

4.1 Technical Level

The data of juvenile delinquency involves the personal information of juvenile delinquents, and my country attaches great importance to the protection of the personal information of minors. We need to consider how to reduce the risk of data theft or loss during transmission, how to deal with establishing and closing connections, and exceptions caused by connection interruptions. Avoid data disconnection during transmission, resulting in data loss. Complete the verification and confirmation of the data, reduce the error retransmission, provide multiple paths, arrange them in sequence, and automatically adjust the timeout value. It is necessary to use the TCP protocol. In the case of interruption of the communication line, TCP reports an error, and the application program re-establishes the connection and transmits the data again. However, in the intermediate transmission process, it is difficult to guarantee whether there is interference from a third party. Therefore, it must be controlled by the protocol of the application layer.

If it is in blocking mode, it must be confirmed by the other party before returning. You can test it as follows. After the connection is established, the physical line is disconnected. The operating system will not immediately know that the physical link is disconnected (such as dialing up), and the program calls send again. If the return fails, it means that send waits for confirmation before returning. If the return is successful, it means that send only needs to send to the local TCP to return.

But if the amount of data is too large, other problems will arise, as follows:

1. If the Nagle algorithm is not enabled, the sender's TCP/IP protocol will execute the sending action.
2. If enabled, whether the sending conditions can be met. Accordingly, it is impossible to judge whether the condition is satisfied.

TCP itself uses a sliding window model, and the use of TCP connections is concerned with handling the establishment and closing of connections, as well as exceptions caused by connection interruptions.

4.2 Data Collection

The deep mining and fusion application of data is a significant feature of big data technology. It can help us make predictions. After years of data accumulation, the people's courts already have a large amount of judicial statistics. However, there are still problems such as the narrow scope of statistical investigation, insufficient statistical indicators, and slow updating of data and errors. Using this technology, the judicial statistics system can be optimized and refined, and it can help local courts to make reference and comparison in the judgment of related cases, and reduce the problem of excessive or light sentences. At the same time, the data collected from various regions can analyze the reasons of the case, summarize and summarize, break the information island, and provide diversified guarantees for subsequent judicial trials.

When collecting data, ensure its accuracy and authenticity. You can use python to write a script to crawl data in batches, and use the IP pool to prevent blocking, simulate login, crack the verification code, crack the anti-crawling mechanism, parse the picture, etc., and finally process it into a standard format for storage. At the same time, in order to ensure the personal privacy of minors, it is necessary to further encrypt the data. When data is transmitted on the Internet, it may be attacked by man-in-the-middle, thereby intercepting data, falsifying data, and causing four problems of eavesdropping, counterfeiting, tampering, and post-event denial. Using python to write scripts to crawl data in batches, coupled with the IP pool, can protect data security to a certain extent. The core of data security is to ensure the safety and legal and orderly flow of data. Currently, data is a new type of production factor that affects national security. Because juvenile cases involve the protection of the privacy of minors, the personal privacy of juvenile offenders will not be illegally violated due to problems in data transmission. While ensuring data security, it also protects the legitimate rights and interests of juvenile offenders to a certain extent (Fig. 2).

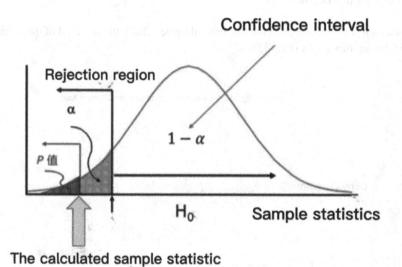

Fig. 2. China Data Research

4.3　Later Protection

Carry out a significance test, make a hypothesis prediction on the overall parameters or overall distribution, use the sample information to judge the rationality of the hypothesis itself, and judge whether there is a significant difference between the data. The collected data can be further tested to provide a certain guarantee for the accuracy of the data. Improve statistical power and increase alpha levels. Using saliency detection, the data is estimated and detected again to avoid data statistics errors due to midway program errors. Carry out prediction test, reflect internal laws, reflect the internal relationship of things, analyze the correlation between two factors, and ensure accuracy. Provide predictive data for follow-up research to help predict in advance and achieve the purpose of prevention.

1. Propose the null and alternative hypotheses

   $H 0$: _____
   $H1$: _____

   The alternative hypothesis is corresponding, indicating whether the test data is a two-tailed test or a left one-tailed or right one-tailed test.
2. Construct the test statistic, collect sample data, and calculate the sample observation value of the test statistic.
3. According to the proposed significance level, determine the critical value and rejection domain
4. Calculate the value of the test statistic.
5. Make inspection decisions.

   Based on a data sample, compare to a critical value. Check the standard of the value and perform another check (Fig. 3).

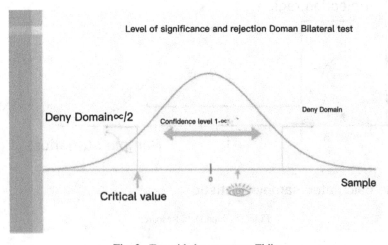

Fig. 3. Two-sided test source: Zhihu

5 Conclusion

Using big data statistics to integrate and analyze various types of cases, provide a solid basis for judgment and punishment for subsequent similar cases, provide a scientific basis for handling and preventing juvenile theft, and improve the problems faced in the process of data transmission. It can correct and estimate the data while ensuring the safe transmission of data. It has practical significance for judging and helping juvenile thieves in the future. Integrating the Internet of Things into judicial issues, providing better legal services through technology, and contributing to the prevention of juvenile crimes.

Acknowledgments. This research was supported by Social Science Foundation of Fu-jian Province, China (Grant No. FJ2021B059) (Topic: Legalization of Credit Management of Cross-Strait, Hong Kong and Macao); Educa-tional Commission of Fujian Province, China (Grant No. JAS21106); and Research Foundation of Jimei University (Grant No. Q202112).

References

Shen, Y., Tang, G.: An analysis of juvenile re-offending. J. Natl. Prosecutors Coll. 17-5

Huang, X., Zeng, Y., Kong, Y.: Research on the prediction of juvenile first offenders: an empirical study on the possibility of juvenile offenders in Zhejiang Province. Chin. J. Crim. Law (2004)

Wang, C.: Re-Criminal Research on Rural Minors. Master's Thesis, Shanghai Jiaotong University Sociology (2008)

David, P.: Sociology: Renmin University of China Press, Prentice Hall Publishing Company (1999)

He, Q.: We should pay attention to the prevention of juvenile delinquency "secondary crime", in Consumer Guide (2007)

Yang, H.: Research on grid data transmission technology supporting dynamic update (2008)

Su, Z., Zhang, L., You, X.: Data transmission technology of converged access network (2017)

Song, W., Jiang, X.: Data security and encryption technology analysis in network transmission (2021)

Liu, W.: Security research and development of network applications

Guo, L.: Research on industrial internet data transmission security issues and improvement strategies (2019)

A Cross-Domain Authentication Scheme Based Master-Slave Chain in Edge Computing

Zhiyuan Li[✉] and Zhenjiang Zhang

Department of Electronic and Information Engineering, Key Laboratory of Communication and Information Systems, Beijing Municipal Commission of Education, Beijing Jiaotong University, Beijing 100044, China
{19120091,zhangzhenjiang}@bjtu.edu.cn

Abstract. As an emerging technology, edge computing can solve the problem of limited computing resources of IoT devices under the premise of lower latency. However, the existing mobile edge computing architecture cannot well solve the security problem of the identity authentication of the terminal device. In particular, the cross-domain authentication of the device cannot be completed efficiently when the device is switched between different IoT domains. To address these challenging issues, in this article, a lightweight edge computing cross-domain identity authentication scheme which combines edge computing with blockchain based on master-slave chain is proposed. The scheme uses the consortium blockchain as the master chain, that is, a decentralized authentication platform, realizes cross-domain authentication when the device switches domains, and can also solve the single point of failure problem of traditional authentication. The slave chain is maintained by edge computing nodes and terminal devices in each domain. When devices in the domain are mutually authenticated, the efficiency of authentication can be improved. During authentication, ring signature technology is used to ensure the security of the system, and at the same time, it can effectively save the storage space of the blockchain. Finally, the performance evaluation and security analysis of this scheme have been carried out to prove the safety and effectiveness of our scheme.

Keywords: Edge Computing · Master-slave chain · Ring Signature · Cross-domain authentication

1 Introduction

The appearance of edge computing can share the computing pressure of terminal devices, improve the quality of service (QoS), and respond to users' needs more quickly. However, the security problems caused by edge computing can not be ignored. Specifically, in the current edge computing system framework, edge node deployment is very flexible, and part of terminal device movement in the area covered by edge node is common. This brings new challenges to maintaining the security of equipment in the system and preventing it from external attacks [1].

D.-J. Deng et al. (Eds.): SGIoT 2022, LNICST 497, pp. 48–57, 2023.
https://doi.org/10.1007/978-3-031-31275-5_5

Identity authentication plays an important role in ensuring the safe operation of the whole system. In the current mature cloud computing architecture, cloud location is relatively fixed and centralized, which is convenient for cloud service providers to strictly protect cloud infrastructure and network [2]. However, the existing mature cloud computing security solutions cannot be directly extended to edge computing because the deployment characteristics and operating environment of edge computing are quite different from cloud computing.

Blockchains have a specially designed distributed ledger structure that connects blocks in chronological order. All nodes in a decentralized environment share and maintain the saved data. The main advantages of blockchain are decentralization, open autonomy and anonymous traceability [3]. However, the existing blockchain authentication scheme is not efficient and vulnerable to external threats.

The primary goal of this paper is to propose a cross-domain authentication scheme based on blockchain in edge computing environments. The main contributions of this paper are as follows:

1. An efficient cross-domain authentication scheme is designed in which blockchain is used to replace trusted third parties and can resist single point of failure. Specifically, a master-slave blockchain architecture is designed to store certificate information for devices and assist in cross-domain authentication. Slave chains are used to maintain intra-domain devices and implement intra-domain authentication.
2. Based on this scheme, ring signature technology is used to guarantee the validity of authentication, which improves the verification efficiency of each node in the consensus stage of block generation. Effectively resist malicious attacks inside the system, for the authentication process, can trace the source of the signer.
3. Security analysis and extensive performance evaluations demonstrate the effectiveness and the efficiency of our proposed schemes. Specifically, on the premise of realizing multiple security indexes and resisting threat attack, the authentication performance of our scheme is excellent.

The remainder of this article is organized as follows. Section 2 presents the related work of authentication. In Sect. 3, we describe the master-slave architecture. Detailed authentication scheme based on master-slave chain is proposed in Sect. 4. The security analysis and performance are described in Sect. 5. Section 6 is the conclusion.

2 Related Work

In view of the identity authentication technology of edge computing, some improved authentication schemes applied to edge are proposed based on joint cloud computing and P2P computing. For example, Donald et al. designed a centralized authentication mechanism for mobile cloud computing [4], but this method requires authentication services to be accessible all the time, resulting in limited availability. AMOR et al. proposed an authentication system that allows any fog computing user and fog node to authenticate each other [5], but this system forces all nodes to store the certificate information of all users in the trusted domain. Shouhuai et al. put forward the concept of situational authentication [6], based on different time, place and interacting objects such as situational use different authentication methods. However, these schemes usually need to be connected to a centralized authentication server, so the performance can be improved to some extent.

At present, with the maturity of blockchain technology, it is a research idea to combine blockchain to realize trusted authentication. In [7, 8], Satoshi Nakamoto proposed a decentralized peer-to-peer (P2P) network platform that verifies the integrity and validity of the network through computationally intensive tasks such as proof of work. In [9], Almadhoun et al. applied blockchain authentication to iot scenarios. In [10], Dorri et al. proposed the application of blockchain technology to protect Internet of Things security and privacy technology in smart home scenarios. In [11], Li et al. applied blockchain to large-scale data storage and protection. In [12], Bao et al. constructed a three-tier security authentication architecture based on blockchain. In [13], Zhouglin et al. proposed a security authentication scheme for 5G super-dense network based on block chain to solve the identity authentication problem of mobile edge computing. In [14], Wang et al. proposed a cross-domain authentication model based on blockchain in a distributed environment. However, these studies do not put forward higher requirements for the performance of the system, which cannot meet the real-time requirements of edge computing scenarios.

3   System Architecture

According to the background proposed in Sect. 1, the edge computing authentication architecture based on the master-slave chain is shown in Fig. 1. The architecture is a two-tier architecture. The upper layer consists of multiple edge computing nodes to form a consortium chain for device management; the lower layer consists of edge computing nodes and devices distributed in different domains. The edge computing nodes in the domain form a blockchain to assist devices to achieve intra-domain authentication and cross-domain authentication. The functions of each part are described as follows:

1. Master chain node: Record the device certificate and other information on the blockchain after reaching a consensus. Therefore, when the device sends an authentication request, the query function is provided through the smart contract.
2. Slave chain node: Realize the management of the devices in the domain, and write the information into the blockchain through the consensus mechanism. It communicates with the master node and assist the device with authentication.
3. Device: Implement active application to join a domain and complete the identity registration and authentication process.

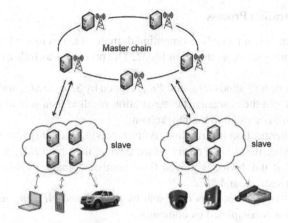

Fig. 1. Overview of the master-slave chain system architecture

4 Proposed Authentication Scheme Based on Master-Slave Chain

This section proposes the detailed process of device registration, intra-domain authentication and cross-domain authentication based on the master-slave chain system architecture. All the used notations are listed in Table 1.

Table 1. Notation description

Parameters	Description
d_{ij}	The j-th device in domain i
SE_j^i	The j-th slave chain edge server in domain i
ME_i	The i-th master chain edge server
ID_{ij}	Identity of d_{ij}
ID_{sij}	Identity of SE_j^i
SK_{ij}	Secret key of d_{ij}
SK_{sij}	Secret key of SE_j^i
SK_{mij}	Secret key of ME_i
PK_{ij}	Public key of d_{ij}
PK_{sij}	Public key of SE_j^i
PK_{dij}	Public key of ME_i
K	The key for the temporary session
Ring{*}	2n + 1 tuple of the ring signature
TS	Timestamp

4.1 Device Registration Process

If a new device wants to join an edge computing domain, it needs to send a request to a nearby edge computing node, as shown in Fig. 2. The process is as follows:

1. Apply to SE_j^i. A new d_{ij} sends ID_{dij} and PK_{dij} signed by SK_{dij} to SE_j^i, and SE_j^i verifies whether d_{ij} can join the domain. The registration result is then sent to ME_i and d_{ij}. Finally, the result is written to the blockchain.
2. ME_i Stores authentication information. After receiving the ID_{dij} sent by SE_j^i, ME_i will query whether the d_{ij} is a newly added device, then bind ID_{dij} and ID_{Sij} into the blockchain. If the device is moved from another domain, modify the binding information between d_{ij} and ME_i.
3. Check ID_{Sij}. After ID_{dij} receives ID_{Sij} sent by the SE_j^i and ME_i, the authentication of the slave chain is completed by comparison.

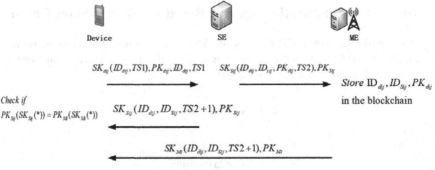

Fig. 2. Registration process for a new device

4.2 Intra-domain Authentication Process

After the registration is completed, the device can achieve mutual authentication with another device through the slave chain node in the domain as required, as shown in Fig. 3. The certification process is as follows:

1. Apply to SE_j^i. d_{ij} Sends ID_{dij} and ID_{dik} to SE_j^i through PK_{Sij} encryption, and applies for authentication with d_{ik}.
2. Send to d_{ik}. SE_j^i checks whether d_{ij} and d_{ik} are successfully registered devices in this domain. If d_{ik} is not a device in this domain, apply for cross-domain authentication to ME_i. This part is explained in cross-domain authentication. If d_{ik} is a device in this domain. Then ID_{dij} and PK_{dij} are encrypted by PK_{dik} and sent to d_{ij}.
3. Key agreement between d_{ij} and d_{ik}. d_{ik} Generates a session key K randomly, and encrypts ID_{dik} and K by PK_{dij} and sends it to d_{ij}. Complete the authentication of two devices in the domain.

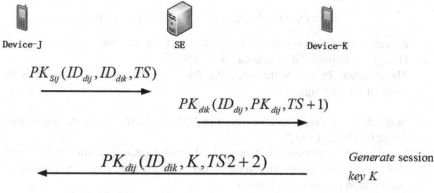

Fig. 3. Intra-domain authentication process between two devices

4.3 Cross-Domain Authentication Process

If the registered device wants to request data across domains, it needs the assistance of the slave chain node to complete the communication with the master chain. After that, the master chain node sends a request to the target device, as shown in Fig. 4. In the process of cross-domain authentication, the ring signature can realize the anonymity of the request initiator under the premise of ensuring the correctness of the signature. The specific certification process is as follows:

1. d_{ij} Applies to SE_j^i. Similar to the intra-domain authentication step 1, d_{ij} sends the ID_{dmn} and request $message1$ encrypted by PK_{Sij} to SE_j^i.
2. SE_j^i Generates ring signature. If d_{mn} is found not in this domain after the query, a ring signature will be generated to ensure the anonymity of d_{ij}. The process is as follows:

   a. Generate a symmetric k from $message1$ through a hash function:

   $$k = hash(\text{message}1) \tag{1}$$

   b. Generate a random number r.
   c. Randomly generate n-1 values $\{x_1, x_2, \ldots, x_{n-1}\}$. Use the public keys of other n-1 slave chain nodes to encrypt separately, and calculate $y_i = PK_i(x_i)$. Aggregate to get $\{y_1, y_2, \ldots, y_{n-1}\}$.
   d. Substitute k, r and $\{y_1, y_2, \ldots, y_{n-1}, y_n\}$ into the function $C_{k,r}()$ to solve for y_n.

   $$C_{k,r}(y_1, y_2, \ldots, y_n) = r \tag{2}$$

   The solution process is as follows:

   $$C_{k,r}(y_1, y_2, \ldots, y_n) = E_k(y_n \oplus E_k(y_{n-1} \oplus E_k(\cdots \oplus E_k(y_1 \oplus r)\ldots))) = r$$

   $$y_n \oplus E_k(y_{n-1} \oplus E_k(\cdots \oplus E_k(y_1 \oplus r)\ldots)) = D_k(r)$$

$$y_n = D_k(r) \oplus E_k(y_{n-1} \oplus E_k(\cdots \oplus E_k(y_1 \oplus r)\ldots))$$

E_k means use k for encryption, D_k means use k for decryption.

e. Decrypt y_n through SK_{Sij} to get $x_n = SK_{Sij}(y_n)$
f. The obtained $2n + 1$ tuple $Ring\{PK_1, PK_2, \ldots, PK_n; r; x_1, x_2, \ldots, x_n\}$ is the result of the ring signature.

3. SE_j^i sends $Ring\{*\}$, ID_{dmn} and $message1$ to ME_k. And ME_k sends the information encrypted by PK_{Smn} to SE_n^m.
4. SE_n^m verifies ring signature. Verification of the ring signature result can determine whether the signature is correct, and the sender of the message cannot be determined. The verification process is as follows:

a. Encrypt y_i through PK_i to get $y_i = PK_i(X_i)$. Therefore, it can be obtained $\{y_1, y_2, \ldots, y_n\}$.
b. Substitute $message1$ into Eq. (1) to get k.
c. Verify the Eq. (2) holds.

5. SE_n^m sends request to d_{mn}. After completing the ring signature verification, SE_n^m sends the information encrypted by PK_{dmn} to d_{mn}.
6. d_{mn} replies to request. d_{mn} Generates a response $message2$ and sends $message2$ back through the above steps.

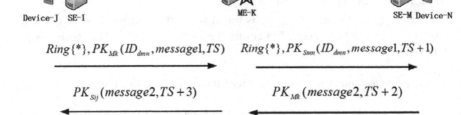

Device-J SE-I   ME-K   SE-M Device-N

$Ring\{*\}, PK_{Mk}(ID_{dmn}, message1, TS)$ $Ring\{*\}, PK_{Smn}(ID_{dmn}, message1, TS+1)$

$PK_{Sij}(message2, TS+3)$ $PK_{Mk}(message2, TS+2)$

Fig. 4. Cross-domain authentication process between two devices

5   Security and Performance

In this section, the performance and security of the proposed master-slave chain authentication scheme will be analyzed. The feasibility of the scheme will be evaluated by comparing the schemes in other references.

5.1   Performance Evaluation

This section compares the computational overheads of the other three references for performance analysis. The overheads of different authentication schemes are shown in

Table 2. The values in the table represent the cumulative operation times of a certain operation.

Table 2. Calculation cost comparison

Scheme	Digital Signature and Verification	Hash Operation	Public Key Encryption and Decryption	Bilinear Pair	Exponential Operation
[9]	2	4	4	6	4
[11]	6	2	8	2	8
[12]	8	3	4	2	4
Our Scheme	5	2	7	0	3

According to the data in Table 2, our scheme performs less times for some operations with high computational cost (e.g. bilinear pair and exponential operation). To sum up, the implementation efficiency of our scheme is higher than that of other schemes.

5.2 Security Analysis

This paper analyzes the impact of various common attack methods on this scheme, and compares other reference schemes, as shown in Table 3. Through analysis, it is concluded that the safety indicators listed in this paper can be realized in our scheme. The specific analysis contents are as follows:

1. Anonymity: This scheme uses ring signatures to ensure that the verifier cannot determine the sender of the message on the premise of ensuring the accuracy of the information.
2. Mutual authentication: we use the master chain node to realize the mutual authentication between the slave chain node and the device when the device is registered. In the identity authentication stage, the mutual authentication between different devices is realized by using the slave chain nodes.
3. Message substitution: In the registration phase, the information of the device is digitally signed to ensure that it is not tampered with by attackers during the transmission process.
4. Cross-domain authentication: This article uses a two-tier blockchain to ensure efficient cross-domain authentication between devices belonging to different IoT domains.
5. Data security: Before the message is transmitted, the asymmetric key will be generated through the elliptic curve, and the public key will be transmitted through the master-slave chain. After that, the two sides negotiate the session key and encrypt the message to ensure the security of data transmission.

6. Message replay: A timestamp is added to each transmitted datagram to prevent frequent message sending and to ensure that the entire architecture is resistant to message replay attacks.

Table 3. Security comparison of different schemes

Attacks	[9]	[11]	[12]	Our Scheme
Anonymity	✗	✗	✗	✓
Mutual authentication	✗	✗	✓	✓
Message substitution	✓	✓	✓	✓
Cross-domain authentication	✗	✓	✗	✓
Data security	✓	✓	✓	✓
Message replay	✓	✗	✓	✓

6 Conclusion

In this article, we expound the potential security risks of current IoT device authentication, and propose a cross-domain authentication scheme based on master-slave chain and edge computing. In this scheme, the device registration process is lightweight, so that the device can quickly join an IoT domain, and the mobility of the device is considered. At the same time, this scheme can also realize intra-domain authentication and cross-domain authentication between different devices. A ring signature method is proposed to ensure the anonymity of the authentication process. Compared with the existing IoT device authentication schemes, the scheme proposed in this paper has less computational overhead and can resist a variety of common threat attacks. It is suitable for resource-constrained devices for registration and identity authentication.

In the future, we will make a more comprehensive evaluation of the performance for our scheme. Besides, we will focus on the privacy protection issue after the device is authenticated, making the architecture proposed in this paper more practical.

Acknowledgement. The authors gratefully acknowledge the support and financial assistance provided by the National Natural Science Foundation under Grant No. 62173026. The authors thank the anonymous reviewers who provided constructive feedback on earlier work of this paper.

References

1. Mao, Y., You, C., Zhang, J., Huang, K., Letaief, K.B.: A survey on mobile edge computing: the communication perspective. IEEE Commun. Surv. Tutor. **19**(4), 2322–2358 (2017)
2. Mukherjee, M., et al.: Security and privacy in fog computing: challenges. IEEE Access **5**, 19293–19304 (2017)

3. Ma, L., Pei, Q., Qu, Y., Fan, K., Lai, X.: Decentralized privacy-preserving reputation management for mobile crowdsensing. In: Chen, S., Choo, K.-K.R., Fu, X., Lou, W., Mohaisen, A. (eds.) SecureComm 2019. LNICSSITE, vol. 304, pp. 532–548. Springer, Cham (2019). https://doi.org/10.1007/978-3-030-37228-6_26

4. Donald, A.C., Arockiam, L.: A secure authentication scheme for MobiCloud. In: 2015 International Conference on Computer Communication and Informatics (ICCCI), Coimbatore (2015)

5. Amor, A.B., Abid, M., Meddeb, A.: SAMAFog: service-aware mutual authentication fog-based protocol. In: 2019 15th International Wireless Communications & Mobile Computing Conference (IWCMC), Tangier, Morocco (2019)

6. Zhu, S., Xu, S., Setia, S., et al.: LHAP: a lightweight network access control protocol for ad hoc networks. Ad Hoc Netw. **4**(5), 567–585 (2006)

7. Zheng, Z., Xie, S., Dai, H., Chen, X., Wang, H.: An overview of blockchain technology: architecture consensus and future trends. In: Proceedings of the IEEE International Congress on Big Data, pp. 557–564 (2017)

8. Nakamoto, S.: Bit coin: a peer to peer electronic cash system (2009)

9. Almadhoun, R., Kadadha, M., Alhemeiri, M., et al.: A user authentication scheme of IoT devices using blockchain-enabled fog nodes. In: 2018 IEEE/ACS 15th International Conference on Computer Systems and Applications (AICCSA). IEEE (2018)

10. Dorri, A., Kanhere, S.S., Jurdak, R., Gauravaram, P.: Blockchain for IoT security and privacy: the case study of a smart home. In: Proceedings of the IEEE International Conference on Pervasive Computing and Communications Workshops, pp. 618–623 (2017)

11. Li, R., Song, T., Mei, B., et al.: Blockchain for large-scale internet of things data storage and protection. IEEE Trans. Serv. Comput. **12**, 762–771 (2018)

12. Bao, Z., Shi, W., He, D., et al.: IoTChain: a three-tier blockchain-based IoT security architecture (2018)

13. Chen, Z., Chen, S., Xu, H., Hu, B.: A security authentication scheme of 5G ultra-dense network based on block chain. IEEE Access **6**, 55372–55379 (2018)

14. Wang, W., Hu, N., Liu, X.: BlockCAM: a blockchain-based cross-domain authentication model. In: Proceedings of the IEEE 3rd International Conference on Data Science Cyberspace (DSC), pp. 896–901 (2018)

Balance of Interests: The Legal Path of Data Circulation and Utilization in the Internet of Things Era

Shen Xie[1][(✉)] and Cheng Chen[2]

[1] Department of Law, Jimei University, Xiamen, China
xie761@163.com
[2] Xiamen Institute of Technology, Xiamen, China
chengchen_cy@yeah.net

Abstract. In the era of the Internet of Things, data circulation and utilization forms a trend. Judicial practice has clarified the "triple authorization rules", that is, data circulation and utilization need to obtain the user's authorization for data collection and users and data holders' authorization for data circulation and utilization, which seriously affects the data flow and big data market development. The data circulation and utilization mechanism needs to be improved urgently. Based on big data industry development demand and commercial interests protection, rebuild the data circulation utilization benefit distribution mechanism, improve the benefit distribution mechanism between data holders and users, confirm the interests of data business subject, priority data holders in the conflict of interest interests protection, fully arouse the enthusiasm of the data business subject to participate in data circulation utilization.

Keywords: Internet of Things technology · Internet of Things cloud data sharing · Legal mechanism

1 Introduction

The Internet of Things technology is a new technology for connecting various sensors and the existing Internet. It uses various terminal sensors to collect user information, and transmit the information to the cloud or other information terminals in the way of data. Using smooth network transmission, the world can form an interconnected information network, namely the Internet of Things. The development of the whole Internet of Things. The Internet of Things technology is booming, the interconnected network is the infrastructure, and the "data and information" collected, transmitted and shared by sensors is the "blood" of the boom of the Internet of Things technology. The interconnection of information network and the sharing of data and information play a very important role in the development of the Internet of Things technology.

Iot cloud data refers to the production data that can identify user information when identified and collected by terminal devices that use the Internet of Things technology

D.-J. Deng et al. (Eds.): SGIoT 2022, LNICST 497, pp. 58–64, 2023.
https://doi.org/10.1007/978-3-031-31275-5_6

and collected in the form of data. The Iot cloud data is formed by the user terminal device collecting user information, and then the iot information network transmits the user data back to the information processing center, and screened, analyzed, processed and sorted out the data. Finally, the processed data is stored in the cloud for subsequent utilization. The entire iot cloud data, from collection, to storage, and then to utilization, involves the data subject (i.e., the user), the data holder (i. e., the Internet of Things technology provider or operator) and the data user respectively. The data can be used for self-use, shared to other subjects, or sold to other subjects.

Content cloud data sharing usually does not affect the data holder of the possession and use of data, therefore, content cloud data sharing is more common, usually by the data controller, namely the platform open IDP port to other users, the use of other use subject behavior to monitor, other use subject within the scope of authorization to obtain data.

The use of IOT cloud data is diverse, and can be used for both commercial and public purposes. Such as the user information analysis of report feedback to users, or use the collected information analysis of user or user group instructions and demand, can accurate positioning and analysis of users, or as the basis for further monitoring user demand, further follow up and feedback to user needs, or use of content cloud data analysis and forecast of user or user groups, provide reference for public policy, and so on. At the same time, in the whole process of collection, analysis or circulation and sharing of IOT cloud data, the data may be cleaned and become pure data for different use purposes, and the personal information cannot be recognized, or the corresponding personal information can still be identified without processing, usually based on the data that can identify the personal information.

In the case of "Sina Weibo v. Mai Mai", the court of second instance in the case initiated the "triple authorization principle", that is, the first authorization for users to obtain data from the platform; the second and third authorization of the user and the platform to use the subsequent data acquisition. Based on the "triple authorization principle", the platform still needs to obtain explicit authorization or consent from users when sharing data with subsequent users. It can be seen that although the sharing and sharing of IOT cloud data is a simple process of data transmission and utilization, the subject relationship involved is relatively complex and involves the construction of many mechanisms. This paper will combine the above issues, starting from the national industrial policy positioning, discuss the ownership of data, ot cloud data personal information protection and sharing of the balance of interests and other mechanisms.

2 Analysis of the Benefit Balance Mechanism of Data Circulation and Utilization

2.1 Practical Dilemma of Data Circulation and Utilization and the Proposal of Industrial Policies

Sharing and sharing of the data, that is, sharing the data to other entities (including public parts such as the government or other commercial entities) in the form of packaging the transmission or opening the sharing port without affecting the data holder's use of the data. Usually, the former is mostly open port shared.

However, at present, it is still difficult to achieve cross-platform and cross-regional data sharing and sharing, which seriously hinders the development of the digital economy industry. The reason is that the rights and interests of data resources are not clear enough, and the data circulation and utilization mechanism has not been established. In particular, the "triple authorization mechanism" formed by the court has seriously affected the collection and circulation of data. Therefore, breaking down the barriers of data islands and establishing a perfect legal mechanism for the sharing and sharing of data resources are the only ways to promote the development and prosperity of the digital economy. To promote data circulation and utilization requires the balance of interests of all parties and constructs a reasonable benefit distribution mechanism. Data is often held by the technology provider or operator of the Internet of Things technology, and the data circulation and utilization is also subject to the sharing willingness of the data holder. Because data contains huge value benefits, it is common to reject data sharing or overpricing; how in the process of data sharing and protecting the interests of data parties and how to price data information are all pending issues. Data circulation cannot be normalized, which will have a significant impact on boosting the development of the data industry.

Thus, it leads to the industrial policy positioning problem of data circulation and utilization. It is not difficult to find that the above difficulties reflect the certain value conflict between data circulation and utilization and personal information protection and data privatization. For the problem of value conflict, we need to provide solutions from the perspective of industrial policy; now we cannot eliminate the conflict, but can only balance the interests of both sides.

We propose the purpose of industrial policy: first, we hope to provide the solution of national industrial policy from the perspective of the development of data factor market: to guarantee the personal information of data, and emphasize the initial rights of data holders and the utilization rights of data utilization, so as to improve the efficiency of data circulation and further stimulate the market potential of data factors. Second, industrial policy orientation is the basis of the legal mechanism. Only when the state determines the direction of industrial development can it guide the improvement of the legal mechanism. To solve these two problems is an industrial policy bias in value conflict, rather than a pure legal problem. The legal mechanism lies in the implementation, and the industrial policy gives the macro guidance. Under normal circumstances, to advocate the scale of data circulation and utilization and personal information protection, the country needs to balance the interests and conflicts of various parties and seek "optimal solutions" from the perspective of industrial development, so as to realize the balance of interests of all parties. With the help of industrial policy positioning, a set of basic legal framework system is established for the data factor market, and the legal mechanism and specific rules of data circulation and utilization are implemented. Third, from the target level, it helps to eliminate the uncertainty of the commercial market. Whether data is shared basically depends on the private or private sector's judgment and consideration of their own economic interests, rather than starting from the goals of economic and social development. Whether the data can be shared together depends on the case study of the market participants, which cannot make useful predictions for the market participants, or form trends and trends. Unified industrial policy is of great significance to the formation of a unified and perfect data factor market.

This paper believes that for the data factor market, it is an important way to accelerate the construction of the data factor market, cultivate and improve the market and activate the market vitality to form the basic market mechanism and norms based on this demand. At the level of national industrial policy, two major issues should be considered: first, how to balance the interests of the conflict under the background of data circulation and utilization; second, how to form a legal mechanism to promote data marketization and sharing under the guidance of industrial policy.

2.2 Balance of Interests Between Data Holders and Users in Data Circulation and Utilization Under Industrial Policy

In the "Sina Weibo v. Mai Mai" case, the court of second instance has also established a rule that the data user should obtain the consent or authorization from the data holder to use the data. The reason is: first, the data holder has paid the necessary labor for the data, should confirm the data holder on the use of data decision; second, if the data user without consent or authorization mechanism, without consent or authorization, of course, without pay, then will cause the market disorder, impact the interests of the data practitioners, cause the development power, the development of the big data industry growth.

Some scholars believe that data is formed in the operation process of business entities, and commercial entities should decide whether to share it in circulation. No subject or reason can force the sharing of data. Of course, some scholars believe that from the perspective of social and economic development, the full use of data resources should promote the sharing and utilization of data. At present, many scholars can hold shared utilization. However, the conditions for data sharing and utilization need to be clarified according to the specific situation of the data.

It is necessary for us to analyze the basic principles and scales of promoting data circulation and utilization from the policy level first. How to achieve a win-win situation between public interests and commercial private interests in the big data industry. How to set industrial policies for the data circulation between data controllers and data users is the logical starting point of this problem, and also the basis for discussing the data circulation and utilization mechanism. As we all know, compared with data privatization, the circulation and sharing of data resources can stimulate the potential of big data and obtain positive externalities. The value of data circulation and utilization to industrial development and social and economic development is obvious. The policy should promote the sharing of data. However, industrial policy is not so simple. The development of big data is often faced with the constraints of external and internal factors, which mainly refer to the personal information protection and data security issues involved in the data, and the internal factors mainly refer to the interests generated by the use of data subjects.

The problem of the data controller's willingness to use the data circulation is itself a matter of interest. In essence, this problem is the balance of interests between the data holder and the data user, which is shown as: one is the decision right of the data holder in the data circulation and utilization; the other is the profit right of the data holder in the data circulation and utilization. All of these will affect the willingness of the holders of the data to share it. For the data controllers, from the perspective of commercial interests, whether to share the data for sharing and sharing depends on the profit comparison between the data self-use and the data sharing. In the absence of perfect industrial policy guidance and legal mechanism application, commercial subjects can only rely on the consideration of business environment and individual cases. From the perspective of market development, we propose effective solutions to balance the interests, which is a good mechanism to solve this problem.

Therefore, in promoting data circulation and utilization, attention should be paid to the balance between social benefits and private benefits of data circulation. This paper holds that first, based on the needs of industrial and social development, data sharing and sharing should be promoted in an orderly manner, implementing data sharing and sharing in policies, or even restricting or prohibiting monopoly data behavior; second, attention should be paid to promoting data circulation and utilization, while protecting the interests of data holders, respecting creation, and paying for labor value added. Therefore, based on the importance of the development of the big data market, it plays a decisive role in promoting the sharing, circulation and shared utilization of factors in the data factor market. Therefore, instead of the "industrial policy to promote the data circulation and utilization", the problem of "how to promote the circulation of data between the data control party and the data utilization party" is proposed.

From the perspective of industrial policy, to realize the data circulation and utilization of data resources between the data controller and the data user, it is necessary to solve the pain points of the data controller and the data circulation and utilization, first, how to realize the appreciation of data circulation and utilization from the perspective of the data controller; second, from the perspective of the data user, how to avoid the wrong, incomplete or unneeded data to ensure the usefulness, integrity and correctness of the data provided.

3 Distribution Mechanism of Benefits for Data Circulation and Utilization

Data circulation and utilization of how to allocate the benefits generated by data circulation in multiple subjects, this paper believes that there are three main implementation mechanisms:

First, Confirmation of benefits during data circulation and utilization. First, the data cannot generate profit at the generation level, that is, the data subject, the user himself, cannot claim the data profit. This paper holds that, if analyzed from the level of rights, although individuals are the subject of digital rights, but only based on personality rights and interests, and no property rights and interests; individuals cannot sell their personal information in exchange for consideration. Property rights are only generated in subjects with commercial property value to user data. The data of personal information in business should only protect the corresponding personality rights and interests from infringement. Why can't individuals enjoy property rights in their personal information? Personal information cannot be obtained in the person, only the flow can produce possible property benefits. This interest is actually an interest generated from being exploited.

Avoid personal profit from selling their personal information. In addition, as property rights and interests are based on the value created by the subject through labor, while users provide their own information to the Internet of Things to enhance the life service experience, which cannot be used as the source of property rights and interests.

Second, data can generate profits at the utilization level. Based on Locke's theory of labor empowerment, whether it is the profit of data circulation or utilization level, we should confirm the benefits of data processing and innovation addition.

As a data holder, there are two ways to obtain property rights: one is to analyze, process and conduct possible profit activities; the other is to package and share the collected data with other commercial entities for profit. From the perspective of promoting the balance of the efficient utilization of data resources and personal information protection, the sharing and sharing of data and information should limit the scope of its utilization and profit. This paper believes that the sharing of data information should be limited by two aspects: one is the limited field, namely the collected data can only be used for the Internet of things services; the second is the limit of profit, data can only be shared and shared, rather than the data resources, after sharing is still the control body, the data control and security obligations. At this time, the source of the property rights acquired by the data control subject is not the value of the data itself, but the value-added value obtained based on the collection, analysis, collation and processing of the data.

As the subject of data utilization, usually only the authorized data information can be used, and only limited to the use within the scope of authorization and pay the corresponding consideration. At the same time, the transfer of IOT data information is prohibited to make a profit.

Second, the pricing in the data circulation process. In order to avoid the illegal or improper profits of the data holders from the data and affect the healthy development of the big data market, the benefits of the data holders should be limited to a certain range. At present, the data value basis includes: the information value reflected in the data itself (the profit value generated by the data), the processing value (including screening, collection and other processing means), and the hidden value of the user itself. This paper holds that the data pricing should be based on the processing value, and should not include the information value of the data itself or the additional value that the data may produce to the user.

Third, the conflict of interest in the process of data utilization, that is, in the process of data circulation and utilization, the interests may conflict among different subjects. For example, it can be competition-oriented. However, competing interests need to be rethink. The competitive interests of data controllers will be affected with the sharing of data, which may affect the economic benefits of data controllers generated by using the data. For example, the data controller and the data user belong to the same class of enterprises, producing a competitive relationship in the business. In such cases, the industrial policy should further consider addressing the competitive interests of the data controllers and the data needs of the data users.

In general, if data collection is a monopoly, sharing of data is normally denied. If the data collection does not form a monopoly, the data user can obtain the data source by himself or through other paths, it can obtain the source through other ways. However, if the subsequent use of data does not affect the competitive interests of the data controller, the data controller should share in principle, unless the data controller can prove that the data may be used for illegal purposes and may harm the social welfare; the data use may infringe the interests of the data subject or the data controller; the business competition and conflict between the data controller; the data user may share the data with the third party; the associated enterprises of the data user, etc.

4 Conclusion

In the era of the Internet of Things, data circulation and utilization has become a kind of balance of power. Based on the demand of the development of big data industry, the data circulation and utilization mechanism needs to be improved urgently. In order to fully tap the potential of data and further promote the development and improvement of data factor market, we should change the existing data subject complete self-determination right of information, change the consent authorization mechanism into informed mechanism, supplement the users' data retrieval right under illegal collection, circulation, utilization, fully mobilize the enthusiasm of data commercial entities, improve the benefit distribution mechanism between data holders and users, confirm and distribute the interests of data commercial subjects, and protect the interests of data holders in conflict of interest.

Hybrid AI-Based iBeacon Indoor Positioning Cybersecurity Attacks and Defenses Thereof

Fang-Yie Leu[1], Chi-Jan Huang[2] (iD), Cheng-Jan Chi[3], and Wei-Tzu Hung[4]([✉]) (iD)

[1] Department of Computer Science, Tunghai University, 407224 Taichung, Taiwan
[2] General Education Center, Ming Chuan University, 111013 Taipei, Taiwan
[3] THLight Company, Ltd., 241409 New Taipei, Taiwan
[4] Department of Civil Engineering, National Taipei University of Technology, 106344 Taipei, Taiwan
jones155376jones@gmail.com

Abstract. Currently, iBeacon systems have been increasingly established in public areas to position people and assist users in indoor for location navigation. People receive the services through the Bluetooth Low Energy (BLE) installed on their mobile phones. However, the positioning and navigation functions of iBeacon system may be compromised when faced with cyberattacks issued by hackers. In other words, its security needs to be further considered and enhanced. This study takes the iBeacon system built in Taipei Main Station, the major transportation hub with daily traffic of at least 300 thousand passengers, as an example for exploring its potential attacks and further studying on the defense technologies under the assistance of AI techniques and human participation. Our experiments demonstrate that the prior information security planning of a iBeacon system and the rolling coding encryption on its issued messages in Taipei Main Station, are the best defense methods.

Keywords: cyberattacks · BLE · information security · rolling encryption · hybrid AI-based · iBeacon systems

1 Introduction

In general, Beacon is a small data transmitter developed for low-power applications of Bluetooth (4.0 and above). It is suitable for being applied to indoor positioning, which solves the problem in that GPS of a mobile phone is unable to receive satellite signals indoors due to obstruction by the building. More importantly, people consider that Beacon systems are the new generation solutions [1] as it meets the accuracy requirements of indoor positioning at a lower power consumption compared to those outdoor positioning systems.

Gradually, applications of iBeacon and BLE Beacon have been increasingly popular on mobile devices since a majority of these devices are with built-in Bluetooth protocol. The potential applications include shopping mall navigation [2] and vehicle management and identification [3]. The higher expansion of iBeacon and BLE Beacon applications

D.-J. Deng et al. (Eds.): SGIoT 2022, LNICST 497, pp. 65–71, 2023.
https://doi.org/10.1007/978-3-031-31275-5_7

often lead to higher risks to these applications. At present, the security issues faced in the use of Beacon include spoofing, piggybacking and privacy concerns, etc. [4]. Also, indoor positioning requests high positioning accuracy and signal availability and accessibility.

As there are rare iBeacon security research involving information security, this study will therefore focus on the information security features of iBeacon and introduce the possible attacks by hackers and their defense approaches.

2 Related Work

2.1 Safety Promotion of iBeacon

Bai et al. [5] proposed an iBeacon base station containing a Bluetooth 4.0 module and an emergency evacuation system to accurately locate users whose mobile phones are now connected to this base station for receiving Bluetooth services, thus able to guide them for evacuation from their current locations when a disaster occurs. Chen & Liu [6] designed a system to guide the evacuation of indoor people, and track the items left by people during the evacuation through the sensor network composed of iBeacon nodes.

Recently, the world's first indoor navigation and evacuation framework with iBeacon IoT positioning has been released to the markets [7]. It can calculate the shortest path from the emergency exits to shorten the time for personnel evacuation so as to safely navigate the user groups to outdoor.

2.2 Information Security Challenges in iBeacon

BLE is a part of Bluetooth 4.0 which is different from the conventional Bluetooth protocols and can be applied to various wearable devices, such as Beacon [8]. However, compared with other BLE technologies, Beacon can be widely applied to various areas/domains due to its low cost and accurate object location identifications. Campos-Cruz et al. [9] analyzed potential threats faced in the practical operation of wireless Beacon systems, and proposed a lightweight cryptography-based security protocol for establishing shared keys. Na et al. [10] revealed the feasibility of attacking iBeacon services via WiFi devices.

3 Research Design

Taipei City is the largest political and economic center in Taiwan, and Taipei Main Station, also the transportation hub for foreign travelers entering and leaving Taipei City. In 2019, the daily passenger traffic of Taipei Main Station consists of 86,000 via high-speed rail, 122,000 via Taiwan Railway, and 319,000 via MRT.

Due to the design of pedestrian passing routes and signs in Taipei Main Station have been increased day by day, the Taipei City Government launched the APP "Taipei Navi" in 2018, which connects to more than 4,000 iBeacons deployed across the station to solve issues such as passenger positioning, wayfinding and commuting. This study therefore adopts Taipei Main Station as the subject in exploring iBeacon security issues.

3.1 iBeacon System Design Architecture

The design architecture of the iBeacon system in this study is shown in Fig. 1. First, the Beacon plaintexts (e.g., a restaurant promotion advertisement) are encrypted by invoking AES algorithm and then transmitted to mobile phones via the BLE protocol through broadcast before encrypted plaintext is transmitted to the server of this iBeacon system for decryption. After that, mobile-phone users may therefore receive the content of plaintext from the server and decide whether to dine at the restaurant or not. Users wishing to have their needs at one of the promoted restaurants may be guided to this restaurant using the indoor navigation function of App Taipei Navi.

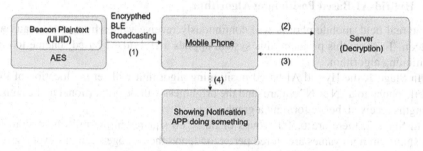

Fig. 1. System diagram of our iBeacon system.

3.2 Positioning Algorithms

The Stage 1, Initial, refers to determining the initial point of a mobile phone. Each Beacon computes its distance to the mobile phone according to the strength of the radio wave and then the Beacon system employs the triangulation method to determine the position of the mobile phone. The strengths are presented in log scale.

The coordinate positioning equations are as follows:

$$x_0 = \frac{\sum_{i=1}^{n} x_i W_i}{\sum_{i=1}^{n} W_i} \quad n = 3 \tag{1}$$

$$y_0 = \frac{\sum_{i=1}^{n} y_i W_i}{\sum_{i=1}^{n} W_i} \quad n = 3 \tag{2}$$

Following the completion of the initial point positioning, it is discovered that instant computation of current location of users is difficult since the Beacon positioning system may only compute the relative position between each Beacon and the mobile phone, while the radio waves require average based on stable readings.

For better user experience, this system refers to Kok et al. [11] in Stage 2 by acceleration computations run by accelerators. In this study, an algorithm is applied to integrate the acceleration from the user's phone position into a velocity which will receive second integration to transform the velocity to a displacement so that a position with the movement direction can be determined according to the gyroscope angle.

Stage 3 concerns data regression. The results gained from stage 2 "Estimate" estimates over user's position once every 30 s. The results are compared with the Initial Points identified in Stage 1. In addition, the Beacon value shall prevail when the error exceeds 15 m since the errors of the accelerometer are accumulated. For specific Beacons, such as the ones near an escalator, Regression will be executed immediately upon numerical strength excess over 70 dB since the user will soon move to another floor when riding the escalator and they will be at near proximity to Beacons as they come near to the floor. At such moment, the Beacon radio wave strength goes extremely high, and a rapid regression, also known as quick regression, is required.

3.3   Hybrid-AI-Based Positioning Algorithm

In the real field, mobile phones will continuously receive values from more than one Beacon. To solve this problem, this system applies a Hybrid AI-based scheme to our positioning algorithm.

In Stage 1, the Hybrid AI-based positioning algorithm will set the location of the mobile phone to a "N × N" square, and the brightness will be proportional to the signal strengths received, hence forming a graph.

In Stage 2, there are 6,500 groups of 80 × 80 squares in the railway station. In this study, strength values are stored per second, and the average strengths every seven seconds as one cycle are mapped into this graph, which will be submitted to TensorFlow immediately [12]; CNN in TensorFlow is then applied for point identification.

In Stage 3: The Hybrid AI-based positioning algorithm will transform the position of a user's mobile phone to a radio wave strength graph. The positions of the Beacons with the strongest wave signal are identified as the user's current position.

3.4   Possible Attacks

Recording and Use. From technical viewpoint, any mobile phone which has BLE protocol can receive and decode the message from the iBeacon system, meaning any mobile application which can obtain the Beacon broadcasts is able to position this mobile phone. Therefore, hackers may use such channel to leak the positioning information. That is, a hacker may walk in the field holding a smartphone to fetch field Beacon codes (ID). Any attacker may enter the field open to the public to obtain data without any beforehand permission.

Impersonation Attack. Beacon broadcasts messages usually are not encrypted, an attacker can detect and replicate the Beacon codes. An attacker can hack a Beacon first and then attack the users who are connected to this Beacon. He/she may even replicate a faked Beacon at another field using the same ID when possible, causing the APP to distribute wrong information in the wrong place.

Obfuscation Attack. Hackers put multiple Beacons at the same location. Since applications mostly rely on Beacon to determine their position, when multiple faked Beacons and Beacons under the original system are placed in the same position, the situation may cause serious interference or delay in the transmission, and affect the integrity and correctness of the data.

Recording and Limited Reproduction. The three types of attacks above can be prevented via rolling coding. However, rolling coding can also be attacked by means of limited reproduction, hackers can record a set of several codes at most for time concerns.

4 Beacon System Defense Methods

This study proposes four methods to defense those attacks mentioned above.

4.1 Data Encryption/Decryption

This method involves simple steps by encrypting Beacon messages and decrypting them by the receiver; however, such method is meaningless in the security of the system, since all the attacks above may still work as long as the issued messages remain unchanged.

4.2 Rolling Coding

This Rolling coding can be divided into two models, i.e., unpredictable and predictable. Unpredictable model means that the code will not be repeated at all; predictable code refers to the code produced following some rules.

The classic descriptive equation of rolling coding is

$$f(t) = f(t+1) \tag{3}$$

Unpredictable Rolling Coding. In the unpredictable model,

$$f(t+1) = g(t, \text{ random}) \tag{4}$$

For example, assuming that the Beacon number is expressed by Code t, and "random" refers to a certain random variable which is a random number for enhancing system security. This series of code can be described as

$$f(t+1) = g(\text{code}, \text{ random}) \tag{5}$$

For example, $f(t+1) = (000,632)$, and after 10 min $f(t+1) = (000,787)$. The variation from $(000,632)$ to $(000,787)$ shows no regularity.

Let $g = AES$, then

$$f(t+1) = AES(\text{code}, \text{ random}) \tag{6}$$

The parameter random of the encrypted variable code may not be applied to predict the next code result even AES is cracked.

Predictable Rolling Coding Method. In the predictable model, $f(t+1)$ in Eq. (3) is the code existing regularity. Generally, the change is once every 10 min, and the count is incremented by 1, i.e., $t+1$. For example, assuming that the coding position is the date, i.e., t, plus 1, and today is the 5th day of the month, $t = 5$, $f(t+1) = f(6)$. The purpose is to reduce the risk of the code being accessed and hacked. It also increases the security of the system.

Basically, predictable rolling coding is added with the predictable mark of Origin = O(code, index, random), i.e., index. For Origin = O(code, index, random) in the original text, the random can be omitted. For example, Eddystone uses PDU Count/Time as an index [13] in Beacon. Line Beacon not only has a timestamp in the plaintext, but also adopts the SHA256 encryption function to encrypt messages. The key length of SHA256 encryption function is 256-bits. It is hard for hackers to crack this function [14].

The advantage of using the predictable rolling coding method is to distinguish whether a message is false or not through timestamps. However, these parameters must be stored in the Flash ROM, and the number of Flash accesses is limited, excessively frequent accesses will damage the hardware [12]. The system owner must carefully consider flash's life time and limit the number of changes.

In the meantime, the watchdog/battery replacement may cause the timestamp to be zero in practical management. When detecting impersonation attack or obfuscation attack, the server must detect whether the constraint T-T' > ΔT or not. The system administrator shall be warned for further processing. Basically, personnel inspections and active monitoring by App are probable solutions.

App Active Monitoring. The APP "Taipei Navi" has accumulated more than 100,000 downloads since its release. The messages received by users using the App from iBeacon will be aggregated into the server at the back end of iBeacon. As shown in Fig. 2, we can compare timestamps for checking to see whether the iBeacon is under a replay attack and then the location of the attacked iBeacon can be identified.

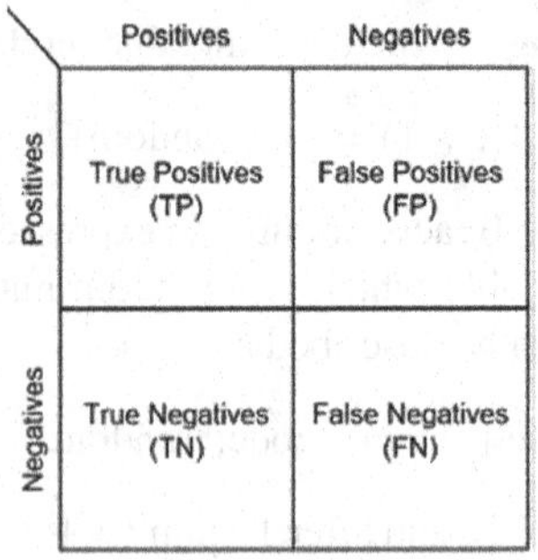

	Positives	Negatives
Positives	True Positives (TP)	False Positives (FP)
Negatives	True Negatives (TN)	False Negatives (FN)

Fig. 2. Confusion matrix.

5   Conclusion and Future Studies

iBeacon is widely used to this date and available for any mobile device that supports BLE; nevertheless, how to protect its security? This study only explores the mainstream iBeacon defenses and attacks due to length constraints of this article. In the future, we will further study the feasibility of other AI-based technologies applications to iBeacon information security protection; furthermore, security personnel on patrol in the station is an intuitive strategy. Therefore, we will also understand the defense method for personnel inspection in our future study.

References

1. Kao, C.L.: The application of beacon micro positioning technology. Arch. Semiannual **20**(1), 88–97 (2021)
2. Meliones, A., Sampson, D.: Blind museum tourer: a system for self-guided tours in museums and blind indoor navigation. Technologies **6**(1), 4 (2018)
3. Zhao, Z.H., Zhang, M.D., Yang, C., Fang, J., Huang, G.Q.: Distributed and collaborative proactive tandem location tracking of vehicle products for warehouse operations. Comput. Ind. Eng. **125**, 637–648 (2018)
4. Spachos, P., Plataniotis, K.: Beacons and the City: Smart Internet of Things, 1st edn. Academic Press, USA (2018)
5. Bai, D.T., Zhang, J.N., Pan, Y.: Research on the principle and technology of indoor positioning navigation escape rescue system. Fire Sci. Technol. **37**(11), 1560–1563 (2018)
6. Chen, L.W., Liu, J.X.: EasyFind: a mobile crowdsourced guiding system with lost item finding based on IoT technologies. In: International Conference on Pervasive Computing and Communication Workshops, pp. 343–345. IEEE, Japan (2019)
7. Chen, L.W., Liu, J.X.: Time-efficient indoor navigation and evacuation with fastest path planning based on internet of things technologies. IEEE Trans. Syst. Man Cybern. Syst. **51**(5), 3125–3135 (2021)
8. Yang, Q., Huang, L.: Inside Radio: An Attack and Defense Guide, 1st edn. Springer, Singapore (2018)
9. Campos-Cruz, K.J., Mancillas-López, C., Ovilla-Martinez, B.: A lightweight security protocol for beacons BLE. In: 18th International Conference on Electrical Engineering, Computing Science and Automatic Control, pp. 1–6. IEEE, Mexico (2021)
10. Na, X., Guo, X., He, Y., Xi, R.: Wi-attack: cross-technology impersonation attack against iBeacon services. In: 18th Annual IEEE International Conference on Sensing, Communication, and Networking, pp. 1–9. IEEE, Italy (2021)
11. Kok, M., Hol, J.D., Sch, T.B.: Using inertial sensors for position and orientation estimation. Found. Trends Signal Process. **11**(1–2), 1–153 (2017)
12. Hu, J., et al.: Efficient graph deep learning in tensorflow with tf_geometric. In: 29th ACM International Conference on Multimedia, pp. 3775–3778. Association for Computing Machinery, China (2021)
13. Sun, M., Kamoto, KM., Liu, Q., Liu, X., Qi, L.: Application of bluetooth low energy beacons and fog computing for smarter environments in emerging economies. In: Zhang, X., Liu, G., Qiu, M., Xiang, W., Huang, T. (eds) Cloud Computing, Smart Grid and Innovative Frontiers in Telecommunications: International Conference on Cloud Computing, pp. 101–110. Springer, Cham (2019). https://doi.org/10.1007/978-3-030-48513-9_8
14. LINE developers. https://developers.line.biz/en/docs/messaging-api/beacon-device-spec/. Accessed 19 July 2022

Digital Transformation Application of Precision Industrial Quotation System

Wen-Hsing Kao[1], Yi-Mei Zeng[2], Zi-Ying Nian[2], and Rung-Shiang Cheng[1](✉)

[1] Department of Information Technology, Overseas Chinese University, Taichung, Taiwan
{star,rscheng}@ocu.edu.tw

[2] Department of Business Administration, Overseas Chinese University, Taichung, Taiwan

Abstract. The digital era is coming. In recent years, due to the continuous improvement of information technology, Artificial Intelligence, Big Data, Cloud Computing and IoT related technology has flourished. For traditional industries, demand is gradually changing from less diverse product to more diverse product. And most of them are customized orders, so the change of production mode has also become an opportunity for the digital transformation of enterprises. In addition, under the impact of the epidemic at the end of 2019, enterprises pay more attention to digital transformation.

This study cooperates with a precision industrial company in Taichung. The company used to record all the data in the quotation process in paper. In addition to the difficulty of data backtracking, quotation data such as cost, delivery period, production process, outsourced manufacturers and prices are also difficult to compare with the actual order data. Also, departments often affect the quotation time due to the cumbersome communication process. In order to solve the above problems and improve the quotation process, this study is discussed in a faster, more accurate, more effective and profitable way.

By building a digital quotation system, digitally optimize the difficulties encountered by quotations, and finally solve the problem to make the quotation system successfully digitally transformed.

Keywords: Digital Transformation · Quotation · Data Mining

1 Introduction

1.1 Background and Motivation

In the process of enterprise operation, it is absolutely related to production operation management, marketing management, human resources management, research and development management, and financial management.

There is a large amount of data that can be used in each management. If the data is not recorded in detail and used properly, it is really a loss to the enterprise. When traditional industries carry out digital transformation, they will always rely on information technology. Such as Industrial Internet of Things ERP system etc. Access to data through cloud

D.-J. Deng et al. (Eds.): SGIoT 2022, LNICST 497, pp. 72–82, 2023.
https://doi.org/10.1007/978-3-031-31275-5_8

computing technology and execute data through multiple ways like data cleaning, data integration, data conversion and other data pre-processing steps to make the data more accurate with the original data. It will not lead to misjudgment due to outlier values or wrong data, and focus on the dimensions of value to enterprises. Finally, through big data analysis, we can understand the competitive edge of enterprises.

In order to achieve the purpose of digital transformation, enterprises must continuously improve and optimize internal working processes. Only when we able to produce diverse customized products and quantitative commodities, we can move forward for the purpose of flexible manufacturing system as to improve our own value. Create a high-tech and high entry barrier, help enterprise to improve the competitive advantages and plays an important role in the manufacturing industry.

1.2 Research Purpose

This study cooperates with a precision industrial company in Taichung. The company used to record all the data in the quotation process in paper. In addition to the difficulty of data backtracking, quotation data such as cost, delivery period, production process, outsourced manufacturers and prices are also difficult to compare with the actual order data. Also, departments often affect the quotation time due to the cumbersome communication process.

In order to solve the above problems and improve the quotation process, this study is discussed in a faster, more accurate, more effective and profitable way. By building a digital quotation system, digitally optimize the difficulties encountered by quotations, and finally solve the problem to make the quotation system successfully digitally transformed.

2 Literature Review

2.1 Digital Transformation

This study integrates the interpretation and definition, application scope and use methods of various experts and scholars for digital transformation. [1] It is mentioned that digital transformation can not only measure the extent to which an organization benefits when applying information technology tools, but also as an evolutionary process. [2] This study builds an integrated model of digital transformation and establishes measurement tools for educational institutions, and evaluates the results in general to determine that this model is suitable for universities. [3] Use the code development platform to provide and promote the technical mechanism of automated software application process development, develop the emerging low-code field on the basis of computer-aided software engineering, and serve as a tool for digital transformation. In the case of digital transformation in European countries, it is mentioned that digital transformation plays an important role in technology and industrial policies, and digitalization is understood as the process of using digital technology and tools to develop business. Through two-stage analysis, this study first evaluates the cluster analysis method (clustering and K-Means) of differences and similarities among EU countries. Then use TOPSIS to rank countries according to the evaluation criteria. The research results found that if EU countries have a similar level of development, they can effectively carry out technical evaluation through social, economic and corporate dimensions. [4] Research on the pharmaceutical industry and complete the digital transformation through the planning and development of the Nerve Live platform. Nerve Live platform has a total of eight models applied to different fields. Since the development of the system launched, the organization has been able to have direct experience, create intelligence, and create value throughout the value chain. Each model combines decades of operating data of multiple internal systems, generates new intelligence pattern through machine learning and advanced analysis, and creates application process modules. Through action and insight planning, tracking, prediction, comparison and monitoring activities, keep the cost down and maximizes both quality and efficiency. For example, a faster, better and cheaper, and eventually create smarter and data-driven decisions throughout the drug development process. And increase information transparency, and all departments can see the same data, so that new strategies can be generated from a complete, comprehensive and common perspective.

2.2 Quotation System

[7] Through research of the value stream mapping (VSM), we provide relevant decision-making bases such as resource utilization rate, delivery time, current products in progress, non-value-added time and number of operators in the quotation process, and achieves concise management to reduce imperfect losses considered by the company in the quotation [8] . Build a quotation model for urgent customers, record all changes and information in the previous quotation process, and be able to propose a more accurate quotation numbers and restore a precise calculation of quotation. In line with the purpose of this study, we hope to speed up the efficiency of quotation and reduce the waiting time of customers through the quotation model.

2.3 Data Mining

When the data warehousing construction is completed, the valuable information that needs to be mined from a large amount of data can be mined through data exploration. [5] This study sorts out the application of data mining in various fields. Because the data generated by the health care exchange is too large to be processed and analyzed through traditional methods, it is necessary to convert the data into useful information through data exploration. From this, it can be seen that data mining technology can extract effective information for a large amount of data. This study analyzed diabetic patients. In 1,778 non-diabetic cases, the decision-making successfully judged 1,728 cases as non-diabetic, with an accuracy of 96.64%. [6] Apply data mining technology to the field of crime analysis, develop a reproducing reporting system based on message extraction technology, and combine natural language processing and cognitive interview methods. Get more information from the testimony of witnesses and victims, and ask questions according to the principle of cognitive interviews through the system to extract answers related to crime, and the overall report exceeds 80% of the accuracy and recall rate. Originally, the police should send manpower to be responsible for the investigation.

Through data exploration-related technology, we can quickly find a response method in various criminal records so far.

3   Method

3.1   Digital Transformation and Data Mining

This study combines Digital Transformation with Data Mining technology (see Fig. 1).

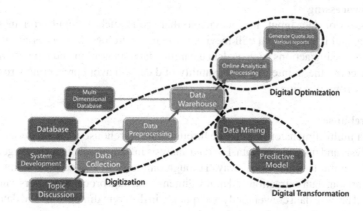

Fig. 1. Concept map of Digital Transformation and Data Mining

3.2   Digitalization

This study will enable the company to move forward in the direction of digital transformation by building a quotation operating system. First of all, change the quotation process from the original paper work to the quotation system to record all the data in the quotation process in detail, plus the principle of feasibility assessment to record the possibilities of the quotation. And the processing of parallel operations to reduce the time spent on the quotation, and then record all the time in the quotation process in detail. Including the time spent by each department in each quotation process or the average length of the total quotation, etc. It also records in detail the reasons why the quotation content has changed during the quotation process. Finally, a variety of charts are generated to explain the quotation status. After completing the quotation operation, the data generated by the process will be constructed as a customer relationship management analysis model. In the future, customer classification will be carried out, so that the company can provide customized services and marketing for each customer.

Data Collection

From the time the business receives the customer's inquiry to the completion of the whole quotation process, the quotation operation system records are adopted. Whether it is customer data, inquiry data, process data, manufacturer data, data generated by the evaluation process, time generated by the evaluation process, etc., in order to establish subsequent data warehousing. The quotation operation system has added parallel operation technology, which shortens the time of quotation, and increases the function of switching operations, and records the communication of various departments. All changes due to the design changes and the adjustment of the process to communicate with customers will be followed up; the above functions cannot be achieved in the previous quotation process. Through feasibility assessment, parallel operations and change operations, the quotation process is more perfect and flexible.

Data Preprocessing

In the process of data input, it is inevitable that errors such as input error messages, empty data, and irregular data will inevitably occur. Therefore, it is necessary to adopt data pre-processing actions such as data cleaning, data integration and data conversion. Ensure the correctness, integrity and usability of data, and avoid presenting wrong data leading to wrong decisions.

Data Warehouse

Establish a multi-dimensional database through data warehouse to facilitate the subsequent analysis and use of large data. For data analysis in data warehouse, data is generally presented in a multi-dimensional way. Through online analysis and processing, query, data comparison, data extraction and multi-dimensional data processing, users can query, analyze and browse data conveniently and quickly in different dimensions and data levels according to specific or professional needs.

3.3 Digital Optimization

Due to the large number of relevant departments involved in the quotation operation, how to shorten the waiting time of customers or business, it is necessary to optimize the quotation operation process. After the digitalization process is stable and the database of each dimension of quotation is built and improved, it can cooperate with the company's customer relationship management. As a reference basis for the urgent order sorting process, it can also be used through the function of quotation grouping and components. Through similar quotation content, the efficiency of quotation is greatly improved to achieve the effect of time optimization, and the previous feasibility assessment is analyzed to increase the success rate of the quotation to avoid the waste of quotation costs.

OLAP

OLAP has six characteristics: 1. Able to provide integrated decision-making information immediately and quickly. 2. The main purpose is to support the analysis of decision-making information rather than OLTP. 3. It is often necessary to extract a large amount of historical data for trend analysis. 4. It is often necessary to carry out complex analysis of multi-dimensional and aggregate information. 5. It is often necessary to present data in different time dimensions. 6. The data required by the user has been defined and calculated in advance, so the query speed is relatively fast.

Generate Various Forms of Quotation Operation
Provide the company's customer relationship management reference basis through OLAP, and then use the quotation group and assembly function. So that the quotation operating system can meet the needs of customers to quote at the same time, improve parallel operations to achieve optimization, and provide urgent authorizations through analysis to achieve the purpose of time optimization. Finally, for the problem of excessive quotation time, the relevant statements are provided for the purpose of improving the accuracy of quotation.

3.4 Digital Transformation

Through quotation data warehouse, using various dimension analysis to learn useful information for the development of the company. For example, through the historical results of the feasibility assessment, we know why the company often evaluates the reasons it cannot process, and finally analyzes the important information that the company has never found in the previous quotation through Data mining.

Data Mining
This study is expected to compare whether the data of the customer's actual order is consistent with the data at the time of quotation through the data exploration tool. For example, estimate the completion time of the quotation, the manufacture procedure and processing order used, the cost and time of the outsourced manufacturer, whether it can be successfully produced, etc. to prove the accuracy of the quotation, analyze the reasons for the closure of the case, and corresponding countermeasures.

Prediction Model
In the future, we hope that when the business receives customer inquiries, it can automatically enter the key attributes of the quotation. Through the data mining results, the success rate of the quotation is counted. It is convenient for the business to judge whether to undertake this quotation, and can provide customers with more accurate quotation time to improve the success rate of the quotation.

4 Results

4.1 Digitalization - Current Situation Results and Discussion

At present, the quotation operation system has been planned. The participating departments have a total of seven departments: business departments, R&D departments, production management departments, production departments, processing departments, procurement departments and quality control departments. By recording all the data in the quotation process, to construct a perfect and rich data table of each dimension, the functions of the system are as follows: (1) Fill in the quotation information in the business. (2) Fill in the graphic data in R&D. (3) R&D feasibility assessment. (4) Internal and external production and manufacturers of production management evaluation. (5) The production management filled in the internal system and work center. (6) External production and manufacturers of production management. (7) Feasibility assessment of filling in the production management. (8) Production Filling in Planning Evaluation. (9) Working hours and working days in the production form. (10) Processing and filling in planning and evaluation. (11) Processing Filling Forms include Working hours and working days. (12) Management Filling in Forms include Working hours and working days. (13) Purchasing forms fill in the working day and amount. (14) Purchasing forms fill in Planning and Evaluation. (15) The quality control filling form only measured the time and the number of working days required for batches. (16) Quality control forms filled in the planning and evaluation. (17) Cartographic upload sheet. (18) Amount filled in in the production management. (19) Business forms fill in the management and sales % and exchange rate. (20) Fill in the working day and order number for business.

Differences before digitalization and after digitization.

Table 1 will list the differences before and after digitalization, and explain in detail the differences before and after improvement for each department:

Table 1. The differences before and after digitalization

project	department	before	after
1	business department	If the quotation is made in paper, if the customer asks about the status of the quotation, the business cannot track the quotation progress and respond to customer questions immediately because it does not know which stage the quotation is on	Through the quotation operation system, you can see the progress of all quotations from the inquiry list and screen all the customers. The total number of quotations of customer and the status of individual quotations will be listed
2	business department	Impossible to know how many quotations have not been closed so far, and it is difficult to track and control	The business can screen the undone quotation documents in order to track the progress, and confirm whether it is necessary to ask departments to speed up the quotation

(*continued*)

Table 1. (*continued*)

project	department	before	after
3	business department	If there is a change in the previous quotation process, it is difficult to trace back to the reason why the change was caused, and the evaluation	At present, when the change needs to be made, it is necessary to record the reasons why it is not feasible, as well as the personnel who record the evaluation. If there is any problems in the follow-up, you can also find the reason for the change and understand the situation at that time
4	production department	Because production is divided into three departments, in the past, it was necessary to manually judge which processes each department was responsible for	The system determines which production department should make this process to avoid manual judgment errors, and can also record which processes and evaluation personnel evaluated by each department at that time
5	procurement departments	The previous quotation process has not recorded material data	Building material data in the system can not only record the amount of materials to provide cost calculation, but also build a database of materials
6	quality control department	The previous quotation process has not recorded the quality data	At present, the quality data can be recorded in the system to record the measurement method at that time
7	All departments	The previous quotation process completed one item and then carried out another, resulting in an extended quotation time	Through the concept of parallel operation, projects that do not affect each other are evaluated at the same time to speed up the quotation

(*continued*)

Table 1. (*continued*)

project	department	before	after
8	All departments	It is difficult to record the time and completion in paper work when each department receives the quotation	Because the system can record the time of state change, it can record the time spent by each department in each state to achieve the purpose of time control

4.2 Digital Optimization - Problem Discussion

When the quotation process is changed to use digital recording and the data warehousing, it can then be able to carry out some analysis and discussion through data.

For example, how to speed up the quotation efficiency, improve the success rate of customers to place orders, or how to improve the accuracy of quotation, so as to accurately grasp all the time and cost spent in the quotation process, use it as a follow-up production management order, and how to ensure that the quotation is profitable. For an enterprise, making profits is the most basic and important thing. Therefore, whether the management and marketing expenses incurred in the quotation process are reasonable or not, and whether the subsequent pricing can enable the company to obtain profits after the formal order, it must be understood through analysis. These contents are information that could not be known during previous paperwork (see Table 2).

Table 2. The differences before and after Digital Optimization

project	department	before	after
1	business department	It is impossible to provide corresponding services for the customer's quotation model	After analysis, you can know the customer's quotation model and provide a quotation process that is more in line with this customer. For example, customers who often place orders immediately after the quotation should pay attention to the quotation time and delivery date
2	procurement departments	Only the materials used are recorded in the digitalization of quotation operations	Through analysis, the materials that often appear in the quotation process can be used to provide procurement reference to ensure sufficient inventory

(*continued*)

Table 2. (*continued*)

project	department	before	after
3	All departments	Previous data are only recorded in their respective databases, so it is difficult to compare	Improve the accuracy of quotation by comparing quotation data with order data

4.3 Digital Transformation - Problem Discussion

After the digital optimization step, the quotation efficiency and quotation accuracy will be improved. Then this study will explore how to save work time through the surface. Data warehouse has been built when the quotation operation is digitalize. Through key information, it can provide departments with data adjustments without enter data (see Tables 3 and 2). And when the business personnel receive the inquiry request, they can judge whether there has been a similar quotation before through the previous quotation information, and provide the information at that time for reference to the decision makers, or the success rate of the quotation to determine whether this quotation needs to be undertaken.

Table 3. The differences before and after Digital transformation

project	department	before	after
1	business department	Can't know which quotations are interrelated	Through the document association function, you can know what similar or related quotations are
2	All departments	Previously, because all the reasons for the closure of the case had not been recorded, it was difficult to find out the bottleneck of the company's quotation	Through the feasibility assessment, we can understand the company's current bottlenecks and transformation direction, such as purchasing machinery and equipment or adjusting materials, processes, etc
3	All departments	When each department previously filled in the quotation content, the information that may be filled in will not change much, but it needs to be filled in again every time	The quotation process can tend to be automated, and suggested data can be made through historical data

5 Conclusion and Future Research

This study has now completed the digitalization of the quotation operation. In-depth research will continue in the direction of digital optimization and digital transformation in the future. Provide a corresponding reference basis for the three-oriented roles of the company. For the decision-making side, because the quotation operation system is an open system, the data presented is absolutely true. Through the two aspects of time and cost, decision makers can understand the current quotation status of the company in order to make correct decisions; For the management side, it can understand which bottlenecks and problems in the current operation have not been found before, and put forward improvement policies in time to improve departmental problems. For the user side, in addition to being able to record all the time points of the quotation and remind the current quotation progress, the efficiency of quotation will be greatly improved after the system function is more stable. Digitalize the existing quotation operation, optimize the quotation process by collecting a large amount of information, and finally make the quotation direction towards business intelligence through data mining.

References

1. Rodríguez-Abitia, G., Bribiesca-Correa, G.: Assessing digital transformation in universities. Future Internet **13**(2), 52 (2021)
2. Sanchis, R., García-Perales, Ó., Fraile, F., Poler, R.: Low-code as enabler of digital transformation in manufacturing industry. Appl. Sci. **10**(1), 12 (2019)
3. Małkowska, A., Urbaniec, M., Kosała, M.: The impact of digital transformation on European countries: Insights from a comparative analysis. Equilib. Q. J. Econ. Econ. Policy **16**(2), 325–355 (2021)
4. Finelli, L.A., Narasimhan, V.: Leading a digital transformation in the pharmaceutical industry: reimagining the way we work in global drug development. Clin. Pharmacol. Ther. **108**(4), 756–761 (2020)
5. Koh, H.C., Tan, G.: Data mining applications in healthcare. J. Healthc. Inf. Manag. **19**(2), 65 (2011)
6. Hassani, H., Huang, X., Silva, E.S., Ghodsi, M.: A review of data mining applications in crime. Stat. Anal. Data Min.: ASA Data Sci. J. **9**(3), 139–154 (2016)
7. Terpend, R., Shannon, P.: Teaching lean principles in nonmanufacturing settings using a computer equipment order quotation administrative process. Decis. Sci. J. Innov. Educ. **19**(1), 63–89 (2021)
8. Fishe, R.P., Roberts, J.S.: Competitive Quote Flipping and Trade Clusters (2020). Available at SSRN 3652630

Balance Between Data Circulation and Personal Information Protection
Based on the Analysis of the Development of the Digital Industry in the Internet of Things Era

Shen Xie[1] and Cheng Chen[2]([✉])

[1] Department of Law, Jimei University, Xiamen, China
[2] Xiamen Institute of Technology, Xiamen, China
chengchen_cy@yeah.net

Abstract. In the era of the Internet of Things, data sharing has formed a trend. Judicial practice has clarified the "triple authorization rules", that is, data sharing and sharing requires users to obtain the authorization of data collection and the authorization of users and data holders for data circulation and utilization, which seriously affects the data circulation. Starting from the needs of the development of the big data industry, to reflect on the hindering impact of the current authorization mechanism on the big data industry, the data control mechanism of data sharing should be rebuilt. In order to fully tap the potential of data and further promote the development and improvement of the data factor market, the existing data subject should change the complete right of self-determination of data, change the consent authorization mechanism into the informed mechanism, supplemented by the user's right of data retrieval under the circumstances of illegal collection, circulation and utilization.

Keywords: Internet of Things technology · Internet of Things · Cloud data sharing

1 Introduction

The Internet of Things technology is a new technology for connecting various sensors and the existing Internet. It uses various terminal sensors to collect user information, and transmit the information to the cloud or other information terminals in the way of data. Using smooth network transmission, the world can form an interconnected information network, namely the Internet of Things. The development of the whole Internet of Things. The Internet of Things technology is booming, the interconnected network is the infrastructure, and the "data and information" collected, transmitted and shared by sensors is the "blood" of the boom of the Internet of Things technology. The interconnection of information network and the sharing of data and information play a very important role in the development of the Internet of Things technology.

Iot cloud data refers to the production data that can identify user information when identified and collected by terminal devices that use the Internet of Things technology

D.-J. Deng et al. (Eds.): SGIoT 2022, LNICST 497, pp. 83–88, 2023.
https://doi.org/10.1007/978-3-031-31275-5_9

and collected in the form of data. IOT cloud data is formed by collecting user information by the terminal equipment on the user end, and then the Internet of Things information network transmits the user data back to the information processing center, and screened, analyzed, processed and sorted out the data. Finally, the processed data is stored in the cloud for subsequent utilization. The whole Internet of Things cloud data, from collection to storage, and then to utilization, involves the data subject (i. e., user), data holder (i. e., Internet of Things technology provider or operator) and data user respectively. The data can be used for self-use, shared to other subjects, or sold to other subjects.

Based on the protection of personal information in the data circulation, Three mechanisms have been established: whether the data is anonymized, Decple personal information from individuals, No personal identifiability; Second, if the data can not be completely anonymized, Then the data involving personal information shall be agreed to and authorized by the individual corresponding to the information; Third, in the use process, If there is an abuse of data containing personal information, Individuals have the right to exercise the "right to carry personal data", The EU General Data Protection Regulation is based on the data subject's right of self-determination of their personal data, It clearly stipulates the "right to carry personal data", That is, the data subject has the right to obtain the personal data provided to the data controller in a structured, common, and machine-readable format, Or have the right to freely transmit such data from the data controller that it provides to another data controller.

Iot cloud data sharing involves personal information protection, which lies in the collection, sharing and utilization. Currently, it is common practice to grant users "self-determination on personal information", including users taking control over data containing personal information. In the case of "Sina Weibo v. Mai Mai", the court of second instance in the case initiated the "triple authorization principle", that is, the first authorization for users to obtain data from the platform; the second and third authorization for the user and the platform to use the subsequent data acquisition. Based on the "triple authorization principle", the platform still needs to obtain explicit authorization or consent from users when sharing data with subsequent users. Based on the requirements of various countries for the protection of personal information, to avoid and prevent the leakage of personal information and privacy directed by the Internet of Things cloud data, various countries tend to leave the whole operation process after data collection to the users corresponding to the personal information for control.

This leads to a value conflict between user data control and the free circulation of data. It is conceivable that if users do not agree to share the data, the data flow will be limited, and the development potential of the entire industry should also be affected. In other words, the development of the entire big data industry will be presented with various uncertainties. Then, from the perspective of industrial policy, how to further weigh the value conflict between personal information protection and the development of big data industry, so that the two can obtain the optimal solution in the value combination, is the problem to be discussed and solved in this paper. It can be seen that although the sharing and sharing of IOT cloud data is a simple process of data transmission and utilization, the subject relationship involved is relatively complex and involves the construction of many mechanisms.

2 Conflict and Balance of the Interests of All Parties in the Data Sharing and Sharing Under the Industrial Policy

Information self-determination is seen as an important sign of the free development of personality. The sharing of data may cause the dissemination and diffusion of personal information. The data control right belongs to the subject of digital rights is a means to protect the right of information self-determination of the data subject. In the specific mechanism, it is the consent or authorization mechanism of data collection and use.

However, more and more scholars believe that it is undesirable to give information subjects absolute control over personal information. First, from the perspective of personal information protection, without considering the development of data industry and data public value, the private interest of data is not comparable to the public value, and the right to self-determination of personal information will more or less affect the circulation and utilization of data, and produce value conflicts. Second, users are not the appropriate subject of the decision power of personal information. Users have no industrial foundation, and can only control the data through consent or authorization, which will also lead to more illegal means to illegally obtain or disclose personal information.

From the value orientation of data sharing and sharing, data development and personal information protection should not be ignored. The public interest of data mainly includes the data development right and the public value, while the protection of personal information is the private interest right of data. This paper holds that the conflict between the two should be balanced, rather than biased on one side, especially in the case that industrial policy does not affect personal information and private interests, starting from social development, maintaining social welfare means human development. Second, the possible infringement of the rights and interests of data subjects or the existence of transmission security risk caused by data sharing means that the cancellation of sharing sharing, is not the way to solve the problem. Data sharing is not the root cause of the problem. The root cause of the problem lies in the legal relationship of multiple parties in sharing. We should not give up eating for fear of choking. We should explore and find a suitable path for development and sharing, and find a balance limit and a reasonable scale between sharing and sharing. The author believes that in the process of data sharing and sharing, the personal information contained in the data should be reasonably protected, and the data sharing should be carried out on the basis of personal information protection. However, based on the development of the data industry, it is also necessary to reduce the personal absolute control of the information to some extent. Since it is inevitable that personal information will be used and gain value in the industry, what we should solve instead is how to build a reasonable mechanism to avoid abuse for the use of personal information.

What is the reasonable premise for the reduction of the information self-determination of the data subject? This article thinks there are two: one is the data containing personal information will be used for public purposes, such as epidemic prevention and control of personal whereabouts flow, will involve personal positioning information, such as annual statistics in the annual data may involve personal income, etc., these use alone or collection, more or less will cause certain impact on personal information, but based on public purposes, should be given to a certain extent. Second, based on the development needs of the big data industry, a reasonable data circulation mechanism is established to exempt the authorization and consent procedures of the data subjects to a certain extent. Advocate the whole society to form an efficient and orderly data circulation factor market, promote the free circulation of valuable data, and meet the needs of the development of big data industry. However, the data protection related to personal information should still be adhered to. This paper believes that there should be several standards and principles: first, the protection of personal data in the process of data circulation; second, based on the use of data resale and illegal profits; third, the data subject can exercise the "right to carry personal information" to retrieve the data at any time based on the abuse in the data circulation. Fourth, take the corresponding data security protection measures.

3 Control and Utilization Mechanism of Data Circulation Under the Background of Data Sharing

3.1 Conform from Prior Consent Mechanism into "PRior Knowledge + post Control" Mechanism

Based on the consideration of industrial base and effect, data control party and utilization party are the backbone of promoting data circulation control. From the point of view of the data subject, holder and utilization subject, because the data information is generated by the Internet of Things service provider, the data control subject of the data information is more professional than the user private, so the control of the data information should belong to the data holder; this essentially forms the right of self-determination of the data subject information.

First, the reduction of the right to self-determination of data subjects does not mean denying the personal information protection mechanism, but this protection should be changed from the original consent authorization mechanism to the informed mechanism. This paper holds that for the protection of personal information, passive restriction mechanism rather than active restriction mechanism, that is, for the collection and circulation of personal data, in principle, only the user knows without full consent or authorization of personal information; moreover, the cost of collection and circulation, consent or authorization and monitoring of personal data is high. In principle, as long as there is no illegal operation and abuse of personal information, the restrictions on the collection and circulation of data should not be increased. At the same time, the collection and circulation for public purposes can exempt users from personal knowledge, as long as there is no abuse of information.

Second, emphasizing the data holder's control over the data information does not mean that the subject enjoys complete control over the data information. Data subjects still have the requirement to protect personal information. The control interest of the data control subject means that the control subject can occupy and use the data information, and also undertakes the security obligation of the data control and transmission and the protection obligation of the data information. At the same time, the digital power subject, the user, can exercise the right to retrieve the data information, or the illegal utilization of the data control subject, or the purpose of personal protection of the data information. The data retrieval right of the trigger data subject only comes from the protection of personal information data (Table 1).

Table 1. Premise of personal information protection for table data sharing

User informed	Identification mechanism of user information	Whether public use	Data circulation
yes	yes	yes	can
deny	yes	yes	
deny	deny	yes	
deny	deny	deny	cannot
yes	deny	yes	can
deny	yes	deny	cannot
yes	yes	deny	can
yes	deny	deny	can

3.2 Control Mechanism at the Common Level of Data Sharing

Data sharing and sharing under the condition of personal information protection is essentially a dispute over the control rights and interests of data, that is, the control right of the data subject, the data controller and the data user over the data. The control mechanism of data generation and utilization is formed, which includes three parts: authorization mechanism (data flow direction, dynamic), utilization mechanism (data possession and use, static) and confrontation mechanism. Among them, the authorization mechanism is the data control mechanism between different subject (this is the generation of data control), using the mechanism is the subject of data utilization of independent decision-making mechanism (the exercise of data control), confrontation mechanism is a main body based on some reason against the data control of another subject (data control to eliminate or pause).

First, data control does not absolutely belong to a certain subject, which is the characteristic of data different from traditional objects, its control rights can be shared, and the actual control of data does not mean the control of equity level.

Second, data control for the different entities. First, the control right of the data subject includes: a) the data generation level, that is, to independently decide whether to form the data; b) the data subject shall be informed of the collection of the data; or requires that the collected data will not affect the subsequent utilization of the data. At the same time, based on the smooth and efficiency of commercial data utilization, this knowledge should usually be a package, rather than such case or personalized processing. Second, the control right of the data holder includes: a) the decision at the data circulation level, that is, the data holder can decide whether to share the data; b) the data utilization level, that is, the data holder has the right to decide whether and how the data is used, including the right of the authorized data user to use the data, of course, the utilization level should comply with the laws and regulations and the authorized content of the data subject. Third, the control of the data user, that is the decision power at the data utilization level. After obtaining the shared data, the data user can decide to use the data independently according to the authorized content. However, the data user cannot exercise the decision power on the data circulation, that is, when the data user can only use the data and use the data within the authorization of the data holder.

Third, the data utilization level, such as the confrontation subject's control over data. Control is not completely free, or based on authorized restrictions, or based on public interest industrial policy restrictions, produce a confrontation mechanism. In essence, the confrontation right is generated by the control right. Under the premise that the control right is multi-oriented, the right of confrontation should also be multi-oriented and can be exercised by different subjects. First, the control right of the data holder is not completely unrestricted. At the level of decision power at the utilization level, the data subject returns the control when it makes illegal use. At the data utilization level, the data is also based on the balance of interests between the data subject, data holder and data user. The data subjects oppose the control rights of other subjects based on their control rights. Although the data subject should not control the use of the data in the whole chain, the data subject can only control the illegal use of the data, that is, it can exercise the right to retrieve or be forgotten when the data is illegally used. Second, based on the needs of industrial development, the improper interference of the data subject in the subsequent circulation and utilization is opposed. If the data user uses the data under the authorization of the data holder, the improper interference of the data subject and the data holder can be excluded. The behavior of the data user is limited to the utilization purpose, and cannot be similar to the data holder enjoying the control of the data circulation level.

4 Conclusion

In the era of the Internet of Things, data sharing has become a balance of power. Based on the needs of the development of the big data industry, the data sharing and sharing mechanism needs to be improved urgently. In order to fully tap the potential of data and further promote the development and improvement of the data factor market, the existing data subject should change the complete right of self-determination of data, change the consent authorization mechanism into the informed mechanism, supplemented by the user's right of data retrieval under the circumstances of illegal collection, circulation and utilization.

Artificial Intelligence, Machine Leaning, Deep Learning and Neural Network

Combined Short-Term Load Forecasting Method Based on HHT

Yuan Zhang[1], Shu Xia[1], Chihao Chen[2], Fan Yang[1], and Xing He[2(✉)]

[1] State Grid Shanghai Municipal Electric Power Company, Shanghai 200122, China
[2] Department of Automation, Shanghai Jiao Tong University, Shanghai 200240, China
xhe@sjtu.edu.cn

Abstract. Short-term load forecasting of the power grid can realize the optimal configuration of power generation and dispatch of the power grid which saves energy to the greatest extent and ensures the stable operation of the power system. The power load data is affected by many factors and presents complex volatility. It is difficult for a single prediction method to obtain accurate prediction results. In this paper, a combined optimization prediction method based on Hilbert-Huang transform (HHT) is proposed. By acquiring more regular component sequences of load data, its essential characteristics are explored and then combined with different neural network models for prediction to improve the accuracy and stability of short-term load forecasting. Simulation experiment results verify the prediction accuracy of the combined prediction method.

Keywords: Short-term Load Forecasting · Hilbert-Huang Transform · Neural Network

1 Introduction

With the continuous popularization and development of smart grid, the accuracy of load forecasting is vital for improving the scientificity of power generation and distribution and dispatching in the power system [1]. The short-term load forecasting is used to forecast the load data in the next day or next few days, which is affected by many factors. The forecasting method is continuously improved, and the forecasting accuracy also remains to be further improved. The method for short-term load forecasting is mainly classified as classical forecasting method and modern forecasting method. The classical forecasting method includes empirical forecasting method and traditional forecasting method, of which the machine learning algorithm is used in the modern forecasting method for analysis modeling through historical load data and relevant factors of impact load, such as air temperature and special event. The research methods include support vector machine, random forest and neural network at present [2].

In recent years, the dynamic equilibrium of power supply and demand is provided with higher requirement with the development and reform of power market, so that the requirement for accuracy of short-term load forecasting becomes higher and higher;

D.-J. Deng et al. (Eds.): SGIoT 2022, LNICST 497, pp. 91–101, 2023.
https://doi.org/10.1007/978-3-031-31275-5_10

at the same time, with the continuous renewal of research method in short-term load forecasting field, many experts put forward the method for combination forecasting. The combination forecasting model not only overcomes the limitation of single model algorithm, but also realizes the complementary advantages between different neural networks by virtue of multi-feature characteristics of load data. It is widely applied and deeply researched in the short-term load forecasting field at present. The common thoughts in combination forecasting model include: firstly, combine with different neural network models to realize combination forecasting for load data, such as CNN-LSTM and GRU-NN combination forecasting model [3, 4]; secondly, preprocess the original load sequence, take different methods to extract features, then establish the forecasting model respectively, such as variational mode decomposition (VMD) and local mean decomposition (LMD) selected [5, 6], and execute load forecasting in combination with different forecasting models.

On the basis of existing scientific research achievements of combination forecasting method and characteristics of periodicity, non-linearity, non-stationarity and strong randomness of short-term load forecasting sequence, a short-term load combination forecasting method for power grid based on Hilbert-Huang Transform is proposed in this paper. HHT is a time-frequency analysis method characterized by self-adaptability and decomposing signal locally. Firstly, the load data is decomposed by empirical mode decomposition (EMD) algorithm to get IMF component and get different components of instantaneous frequency by Hilbert conversion; secondly, the different load forecasting models are selected to forecast the high-frequency, medium-frequency and low-frequency components respectively. Such a combination model can not only make full use of the most of character of different components, but also realize the complementary advantage between different forecasting models. The rationality and effectiveness of the combination model are validated by test in this paper.

2   Theoretical Basis of Combination Model

2.1   Empirical Mode Decomposition (*EMD*)

HHT include EMD and Hilbert conversion. EMD decomposition is the core part of HHT conversion, as well as the truly innovative point. EMD process is an iterative process of data processing by envelope fit by extreme value. After the data column iterated meets the certain conditions, it will become the intrinsic mode function (IMF), calling as screening. IMF is characterized by two points: 1) In sequence, the number of extreme point is equal to that of zero crossing point or the difference is not greater than 1; 2) At any time, the local value of upper envelope and lower envelope defined by extreme point is zero [7]. The general steps of EMD decomposition include:

1) The maximum value and minimum value of input signal $x(t)$ are evaluated to fit the envelope. The curve fitting mentioned here is an important issue in *EMD*. The effect of the interpolation method selected on envelope fitting will have a direct influence on *EMD* decomposition result, and the cubic spline interpolation method is used in this paper.

2) The mean $m(t)$ of upper envelope and lower envelope is evaluated, and $h(t)$ is evaluated by $h(t) = x(t) - m(t)$;

3) *IMF* end condition of $h(t)$ is judged. If two features of *IMF* mentioned above are met, $h(t)$ is the first *IMF* evaluated by decomposition, recorded as $h_1(t)$; if not, Step 1 and Step 2 are cycled and repeated through assuming $h(t) = x(t)$ as the new sequence;

4) The new sequence $r(t)$ is gotten by $r(t) = x(t) - h_n(t)$, and the decomposition end condition is judged. If it is met, the decomposition is ended; $r(t)$ is the residual component, and n *IMF* components are gotten by decomposition; if not, the above steps are cycled and repeated through assuming $r(t) = x(t)$.

A certain number of *IMF* and residual component r are gotten through decomposition of original sequence signal $x(t)$, of which $x(t)$ is expressed as:

$$x(t) = \sum_{i=1}^{n} h_i(t) + r(t) \tag{1}$$

wherein, $h_i(t)$ is the i*IMF* component, and $r(t)$ is the residual component. Each *IMF* component gotten here is the independent data sequence of a characteristic scale [8].

2.2 Hilbert Spectrum Analysis

After *EMD* decomposition screening, *Hilbert* conversion is applied in each independent *IMF* component, so as to get the instantaneous frequency and instantaneous amplitude to analyze the components. *Hilbert* conversion can realize the $90°$ phase shift of base frequency and harmonic wave accurately, and remain constant amplitude [9]. With regard to the given signal $x(t)$, *Hilbert* conversion may be defined as:

$$H[x(t)] = \frac{1}{\pi} \int_{-\infty}^{+\infty} \frac{x(\tau)}{t - \tau} d\tau = x(t) * \frac{1}{\pi t} \tag{2}$$

The analytic signal is gotten through *Hilbert* conversion for signal $x(t)$:

$$z(t) = x(t) + jH[x(t)] = a(t)e^{j\theta(t)} \tag{3}$$

So the instantaneous frequency ω:

$$f_i = \frac{1}{2\pi} \omega_i(t) = \frac{1}{2\pi} \frac{d\theta_i(t)}{dt} \tag{4}$$

Through *Hilbert* conversion, the analytic function of each IMF component $h_i(t)$:

$$z_i(t) = h_i(t) + j\tilde{h}_i(t) = a_i(t)e^{j\theta_i(t)} \tag{5}$$

The instantaneous frequency and instantaneous amplitude of each *IMF* component are gotten from Eq. (4, 5). In essence, *Hilbert* conversion shows the optimal approximation degree of local signal and sine function, and its localization feature is further reinforced in the differential operation of solving instantaneous frequency [10].

2.3 RBF Neural Network

RBF neural network can approximate arbitrary nonlinear function with good function approximation function, and is widely applied in the load forecasting aspect by virtue of characteristics of simple structure and rapid learning convergence rate. *RBF* neural network based on Gaussian kernel is used [11]. It is assumed that the input vector is n dimension, and is denoted as $x = (x_1, x_2, \ldots, x_n)^T$. In addition, there are k hidden nodes and m outputs in the model. $h_i(x)$ represents the i hidden layer node. The Gaussian function is used for conversion of space mapping of input information as the kernel function of hidden layer neuron:

$$h_i(x) = \Phi_i(x) = e^{-\frac{x_i^2}{\delta_i^2}} \tag{6}$$

δ is the extended constant. When the vector is input to neural network through *Gaussian* radial basis function, the output of the j node of hidden layer:

$$\Phi_i(x) = \exp\left(\frac{-\|x_i - c_j\|}{2\sigma_j^2}\right) \tag{7}$$

wherein, c_j is the center of Gaussian function of the j hidden layer; $\|\cdot\|$ is Euclidean norm, and σ_j is the width of Gaussian function of the j hidden layer. The output of *RBF* neural network:

$$Y = (y_1, y_2, \ldots, y_m)^T = \sum_{j=1}^{m} w_j \Phi_j(x) \tag{8}$$

wherein, w_j is the network connection weight between the j hidden layer node and output layer [18]. *RBF* neural network forecasting model can turn the nonlinear mapping from input layer to hidden layer into the linear mapping on the other space, and forecast the signal with high frequency, large volatility and strong randomness better [19].

2.4 LSTM Recurrent Neural Network

LSTM is an improved structure proposed for easy gradient vanishing and gradient explosion of common *RNN* in practical training. It is a mechanism which leads in cell gate from neuron of standard *RNN* model, which consists of input gate, output gate and forget gate [12]. The forget gate is used to decide the forget and update of transitional information. LSTM cell structure is as shown in Fig. 1.

LSTM model can decide which information is forgotten and updated to constitute the long-term and short-term memory network through gate mechanism in cell structure. According to LSTM cell structure chart, C_t is the cell state at t time; x_t is the input at t time; h_t is the output at t time, and f_t, i_t and o_t are output of forget gate, input gate and output gate respectively. The operation process of concrete cell structure:

$$f_t = \sigma\left(W_f[h_{t-1}, x_t] + b_f\right) \tag{9}$$

$$i_t = \sigma\left(W_i[h_{t-1}, x_t] + b_i\right) \tag{10}$$

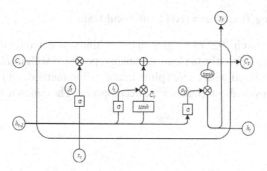

Fig. 1. LSTM Unit Structure Diagram.

$$\overline{C}_t = tanh\big(W_c[h_{t-1}, x_t] + b_c\big) \tag{11}$$

$$o_t = \sigma\big(W_o[h_{t-1}, x_t] + b_o\big) \tag{12}$$

$$C_t = f_t C_{t-1} + i_t \overline{C}_t \tag{13}$$

$$h_t = o_t tanh(C_t) \tag{14}$$

wherein, W_f, W_i, W_c and W_o are weight matrixes, and b_f, b_i, b_c and b_o are bias vectors. *LSTM* model is optimized by "forget gate" additionally, so as to control the convergence of gradient during training data, and solve the gradient vanishing or gradient explosion better.

3 Short-Term Load Forecasting Combination Model Based on HHT

The short-term load data of power grid is affected by human production and life, change of meteorological condition, economic factor, political factor, etc. The system load data includes multiple characteristics for analysis and forecasting, and it is difficult to obtain the essential characteristics. In order to further explore the inherent law of load data, the short-term load forecasting combination model of power grid based on *HHT* is established to decompose the load data as a certain amount of *IMF* by *EMD* algorithm, and then convert and process each component alone by *Hilbert* conversion, so as to get different instantaneous frequencies and instantaneous amplitudes. According to different characteristics of *IMF*, the different neural network models are selected for forecasting, and the result is overlapped to get the forecasted value of load in the end. In the meantime, due to large influence of change of air temperature on fluctuation of load data, the accuracy of load forecasting is promoted in combination with the correlation between temperature data of the region and *IMF* component.

3.1 Hilbert-Huang Transform (HHT) of Load Data

The data sample in March 2021 of a region in East China is selected for test. The load data curve is shown in Fig. 2. Firstly, the load sequence is provided with *EMD* decomposition, then the envelope is fitted with cubic spline interpolation method, and a total of 7 *IMF* components and a residual component *r* are decomposed. The concrete result is as shown in Fig. 3.

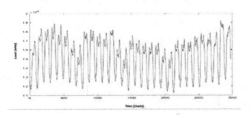

Fig. 2. Load data curve (March, 2021)

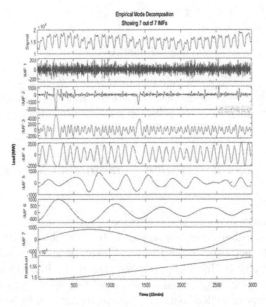

Fig. 3. *EMD* decomposition result

The frequency of IMF_1 component and IMF_2 component is high in Fig. 3, but that of IMF_3 to IMF_7 is decreased progressively in contrast. In order to further analyze each component, *Hilbert* conversion is also applied to obtain the concrete instantaneous frequency curve chart of each component, as shown in Fig. 4.

The mean frequency of each *IMF* component is further calculated in Table 1. It shows that each *IMF* component owns different frequency characteristics in Fig. 4 and

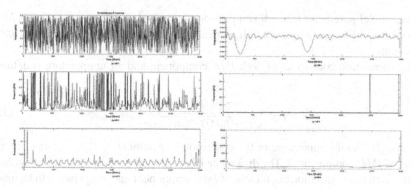

Fig. 4. Instantaneous frequency of *IMF* component

Table 1. It is decreased progressively, and the mean value calculated is also reduced in turn. IMF_1 to IMF_3 is characterized by large fluctuation, strong randomness and high frequency upon calculation as the random part of load; IMF_4 to IMF_5 is characterized by steady fluctuation trend and mean frequency decrease, which represents the periodicity of load; eventually, according to the calculation result of mean frequency in Table 1, IMF_6, IMF_7 and residual term r approach to zero, which represents the trend component of load. The components are divided into random component, periodic component and trend component according to their characteristics. On one hand, they reduce the difficulty of building forecasting model; on the other hand, they emphasize on different characteristics of each component. The model is built by combination of *RBF* neural network model and recurrent neural network based on *LSTM*. It not only takes advantage of high learning rate of *RBF* neural network to process the data signal with large volatility and high frequency, but also processes the problems with strong periodicity and highly correlated with time sequence in combination with *LSTM* to effectively improve the forecasting accuracy.

Table 1. Average frequency of IMF component

Component	IMF1	IMF2	IMF3	IMF4	IMF5	IMF6	IMF7
Frequency (Hz)	0.2792	0.0992	0.0204	0.0097	0.005	0.0016	0.0006

3.2 Correlation Analysis of *IMF* Component Temperature

The power load data includes multiple properties of power utilizations, i.e., industrial load, appliance load and transportation load. Different *IMF* components represent different properties of power utilization data, and the meteorological influence is also different, so it should be analyzed in preliminary data processing in combination with meteorological factors. For example, the air temperature is selected as the representation of meteorological factors, the meteorological factor is integrated to adjust the input data and model parameter through comparison with correlation between different *IMF* components and temperatures as well as neural network modeling for different *IMF* components.

The correlation coefficient of each *IMF* component and air temperature is defined as

$$r_i = \frac{cov(h_i(t), c_i(t))}{\sqrt{cov(h_i(t))}\sqrt{cov(c_i(t))}} \tag{15}$$

wherein, $c_i(t)$ is air temperature of the corresponding point ($i = 1, 2, \ldots, n$; n is total number of *IMF* components). The difference in correlation of different seasons is obvious, of which the correlation coefficient of *IMF* component and temperature in summer and winter is high, and the load data in March is selected; the correlation of *IMF* component and air temperature data gotten by decomposition is small on the whole, and the curve chart of correlation coefficient in Fig. 5 is obtained. Specially, it is shown that the correlation between IMF_1 component and IMF_2 component and air temperature data scarcely exists. IMF_3 and IMF_4 are positively correlated with air temperature data, but IMF_5 and IMF_7 are negatively correlated with air temperature data, so the short-term load forecasting combination model is trained for different *IMF* components respectively. As an example of IMF_4 component, it shows that IMF_4 component is greatly affected by weather in contrast in Fig. 5, and the forecasting difficulty is high. In the short-term load forecasting combination modeling of power grid corresponding to IMF_4 component, the proportion of training data, validation data and test data is about 90%, 5% and 5% respectively.

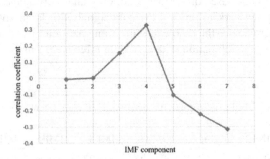

Fig. 5. Correlation between IMF components and temperature

3.3 Short-Term Load Forecasting Combination Model of Power Grid

The load sequence of power system is characterized by volatility and special periodicity, and it is greatly affected by actual scenes, for example, the difference of geographic position and living habit of the southern and northern China, economic and social difference of the first-tier and second-tier cities and the third-tier and fourth-tier cities will cause different periodicities and volatilities of load data due to climate, major events, electricity price fluctuation, etc. The short-term load combination forecasting model of power grid based on *HHT* proposed herein is applied to study the essence of load data through decomposition of short-term load data of power grid, and then forecast in combination with the appropriate neural network forecasting model according to characteristics of different components, so as to improve the forecasting accuracy and stability.

The concrete steps of short-term load combination forecasting model of power grid based on *HHT* is:

(1) Preprocess the historical load data and specify the evaluation index;
(2) Decompose the load data by *EMD* algorithm, provide *Hilbert* conversion for *IMF* component, and get the instantaneous frequency;
(3) Apply appropriate neural network model for forecasting respectively according to characteristics of different frequencies of each component;
(4) Add the forecasted result of each component to get the final result;
(5) Eventually, get the accuracy index through comparison with the non-compositional method.

4 Simulated Analysis

The short-term load forecasting model is applied, and the load data in March 2021 of one region in eastern China is selected to forecast the load value for 24 h on April 1, 2021 as the training sample, and analyze the accuracy of forecasted result. The curve chart of actual load and forecasted load is as shown in Fig. 6. The error of concrete forecasted result value and relative percentage of forecasting is as shown in Table 2, of which the forecasting percentage error is defined as:

$$APE = \left| \frac{A_t - P_t}{A_t} \right| \times 100\% \tag{16}$$

wherein, A_t is the real load value; P_t is the load value gotten by forecasting.

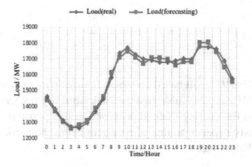

Fig. 6. Comparison between real load and forecasting load

Table 2. APE of forecasting load

Time/H	APE/%	Time/H	APE/%	Time/H	APE/%	Time/H	APE/%
0:00	1.52	1:00	0.78	2:00	0.64	3:00	0.67
4:00	1.34	5:00	0.96	6:00	1.48	7:00	0.82
8:00	1.89	9:00	1.45	10:00	1.17	11:00	0.97
12:00	1.78	13:00	0.91	14:00	1.74	15:00	1.05
16:00	1.62	17:00	1.20	18:00	0.95	19:00	1.34
20:00	1.74	21:00	1.06	22:00	2.27	23:00	1.13

In order to compare with other methods, the mean absolute percentage error (*MAPE*) is selected to measure the forecasted result as the evaluation index of short-term load forecasting of power grid.

$$MAPE = \frac{1}{n} \sum_{t=1}^{n} \left| \frac{A_t - P_t}{A_t} \right| \times 100\% \tag{17}$$

The result which shows the higher forecasting accuracy and better effect of the method proposed herein is presented in Table 3 by comparison of the method proposed herein and forecasted result of *RNN* recurrent neural network and *LSTM* recurrent neural network forecasting model for mean load of one region.

Table 3. MAPE of short-term load forecasting

Date	Proposed method/%	LSTM/%	RNN/%
Apr. 1	1.27	2.26	2.53
Apr. 2	1.67	2.07	3.22
Apr. 3	1.36	2.72	3.05
Apr. 4	1.94	2.45	3.52
Apr. 5	1.44	2.31	2.47

In contrast with *MAPE* result based on the combination method and network model method based on *LSTM* and *RNN*, although the forecasting accuracy is fluctuated, *MAPE* index of combination forecasting method proposed in this paper is basically less than 2%, which is obviously superior to that of recurrent neural network forecasting model based on *LSTM* applied alone.

5 Conclusions

In this paper, the short-term load combination forecasting model of power grid based on *HHT* is studied. The original load sequence is decomposed by *EMD* decomposition algorithm, and then each *IMF* component is changed along by *HT*. According to characteristics of different components and analysis on correlation of air temperature data, it is forecasted in combination with the forecasting model of neural network based on *RBF* and recurrent neural network based on *LSTM*. It not only takes advantage of *HHT* to process nonlinear and non-stable signal, but also realizes the complementary advantages between different neural networks. It is discovered that the accuracy of short-term load forecasting combination method of power grid based on *HHT* is higher through experimental result. Certainly, the characteristic analysis on IMF component should remain to be further studied and explored in contrast with correlation analysis of other factors, such as social experience factors and holiday activity factors. The combined neural network model also remains to be further improved and tried to promote the load forecasting accuracy to a greater extent.

References

1. Yao, J.G., Yang, S.C., Gao, Z.H., et al.: Development trend prospects of power dispatching automation system. Autom. Electr. Power Syst. **31**(13), 7–11 (2007)
2. Osman, Z.H., Awad, M.L., Mahmoud, T.K.: Neural network based approach for short-term load forecasting. In: 2009 IEEE/PES Power Systems Conference and Exposition, pp. 1–8. Seattle, WA (2009)
3. Lu, J.X., Zhang, Q.P., Yang, Z.H., et al.: Short-term load forecasting method based on CNN-LSTM hybrid neural network model. Autom. Electr. Power Syst. **43**(8), 131–137 (2019)
4. Wu, L.Z., Kong, C., Hao, X.H., et al.: A short-term load forecasting method based on GRU-CNN hybrid neural network model. Math. Probl. Eng. **2020**, 1–10 (2020)
5. Liang, Z., Sun, G.Q., Li, H.C., et al.: Short-term load forecasting based on VMD and PSO optimized deep belief network. Power Syst. Technol. **42**(2), 598–606 (2018)
6. Kong, X.Y., Li, C., Zheng, F., et al.: Short-term load forecasting method based on empirical mode decomposition and feature correlation analysis. Autom. Electr. Power Syst. **43**(5), 46–51 (2019)
7. Huang, N.E., Shen, Z., Long, S.R., et al.: The empirical mode decomposition and the Hilbert spectrum for nonlinear and non-stationary time series analysis. In: Proceedings of the Royal Society of London. Series A: Mathematical, Physical and Engineering Sciences, pp. 903–995 (1998)
8. Zhu, Z.H., Sun, Y.L., Ji, Y.: Short-term load forecasting based on EMD and SVM. High Volt. Eng. **33**(5), 118–122 (2007)
9. Huang, C.G.: Hilbert transform and its applications. J. Chengdu Inst. Meteorol. **14**(3), 273–276 (1999)
10. Munir, B.S., Reza, M., Trisetyarso, A., et al.: Feature extraction using Hilbert-Huang transform for power system oscillation measurements. In: 2017 4th International Conference on Information Technology, Computer, and Electrical Engineering (ICITACEE), pp. 93–96. Semarang, Indonesia (2017)
11. Schilling, R.J., Carroll, J.J., Al-Ajlouni, A.F.: Approximation of nonlinear systems with radial basis function neural networks. IEEE Trans. Neural Netw. **12**(1), 1–15 (2001)
12. Gers, F.A., Schmidhuber, J., Cummins F.: Learning to forget: continual prediction with LSTM. In: Ninth International Conference on Artificial Neural Networks (ICANN), pp. 850–855. Edinburgh, UK (1999)

Research on Edge Computing Offloading Based on Reinforcement Learning in Multi-user Scenarios

Zi-Hang Yu[1], Jian-Jun Zeng[2], Sai Liu[1], and Zhen-Jiang Zhang[1]([⊠])

[1] Department of Electronic and Information Engineering, Key Laboratory of Communication and Information Systems, Beijing Municipal Commission of Education, Beijing Jiaotong University, Beijing 100044, China
{22110021,20120073,zhangzhenjiang}@bjtu.edu.cn
[2] College of Intelligence and Computing, Beijing InchTek Technology, Tianjin University, 100044 Beijing, China
jj@inchtek.ai

Abstract. Under the blessing of the new generation of information technology represented by 5G, a large number of new models and new businesses represented by smart logistics, industrial Internet, and smart transportation have emerged one after another, and the door to the intelligent interconnection of all things has officially opened. However, due to IoT sensor devices are usually responsible for data acquisition and transmission, they have certain limitations in terms of computing and storage capabilities. How to expand the performance of devices located at the edge of the network has become a focus of attention. Aiming at the problems of high energy consumption, prolonged time and high task failure rate in traditional IoT edge computing methods, this paper introduces deep reinforcement learning technology to optimize IoT edge computing offload methods. This paper models a single edge server multi-user scenario, and designs a function that comprehensively considers task delay and task failure rate as the goal of further optimization. At the same time, aiming at the problem of state space dimension explosion in traditional reinforcement learning, a computing task offloading method based on deep Q network is further proposed. Through simulation experiments, the results show that the proposed method has certain advantages in time delay and task success rate under the condition of different number of IoT devices.

Keywords: Edge computing · Reinforcement learning · Computing offload · Deep Q network

1 Introduction

With the rapid development of portable devices, the Internet of Things, and other fields, the need for more stringent requirements, computational sensitivity, and low latency has followed. With the advent of the 5G era, the network speed has once again increased rapidly, and many emerging fields and scenarios have emerged, such as Augmented

© ICST Institute for Computer Sciences, Social Informatics and Telecommunications Engineering 2023
Published by Springer Nature Switzerland AG 2023. All Rights Reserved
D.-J. Deng et al. (Eds.): SGIoT 2022, LNICST 497, pp. 102–112, 2023.
https://doi.org/10.1007/978-3-031-31275-5_11

Reality, Virtual Reality [1]. Not only to meet the requirements of low-latency and high-reliability communication, but also to ensure service quality. In addition, in daily life, study and work, there is a huge amount of data that needs to be processed, and these problems have an urgent need for powerful computing hardware.

In order to solve the above problems, the European Telecommunications Standardization Institute proposed mobile edge computing in 2014. Mobile edge computing is to solve the problems of computing delay of mobile cloud computing and insufficient computing equipment for big data processing. It is defined as providing cloud computing capability and IT service environment to application developers and content providers at the network edge [2]. Compared with mobile cloud computing, mobile edge computing can offload computing tasks to edge servers without going through a wide area network, thereby reducing latency and energy consumption and alleviating network bandwidth pressure [3].

Mobile edge computing also has its own shortcomings, limited by factors such as equipment and location, and the choice of task offloading strategy is particularly important in mobile edge computing [4]. When the user's own terminal cannot meet the data or business needs, need to choose a reasonable offload strategy, whether to offload this task, where to offload this task, these are all questions to consider. The goal of the offloading strategy is to optimize energy consumption, delay, cost, load balancing, etc. [5]. As for which weight is higher, it needs to be determined according to the specific application scenario. Moreover, in the actual scene, the environment is constantly changing, and the strategy cannot be static [9]. It needs to learn in the dynamic to achieve the best effect, so as to improve the service quality and user experience. Therefore, a reasonable offloading strategy can make MEC play the biggest role, utilize resources to the greatest extent [10], reduce service delay, reduce energy consumption of computing equipment, balance various loads in the system, and allow more users to obtain better user experience [11].

2   Related Work

One of the basic functions of the MEC system is to provide computing services to the edge of the network. In order to improve the quality of service (QoS), proper task offloading strategy is very important. In recent years, task offloading has received extensive attention from academia and industry. According to existing theoretical research, the task offloading problem in edge computing is a combinatorial optimization problem. From the current computing offloading task model, there are two main directions of existing research: Binary Offloading model and Partial Offloading model. In the binary offloading model, in order to simplify the problem, the tasks can no longer be divided, and the tasks can only be executed locally or on the edge server. The binary unloading model is still NP-Hard in most MEC scenarios. Dinh et al. aimed to find an offload schedule for a set of tasks between different access points and MEC service hosts to achieve the minimum goal of combining latency and energy consumption [6]. To obtain the best user experience quality as the goal, Hong et al. used approximate dynamic programming to solve it effectively [7]. Binary computing task offloading In addition to heuristic solutions, convex optimization methods are also used to solve binary offloading problems. Due to the constraints of the unloading problem, the unloading problem is usually non-convex.

Existing studies use approximation or relaxation methods to transform the non-convex problem into a convex optimization problem. Wang et al. adopted a relaxed approach to transform the joint allocation problem of cache and resources into a convex optimization problem [8]. However, with the emergence of time-sensitive tasks such as AR/VR and autonomous driving, traditional optimization algorithms cannot meet the needs well [12]. In response to the above problems, this paper integrates deep reinforcement learning into the edge computing of the Internet of Things, combines the perception ability of deep learning with the decision-making ability of reinforcement learning, and optimizes the computing offloading problem in the original edge computing of the Internet of Things.

3   System Model

3.1   Network Model

This article discusses the MEC system consisting of an Access Point (AP) and multiple mobile devices. The wireless AP can be a small cell base station or a Wi-Fi AP. In addition to the conventional AP, it has an MEC server. The MEC network model is shown in the Fig. 1.

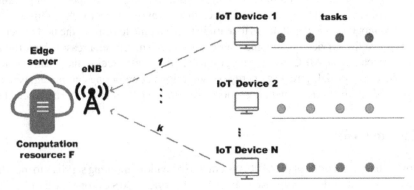

Fig. 1. MEC network model diagram

In the MEC network, there is one edge server and N IoT devices, and the edge server can provide computing services for the IoT devices within its coverage. Assuming that each IoT device has multiple computing tasks, these tasks can be selected to be executed locally or offloaded to the MEC server for execution. A collection of IoT devices can be represented as $\{1, 2, \ldots N\}$. The total computing resources of the MEC server are F. Divide time into multiple slots,the length of each slot is set to τ. Assume that the computing tasks of IoT devices follow a Poisson process. Its speed is λ.

Get a parameter as p, where $p = \lambda t_0$. This process is a Bernoulli process with parameter p. That is, the arrival time of each device computing task is an independent random variable.

The arriving task is defined by a triple $task_{i,j} = (b_{i,j}, c_{i,j}, \tau)$. Where $b_{i,j}$ represents the size of the input computational task. $c_{i,j}$ represents the number of CPU cycles required to complete the computing task. τ represents the deadline for completing the calculation task, used for delay constraints. The variable $a_{i,j} \in \{0, 1\}$ is used to represent the offloading decision of the computing task. If $a_{i,j} = 0$, it means that the computing task is executed locally, if $a_{i,j} = 1$, it means that the computing task is offloaded to the edge server for execution.

3.2 Communication Model

Since this paper pays more attention to the computational offloading decision problem of the MEC server shared by multiple users, the wireless communication part is simplified, and the situation of users working on orthogonal channels is considered. Therefore, users do not suffer from multi-user interference with each other, which is a common situation in communication systems such as LTE (Long Term Evolution) at present. Since the wireless arrival state changes over time and is affected by the mobility of the terminal equipment, when a task arrives and the channel state is not good, it is chosen to be processed locally instead of waiting for better channel conditions. Suppose $h_{i,j}$ is the small-scale channel gain of the th terminal device to the MEC server in the j-th slot. The channel transmission rate calculated by Shannon's theorem is shown in the formula (1):

$$R_{i,j} = log\left(1 + \frac{d_{i,j}^{-\alpha}|h_{i,j}|^2 P_{i,j}}{\sigma^2}\right), i, j = 1, 2, \cdots, N \tag{1}$$

where d_i represents the distance from the device to the MEC server, α represents the path loss index, P_i represents the transmit power of the device, σ^2 represents the noise power of the MEC server.

3.3 Computational Model

According to the result of computing offloading, the computing tasks executed locally are waiting to be executed in the local buffer queue, and the computing tasks that are offloaded to the MEC server are waiting for computing in the buffer of the server.

Local Computing Model. If you choose to execute task$_{i,j}$ locally, the calculation formula of the processing delay $t_{i,j}^l$ of the task is as follows:

$$t_{i,j}^l = c_{i,j}/f_i^l \tag{2}$$

Among them, $c_{i,j}$ represents the amount of computation that the task needs to complete, and f_i^l represents the computing capability of the local device. At the same time, taking into account the time limit of task processing, propose a penalty $\beta_{i,j}$ for not completing the task within the deadline, the calculation formula is as (3):

$$\beta_{i,j} = 1_{\{t_{i,j}^l > \tau\}} \tag{3}$$

where $1_{\{\mu\}}$ is an indicator function whose value is 1 only when the condition is true, and 0 otherwise.

Edge Computing Model. The process of offloading tasks to the edge server mainly includes three processes. First, the terminal device uploads the input data to the edge server through the wireless network, then the edge server executes the calculation task, and finally returns the calculation result to the corresponding terminal device. The delay calculation formula of the unloading process is as follows:

$$t_{i,j}^{off} = t_{i,j}^{trans} + t_{i,j}^{comp} \tag{4}$$

$$t_{i,j}^{trans} = b_{i,j}/R_{i,j} \tag{5}$$

$$t_{i,j}^{comp} = c_{i,j}/f_{i,j} \tag{6}$$

which $t_{i,j}^{trans}$ represents the transmission time that will calculate the data sent from the terminal device with the MEC server. $t_{i,j}^{comp}$ represents the processing time of computing tasks performed by the MEC server, $b_{i,j}$ represents the calculated data size transferred. $R_{i,j}$ represents the transmission speed of the i-th terminal device between the j-th slot and the server. $f_{i,j}$ represents the computing power allocated by the MEC server to the terminal device. Since the computing resources of the server are limited, the computing resources allocated by the MEC server to each terminal device should be smaller than the computing resources possessed by the MEC server, that is, the following constraints are satisfied:

$$\sum_{i=1}^{N} f_{i,j} \leq F, \forall j \tag{7}$$

Also taking into account the time limit of task processing, it is proposed to represent the penalty for not completing the task within the deadline. The calculation formula is as follows:

$$\beta_{i,j} = 1_{\{t_{i,j}^{off} > \tau\}} \tag{8}$$

3.4 Problem Modeling

According to formula (2) (4) (5) (6), the computational task delay can be expressed as

$$t_{i,j} = a_{i,j} t_{i,j}^{off} + (1 - a_{i,j}) t_{i,j}^{l} \tag{9}$$

where $a_{i,j}$ represents the unloading decision vector of the terminal device. Considering the task processing delay and the task timeout failure rate, the objective function is obtained, as follows:

$$U = \frac{1}{T} \frac{1}{N} \sum_{j=1}^{T} \sum_{i=1}^{N} \left(\omega_1 t_{i,j}/\tau + \omega_2 \beta_{i,j} \right)$$

$$s.t. \ C1 : a_{i,j} \in \{0, 1\}, \forall i, j \tag{10}$$

$$C2 : \sum_{i=1}^{N} f_{i,j} \leq F, \forall j$$

Which $C1$ means that the type of computational unloading considered in this paper is binary unloading, $C2$ indicates computing resource constraints. The objective function consists of two parts, which $\frac{1}{T}\frac{1}{N}\sum_{j=1}^{T}\sum_{i=1}^{N}(\omega_1 t_{i,j}/\tau)$ represents the computing task delay, $\frac{1}{T}\frac{1}{N}\sum_{j=1}^{T}\sum_{i=1}^{N}\omega_2\beta_{i,j}$ represents the timeout task penalty item. ω_1, ω_2 represents the weighted value of these two terms.

4　Computational Offloading Algorithm Based on Reinforcement Learning

This section defines the three elements of reinforcement learning, state, action, and reward in detail. And introduced the reinforcement learning algorithm Q-Learning and DQN algorithm, combined with the computational offloading scenario designed above, the multi-objective optimization problem with computational offloading constraints is transformed into a problem of maximizing the Q value. Among them, Q-Learning stores the Q value in the Q table. As the number of user devices increases, the problem of excessive dimension may occur. The DQN algorithm is further proposed, which replaces the Q table with a deep neural network and uses it to approximate the Q function.

4.1　Q-Learning Algorithm

Reinforcement learning algorithms differ from MDPs in that RL algorithms attempt to derive optimal policies without an explicit model of the environment's dynamics. Reinforcement learning agents learn in real-world interactions with the environment and refine their behavioral policies through the experience gained from interacting with the environment. In the scenario of edge computing offloading, the observation information of the agent should include the transmission rate between the terminal device and the edge server $R_{i,j}$, the amount of data sent by the terminal device to the server $b_{i,j}$, and computing resources required for computing tasks $c_{i,j}$, That is, the state vector is $s(j) = [R_1, R_2, ...R_N, b_1, b_2...b_N, c_1, c_2, ...c_N]$.

The action vector of the agent includes the unloading decision of each terminal device and the computing resources allocated to the terminal device by the MEC server. That is, the action vector is $a(j) = [a_1, a_2, ...a_N, f_1, f_2..f_N]$. The reward function of the agent is set according to the optimization goal in the edge computing offloading scenario. Since the optimization goal is to obtain the minimum value of the function, and reinforcement learning is to obtain the maximum reward, the reward function needs to take a negative value on the joint optimization goal. That is, the reward $r(i,j)$ is $-\sum_{j=1}^{T}\sum_{i=1}^{N}(\omega_1 t_{i,j}/\tau + \omega_2\beta_{i,j})$. Q-Learning is a classic off-policy algorithm based on time difference. It directly approximates the Q-value, and the agent state transitions are independent of the policy it is learning. The RL agent will learn from actual interactions with the environment and adjust its behavior after experiencing the consequences of its behavior to maximize the expected discounted return. The formula for estimating the value of Q is as follow:

$$Q(s, a) \leftarrow Q(s, a) + \alpha(r(s, a) + \gamma\max Q(s', a') - Q(s, a)) \tag{11}$$

where α represents the learning rate, in the iterative process, it is responsible for controlling the learning progress of the agent. $r(s, a) + \gamma \max Q(s', a') - Q(s, a)$ represent TD-error. The current Q value can be updated by this increment. Indicates the value obtained by taking action in the current state, s' represents the state reached after taking an action a in the state s.a' represents the action of obtaining the maximum Q value in state s. The parameter γ represents the discount factor, which represents the importance of future rewards. When γ approaches 0, the agent will only consider the rewards obtained in the current state, and when it approaches 1, the agent will also pay attention to the rewards obtained in the future.

The process of the Q-Learning algorithm is as follows: first, initialize the Q table randomly, and in each training episode, read the state information between the terminal device and the MEC server, select the largest Q value according to the greedy strategy, and get its corresponding action, then send the computing offload and resource allocation information to the terminal device, then enter the next state. Update the Q table according to the formula (12), and iterate continuously.

In the Q-Learning algorithm, the Q table is used to access the Q value corresponding to each state and behavior. However, due to the large number of terminal devices connected to an MEC server, it is difficult for computer memory to store all of them. Therefore, the neural network in machine learning is introduced, and the set of states and actions is used as the input of the neural network, after the convolution and activation functions in the neural network, Output state - Q value of action set. That is, the network f with parameter θ is used to estimate the Q value. The formula is as follows:

4.2 DQN Algorithm

Deep Q network (DQN) adopts the convolutional neural network in deep learning as the generalization model of the state-action value function; at the same time, it uses the classical algorithm of reinforcement learning-Q-Learning to update the model parameters of the state-action value function, so that the model eventually a better strategy can be learned.

$$f(s, a, \theta) = Q^*(s, a) \qquad (12)$$

Deep Q networks have two very important mechanisms. First, DQN has a memory pool for storing previous experiences. Each time DQN is updated, some previous experience can be randomly selected for learning. Second, there are two neural networks with the same structure but different parameters. The neural network for predicting the Q value has the latest parameters, while the neural network for the target Q value uses parameters from a period of time ago and remains unchanged for a period of time. So that the difference between the two network outputs can be used for continuous training, and the stability during the training process can be enhanced at the same time.

For the DQN algorithm, its execution process is as follows: First initialize the experience pool space to N, use random weights θ, θ^-. Initialize the evaluation network and the target network. At this time, the parameters of the target network and the evaluation network are the same. Perform operations for each episode: obtain status information between the terminal device and the MEC server, get the initial state. For each time slot, the action a_t is selected according to the ε-greedy algorithm. After that, the terminal device calculates reward r_t according to the unloading decision and resource allocation. And get the observation state s_{t+1} in the next slot.Store the results (s_t, a_t, r_t, s_{t+1}) obtained in the above process into the experience pool. Randomly select min-batch data from the experience pool to update the evaluation network parameters θ, the target network parameters θ^- are updated at intervals of C steps. The DQN algorithm is deployed in the MEC server, and a centralized method is used to obtain the state between the terminal device and MEC server. At the same time, due to the obvious correlation between each continuous state in reinforcement learning, it cannot meet the requirement of independent and identical distribution of data in neural network training, so the experience replay mechanism is introduced. The experience is stored in the experience pool, and during training, data is randomly selected for neural network training. The training process is shown in Fig. 2.

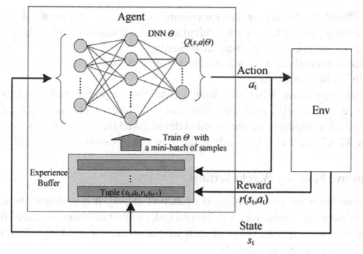

Fig. 2. DQN training process diagram

Select $l(\theta)$ as the loss function for training, in which the network parameters of the target network are updated after C steps to ensure the stability of the training process. The formula for calculating $l(\theta)$ is as follows:

$$l(\theta) = \left[r_t + \gamma \max Q^- \left(s_{t+1}, a'; \theta^- \right) - Q \left(s_{t+1}, a'; \theta \right) \right]^2 \tag{13}$$

5 Experimental Simulation

5.1 Simulation Parameter Settings

The simulation parameters are set as shown in Table 1.

In order to describe the performance of the algorithm proposed in this paper, three algorithms are selected as benchmark algorithms for comparison:

Table 1. Simulation parameter table.

parameter	value
Number of terminal devices N	4
MEC server performance F	40 GHZ
Terminal equipment performance f	3 GHz
task data size l	[20,40] kb
The size of the task calculation c	[0.5,3] GHz
length of a slot τ	1 s
target parameter ω_1	5
target parameter ω_2	5

(1) **All offload to the server for execution:** All tasks on the terminal device are offloaded to the MEC server for calculation, and at the same time, the computing resources are selected and distributed evenly.

(2) **All local execution:** The task on the terminal device is selected to be executed locally without offloading.

(3) **Greedy algorithm:** When the channel condition is optimal, task is selected to be offloaded to the MEC server for execution, and under other conditions, the computing task is executed on the terminal device. And the computing tasks offloaded to the MEC server evenly distribute the computing resources of the MEC server.

5.2 Objective Function Weight Setting

To determine the weight of the objective function ω_1, ω_2, it is necessary to study the influence of the weight value on the delay and task failure rate under the use of the DQN algorithm. As for ω_1, ω_2, the effect of each weight on latency and task failure rate was studied by fixing one of the values to 1.

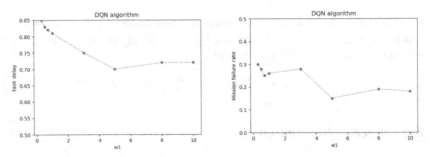

Fig. 3. The effect of parameter ω_1 on task delay and Mission failure rate

The above Fig. 3 represents the impact of different values on the delay and mission failure rate. It can be seen from the figure that with the increase of ω_1, the overall delay first decreases and then increases, and when equal to 5 time to get the minimum value. With the increase of ω_1, the task failure rate decreases first and then increases as a whole, and it is also obtained near 5. Therefore, the selected value is 5. Using the same experimental method, it is determined that the value of ω_2 is also 5.

5.3 The Effect of the Number of End Devices

This part studies the effect of changes in the number of IoT devices in the entire MEC system on the overall objective function when other conditions remain unchanged. The values of ω_1 and ω_2 are both 5.

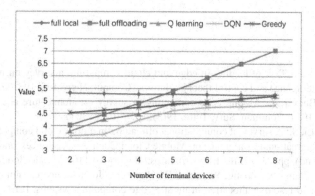

Fig. 4. The influence of the number of terminal devices on the objective function value

Figure 4 represents the effect of the number of end devices on the overall objective function. As can be seen from the figure, as the number of terminal devices increases, it can be seen from the figure that for policies that are all executed locally, the increase in the number of IoT devices will not affect their objective function. With the increase of the number of IoT devices, the total utility function of the strategy, greedy algorithm, Q learning and DQN strategy that are all offloaded to the edge server for execution gradually increases, and the growth rate of the all offloading strategy is the largest. When the number of IoT devices is less than or equal to 4, the full offloading strategy is better than the all locally executed strategy. When the number of terminal devices is greater than 5, the local offloading strategy is better than the all offloading strategy. At the same time, the advantages of the DQN algorithm are more obvious.

6 Future Work

This paper mainly models for multi-user edge computing scenarios, and designs a function that comprehensively considers task delay and task failure rate as the goal of further optimization. Combining the Q-Learning algorithm and the DQN algorithm, and conducting simulation experiments with different numbers of terminal devices, the simulation results show that it has certain advantages in time delay and task success rate. Some algorithms proposed in this paper based on deep reinforcement learning are applied to the problem of computational offloading, but only the task delay and task failure rate are considered. In real edge computing scenarios, the power of terminal devices is usually limited. How to reduce energy consumption as much as possible in the process of computing offloading while ensuring that the delay is met is a problem that needs to be considered in the future. In real scenarios, the number of terminal devices changes dynamically, and how the algorithm performs adaptive adjustment is also a problem worthy of consideration.

Acknowledgment. This work was supported by the National Natural Science Foundation of China (No. 62173026).

References

1. Saeik, F., et al.: Task offloading in edge and cloud computing: a survey on mathematical, artificial intelligence and control theory solutions. Comput. Netw. **195**, 108177 (2021)
2. Mach, P., Becvar, Z.: Mobile edge computing: a survey on architecture and computation offloading. IEEE Commun. Surv. Tutor. **19**(3), 1628–1656 (2017)
3. Zhang, Z., Li, S.: A survey of computational offloading in mobile cloud computing. In: 2016 4th IEEE International Conference on Mobile Cloud Computing, Services, and Engineering (MobileCloud), pp. 81–82. IEEE (2016). https://doi.org/10.1109/MobileCloud.2016.15
4. Zhang, G., Zhang, S., Zhang, W., Shen, Z., Wang, L.: Joint service caching, computation offloading and resource allocation in mobile edge computing systems. IEEE Trans. Wirel. Commun. **20**(8), 5288–5300 (2021)
5. Zhan, Y., Guo, S., Li, P., Zhang, J.: A deep reinforcement learning based offloading game in edge computing. IEEE Trans. Comput. **69**(6), 883–893 (2020)
6. Dinh, T.Q., Tang, J., La, Q.D., Quek, T.Q.: Offloading in mobile edge computing: task allocation and computational frequency scaling. IEEE Trans. Commun. **65**(8), 3571–3584 (2017)
7. Hong, S.T., Kim, H.: QoE-aware computation offloading to capture energy-latency-pricing tradeoff in mobile clouds. IEEE Trans. Mob. Comput. **18**(9), 2174–2189 (2018)
8. Wang, C., Liang, C., Yu, F.R., Chen, Q., Tang, L.: Computation offloading and resource allocation in wireless cellular networks with mobile edge computing. IEEE Trans. Wirel. Commun. **16**(8), 4924–4938 (2017)
9. Lu, J., et al.: A multi-task oriented framework for mobile computation offloading. IEEE Trans. Cloud Comput. **10**(1), 187–201 (2019). https://doi.org/10.1109/TCC.2019.2952346
10. Huang, C.M., Wu, Z.Y., Lin, S.Y.: The mobile edge computing (MEC)-based VANET data offloading using the staying-time-oriented k-hop away offloading agent. In: 2019 International Conference on Information Networking (ICOIN), pp. 357–362. IEEE (2019). https://doi.org/10.1109/ICOIN.2019.8718188
11. Aiwen, Z., Leyuan, L.: Energy-optimal task offloading algorithm of resources cooperation in mobile edge computing. In: 2021 4th International Conference on Advanced Electronic Materials, Computers and Software Engineering (AEMCSE), pp. 707–710. IEEE (2021). https://doi.org/10.1109/AEMCSE51986.2021.00146
12. Ko, H., Pack, S., Leung, V.C.: Performance optimization of serverless computing for latency-guaranteed and energy-efficient task offloading in energy harvesting industrial IoT. IEEE Internet Things J. (2021). https://doi.org/10.1109/JIOT.2021.3137291

Design of Malicious Code Detection System Based on Convolutional Neural Network

Yumeng Wu[1]([✉]), Jianjun Zeng[2,3], Zhenjiang Zhang[1], Wei Li[4,5], Zhiyuan Zhang[1], and Yang Zhang[1]

[1] School of Electronic and Information Engineering, Key Laboratory of Communication and Information Systems, Beijing Municipal Commission of Education, Beijing Jiaotong University, Beijing 100044, China
{21120146,zhangzhenjiang,zhangzhiyuan,zhangyang1}@bjtu.edu.cn
[2] College of Intelligence and Computing, Tianjin University, Tianjin, China
jj@inchtek.ai
[3] Beijing InchTek Technology Co., Ltd., Beijing 100012, China
[4] The Classified Information Carrier Safety Management Engineering Technology Research Center of Beijing, Beijing, China
[5] Beijing Jinghang Computation and Communication Research Institute, Beijing, China

Abstract. With the rapid development of Internet of things, cloud computing, edge computing and other technologies, malicious code attacks users and even enterprises more and more frequently with the help of software and system security vulnerabilities, which poses a serious threat to network security. The traditional static or dynamic malicious code detection technology is difficult to solve the problem of high-speed iteration and camouflage of malicious code. The detection method based on machine learning algorithm and data mining idea depends on manual feature extraction, and can not automatically and effectively extract the deeper features of malicious code. In view of the traditional malicious code detection methods and the related technologies of deep learning, this paper integrates deep learning into the dynamic malicious code detection system, and proposes a malicious code detection system based on convolutional neural network.

Keywords: convolutional neural network · malicious code detection · network security · deep learning

1 Introduction

In recent years, malicious code and network attacks have become more frequent, and new threats have emerged. The increasingly serious information security problem not only makes enterprises and users suffer huge economic losses, but also makes the national security is facing a serious threat. Viruses multiply and iterate quickly [1]. It can easily escape traditional detection methods by changing their signature concealment behavior. In order to keep up with the increasingly frequent and rapidly evolving pace of malicious code changes and improve the speed of emergency response to malicious attacks, it is

D.-J. Deng et al. (Eds.): SGIoT 2022, LNICST 497, pp. 113–124, 2023.
https://doi.org/10.1007/978-3-031-31275-5_12

necessary to timely analyze the attack methods and characteristics of malicious code quickly and accurately.

The traditional malicious code detection model needs to be trained by manually extracting features. The number of malicious code and the content of feature extraction greatly affect the detection effect of the model. Traditional malicious code detection methods include analysis methods based on dynamic behaviour [2, 3] and static signature [4]. The working principle is to obtain the relevant feature information through static scanning or dynamic analysis, and then compare it with the existing feature library. The feature library is limited and needs to be updated in time. The existing feature library is difficult to deal with the current surge in malicious code detection. In addition, this method of feature comparison will occupy a lot of running memory and low detection efficiency. Therefore, the traditional malicious code detection technology has been unable to effectively resist the new threats and attacks on the computer system and the Internet [5].

In recent years, machine learning has developed rapidly, especially in the fields of computer vision [6] and natural language processing [7]. Data mining is a process of finding anomalies, patterns and correlations in large data sets to predict results. Therefore, it is a popular application field to mine the potential value in the field of big data and discover the relationship between data by using the set of data mining and machine learning [8, 9]. However, the detection method based on machine learning algorithm and data mining idea can not automatically and effectively extract the deeper features of malicious code, which depends on manual extraction. These shallow features can not fully and accurately describe malicious code, and feature extraction largely determines the results of malicious code detection, resulting in the low accuracy of malicious code detection.

Aiming at the shortcomings of machine learning based detection technology, the deep learning model can automatically extract deeper features of malicious code, which can more accurately describe malicious code [10]. Compared with the artificial dependence of machine learning detection, the deep learning model has self-learning ability, and can learn the characteristic differences between malicious code samples and normal samples, so as to better complete the task of malicious code detection.

Combined with the traditional dynamic analysis method of malicious code detection and CNN model, this paper proposes a malicious code detection system model based on convolutional neural network. The system uses the sandbox to extract the malicious code API call sequence, and then takes its one-hot vectorization as the characteristic input of the malicious code detection system. The neural network parameters are adjusted by the optimization algorithm. Finally, the usability and superiority of the system are verified by experimental analysis.

2 Related Work

Many scholars have begun to study malicious code detection technology. Tahan et al. [11] proposed a new automatic signature generation method, which is based on deep packet inspection and runs in real time. This method can be used for large-scale malware detection by ignoring the signatures in benign executable files. Signature based detection is the most common method for commercial anti malware, but it can not identify new and unknown malware, so it is necessary to constantly update the malicious code signature database. With the rapid growth of the number and types of malicious code in recent years, this method relies on manual extraction, and the performance has become a big problem.

The behavior based malicious code detection method mainly collects the malicious behavior of malware instances and detects according to the collected behavior information. Firstly, it is necessary to perform dynamic analysis on relatively new malware data sets in a controlled virtual environment, and capture the API call information executed by malware instances. Firdausi et al. [12] extract the behavior information of malware in sandbox environment and generate behavior reports. These reports are preprocessed into sparse vector model, and then trained for classification through machine learning classification model. Burguera et al. [13] proposed a behavior based malware detection system crowdroid for Android, which dynamically analyzes the behavior of malicious code, and takes the behavior information extracted from the dynamic analysis as the feature of detecting malicious code on Android platform. Behavior based malicious code detection technology has the risk of being attacked by malicious code and occupies more resources.

In order to solve the shortcomings of traditional malicious code detection technology, research experts focus on the field of machine learning. Santos et al. [14] thought that the practical difficulty was that the detection method based on machine learning needed a large amount of labeled data, so they proposed llgc semi supervised learning to expand the training samples. The detection methods based on data mining [15] and traditional machine learning usually extract the features of malicious code and use the classifier algorithm of machine learning for detection and classification. The traditional classification model of machine learning can not effectively and automatically extract deep-seated features. It depends on manual feature extraction, and the experimental accuracy is low.

The above malicious code detection methods have some disadvantages. In recent years, the emerging deep learning methods can still show good detection effect in the case of insufficient feature extraction. Researchers are trying to apply the deep learning algorithm to the field of malicious code detection, which has research significance and development prospects at present. The advantages of deep learning, such as many feature dimensions, feature self-learning and large number of samples, mean that deep learning can play a great role in the field of malicious code detection. For example, feedforward neural network is used to analyze malicious code [16], and cyclic neural network is used to model system call sequence to build the language model of malicious code [17]. Most studies focus on the improvement of malicious code detection algorithm, and do not build a specific system model of malicious code detection. This paper draws lessons from the analysis methods of natural language processing, pays attention to the dynamic characteristics of malicious code, proposes a malicious code detection system model based on convolutional neural network, and makes an in-depth study on the feature extraction of malicious code, the feature vectorization representation of malicious code, and the detection and classification model of malicious code.

3 System Model

This section introduces the overall architecture of malicious code detection system based on convolutional neural network and the key technologies of feature extraction and neural network construction.

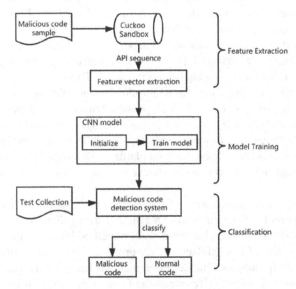

Fig. 1. Malicious code detection model framework

3.1 Overall Architecture

The model of malicious code detection system based on convolutional neural network is mainly divided into three stages: feature extraction, model training and classification detection. In the feature extraction stage, the API call log of malicious code is obtained through the open source automatic malware analysis tool cuckoo sandbox, and the API features are vectorized to obtain the feature vector. In the second stage, the convolutional neural network model is constructed and trained to the best state through the training set. In the third stage, the malicious code detection system detects unknown code and obtains malicious or benign classification results. Figure 1 is the overall framework of malicious code detection model based on CNN.

3.2 API Based Dynamic Behavior Capture

Sandbox. Sandbox is a lightweight virtual machine that can intercept system calls and restrict program execution in violation of security policies. Its core is to establish an execution environment with limited behavior. We put the sample program into the environment and run it. The path of file operation and registry operation in the sandbox will be redirected to the specified location of the sandbox. Some dangerous behaviors of the program, such as underlying disk operation and installation driver, will be prohibited by the sandbox, which ensures that the system environment will not be affected, The system state is rolled back after the operation. Thanks to the modular design and powerful scripting function of cuckoo, it can be used as an independent application or integrated into a larger framework. Cuckoo can be used to analyze windows executable files, DLL files, office files, URL and HTML files, VB scripts and other types of files.

In this paper, the open source automatic malware analysis sandbox cuckoo is built to automatically analyze and collect the behavior of samples in the isolated windows operating system. Cuckoo sandbox environment is mainly used for dynamic analysis of malicious code. It can execute and monitor malicious files in real time. The standard process of dynamic analysis of malicious code is to run PE files in an independent, transparent and secure analysis environment and monitor the dynamic behavior of samples. Through a variety of virtual sandboxes and the establishment of simulation technology to simulate the file running environment.

Cuckoo Sandbox mainly includes host machine (central management module) and guest machine (guest virtual machine module), which communicate with each other by establishing a virtual network. Host machine includes cuckoo sandbox software, virtual box software and various analysis components to manage the startup analysis, behavior monitoring and report generation analysis process of sandbox. Guest machine is an isolated environment where malicious code samples can be safely executed and analyzed, and finally report the analysis results to the central management module. Figure 2 shows the structure of Cuckoo Sandbox.

API Sequence Acquisition. First, put the code file sample into the cuckoo sandbox to get the analysis report in JSON format. The original JSON format API information includes: API type, API name, API parameter value, API return value, etc. Match it with the fields (category and API) to be extracted by the python script. If the matching is successful, the values corresponding to category and API in the API information are extracted and saved in the TXT format document as the original data of the feature vector.

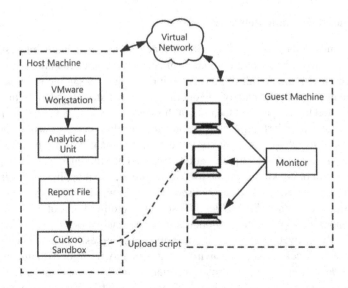

Fig. 2. Cuckoo Sandbox structure

3.3   Construction of Convolutional Neural Network

Convolution neural network is a deep feedforward neural network with the character-istics of local connection and weight sharing. The convolution layer uses convolution filter to extract features from data samples. In the field of image processing, convolution filter is mainly used to identify features from images. Similar to image, convolution filter is used to extract information and detect high-level features of short text in text processing. Because the logs containing malicious executable program instructions are composed of sequences, there are obvious similarities with natural language process-ing when selecting modeling methods. At present, convolutional neural networks are generally composed of convolution layer, convergence layer and full connection layer. Referring to the convolutional neural network structure, this paper uses the convolu-tional neural network to detect the malicious behavior of samples. Convolutional neural network architecture is shown in Fig. 3.

One-Hot Feature Vectorization. The convolution neural network model takes the word vector as the input of the input layer. The purpose of feature vectorization is to generate feature vectors for algorithm processing by using the API call information sequence obtained by sandbox. The whole process fully excavates sensitive information and maintains the behavior characteristics of malicious code. In the process of generating eigenvectors, one-hot model is selected.

One-hot coding is one of the methods of text vectorization, as shown in Fig. 4. One-hot encoding uses an n-bit status register to encode N states, and only one bit is valid. It associates the unique integer index i with each word, and then converts the index i into a binary vector with length n (n is the dictionary size, corresponding to the above n-bit status register). The characteristic of this vector is that only the ith element is 1 and the other elements are 0.

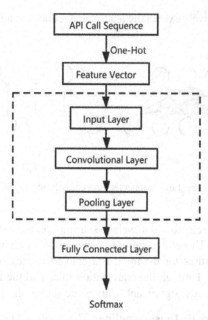

Fig. 3. Convolutional neural network architecture

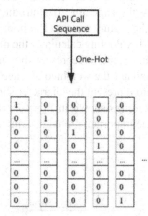

Fig. 4. One-hot Feature Vectorization

Convolution Layer Feature Extraction. Convolution layer mainly includes local perception and weight sharing. Different from the ordinary neural network, which designs the input layer and hidden layer as a fully connected form, the convolution layer of convolution neural network designs each hidden unit to connect only a part of the input unit.,as shown in Fig. 5. This local sensing structure can sense small areas, so as to reduce the number of parameters.

On the one hand, weight sharing enables the repeating unit to recognize the feature without considering the position of the feature in the visual domain. On the other hand, weight sharing can effectively extract the feature and reduce the number of free variables to be learned.

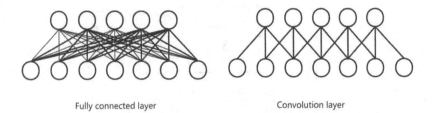

Fully connected layer   Convolution layer

Fig. 5. Fully connected and convolution layer

The way of local perception and weight sharing has the disadvantage of insufficient feature extraction. Therefore, multiple convolution filters with different weights can extract different features for the input and convert the text information into two-dimensional image data. Through the convolution filter and the feature RE Extraction of the pooling layer, the most significant features are sent to the softmax classifier.

Max Pooling Characteristic Downsampling. The pooling layer takes the results of the local features extracted by the convolution layer as the input, and then extracts the most significant features, so as to reduce the dimension of the feature matrix and solve the problem of model over fitting. At the same time, the introduction of pooling also ensures the deformation invariance of the feature matrix. The pool layer mainly includes Max pooling and Average Pooling. Max Pooling calculates the maximum value in the image pooling window as the sampling value to represent the characteristics of the region; The Average Pooling layer calculates the weighted average value in the image pooling window as the sampling value to represent the characteristics of the region. The model in this paper adopts Max pooling (as shown in Fig. 6), which can reduce the output dimension while maintaining the important global information captured by the filter.

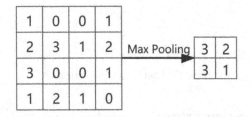

Fig. 6. Max Pooling sample (window2*2)

Model Optimization Algorithm. In this paper, SGD random gradient descent algorithm is selected as the optimization algorithm. After calculating the loss, the optimizer optimizes the constructed network model. In a complex neural network model, the optimizer optimization process changes the parameters of each layer of the network. In each iteration, the parameter value stabilizes to the optimal value in the specified direction, and finally makes the loss (the proximity between the classified predicted value and the actual value) tend to be the minimum.

SGD random gradient descent algorithm can randomly use one sample for parameter optimization in each iteration and one sample for gradient descent in each update. Because the samples are random, the accurate gradient cannot be obtained. θTherefore, the loss function obtained in each iteration is generally close to the direction of the global optimal solution. Stochastic descent gradient algorithm SGD is a common optimization algorithm in general neural network models. The algorithm formula is as shown in Table 1.

Table 1. SGD algorithm

SGD algorithm
Loop{
For i in range(m): {
$\theta_j = \theta_j + \alpha(y^{(i)} - h_\theta(x^{(i)}))\, x^{(i)}_j$
}
}

4 Simulation and Analysis

4.1 Experimental Environment

This paper selects the public website to download the windows malicious PE file set, a total of 2000 samples; In addition, Download 1000 samples of the normal sample set from Baidu app store, and finally a total of 3000 samples.

The environment configuration of cuckoo sandbox is shown in the Table 2.

Table 2. Configuration environment

Environment	Configuration
CPU	Intel(R)Core(TM)i7-8550U
Memory	8G
Operating System	Ubuntu 16.04
Software environment	Python2.7, Cuckoo2.0.4

Table 3. Confusion matrix

		Predicted class	
		$y^\wedge = c$	$y^\wedge \neq c$
Real class	$y = c$	TP_c	FN_c
	$y \neq c$	FP_c	TN_c

4.2 Evaluation Index

The confusion matrix is defined to represent the relationship between classification results and actual results, as shown in Table 3.

Define the accuracy rate, recall rate and F value according to the contents in the table. The accuracy rate of category c is the proportion of correct prediction in all samples predicted as category c.

$$\alpha_c = \frac{TP_c}{TP_c + FP_c} \tag{1}$$

The recall rate of category c is the correct proportion predicted in all samples with real label of category c.

$$R_c = \frac{TP_c}{TP_c + FN_c} \tag{2}$$

F measure is a comprehensive index, which is the harmonic average of accuracy rate and recall rate (generally, the value of β is 1):

$$F_c = \frac{\left(1 + \beta^2\right) \times \alpha_c \times R_c}{\beta^2 \times \alpha_c + R_c} \tag{3}$$

4.3 Experimental Analysis

The data set is randomly divided into two partitions of the same size as the training set and the test set. The experiment was repeated three times, leaving a different partition for testing each time. Finally, a reliable measurement method is obtained to measure the performance of the proposed convolutional neural network model on the whole data set. CNN is compared with NaiveBayes, MLP and SVM to detect the performance of the model.

The performance of the convolutional neural network model was quantitatively evaluated using three indicators: accuracy, recall and F. The experimental results are shown in Table 4. The overall results of CNN model in accuracy, recall and F ($\beta = 1$) are higher than those of other common machine learning algorithms, so CNN has more advantages than other machine learning algorithms.

Table 4. Comparison of model performance

Model	Accuracy	Recall	F1
CNN	0.93	0.91	0.92
NaiveBayes	0.83	0.72	0.77
MLP	0.91	0.89	0.90
SVM	0.89	0.84	0.86

5 Conclusion

Aiming at the shortcomings of traditional malicious code detection methods and machine learning methods, this paper introduces convolutional neural network into the traditional malicious code dynamic behavior detection system, and proposes a malicious code detection system based on convolutional neural network. The usability of the system and its superiority over other machine learning models are proved by experiments. In the next step, the feature extraction method and depth learning model parameters will be optimized to achieve better training effect.

Acknowledgement. This research is supported by the National Natural Science Foundation of China (NO. 62173026).

References

1. Zhang, Y., Li, B.: Malicious code detection based on code semantic features. IEEE Access **8**, 176728–176737 (2020)
2. Kang, B.B.H., Srivastava, A.: Dynamic malware analysis. In: van Tilborg, H.C.A., Jajodia, S. (eds.) Encyclopedia of Cryptography and Security, pp. 367–368. Springer, Boston (2011). https://doi.org/10.1007/978-1-4419-5906-5_846
3. Zhang, B., Qianmua, L., Ma, Y.: Research on dynamic heuristic scanning technique and the application of the malicious code detection model. Inf. Process. Lett. **117**(jan.), 19–24 (2017)
4. Sung, A.H., Xu, J., Chavez, P., et al.: Static analyzer of vicious executables (SAVE). In: 2004 20th Annual Computer Security Applications Conference. IEEE Computer Society (2005)
5. Han, L., Qian, M., Xu, X., et al.: Malicious code detection model based on behavior association. Tsinghua Sci. Technol. **19**(5), 508–515 (2014)
6. Krizhevsky, A., Sutskever, I., Hinton, G.E.: ImageNet classification with deep convolutional neural networks. In: Advances in Neural Information Processing Systems, pp. 1097–1105 (2012)
7. Collobert, R., Weston, J., Bottou, L., et al.: Natural language processing (almost) from scratch. J. Mach. Learn. Res. **12**(8), 2493–2537 (2011)
8. Chayal, N.M., Patel, N.P.: Review of machine learning and data mining methods to predict different cyberattacks. In: Kotecha, K., Piuri, V., Shah, H., Patel, R. (eds.) Data Science and Intelligent Applications. Lecture Notes on Data Engineering and Communications Technologies, vol. 52, pp. 43–51. Springer, Singapore (2021). https://doi.org/10.1007/978-981-15-4474-3_5

9. Yang, H., Li, S., Wu, X., et al.: A novel solutions for malicious code detection and family clustering based on machine learning. IEEE Access **7**, 1 (2019)
10. Cui, Z., Xue, F., Cai, X., et al.: Detection of malicious code variants based on deep learning. IEEE Trans. Industr. Inform. 1 (2018)
11. Tahan, G., Glezer, C., Elovici, Y., Rokach, L.: Auto-Sign: an automatic signature generator for high-speed malware filtering devices. J. Comput. Virol. **6**(2), 91–103 (2010)
12. Firdausi, I., Erwin, A., Nugroho, A.S.: Analysis of machine learning techniques used in behavior-based malware detection. In: 2010 Second International Conference on Advances in Computing, Control, and Telecommunication Technologies, pp. 201–203 (2010)
13. Burguera, I., Zurutuza, U., Nadjm-Tehrani, S.: Crowdroid: behavior-Based malware detection system for android. In: Proceedings of the 1st ACM Workshop on Security and Privacy in Smartphones and Mobile Devices, pp. 15–26 (2011)
14. Santos, I., Laorden, C., Bringas, P.G.: Collective classification for unknown malware detection. In: Proceedings of the International Conference on Security and Cryptography, pp. 251-256 (2011)
15. Yang, Y., Yang, Z., Liu, X.: The algorithm of malicious code detection based on data mining. In: Green Energy and Sustainable Development I: Proceedings of the International Conference on Green Energy and Sustainable Development (GESD 2017) (2017)
16. Saxe, J., Berlin, K.: Deep neural network based malware detection using two dimensional binary program features. arXiv preprint arXiv:1508.03096 (2015)
17. Pascanu, R., Stokes, J.W., Sanossian, H., Marinescu, M., Thomas, A.: Malware classification with recurrent networks. In: IEEE International Conference on Acoustics, Speech and Signal Processing (ICASSP) (2015)

Comprehensive Task Priority Queue for Resource Allocation in Vehicle Edge Computing Network Based on Deep Reinforcement Learning

Zhaonian Li[1]([✉]), Changxiang Chen[2], and ZhenJiang Zhang[1]

[1] Department of Electronic and Information Engineering, Key Laboratory of Communication and Information Systems, Beijing Municipal Commission of Education Beijing Jiaotong University, Beijing 100044, China
{20120083,zhangzhenjiang}@bjtu.edu.cn
[2] Westone Information Industry INC, Chengdu 610041, Sichuan, China

Abstract. The rapid increase in the number of vehicles and their intelligence have led to the lack of calculation resource of original network. However, the framework like vehicle-to-roadside infrastructure is still faced with the challenge of balancing the impact of time and energy consumption. To overcome these drawbacks, this paper establishes a comprehensive task priority queue on the basis of software defined network (SDN) based vehicular network instead of randomly offloading the tasks. According to the task type and vehicle speed, different tasks are graded and a joint optimization problem for minimizing the vehicles' time and energy consumption is formulated. Deep deterministic policy gradient (DDPG) algorithm is proposed to simulate the optimal resource allocation strategy of VEC model in the paper. Finally, this paper analyze the significance of the proposed model by giving numerical results.

Keywords: vehicle edge computing network · SDN · comprehensive task priority queue · task offloading · DDPG

1 Introduction

With the rapid development of technology and economic, everything becomes more intelligent and are connected to each other via Internet of Things. As for vehicles, it is important to build an efficient and practical task offloading model to guarantee the demands of different vehicles. In this model, new energy vehicles should be paid more attention, which is more sensitive to energy. As introduced in [1, 2], vehicle-to-vehicle, vehicle-to-roadside infrastructure and vehicle-to-cloud are the basic models of vehicular communication network. However, different types of tasks existed by vehicles have different demands. For example, vehicular application like autonomous driving is not suitable to be offloaded to remote cloud in order to save time instead of energy. So, how to assign tasks and ensure the service quality of the system becomes very important.

© ICST Institute for Computer Sciences, Social Informatics and Telecommunications Engineering 2023
Published by Springer Nature Switzerland AG 2023. All Rights Reserved
D.-J. Deng et al. (Eds.): SGIoT 2022, LNICST 497, pp. 125–132, 2023.
https://doi.org/10.1007/978-3-031-31275-5_13

So as to make overall decisions, SDN-based vehicle edge computing network [3, 4] can gather the information of the whole vehicular network. In this model, the SDN controller can obtain all of the task information and the servers' capacity information. Meanwhile, different types of tasks' demands [5] should be taken into consideration to make the model more realistic and meaningful. In the recent years, lots of researchers focus on the VEC and have done a series of signification contribution in the area of reducing time consumption, encouraging the collaboration between vehicles and so on. Whatever the starting point, researchers try to improve the quality of service of intelligent vehicular network, while saving more resources.

Previous studies have provided many research directions and methods for the problem. However, most of them belongs to the area of offline scenario vehicular network when discussing the optimization of task offloading [6]. Some environment parameters and task offloading conditions are over idealization or determined in a more fixed way. In the past few years, the tasks with different types or velocities are identified as different priorities [5, 7], which cannot objectively describe the real traffic situation. For example, a high grade task with a low vehicle velocity has a lower priority compared with a middle grade task with a high vehicle velocity. [8] introduces a method that the weight of energy consumption is redefined by the battery's remaining energy rate aiming at saving more energy for vehicles, while still in the range of adjusting the hyper parameters of the model. As for the tasking offloading direction and path, [9] proposes a novel communication model: the vehicle send the task to the server along its moving direction via vehicle-to-vehicle (V2V) multi hop mode. The authors of [10] chooses a binary offloading directions, executing the task locally or transmitting it to the edge node. Combining V2V and V2I [11], the task can be executed in the local, other vehicles or RSU. Apart from the research in the scenario of typical urban, the authors of [12] do researches in the unmanned-aerial-vehicle assisted edge computing environment. With the help of satellites and UAV network, it realizes the interaction in remote network scenarios.

Meanwhile, with the popular of machine learning, it is conveniently to use it to forecast future arrival data and make decisions. The authors of [14] uses the LSTM algorithm to make a dynamic prediction of edge communication and computing resources using mobile users' space-time. Besides, reinforcement learning is used to make task offloading decisions. DDPG algorithm is available to solve the problem of continues decision-making and be applied to high dimensional inputs [15].

Inspired by the previous studies, we propose a latency and energy aware deep deterministic policy gradient algorithm, which allows the agent to make intelligent and dynamic decisions on observation state based on reward and punishment mechanism. So, in the following part of this paper, the resource allocation problems are discussed in the SDN-based VEC model. When building the model of data transmission, we consider the interaction among edge computing devices and their operation modes. Specially, this paper adopts a comprehensive task priority queue and use the available computing resources in the network as far as possible to obtain the optimal resource allocation strategy, balancing the impact of the consumption of time and energy. In the paper, DDPG algorithm is deployed in the SDN controller, which uses the mode of centralized learning and distributed application in the roadside units (RSUs) or vehicle's processor to seek the optimal strategy via learning.

2 System Model

2.1 System Architecture

As illustrated in Fig. 1, we construct a SDN-based vehicular network model (SDN-VN), taking vehicles and multiple roadside units (RSU) into consideration. In the controller plane, it contains several RSU-controllers and a center SDN controller [3]. The RSU-controller is in charge of collecting the data from the data plane, including the data provided by vehicles and RSUs, as well as the resources like computing, communication, remaining energy. After gathering the information, the center SDN controller can make a global resource management rule, which is forwarded by the RSU-controllers. In this way, the model achieves the optimal overall strategy of task offloading in the vehicular network.

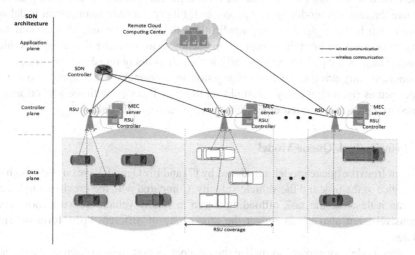

Fig. 1. The architecture of SDN-based vehicular network

We set that there is an one-direction road covered by RSUs and they can communicate with their neighbours via backbone network. The set of RSUs is given by $M = \{1, 2, ..., m\}$. Located along the roadside, RSUs can obtain ample energy through various paths. In this paper, we assume that the coverage of each RSU is the same and the adjacent ones do not overlap. Besides, each RSU is equipped with a MEC server, providing huge calculation resource to handle the tasks in vehicular edge network. In order to simplify the problem, using the diameter of the coverage area to represent the working range of RSU, recorded as L_{RSU}. We set the set of vehicles in a cell as $N = \{1, 2, ..., n\}$. Vehicles can only establish the connection with the RSU in its cell via wireless network. However, we still assume that the vehicle can receive the computed result from the previous MEC server when it enter the next cell because the latency of computing task is quite small.

2.2 Vehicular Velocity Model

Similar to [11, 16], we take a free traffic model into consideration in order to describe the velocity information. In a cell, all of vehicles drive at a constant speed, which follows the Gaussian speed distribution. Thus, the relationship between traffic density and vehicle's average velocity is described as $\bar{v} = v_{max}\left(1 - \frac{\rho}{\rho_{max}}\right)$, where ρ represents the traffic density of a cell, v_{max} and ρ_{max} are the maximum value of velocity and traffic density. The vehicles initialize its speed independently and randomly in each time slot, recorded as $v \sim F(\bar{v}, \sigma_v^2)$. In the reality traffic situation, the difference among vehicles' velocity should be lower when the traffic density becomes higher so as to reduce the probability of vehicle impact. So, similar to [16], we set the variance of vehicle speed is positive correlation to the average velocity, given as $\sigma_v \propto \bar{v}$.

2.3 Task Model

In the vehicular network (VN), we define three different priorities of computing tasks to simulate the real VN model, $\Phi = \{\phi_1, \phi_2, \phi_3\}$. Firstly, security information is defined as ϕ_1, which is the highest priority application. Related to the auto driving and road safety tasks, we need limit the computation latency so as to ensure the safety of vehicle driving. Thus, task ϕ_1 is executed locally with a short delay threshold, set to τ_{max}^1. As for some auxiliary driving tasks, like navigation and optional security applications, they are defined as ϕ_2, with a delay threshold set to τ_{max}^2. Tasks ϕ_3 with the low priority, is defined to represent vehicular entertainment applications with delay τ_{max}^3.

2.4 Priority Task Queue Model

Different from the queue model introduced by [7] and FIFO model, we consider both the importance of the task and the vehicle velocity. Compared with the previous model, not only can it describe the task offloading arisen in reality vehicle network more comprehensively, but also it can reflect the emergency of different tasks form different vehicles.

In this model, we should normalize the parameters first so as to balance the impacts of different parameters. So we use normalization of arctangent function and a method similar to min-max normalization to normalize the velocity and task type, where.

Then, we set $I_m = \alpha'\phi' + \beta'v'$ to show the priority of task, where α' and β' are the constants. The RSU controller obtain the information of vehicles' tasks and determine the offloading policy based on the priority task queue model and the resource consumption. So, the tasks in a slot are remarked as $K = \{1, 2, ..., k\}$, where k is the processing sequence number. We set that the MEC can only handle a task at a time, so the total execution time delay should include the waiting time. Let $t_w = \{t_{local}, t_{RSU}\}$ represent the set of waiting time of different processors.

2.5 Task Execution Latency and Energy Analysis

In this model, if the task is executed locally, we just consider the process of task calculation. If the task is executed in the edge side, we should consider the transmission process, including upload and download. However, we just take the transmission energy consumption into consideration. The resource offloading policy is influenced by the time delay and energy execution during the whole progress. Thus, we set a formula with two constants α and β to describe the relationship between them, shaped like $P_k = \alpha \frac{\bar{t}-T_k}{\bar{t}} + \beta \frac{\bar{e}-E_k}{\bar{e}}$. The constants show the relation between latency and energy and their sum is one. The total latency T_k includes task execution latency and waiting time. The minuends on numerator are the standard values for unifying the unit of calculation. Thus, the problem can be formulated as the following function (P):

$$P : \text{maxmize } R$$
$$\text{subject to } X = \{0, 1\}$$
$$p_n \in (0, P_n]$$
$$f_n^{loc} \in (0, F_n^{loc}], f^{RSU} \in (0, F^{RSU}]$$
$$T_k \leq \tau_{\max,k}$$

$$R = \sum_{n=1}^{N} \sum_{k=1}^{K} \iota_n \times P_k \times X = \sum_{n=0}^{N} \iota_n \times \begin{bmatrix} (1 - X_k)P_1 \\ X_k P_2 \\ X_k P_3 \end{bmatrix},$$

where X represents the offloading direction and ι represents the existence of tasks.

3   Resource Allocation Algorithm Based on Deep Reinforcement Learning and Simulation Results

Because the task is a multi-processor cooperated computing problem, which is a NP hard problem. So, we use the deep reinforcement learning algorithm to solve the optimal resource allocation and task offloading question. In the following, the DDPG algorithm is introduced in detail.

State space: we define the state space of vehicle n as $s_n(t)$, including reduced task information and waiting time information, which is depicted as $s_n(t) = [\tau_{\max,k}, E_{r,n}, E_n(t), t_{w,n}]$. In this set, $\tau_{\max,k}$ is the maximum latency of task k of vehicle n. $E_{r,n}$ is the remaining energy of vehicle n. $E_n(t)$ is the virtual energy queue of vehicle n. And in the part of waiting information, it just contains that of task vehicle n apart from RSUs. Therefore, the state space of the system can be defined as: $S_t = (s_1(t), s_2(t), \cdots, s_n(t))$.

The specific simulation parameters are shown in Table 1 and Table 2.

In this paper, the algorithms compared are as follows:

All Local Consumption (ALC): All tasks are executed locally.
Random Offloading (RD): The tasks of type 1 are executed locally and the others are calculated randomly.
First-In-First-Out Greedy (FIFO): The task queue is without priority, but obey latency and energy greedy algorithm (Fig. 3).

In Fig. 2, we show the convergence situation of our algorithm. This model becomes stable after 300 iterations of training. And in the next figure, we present the comparison

Table 1. Simulation parameters of model

Parameter	Value	Parameter	Value
Number of vehicles	20	Size of task	0.1 Mb
Average speed of vehicle	60 km/h	Average energy of vehicle	60%
Channel model	Typical Urban	Output/Input ratio	0.1
Delay Threshold	2, 20, 40 ms	Power of vehicle	0.25 W
Computation capacity of RSU	10 G cycles/s	Computation capacity of vehicle	1 G cycles/s

Table 2. Parameters of the neural network

Parameter	Value	Parameter	Value
Layers	3	Layer Type	Fully Connected
Learning Rate of Actor	10^{-6}	Learning Rate of Critic	10^{-6}
Episode	500	Batch	128

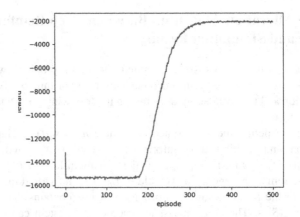

Fig. 2. Algorithm convergence diagram

of reward, execution time and consumption energy with different algorithms. Compared with ALC, RD and FIFO algorithm, our comprehensive task priority queue model can always obtain the maximize reward.

Meanwhile, it can balance the importance of time and energy consumption for different vehicle conditions, appropriately spending more time to save energy and obtain larger reward.

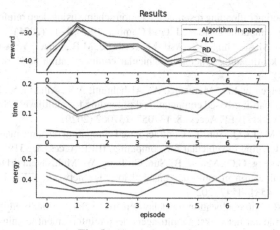

Fig. 3. Simulation results

4   Conclusion

In this paper, we propose a comprehensive task priority queue for resource allocation to achieve the goal of energy-efficiency and time-save for all vehicles in the model within task latency threshold constraint. First, we establish the model of task queue and communication model. Then, the DDPG method is used to obtain the offloading strategy. Simulation results shows that the our algorithm can improve the performance of model while saving energy.

Acknowledgement. The authors gratefully acknowledge the support and financial assistance provided by the National Natural Science Foundation of China (NO. 62173026).

References

1. Liu, C., Liu, K., Guo, S., Xie, R., Lee, V.C., Son, S.H.: Adaptive offloading for time-critical tasks in heterogeneous internet of vehicles. IEEE Internet Things J. **7**(9), 7999–8011 (2020)
2. Liu, K., Xu, X., Chen, M., Liu, B., Wu, L., Lee, V.C.S.: A hierarchical architecture for the future internet of vehicles. IEEE Commun. Mag. **57**(7), 41–47 (2019)
3. Zhang, J., Guo, H., Liu, J., Zhang, Y.: Task offloading in vehicular edge computing networks: a load-balancing solution. IEEE Trans. Veh. Technol. **69**(2), 2092–2104 (2019)
4. Zhang, J., Guo, H., Liu, J.: Adaptive task offloading vehicular edge computing networks: a reinforcement learning based scheme. Mob. Netw. Appl. **25**(5), 1736–1745 (2020)
5. Huang, X., He, L., Zhang, W.: Vehicle speed aware computing task offloading and resource allocation based on multi-agent reinforcement learning in a vehicular edge computing network. In: 2020 IEEE International Conference on Edge Computing (EDGE), pp. 1–8. IEEE (2020)
6. Cho, H., Cui, Y., Lee, J.: Energy-efficient cooperative offloading for edge computing-enabled vehicular networks. IEEE Trans. Wireless Commun. **21**(12), 10709–10723 (2022)
7. Shi, J., Du, J., Wang, J., Wang, J., Yuan, J.: Priority-aware task offloading in vehicular fog computing based on deep reinforcement learning. IEEE Trans. Veh. Technol. **69**(12), 16067–16081 (2020)

8. Li, X.: A computing offloading resource allocation scheme using deep reinforcement learning in mobile edge computing systems. J. Grid Comput. **19**(3), 1–12 (2021)

9. Raza, S., Mirza, M.A., Ahmad, S., Asif, M., Rasheed, M.B., Ghadi, Y.: A vehicle to vehicle relay-based task offloading scheme in vehicular communication networks. PeerJ Comput. Sci. **7**, e486 (2021)

10. Khayyat, M., Elgendy, I.A., Muthanna, A., Alshahrani, A.S., Alharbi, S., Koucheryavy, A.: Advanced deep learning-based computational offloading for multilevel vehicular edge-cloud computing networks. IEEE Access **8**, 137052–137062 (2020)

11. Zhao, J., Kong, M., Li, Q., Sun, X.: Contract-based computing resource management via deep reinforcement learning in vehicular fog computing. IEEE Access **8**, 3319–3329 (2019)

12. Seid, A.M., Boateng, G.O., Mareri, B., Sun, G., Jiang, W.: Multi-agent drl for task offloading and resource allocation in multi-uav enabled iot edge network. IEEE Trans. Netw. Serv. Manage. **18**(4), 4531–4547 (2021)

13. Wu, J., et al.: Resource allocation for delay-sensitive vehicleto-multi-edges (v2es) communications in vehicular networks: a multi-agent deep reinforcement learning approach. IEEE Trans. Netw. Sci. Eng. **8**(2), 1873–1886 (2021)

14. Zhang, K., Cao, J., Zhang, Y.: Adaptive digital twin and multiagent deep reinforcement learning for vehicular edge computing and networks. IEEE Trans. Industr. Inf. **18**(2), 1405–1413 (2021)

15. Zheng, C., Liu, S., Huang, Y., Yang, L.: Hybrid policy learning for energy-latency tradeoff in MEC-assisted VR video service. IEEE Trans. Veh. Technol. **70**(9), 9006–9021 (2021)

16. Tan, W.L., Lau, W.C., Yue, O., Hui, T.H.: Analytical models and performance evaluation of drive-thru internet systems. IEEE J. Sel. Areas Commun. **29**(1), 207–222 (2011)

17. Su, Z., Hui, Y., Luan, T.H.: Distributed task allocation to enable collaborative autonomous driving with network softwarization. IEEE J. Sel. Areas Commun. **36**(10), 2175–2189 (2018)

Applying the Shapley Value Method to Predict Mortality in Liver Cancer Based on Explainable AI

Lun-Ping Hung[1]($\boxtimes$), Chong-Huai Xu[1], Ching-Sheng Wang[2], and Chien-Liang Chen[3]

[1] Department of Information Management, National Taipei University of Nursing and Health Sciences, Taipei 112303, Taiwan
lunping@ntunhs.edu.tw

[2] Department of Computer Science and Information Engineering, Aletheia University, Taipei 25103, Taiwan

[3] Department of Innovative Living Design, Overseas Chinese University, Taichung 40721, Taiwan

Abstract. Hepatocellular carcinoma (HCC) is the sixth-leading cause of death worldwide and has the highest mortality rate among all types of cancers. In most cases, the patient has entered the terminal phase of a cancer disease when hepatocellular carcinoma occurs. Therefore, if the cause of cancer can be identified, disease deterioration can be prevented. With the rise of artificial intelligence (A.I.) technology in recent years, many scholars have used machine learning technology to predict the probability of dying from hepatocellular carcinoma and have obtained good results. However, the studies lack interpretability and do not facilitate the further analyses of medical experts. Therefore, this study proposes a deep learning model based on XGBoost and uses the data evaluation method of Shapley value to study the characteristics of machine learning and verify the results using the hepatocellular carcinoma dataset. The proposed model delivered strong prediction performance, with an accuracy of 92.68%, and accurately interpreted the dataset features, supporting analyses by medical experts.

Keywords: Machine learning · Hepatocellular carcinoma · Risk factors · SHapley Additive exPlanations (SHAP) · Extreme gradient boosting (XGBoost)

1 Introduction

Hepatocellular carcinoma is the sixth-leading cause of death worldwide and has the highest mortality rate among all cancer types. In most of the cases, there is no significant symptom of HCC in the early phase of cancer, and the patient has entered the terminal phase when HCC occurs [1]. Therefore, if HCC is identified at an earlier stage for prevention and treatment, the mortality can be reduced. With scientific and technological advancement, scholars began to explore the application of machine learning in the medical care of diseases [2], such as lung [3], breast [4] and liver cancer [5]. Also, machine learning can be used to conduct clinical research in a virtual environment [6].

© ICST Institute for Computer Sciences, Social Informatics and Telecommunications Engineering 2023
Published by Springer Nature Switzerland AG 2023. All Rights Reserved
D.-J. Deng et al. (Eds.): SGIoT 2022, LNICST 497, pp. 133–143, 2023.
https://doi.org/10.1007/978-3-031-31275-5_14

The goal of machine learning research is mostly to improve algorithm accuracy, which is vital to medical diagnosis. However, in clinical practice, physicians often encounter complex situations that cannot be solved only with accuracy. For example, in deep learning methods with high precision, the characteristics of black box techniques will cause difficulties for physicians in understanding and evaluation, and they cannot accept the advice without a scientific basis when faced with serious diseases. Additionally, many medical institutions lacked the medical data to satisfy the criteria of a training set for deep learning.

Many researchers have focused on how to interpret complex and powerful models such as CNN [7], XNN [8] and LSTM [9], which were all common and practical machine learning tools. However, the explanations given by researchers regarding the information of the models were still incomprehensible for physicians; some new studies attempt to provide a more comprehensible model interpretation for physicians, to ease their worries and support their decision-making process. For example, Bas H.M. et al. used the Explainable AI (XAI) standard framework for classification in medical image analysis and conducted investigations and classification in a paper about XAI techniques based on frameworks and anatomical location [10]. Andreas et al. proposed using explainable AI via multi-modal and multi-center data fusion to address the lack of interpretability and transparency [11].

A challenge remains in how to strike a balance between accuracy, interpretability, and other AI factors in the medical field. Therefore, this study attempts to integrate the methods of solving these problems into the prediction of liver cancer mortality by proposing a method of predicting liver cancer mortality incorporating Shapley value and ensemble learning. Compared with the traditional method of machine learning that trains a single classifier, ensemble learning, or the method that combines multiple classifiers, can improve generalizability or accuracy [12]. We use the eXtreme Gradient Boosting (XGBoost) machine learning framework to predict the risk of liver cancer mortality and use Shapley value to interpret the causes of the prediction results. This approach has the following advantages: 1. Allowing physicians to understand the importance of each dataset attribute, compared with other attributes. 2. Effectively improving physicians' disease diagnosis and prognosis decision-making. 3. No necessity of having a large amount of training data, and the accuracy of predicting liver cancer mortality is relatively high.

2   Related Works

As the techniques designed for machine learning are increasingly popular, the studies of applying machine learning to cancer diagnoses are also maturing. The intervention of machine learning has successfully improved research efficiency and generated results with low error rates, effectively helping cancer diagnosis [13]. Except for this, the subfield of machine learning known as XAI can interpret complex artificial intelligence models [14], and studies have found that the machine learning systems that have been interpreted can support clinical cancer diagnosis [15]. Therefore, in the following paragraphs, this study categorizes and explains the relevant literature about the interpretable prediction of liver cancer diagnosis:

2.1 Shapley Additive Explanation (SHAP)

SHAP (SHapley Additive exPlanations) is a game theoretic approach to interpret the output of any machine learning model. It connects optimal credit allocation with local explanations using the classic Shapley values from game theory and their related extensions [16]. The goal of SHAP is to explain the prediction of an instance x by computing the contribution of each feature to the prediction. Compared with the traditional method that analyzes the differences in the features' importance, SHAP only clarifies which of the features are more important to the model, without explaining how the features affect the results. The positive and negative values of SHAP correspond to the effect of each sample's features, which reveals the effects of which features in the dataset are the most important. The interpretation of SHAP itself is an additive feature attribution method and is similar to the linear regression method [17].

2.2 XGBoost

XGBoost (eXtreme Gradient Boosting) is a framework based on gradient boosting that integrates the advantages of bagging and boosting and is mainly used for monitoring and learning, while it can also be applied to classification and regression analysis. XGBoost is composed of a set of classification and regression trees (CART). Each leaf of the regression trees is assigned a set of scores, which are the basis for the subsequent classification. The trees are interrelated and the goal is to generate news trees that can correct the mistakes of the previous tree [18]. As shown in Fig. 1, each person is assigned to

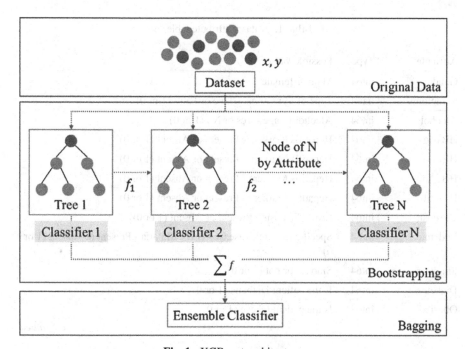

Fig. 1. XGBoost architecture.

different leaves, and is assigned a score based on the leaf the person belongs to. The difference between CART and decision trees is that the leaves of decision trees only contain decision values, while the scores of CART are related to all leaves, and the final individual score of each person is obtained by summing the scores obtained from each tree.

3 Research Methods and Results

This study proposes a new interpretable prediction system based on Shapley value that uses XAI technology to combine XGBoost to predict the death risks by focusing on liver cancer cells, effectively improving physicians' disease diagnosis and prognosis decision-making. This research analyzes and generate ROC curves, ROC performance evaluation and SHAP visualization results, which are explained as follows:

3.1 Patients Data Gathering

The database of liver cancer deaths provided by the UCI Machine Learning Repository is used here, and the data is obtained from a university hospital in Portugal. There are a total of 204 records in the data [19], and the dataset includes 50 variables selected according to EASL-EORTC (European Association for the Study of the Liver-European Organization for Research and Treatment of Cancer), among which the target-dependent variables are: Class (1 denotes death and 0 denotes survival); Table 1 displays the categories and attributes of its data. After reading the data, it is found that there is no missing value.

Table 1. Dataset attribute table.

Attribute	Type	Possible values
Gender	int64	Male or female
Symptoms	int64	Type of Symptoms - True or False (1 or 0)
Alcohol	int64	Alcohol Usage - Yes or No (1 or 0)
HBsAg	int64	Hepatitis Markers - Present or Absent (1 or 0)
HBeAg	int64	Hepatitis Markers - Present or Absent (1 or 0)
HBcAb	int64	Hepatitis Markers - Present or Absent (1 or 0)
HCVAb	int64	Hepatitis Markers - Present or Absent (1 or 0)
Cirrhosis	int64	Liver Cirrhosis - Present or Absent (1 or 0)
Endemic	int64	Specific Endemic disease - (Like Malaria - Present or Absent (1 or 0)
Smoking	int64	Smokes or not (1 or 0)
Diabetes	int64	Is the patient Diabetic (1 or 0)
Obesity	int64	Is the patient Obese (1 or 0)

(continued)

Table 1. (*continued*)

Attribute	Type	Possible values
Hemochro	int64	Body loads too much of Iron - Yes or No (1 or 0)
AHI	int64	AHT Present or not
CRI	int64	Chronic Renal Insufficiency - Yes or no (1 or 0)
HIV	int64	Does the patient have HIV -Yes or No (1 or 0)
NASH	int64	Non-Alcoholic Fatty Liver steatohepatitis (NASH) - Yes or No (1 or 0)
Varices	int64	Presence of Esophageal Varices - (1 or 0)
Spleno	int64	Presence of Gastric Varices like bleeding in upper intestinal tract - (1 or 0)
PHT	int64	Parathyroid Hormone Test - Present or Absent - (1 or 0)
PVT	int64	other Pathology test for HCC confirmation (1 or 0)
Metastasis	int64	Presence of Cancer in Bones and other organs - Present or Absent - (1 or 0)
Hallmark	int64	Cancer Markers Test -Present or Absent (1 or 0)
Age	int64	Age of the patient
Grams_day	int64	Doses given -Grams per day
Packs_year	float64	No of Cigar Packets per Year
PS	int64	Staging of HCC
Encephalopathy	int64	End Stage liver disease
Ascites	int64	Poor Outcome in the absence of Transplantation
INR	float64	Used to assess coagulation function
AFP	float64	Biolevel Markers for early HCC
Hemoglobin	float64	12 to 17.5 gms per deciliter
MCV	float64	80 to 96
Leucocytes	float64	4500 to 11000 WBC per microliter
Platelets	float64	150,000 to 450,000 platelets per microliter
Albumin	float64	3.5 to 5.5 g/dL
Total_Bil	float64	0.1 to 1.2 mg/dL
ALT	int64	7 to 56 Units
AST	int64	10 to 40 units – Normal Range
GGT	int64	9–48 units per liter
ALP	int64	44 to 147

(*continued*)

Table 1. (*continued*)

Attribute	Type	Possible values
TP	float64	6 and 8.3 Range
Creatinine	float64	0.6 to 1.2
Nodule	int64	The size of the nodules determines the liver disease
Major_Dim	float64	Dimension of the Tumor
Dir_Bil	float64	Upto 1.2 mg/dl
Iron	float64	13.5 to 17.5
Sat	float64	Iron related test (in Numerical value)
Ferritin	float64	12 to 300 Range
Class	int64	Present or Absent (1 or 0)

3.2 Predictive Assessment

The following cross-validation method is used to evaluate liver cancer mortality. As the true classification of each condition is known, the values of the absolute performance indicators of a classifier are calculated with a confusion matrix:

- TP (true positive) – died from liver cancer in reality and has been predicted to die from liver cancer.
- TN (true negative) – did not die from liver cancer in reality and has been predicted to die from liver cancer.
- FP (false positive) – died from liver cancer in reality but has not been predicted to die from liver cancer.
- FN (false negative) – did not die from liver cancer in reality and has not been predicted to die from liver cancer.

The corresponding relative indicators: Accuracy is the ratio of correctly classified samples by the classifier to the total sample in the tested dataset, and is a comprehensive score that reflects the overall performance of the classifier.

$$\text{Accuracy} = \frac{TP + TN}{TP + TN + FP + FN} \qquad (1)$$

Recall is the prediction performance on positive cases of the classification model. In the prediction of liver cancer deaths, if the performance of confirming positive cases can be improved, the survival rate can also be improved, as the patients can be treated earlier with earlier diagnosis. Therefore, recall is one of the measurement indicators of performance in machine learning.

$$\text{Recall} = \frac{TP}{TP + FN} \qquad (2)$$

F_β is a score value that combines two types of score values, accuracy and recall. Additionally, in the combination process, the weight of recall is β times that of accuracy, which indicates that β represents the relative importance of accuracy and recall. Considering that cancer treatment may have a negative impact on the patient, β is set to 1 (i.e., F1), while an F1 score represents that accuracy and recall are considered to be equally important.

$$F_\beta = \left(1 + \beta^2\right) \frac{Precision \cdot Recall}{(\beta^2 \cdot Precision + Recall)}, \text{ where Precision}$$

$$= \frac{TP}{TP + FN} \tag{3}$$

The receiver operating characteristic (ROC) curve is used, and a decision threshold is needed for other measurement methods (accuracy, recall and F1 score). In a ROC curve, the model's continuous outputs of probabilities and analogous probabilities are collapsed to become one set of classification prediction results. The ROC curve may come from the continuous outputs of probabilities, and is an efficient method to evaluate the model's performance at the decision threshold. AUC is the area under the ROC curve, and is the most commonly used summary indicator for ROC curves. In general, a higher AUC represents a better performance of the classifier.

3.3 Results

Table 2 compares the accuracy, recall and F1 score of the classifier. The values shown in Table 2 result from 10-fold cross-validation. The results show that the accuracy of XGBoost is 92.68%, and the recall and the F1 score are better than that of other classifiers. Furthermore, the performance of XGBoost is more stable than other classifiers. Although the accuracy of neural networks is relatively high, their performance may be poor when the amount of training data is low, because neural networks can be affected by the characteristic of overfitting.

Figure 2 presents the ROC curves of 10 classifiers, and it shows that the performance of XGBoost is significantly better than most of the other classifiers, and is not inferior to other classifiers in terms of AUC.

Table 2. Predicted performance of the classifier.

Classifier	Accuracy (%)	Recall (%)	F1-score (%)
KNN	85.36	85.23	85.28
Decision Tree	75.60	75.35	7524
Random Forest	90.24	90.11	90.19
Naive Bayes	56.09	56.78	52.69
Linear Regression	87.80	87.85	87.80
Support Vector Machine	92.68	92.85	92.66

(continued)

Table 2. (*continued*)

Classifier	Accuracy (%)	Recall (%)	F1-score (%)
Gradient Boosting Classifier	85.36	85.23	85.28
AdaBoosting Classifier	75.60	75.59	75.59
Neural Network	92.68	92.73	92.68
XGBoost	92.68	92.5	92.61

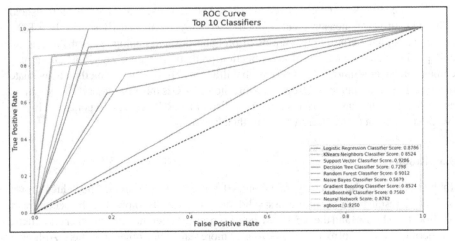

Fig. 2. ROC Curve.

3.4 Using SHapley Additive Explainable

SHAP Summary Chart

The features are ranked according to the sum of SHAP values of all samples to obtain the 20 features that have the greatest impact on the model output, as shown in Fig. 3, while the distribution of the influence of each feature is presented with SHAP values, in which different colors represent different feature values (red represents a high value and blue represents a low value). For example, a higher AFP feature is more likely to affect the probability of dying from liver cancer.

SHAP Feature Map

The SHAP values show how each feature affects the model's output. As SHAP values represent the key to the changes in the model caused by the features, the research results show that there is a great impact on the prediction of liver cancer death as the Albumin feature parameters changes. The vertical discrete value of a single Albumin value has an interactive effect with other features. Different colors are used to help distinguish this feature, as shown in Fig. 4. For example, areas with higher PHT values have a lower effect on the Albumin values that affect the probability of dying from liver cancer.

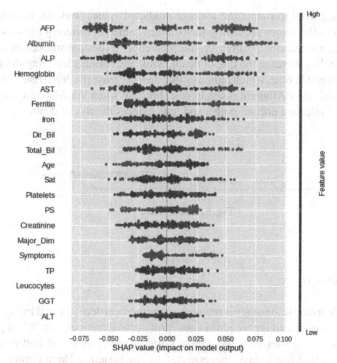

Fig. 3. SHAP values Summary Chart. (Color figure online)

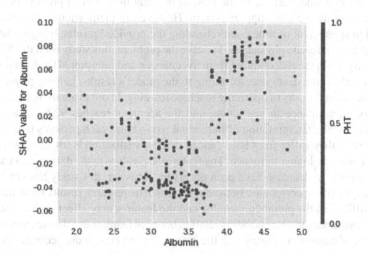

Fig. 4. SHAP dependence plot.

Personal Risk Explanation

The SHAP heatmap is used to explain the individuals' risks, and the outputs are the features of a person's risks of dying from liver cancer, interpreting each risk feature that helps the model to output the average predicted values from the training dataset. Figure 5 shows the values predicting the death of someone suffering from liver cancer. In the figure, the features pushing up the prediction values are marked in red, which indicates that they increase the risk of death, while the features lowering the prediction values are marked in blue, which indicates that they decrease the death risk. For example, the negative effect of Albumin is the largest, because when the Albumin level is equal to 3.2 g/dL, it falls in a normal range, and thus reduces the risk of death.

Fig. 5. SHAP force plot.

4   Conclusion

As machine learning technology is matures, many medical decision-making systems tend to improve accuracy and ignore physicians' professional competence. When physicians need to make a decision with the patient's life at stake, they still find it difficult to trust the prediction result analysis generated by the systems. There remains a lack of specific rules for existing medical decision-making systems. Many studies have applied interpretable machine learning to the field of medical treatment to provide physicians with a trustworthy medical support system. However, in many studies, the physicians still need to spend a lot of time comprehending the provided results, bringing about an additional burden for the physicians. To solve the problem, this study used the XGBoost classifier to predict the risk of dying from liver cancer, and interpreted the features in the dataset that affect the death rate according to the model's results, helping physicians to better understand the way of operating machine learning. In our evaluation, the classifier has a good performance in prediction, and the accuracy reaches 92.68%. Regarding interpretability, the interpretation of individual risks shows each person's potential risk of dying when they suffer from liver cancer, while visualization is used to comprehend the feature with the higher influence. The features and values in the dataset that cause the risks to increase or decrease have been observed. However, this study has not focused on the analysis of the correlation between features. The research results show that some features will affect the prediction results, and the features may affect each other. In the future, it is necessary to discuss the correlation between features in a dataset, and increase the number of datasets, to ensure that the system can generate more accurate results.

References

1. Yan, Q., et al.: Application and progress of the detection technologies in hepatocellular carcinoma. Genes Dis. 2 (2022)

2. Sood, S.K., Rawat, K.S., et al.: A visual review of artificial intelligence and industry 4.0 in healthcare. Comput. Electr. Eng. **101**, 107948–107962 (2022)

3. Saba, T., Sameh, A., Khan, F., Shad, S.A., Sharif, M.: Lung nodule detection based on ensemble of hand crafted and deep features. J. Med. Syst. **43**(12), 1–12 (2019). https://doi.org/10.1007/s10916-019-1455-6

4. Li, J., et al.: Predicting breast cancer 5-year survival using machine learning: a systematic review. PLoS One **16**(4), e0250370 (2021)

5. Oza, P., et al.: A Bottom-up review of image analysis methods for suspicious region detection in mammograms. J. Imaging **7**(9), 1–40 (2021)

6. Moingeon, P., Kuenemann, M., et al.: Artificial intelligence-enhanced drug design and development: toward a computational precision medicine. Drug Discov. Today **27**(1), 215–222 (2022)

7. Maweu, B., et al.: CEFEs: A CNN explainable framework for ECG signals. Artif. Intell. Med. **115**, 102059–102074 (2021)

8. Qi, Z., Li, F.: Embedding deep networks into visual explanations. Artif. Intell. **292**, 1–27 (2017)

9. Yudistira, N., et al.: Learning where to look for COVID-19 growth: multivariate analysis of COVID-19 cases over time using explainable convolution-LSTM. Appl. Soft Comput. **109**, 107469–107487 (2021)

10. van der Velden, B.H.M., et al.: Explainable artificial intelligence (XAI) in deep learning-based medical image analysis. Med. Image Anal. **79**, 102470–102490 (2022)

11. Holzinger, A., et al.: Information fusion as an integrative cross-cutting enabler to achieve robust, explainable, and trustworthy medical artificial intelligence. Inf. Fusion **79**, 263–278 (2022)

12. Kazmaier, J., van Vuuren, J.H.: The power of ensemble learning in sentiment analysis. Expert Syst. Appl. **187**, 115819–115834 (2022)

13. Painuli, D., Bhardwaj, S., et al.: Recent advancement in cancer diagnosis using machine learning and deep learning techniques: a comprehensive review. Comput. Biol. Med. **146**, 105580–105609 (2022)

14. Barredo Arrieta, A., et al.: Explainable Artificial Intelligence (XAI): concepts, taxonomies, opportunities and challenges toward responsible AI. Inf. Fusion **58**, 82–115 (2020)

15. Gu, D., Su, K., et al.: A case-based ensemble learning system for explainable breast cancer recurrence prediction. Artif. Intell. Med. **107**, 101858–101866 (2020)

16. Štrumbelj, E., Kononenko, I.: Explaining prediction models and individual predictions with feature contributions. Knowl. Inf. Syst. **41**(3), 647–665 (2013). https://doi.org/10.1007/s10115-013-0679-x

17. Lundberg, S.M., Lee, S.-I.: A unified approach to interpreting model predictions. In: Proceedings of the 31st International Conference on Neural Information Processing Systems, pp. 4768–4777. Curran Associates Inc., Long Beach (2017)

18. Chen, T., et al.: Xgboost: extreme gradient boosting. R Package Version 0.4-2 **1**(4), 1–4 (2015)

19. Santos, M.S., et al.: A new cluster-based oversampling method for improving survival prediction of hepatocellular carcinoma patients. J. Biomed. Inform. **58**, 49–59 (2015)

Face Emotion Expression Recognition Using DLIB Model and Convolutional Neural Network Approach for Supporting Online Learning

Rita Wiryasaputra[1,2], Chin-Yin Huang[1], Jimmy Juliansyah[2], and Chao-Tung Yang[3,4(✉)]

[1] Department of Industrial Engineering and Enterprise Information, Tunghai University, Taichung 407224, Taiwan
`huangcy@go.thu.edu.tw`
[2] Department of Informatics, Krida Wacana Christian University, Jakarta 11470, Indonesia
`rita.wiryasaputra@ukrida.ac.id`
[3] Department of Computer Science, Tunghai University, Taichung 407224, Taiwan
`ctyang@thu.edu.tw`
[4] Research Center for Smart Sustainable Circular Economy, Tunghai University, Taichung 407224, Taiwan

Abstract. Many sectors have experienced the impact of the COVID-19 outbreak, without exception education. The method of process learning transformed from face-to-face meeting learning became online learning. Learners tried to adapt to this unexpected circumstance. In the online learning approach, the instructors only assumed the degree of learners' understanding with their face emotion expressions spontaneously. Advancement technology enables the machine to learn data fast and accurately. Mostly, the position of the learner's face in front of the camera when attending the online course, and the DLIB's shape detector model map the landmark of the captured face. Deep learning is a subset domain of machine learning. Convolutional Neural Network (CNN) model as a deep learning approach has characteristics in the high computation and ease of implementation. The work proposed a face-emotion expression recognition model for supporting online learning. The combination ratio images dataset was 80% data training and 20% data testing, and the condition expression was determined with a deep learning approach. The experimental results showed that the recognition accuracy of the proposed model achieved 97% for dataset image input.

Keywords: Convolutional Neural Network (CNN) · DLIB · Deep Learning · Face Emotion Expression Recognition · Machine Learning

1 Introduction

The COVID-19 outbreak changes many sectors of human life. The changes transform the learner and white-collar workers to have experience in the new

D.-J. Deng et al. (Eds.): SGIoT 2022, LNICST 497, pp. 144–149, 2023.
https://doi.org/10.1007/978-3-031-31275-5_15

unlimited world. The method of process learning and meeting transformed from physical face-to-face to online learning/meeting. Learners tried to adapt to this unexpected circumstance. In the online learning approach, the instructors only assumed the degree of learners' understanding with their face emotion expressions spontaneously. The instructor's engagement to be more active in the delivery of the course materials is important in synchronous learning. Early detection is needed to measure the involvement of learners' emotions and is the benchmark for the improvement of an online class. Human emotion reflects in their face. Basically, there are seven types of emotions, namely neutral, angry, happy, sadness, disgust, surprise, and fear [7]. The combination of emotions represents the person's understanding level [6]. In terms of face detection, the input mediums are video, images, and live video streaming [1]. Mostly, the position of learners' faces in front of the camera when attending the online course, and the DLIB's shape detector model map the landmark of the captured face into coordinates. The Dlib model provides 68 points of face form coordinates that landmark the vital of the face, eyes, nose, and mouth. DLIB enables identification of the faces from the front [2]. One of the classification models in the machine learning domain is the Convolutional Neural Network (CNN) which has advantages in speed and computation [1] [3]. Using segmented data, the CNN model can increase its accuracy value. The research contributes to building the model that recognizes a human facial emotion expression. The aim of the research is to investigate the performance of the Convolutional Neural Network model to support online learning. The paper is structured as follows: the first section reviews the research background, Sect. 2 describes the previous research relevant to this research, Sect. 3 presents the research methodology, and the experiment and conclusions are outlined in Sects. 4 and Sect. 5, respectively.

2   Related Works

This section describes the literature study stage where review and research article papers were retrieved from Google Scholar, Science Direct, and IEEEXplore repositories. Jadhav revealed the comparison between algorithms for the complex issue in automatic face detection. When comparing the four detection algorithms: Cascade classifier, DLIB CNN, DLIB Histogram of Oriented Gradients (HOG), and Multitask Convolutional Neural Network (MTCNN), the prediction of the Cascade Classifier algorithm was not accurate even though the algorithm supported the real-time detection process that ran on CPU. For easy implementation, DLIB CNN with different parameters such as from the front, with low light, in multiple and side faces robust with various face occlusions, however, the model ran slow on real-time images with CPU [1].

Kamal conducted the research with plant leaves images using background subtraction, segmentation, and Convolutional Neural Network. The foreground image was removed by the background subtraction function, and the segmentation was used to have the region of interest. Took several classes of datasets such as two, four and eight with the result where the fine-tuned DenseNet121 accuracy reached 98.7%, the Inception V3 accuracy 96.7%, and the DenseNet121 accuracy achieved 93.57% [3].

Mukhopadhyay state four continuous human emotions in concert with a learning session. The complexity of human emotions and the psychological states were not enough to reflect the learner through the basic emotion. During a period of time, the combination of two or more emotions enables one to capture the facial emotion. Using the CNN model, the accuracy of emotion classification 65% and 62% for identification of mind state [6].

In terms of the prevention of accidents and fatalities, Mohanty conducted the detection of drowsiness in drivers using the DLIB model. The input of the model was video and the ratios of eyes and mouth reflected as the drowsiness detection. DLIB library is used to localize the facial landmarks where the histogram form represented the frequencies of gradient direction. The maximum accuracy of recognition reached 96.71% [5].

3   Methodology

This section presents the overall research stages, from retrieving the image collection, and step face landmarking, to the evaluation of the model and the image classification. The images from dataset were carried out for the labeling process and the selection data were segmented with a DLIB face detector model which maps the coordinates on the face. The main purpose of data segmentation is easy classification. As a result of data segmentation, so the size of the image was reduced to 224×224 pixels. Then CNN model trained the data.

3.1   Face Emotion Expression

Detecting a person's emotions enable someone to understand other people's feeling. Facial expressions and body gestures reflect human emotions. There are seven kinds of human emotions, namely neutral, angry, sadness, happy, surprise, disgust, and fear [7].

3.2   DLIB

DLIB is an open-source library for shape detection. It maps in the 68 points coordinates of the facial landmarks. The DLIB's points are described as follows: point number 1 to 17 are facial shapes, point number 18 to 22 are used to show the left eyebrows, point 23 to 27 are right eyebrows pattern, point 28 to 22, and point 22 to 36 are the nose shape, point 37 to 42 are the left eye shape, while point 43 to the 48 are the right eye shape, and the mouth form use point 49 until point 68. In terms of face shape detection performance, the DLIB function used the Histogram of Oriented Gradients (HOG) [5].

3.3 Convolutional Neural Network

Convolutional Neural Network (CNN) is one of the deep learning models with its characteristics of ease of implementation and high computation [1]. The impact of the CNN model is experienced on Computer vision tasks, however the performance of the model decrease in the varied dataset images [3].

4 Experiment

The experiment section explains the implementation of the proposed model. The experiment used a total of 901 images in CK+ dataset, which were divided into seven facial expressions: anger, happiness, sadness, fear, disgust, neutral, and surprise. All images in the dataset experienced with labeling process. The DLIB model was trained to identify 68 facial landmarks, then data segmentation eliminated the background images. The images as the result of segmentation were reduced according to the size of the model. Figure 1 presents the image results of before and after data segmentation. The result of data segmentation was adapted and learned by the model. In the architecture, ReLU activation function was used on 3 convolution layers, 2 pooling layers, and 1 fully connected layer. The SoftMax activation and the Adam optimizer were used to produce the output layer which had 7 nodes. The model was evaluated with confusion matrices in the simplest form of a table with two rows and two columns, and represents the four possibility classification outcome: True Positive (TP), False Positive, True Negative (TN) and False Negative (FN) [4]. The performance of the model did not only evaluated in the confusion matrix form, but also measure the model in accuracy, precision, recall, and the F1-score. The model gained 97% accuracy in 100 epochs. All the experiments used ratio of 20% data testing and 30% data testing consecutively. The first architecture model experiments used max-pooling 5×5, and dropout twice after dense. Generally, dense was used to decrease the unnecessary data so the model had an unfitting state. However, in these experiments, both models' results got overfitted and are shown in

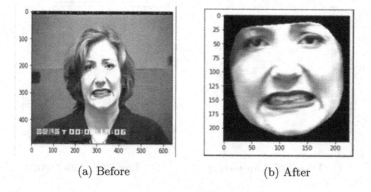

(a) Before   (b) After

Fig. 1. Data Segmentation

Figure 2. The overall model architecture as follow: Input $224 \times 224 \times 1$; Convolution2D 64, 5×5; Max Pooling 5×5; Convolution2D 64, 3×3; Convolution2D 64, 3×3; Average Pooling 3×3; Convolution2D 128, 3×3; Convolution2D 128, 3×3; Average Pooling 3×3; Dense 1024; Dropout 0.2; Dense 1024; Dropout 0.2; Dense 7.   The next experiments still used max-pooling 5×5 in 20% data testing or 30% data testing. Changed the position of dropout and only used it before dense. However, both models' results still experienced overfitting. The detail of model architecture was Input $224 \times 224x1$; Convolution2D 64, 5×5; Max Pooling 5×5; Convolution2D 64, 3×3; Convolution2D 64, 3×3; Average Pooling 3×3; Convolution2D 128, 3×3; Convolution2D 128, 3×3; Average Pooling 3×3; Dropout 0.2; Dense 1024; Dense 1024; Dense 7. Other experiments shifted the max-pooling with the average pooling 5×5 in 20% data testing or 30% data testing, only using dropout once and the position before dense. The pooling layer reduces the input images' spatial size and the number of computations in networks progressively. The purpose of simplifying the architecture was to get better results than previous experiments. The detail of model architecture was Input $224 \times 224x1$; Convolution2D 64, 5×5; Average Pooling 5×5; Convo-

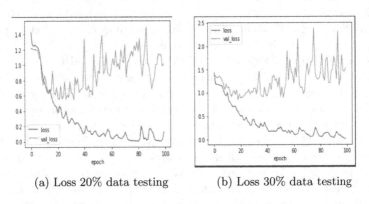

(a) Loss 20% data testing   (b) Loss 30% data testing

Fig. 2. Comparison Accuracy of Architecture1

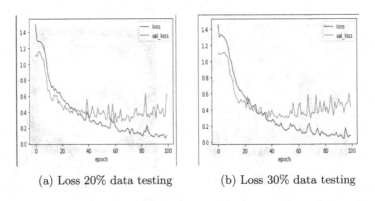

(a) Loss 20% data testing   (b) Loss 30% data testing

Fig. 3. Comparison Accuracy of Architecture3

lution2D 64, 3 × 3; Convolution2D 64, 3 × 3; Average Pooling 3 × 3; Dropout 0.2; Dense 1024; Dense 7. The graphs are better than those of the last experiments significantly, as illustrated in Fig. 3

5 Conclusion

Cutting-edge technology brings a new horizon to the education domain. For supporting the online learning process, the recognition of facial emotion expressions learners can be used as the evaluation for instructors when delivering the course material. With a distribution of 80% data training and 20% data testing, the accuracy of the proposed model to recognize achieved 97%. Although the achievement of the performance model is high, however, increasing the number of data images with high resolution (minimum: 640 × 490 pixels) in the dataset and equalizing the amount of data for each class will make the performance better.

Acknowledgement. This research was supported in part by the National Science and Technology Council (NSTC), Taiwan R.O.C. grants numbers 111-2622-E-029-003, 111-2811-E-029-001, 111-2621-M-029-004, and 110-2221-E-029-020-MY3.

References

1. Survey on face detection algorithms. Int. J. Innov. Sci. Res. Technol. **6** (2021)
2. Bezerra, G.A., Gomes, R.B.: Recognition of occluded and lateral faces using MTCNN, DLIB and homographies, 11 (2018)
3. Kamal, K.C., et al.: Impacts of background removal on convolutional neural networks for plant disease classification in-situ (2021)
4. Krstinić, D., Braović, M., Šerić, L., Božić-Štulić, D.: Multi-label classifier performance evaluation with confusion matrix, pp. 01–14. Academy and Industry Research Collaboration Center (AIRCC) (2020)
5. Mohanty, S., Hegde, S.V., Prasad, S., Manikandan, J.: Design of real-time drowsiness detection system using DLIB (2019)
6. Mukhopadhyay, M., Pal, S., Nayyar, A., Pramanik, P.K.D., Dasgupta, N., Choudhury, P.: Facial emotion detection to assess learner's state of mind in an online learning system. In: ACM International Conference Proceeding Series, pp. 107–115 (2020)
7. Tarnowski, P., Kołodziej, M., Majkowski, A., Rak, R.J.: Emotion recognition using facial expressions. Procedia Comput. Sci. **108**, 1175–1184 (2017)

Image Classification for Smoke and Flame Recognition Using CNN and Transfer Learning on Edge Device

Endah Kristiani[1,2], Yi-Chun Chen[1,4], Chao-Tung Yang[1,3]([⊠]),
and Chia-Hsin Li[4]

[1] Department of Computer Science, Tunghai University,
Taichung 407224, Taiwan, Republic of China
ctyang@thu.edu.tw
[2] Department of Informatics, Krida Wacana Christian Univeristy,
Jakarta 11470, Indonesia
[3] Research Center for Smart Sustainable Circular Economy, Tunghai University,
No. 1727, Sec.4, Taiwan Boulevard, Taichung 407224, Taiwan, Republic of China
[4] iAMBITION TECHNOLOGY CO., LTD., 3F., No. 159-1, Sec. 1, Zhongxing Rd.,
Dali, Taichung 41267, Taiwan, Republic of China

Abstract. This paper implemented image classification for smoke and flame detection. CNN model was trained in three topologies of InceptionV3, MobileNet, and VGG16. These three models were then tested on Raspberry Pi 4 with Intel Neural Compute Stick 2 (NCS 2). The experimental results demonstrated that MobileNetV2 is a superior model to the other two models in terms of training and inference, even if the accuracy rate of the three was as high as 94% when utilizing the test set for evaluation.

Keywords: image classification · CNN · Imagnet · edge computing · transfer learning

1 Introduction

In recent years, there has been a significant increase in the development of computer image vision. In addition, image recognition has significantly improved the widespread adoption of convolutional neural networks. Neural Networks can be broken down into subcategories, one of which is called Convolutional Neural Networks (commonly abbreviated as CNN or ConvNet). These networks are typically implemented for tasks involving image and speech recognition. The high dimensionality of images can be reduced by its built-in convolutional layer without any information being lost in the process. That is the reason why CNNs are particularly well-suited for image classification problems [1–3].

This study uses smoke and flame images to create deep-learning models for detecting the early signs of fire. We trained the models based on CNN and

© ICST Institute for Computer Sciences, Social Informatics and Telecommunications Engineering 2023
Published by Springer Nature Switzerland AG 2023. All Rights Reserved
D.-J. Deng et al. (Eds.): SGIoT 2022, LNICST 497, pp. 150–158, 2023.
https://doi.org/10.1007/978-3-031-31275-5_16

inferred the models on the edge device. In detail, our objectives are listed as follows.

- To train the models based on three types of CNN networks, InceptionV3, MobileNet, and VGG16.
- To infer the trained models on Raspberry Pi 4 and Intel NCS 2.

2   Background Review and Related Works

This section discussed the methods and previous research works as our references, such as image classification and CNN.

2.1   Image Classification

Image Classification (often referred to as Image Recognition) is the process of connecting a given image with a single (single-label classification) or several (multilabel classification) labels. Classification of images is a challenging task that allows for the evaluation of modern architectures and methodologies in the field of computer vision. The most often encountered classification job in supervised image classification is single-label classification. As the name implies, single-label categorization assigns a single label or comment to each picture. As a result, the model generates a single value or prediction for each image seen. The model returns a vector of length equal to the number of classes and a value indicating whether the picture corresponds to that class.

2.2   Convolution Neural Network (CNN)

CNN has always been a significant part of Deep Learning. Its power in image and image recognition is mighty, and it can even be said to be even more potent than human eye recognition. Many image recognition models are also formed from the extension of the CNN architecture. A convolutional neural network uses convolution to use color and size in the image as the input data of the neural network. Compared with the most active neural network, the most significant difference is the sharing of weights. The basic idea of CNN is to use a diversified image database as training data. Then, transfer the image to the output end of the grid using neural network parameters, and calculate the error value of the target and prediction at the output end learned by backpropagation. CNN method constantly updates the weight value of the neural network because this calculation allows the convolutional neural network to solve the problem of large amounts of data. Therefore, convolutional neural network research for high variability and dimensions is very suitable for image recognition. Convolutional neural network architecture often includes single or multiple convolution layers, pooling layers, and a fully connected layer at the output end. The function of the convolutional layer is to capture images. The action of taking features, finding the best features, and then classifying, and the pooling layer is often added between the convolutional layers.

2.3 Smart Edge

Edge Computing is a distributed computing architecture. The data originally processed by the central node is cut and distributed to the edge nodes, which can be closer to the user's terminal equipment and speed up the data. The processing and speed of the network reduce the delay [4]. Edge computing decomposes the work that was originally unified from the center of the network, which is the cloud, and distributes it to the edge nodes for processing. This makes the processing and transmission of data faster and reduces the network transmission The resulting delay. Therefore, when the network connection is interrupted, part of the calculations or services handed over to the edge processing can continue to be completed, achieving high availability of the overall service. In previous applications where AI and terminals were combined, terminal devices' storage and computing capabilities were very limited, so data must be sent back to the cloud for processing through the network. This data will be sent back to the central data center if traditional cloud computing is used. Centralized processing, and then transmitted back to the user's equipment, this method has greatly increased the demand for network bandwidth. However, with the continuous advancement of hardware equipment and algorithms in recent years, edge computing is the key to accelerating the Internet of Things. After the edge node receives the data, it directly analyzes and processes it, thereby reducing cloud computing resources and improving transmission efficiency [5].

2.4 Related Works

Due to the limitations of mobile devices, Jadon et al. [8] proposed a portable method for fire identification and use. Most automatic fire alarm systems will detect fires caused by sensors such as heat, smoke, or flame. One of the new ways to solve this problem is to perform detection using images. The imaging method is promising because it does not require a specific sensor and can be easily embedded in different devices.

In the paper by Jareerat et al. [6], an early warning must be given to reduce the loss of life and property caused by fire. A fire detection system based on light detection and analysis is proposed. The system uses HSV and YCbCr color models under given conditions to separate orange, yellow, and high-brightness light from the background and ambient light. Analyze and calculate fire growth based on frame differences. The overall accuracy of the experiment has exceeded 90%.

Thou-Ho Chen [7] presents a smoke-detection method for early fire-alarming systems based on video processing. The basic strategy of smoke-pixel judgment is composed of two decision rules: a chromaticity-based static decision rule and a diffusion-based dynamic characteristic decision rule. The chromatic decision rule is deduced by the grayish color of the smoke and the dynamic decision rule is dependent on the spreading attributes of smoke.

3 Methods

3.1 Dataset

The research dataset for this study was compiled using web crawlers from daily fire scenes and aerial photos of big forest fires. It will be kept on the server for administration and data enhancement to support later trials. There are 1056 smoke photographs and 2305 fire images in the original collection of the fire dataset. The initial inadequate dataset is supplemented with Keras. The original image has been rotated, turned upside down, and moved to the left and right. Based on the augmentation, 8000 additional photographs were included. Therefore, the dataset increased to 11361 images. Then, for training purposes, the dataset has a distribution ratio of 60% train set, 20% validation set, and 20% test set.

3.2 Model's Training and Inference

After the image preprocessing, we began the construction of the Deep Learning model, using three different CNN networks to train fire image data, that is VGG16, InceptionV3, and MobileNetV3. Tensorflow was used as the basic framework to train the models. Imagenet was used as the transfer learning model in the training. Then, the OpenVINO tool was used for model optimization to speed up operational efficiency in the edge device. Figure 1 shows the Raspberry Pi with Intel NCS 2 as edge devices.

Fig. 1. Raspberry Pi and NCS

3.3 Optimization Development

The Raspberry Pi is being used as an edge device with the optimization development methodology. To accelerate the training and inference procedures, our system made advantage of open-source AI software. The Intel Distribution of the OpenVINO Toolkit optimizes model deployment for inference processing by adapting and optimizing trained models for the downstream hardware target. It supports models trained in TensorFlow, Caffe, and MXNet on the CPU, integrated GPU, VPU (Movidius Myriad 2/Neural Compute Stick), and FPGA.

The system used the TensorFlow framework to improve deep learning modules. The Intel Python distribution and the Data Analytics Acceleration Library are required for machine learning. Deep neural network (DNN) libraries that are open-source offer CPU-optimized functions.

4 Results

4.1 Fire Scene Classification Result

This work selects three algorithms of different depths for transfer learning training, namely Inceptionv3, VGG16, and MobileNetV2. Before training, we used K-fold cross-validation for the collection of datasets. The method is to randomly divide the data into k sets and then use one set as Testing data. The remaining k-1 sets as Training data, repeated until each set is regarded as Testing data, and the final results (Prediction results) are compared with the ground truth (Performance Comparison). Training on scenes of fire and normal conditions. After 100 training cycles, we observed the training curve through the training log until the loss value reached the minimum value and did not change. The VGG16 training curve is shown in Fig. 2 and Table 1, Inceptionv3 training curve is shown in Fig. 3 and Table 2, MobileNetV2 training curve such as Fig. 4 and Table 3.

1. VGG16 Models

Table 1. VGG16 Accuracy and Loss

	Accuracy	Loss
Train	0.9546	0.1284
Validation	0.9234	0.1991

2. InceptionV3 Models

Table 2. InceptionV3 Accuracy and Loss

	Accuracy	Loss
Train	0.9844	0.0412
Validation	0.9820	0.0438

3.MobileNetV2 Models

Three different image classification models through the test set of experimental results, The accuracy of VGG16 is as high as 94%, and the accuracy of

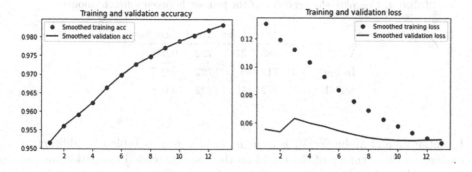

Fig. 2. VGG16 Acc and Loss

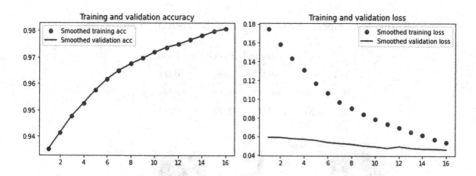

Fig. 3. InceptionV3 Acc and Loss

Table 3. MobileNetV2 Accuracy and Loss

	Accuracy	Loss
Train	0.9880	0.0396
Validation	0.9813	0.0417

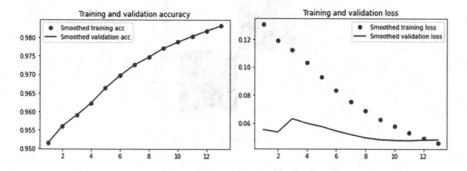

Fig. 4. MobileNetV2 Acc and Loss

Table 4. Compare the accuracy of the test set between different models

	True	False	Total	Accuracy
VGG16	685	37	722	0.9487
InceptionV3	713	9	722	0.9875
MobileNetV2	712	10	722	0.9889

InceptionV3 and MobileNetV2 is as high as 98%, such as Table 4 In addition to comparing the accuracy of the model on the test set, related evaluation indicators are also calculated to verify which model actually performs best, as shown in Fig. 5 and Table 5.

Table 5. Compare evaluation metrics between different models

	Recall	Precision	F1-score
VGG16	0.95	0.96	0.94
InceptionV3	0.99	0.98	0.99
MobileNetV2	0.99	0.99	0.99

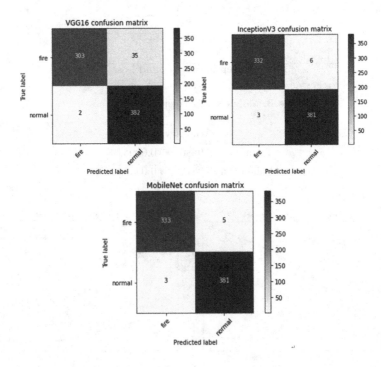

Fig. 5. Models confusion matrix

In addition to the comparison accuracy rate, FP16 (half-precision) and FP32 (single-precision) of the model were also compared. It can be seen from Table 6, the performance of VGG16 is far inferior to the other two models whether it is FP16 or FP32.

Table 6. Compare the operating efficiency between different models

Model Type	FPS
VGG16 FP32	5
VGG16 FP16	5
InceptionV3 FP32	19
InceptionV3 FP16	18
MobileNetV2 FP32	23
MobileNetV2 FP16	25

4.2   Classification Model Comparison

This paper uses three algorithms of CNN, VGG16, InceptionV3, and MobileNetV2. After training the models, we compared these three models' accuracy and related evaluation indicators. Among the three models, MobileNetV2 has the best accuracy and operating efficiency, with an accuracy rate of 98% and an FPS of 25 INF when using the FP16 model. Therefore, this paper chooses to use this model as the final model for subsequent fire scene classification in fire scene classification. The test results are shown in Fig. 6.

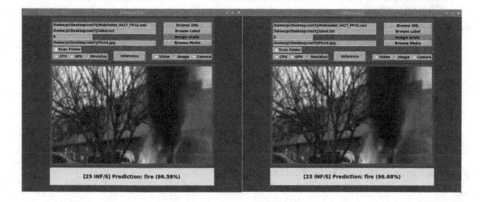

Fig. 6. MobileNetV2 FP16 and FP32 test

5 Conclusions

This paper implemented image classification for smoke and flame recognition. The fire detections employed an image classification method using the CNN model with three networks of VGG16, InceptionV3, and MobileNetV2. Although the accuracy rate of the three was as high as 94%, it can be seen that when using the test set for evaluation, the experimental data showed that MobileNetV2 is an excellent model compared to the other two models in terms of training and inference.

Acknowledgements. This work was supported by the National Science and Technology Council (NSTC), Taiwan (R.O.C.), under grants number 111-2622-E-029-003-, 111-2811-E-029-001-, 111-2621-M-029-004-, and 110-2221-E-029-020-MY3.

References

1. Gaur, A., Singh, A., Kumar, A., Kumar, A., Kapoor, K.: Video flame and smoke based fire detection algorithms: a literature review. Fire Tech. **56**(5), 1943–1980 (2020)
2. Li, P., Zhao, W.: Image fire detection algorithms based on convolutional neural networks. Case Stud. Thermal Eng. **19**, 100625 (2020)
3. Shi, F., et al.: A fire monitoring and alarm system based on YOLOv3 with OHEM. In: 2020 39th Chinese Control Conference (CCC). IEEE (2020)
4. Tang, J., Liu, S., Liu, L., Yu, B., Shi, W.: LoPECS: a low power edge computing system for real-time autonomous driving services. IEEE Access **8**, 30467–30479 (2020)
5. Huynh, L.N., Lee, Y., Balan, R.K.: DeepMon: mobile GPU based deep learning framework for continuous vision applications. In: MobiSys 2017 - Proceedings of 15th Annual Internationsl Conference on Mobile System, Applications and Services, pp. 82–95 (2017)
6. Seebamrungsat, J., Praising, S., Riyamongkol, P.: Fire detection in the buildings using image processing. In: 2014 Third ICT International Student Project Conference (ICT-ISPC), pp. 95–98 (2014). https://doi.org/10.1109/ICT-ISPC.2014.6923226
7. Chen, T., Yin, Y., Huang, S., Ye, Y.: The smoke detection for early fire-alarming system base on video processing. In: 2006 International Conference on Intelligent Information Hiding and Multimedia, pp. 427-430 (2006). https://doi.org/10.1109/IIH-MSP.2006.265033
8. Jadon, A., Varshney, A., Ansari, M.S.: Low-complexity highperformance deep learningdeep learning model for real-time low-cost embedded fire detection systems. Procedia Comput. Sci. **171**(2019), 418–426 (2020)

WLAN, Wireless Internet and 5G

Non-uniform Time Slice Parallel Simulation Method Based on Offline Learning for IEEE 802.11ax

Yangyang Xin, Mao Yang, Zhongjiang Yan$^{(\boxtimes)}$, and Bo Li

School of Electronics and Information, Northwestern Polytechnical University, Xi'an, China
2020262260@mail.nwpu.edu.cn, {yangmao,zhjyan,libo.npu}@nwpu.edu.cn

Abstract. With the rapid development of wireless networks, wireless local area networks (WLAN) are becoming more and more complex and densely deployed, resulting in a significant increase in the time consumption of traditional serial simulations. Aiming at the time consumption problem of traditional discrete-event-based WLAN serial simulation, A parallel simulation method is proposed based on offline learning with non-uniform time slices, which effectively reduces the time consumption. Firstly, the parallel simulation task is modeled as a problem of completing the simulation task within a given time consumption threshold constraint based on the processes pool. Secondly, the time consumption factor is obtained by offline learning of the simulation platform. Thirdly, the parallel simulation algorithm of non-uniform time slice division (NUTSD) based on the time consumption factor is proposed to analyze and solve the problem. Finally, the method is simulated and verified. The simulation results show that this method can greatly reduce time consumption.

Keywords: WLAN · Processes Pool · Offline Learning · Non-Uniform Time Slice · Parallel Simulation

1 Introduction

With the development of WLAN [1], the research on WLAN is deepening, and simulation is one of the main ways to study WLAN [2]. In the study of IEEE 802.11ax [3], due to the diverse services of simulation, the number of nodes is increasing and the deployment is becoming more and more intensive [4], resulting in the traditional serial simulation taking a too long time to meet the needs of simulation. So, it is urgent and necessary to develop a parallel simulation for IEEE 802.11ax.

Parallel simulation is a more effective simulation method compared with serial simulation [5], which includes space parallelism and time parallelism. The space parallel method divides the space into a group of subspaces, such as dividing several nodes into several groups, and each logical process is responsible for

D.-J. Deng et al. (Eds.): SGIoT 2022, LNICST 497, pp. 161–171, 2023.
https://doi.org/10.1007/978-3-031-31275-5_17

completing the tasks of each subspace in the entire simulation time. The time parallel method divides the entire simulation time into a set of consecutive segments, and each logical process is responsible for completing the task in one of the segments. At present, there have been many studies on parallel simulation. For wireless network simulation, the space parallel method is mainly based on NS2 [6] (Network Simulator version 2) and NS3 [7] (Network Simulator version 3), which used MPI [8] (Message Passing Interface) to realize the communication between logical processes. Yuan Jin [9] used NS3 and proposed an algorithm to divide a core network into parts and each part of the network is simulated by one process, which reduced simulation time consumption. Wang Lei [10] designed a parallel network simulation system based on NS2, each function module of the simulation system is simulated on different processes, and MPI is used to provide mutual communication between processes to realize parallel simulation. Wu Qian [11] proposed a method that used MPI to realize multi-machine parallelism based on NS2, the task is assigned to different parallel processes by a parallel scheduler, and the message transmission between parallel processes is completed by the MPI group communication interface, the results show that the simulation acceleration effect is obvious in large scale simulation. Huang Yu et.al [12] completed the parallel detection in the telecommunication network based on MPI for a large-scale backbone communication network, each functional module was implemented on different processes, and the detection rate has improved to some extent. Time parallel simulation method, most of the existing work is to study how to couple time slices after dividing the simulation time. Richard M et. al[5] mentioned that after dividing the time, because the starting state of each process may depend on the state of the simulation ending in the previous period, time slices couple has a great influence on the accuracy of simulation results. However, the above studies have not discussed the time parallel method for high-density wireless networks such as 802.11ax. Since the number of nodes in 802.11ax is too large and interaction between nodes is frequent, performing network simulation using the spatial parallelism method is becoming complex.

We propose a time parallel simulation method with non-uniform time slices based on offline learning to solve the parallel simulation problem of 802.11ax. The simulation verification shows that this method can greatly reduce the simulation time consumption under the premise of guaranteeing the consistency of simulation results with traditional simulation methods.

2   System Model

2.1   Simulation Model Based on Process Pool and Non-uniform Time Slice

A process pool consists of resource processes and management processes. The management process controls communication between internal resource pools and external ports, tasks for controlling internal resource pools include task allocation and process pool status management, and tasks for external communication ports include receiving tasks and status feedback. Resource processes are responsible for internal interprocess communication and task execution, and internal interprocess communication includes task acceptance and status feedback.

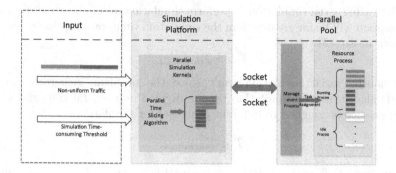

Fig. 1. Simulation model based on process pool and non-uniform time slice.

Figure 1 is a parallel simulation model based on process pools and non-uniform time slices. The inputs of the whole simulation model include non-uniform traffic and simulation time consumption threshold. The process of parallel simulation is the simulation platform divides the simulation time through the non-uniform time slice division algorithm, and then sends the simulation task to the process pool through the socket. The process pool receives the task execution and returns the result to the simulation platform through the socket.

2.2   Problem Description

WLAN simulation tasks can be described as that complete simulation tasks within a given simulation time consumption threshold when the input traffic is non-uniform. It takes a long time for serial simulation to complete the whole simulation, which obviously can't complete the simulation task within the threshold. Therefore, we build a mathematical model based on parallel simulation to solve this problem. The non-uniform traffic is divided into multiple time slices by the NUTSD algorithm. The simulation task of each time slice is completed independently by a process, and the final results are obtained by summarizing the results of all processes.

The mathematical model is as follows, m, T, and $T_{threshold}$ represent the number of idle processes in the process pool, the simulation time consumption, and the time consumption threshold, respectively. $TR_1, TR_2, \cdots, TR_n$ represent the traffic rate, and $t_1, t_2, \cdots, t_n$ represent the simulation time of each traffic rate, where n is the number of traffic rate. The time consumption factor is shown in Eq. (1), indicating the relationship between simulation time and simulation time consumption for different traffic rates, where f is a function, and u is the time consumption factor.

$$u_i = f\left(\mathrm{TR}_i\mathrm{Net}\right) \begin{cases} \mathrm{TR}_i \in (1e3, 1e4, \cdots, 1e9) \\ Net \in (CBR, Possion) \\ i \in (1, 2, 3, \cdots, n) \end{cases} \tag{1}$$

When using serial simulation to perform simulation tasks, the simulation time consumption will be far greater than the simulation time consumption threshold, as shown in Eq. (2).

$$T >> T_{threshold} \tag{2}$$

Obviously, serial simulation can't solve the problem. According to the NUTSD algorithm, the simulation time is divided into several time slices, and each time slice is assigned to different processes for simulation.

$$T < T_{threshold} \tag{3}$$

Equation (3) is satisfied if Eq. (4) is satisfied, where T_{proi} is the simulation time consumption for each process. Therefore, when the longest simulation time consumption in all processes satisfies Eq. (3), the simulation task can be completed.

$$T = \max\left(T_{pro1}, T_{pro2}, \cdots, T_{pron}\right), T_{proi}\left(i \in (1, 2, \cdots n)\right) \tag{4}$$

The estimation of simulation time consumption based on the time consumption factor is shown in Eq. (5), and the number of required processes P is shown in Eq. (6), where $\lceil\ \rceil$ is rounding up the result. The simulation time consumption T_{proi} for each process is shown in Eq. (7).

$$T = t_1 \cdot u_1 + t_2 \cdot u_2 + \cdots + t_n \cdot u_n = \sum_{i=1}^{n} t_i \cdot u_i \tag{5}$$

$$P = \left\lceil \frac{T}{T_{threshold}} \right\rceil \tag{6}$$

$$T_{proi} = \frac{T}{P} \tag{7}$$

Eventually, the simulation duration of each process can be obtained according to Eqs. (1) and (7), and Eq. (3) can be satisfied when the number of execution processes is P.

3   Offline Learning

In this section, we will discuss the time consumption factor, which was mentioned earlier in Sect. 2, and will show the steps to obtain the time consumption factor through offline learning. A data packet will go through several states in the simulation process, and each state generates several events. Moreover, the execution complexity of each event is different, and the time consumption is also different.

Table 1. Package Status and Example of Major Events.

Status	Major Events
Application Layer Generation Package	*IntraApplication*
	StartApplication
Successfully Sent the Package	*SendDataProcess*
Successfully Received the Packet	*SendAck SendCTS*
Retransmit Successful Packets After Receiving Failure	*HandleCTSTimeOut*
	HandleCTSTimeOut
Receive Failure to Retransmit Timeout Packet	*Lowest Level Heading.*
The Remaining Packets in the Queue After the End	*Lowest Level Heading.*

During the IEEE 802.11ax simulation, the data packets are divided into several states and major events as shown in Table 1. When there have enough events, we can assume that the number of events follows the law of large numbers, and we can calculate the average number of events experienced by each data packet from generation to destruction.

Table 2. The Number of Events Corresponding to the Data Packet

	Number of Packages	Number of Events	Total Events
Application Layer Generation Package	X_1	C_1	X_1C_1
Successfully Sent the Package	X_2	C_2	X_2C_2
Successfully Received the Package	X_3	C_3	X_3C_3
Retransmit Successful Packets After Receiving Failuret	X_4	C_4	X_4C_4
Receive Failure to Retransmit Timeout Packet	X_5	C_5	X_5C_5
The Remaining Packets in the Queue After the End	X_6	C_6	X_6C_6

The offline learning can be represented by a mathematical model. t, T, y and X represent the simulation time, the simulation time consumption, the number of events corresponding to t, and the number of data packets corresponding to t, respectively, others are shown in Table 2.

In the IEEE 802.11ax simulation system, when the simulation time is t, X is shown in Eq. (8), and y is shown in Eq. (9).

$$\begin{aligned} X &= X_1 + X_2 + X_3 + X_4 + X_5 + X_6 \\ &= f_1(t) + f_2(t) + f_3(t) + f_4(t) + f_5(t) + f_6(t) \end{aligned} \tag{8}$$

$$y = C_1X_1 + C_2X_2 + C_3X_3 + C_4X_4 + C_5X_5 + C_6X_6 = g(f(t)) \tag{9}$$

$$T = h(y) = h(g(f(t))) \tag{10}$$

T can be calculated by Eq. (10), and the relationship between T and t is very complicated. Therefore, in this paper, a large amount of data is obtained by simulating the 802.11ax simulation system, and the data is fitted to obtain the relationship between T and t, that is, the time consumption factor, denoted by u.

Table 3. Simulation Parameter Table

Simulation Parameters	Parameters
Traffic Type-Topology	*CBR-DL-1AP1STA*
	CBR-DL-6AP3STA
	Possion-DL-1AP3STA
Simulation Time	*10*s
Traffic Rate	*1e8(5 s)–1e3(5 s)*
Packet Size	*1500bits*
Bandwidth	*20M*
MCS Value	*9*

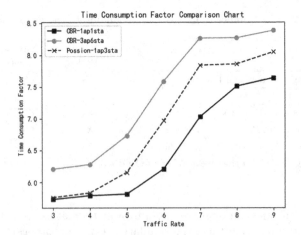

Fig. 2. Different Traffic-Topology Time Consumption Factor Result

A large number of results were obtained through simulation under the simulation parameters shown in Table 3, and the time consumption factor was obtained by fitting the results. Figure 2 shows the time consumption factor results for different traffic rates and different topologies.

4 Non-uniform Time Slice Parallel Simulation Algorithm Based on Offline Learning

Based on Sect. 3, this section proposes a non-uniform time slice parallel simulation algorithm based on offline learning. The inputs of the algorithm include the rate of each traffic, the simulation time of each traffic rate, the time consumption factor, the simulation time consumption threshold, and the total number of processes in the process pool. The output is the simulation time consumption. Firstly, the estimated simulation time of all services is calculated according to the time consumption factor. Then the number of processes required to complete the simulation task within the simulation time consumption threshold and the corresponding simulation time consumption of each process are calculated. Finally, the simulation time required for each process is calculated in reverse. The algorithm can not only complete the simulation task with the least process within the simulation time consumption threshold but also ensures the load balance of the process.

The pseudo-code of the algorithm is as follows:

Algorithm 1: NUTSD Algorithm

---

input : Tacffic Rate TR_i and Simulation Time of Each Rate t_i and Time consumption Factor u_i and Simulation Time consumption Threshold $T_{threshold}$ and Total Number of Processes P_{total}

output: Simulation Time consumption T

Begin

foreach TR_i **do** $T_{total} += u_i \cdot t_i$;

Calculation of Simulation Time Consumption for All Traffic

$P_{need} = \left\lceil \frac{T_{total}}{T_{threshold}} \right\rceil$

Calculate the number of processes required to complete the simulation within the simulation time consumption threshold

$P_{time} = T_{total} / P_{need}$

Calculating simulation time consumption for each process

foreach $i < P_{need}$ **do** $CalculateSimulationtime()$;

Calculate the simulation time for each process

if $P_{need} <= P_{total}$ **then** $StartSimulation()$;

Start Simulation

else Print("Insufficient idle processes");

End

---

5 Simulation

5.1 Simulation Environment and Parameter Settings

This paper is implemented and verified on the IEEE 802.11ax simulation platform [13] of our laboratory. The main simulation verification parameters are shown in Table 4.

Table 4. Simulation Parameter Table

Simulation Parameters	Parameters
Traffic Type-Topology	*CBR-DL-1AP1STA*
	CBR-DL-6AP3STA
	Possion-DL-1AP3STA
Traffic Rate	*1e8(5s)–1e3(5s)*
Packet Size	*1500bits*
Bandwidth	*20M*
MCS Value	*9*
OFDMA	*Open*

5.2 Simulation Results and Analysis

Figure 3(a) shows the results of the serial simulation, uniform divided and non-uniform divided simulation time consumption changes with preset simulation time consumption thresholds in the downlink simulation verification environment of CBR traffic under 1AP1STA topology. Figure 3(b) is the serial simulation, uniformly divided and non-uniformly divided throughputs vary with the preset simulation time consumption threshold, and the packet loss rate is consistent with serial simulation.

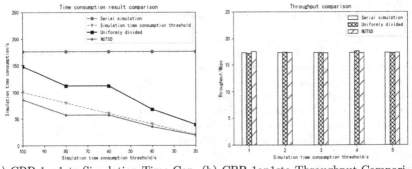

(a) CBR-1ap1sta Simulation Time Consumption Comparison Result   (b) CBR-1ap1sta Throughput Comparison Result

Fig. 3. CBR-1ap1sta Comparison Result

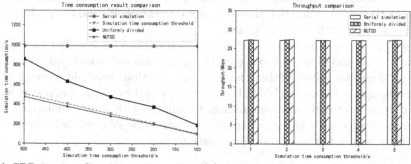

(a) CBR-3ap6sta Simulation Time Consumption Comparison Result (b) CBR-3ap6sta Throughput Comparison Result

Fig. 4. CBR-3ap6sta Comparison Result

Figure 4(a) shows the results of the serial simulation, uniform division, and non-uniform division simulation time consumption changes with the preset simulation time consumption threshold in the downlink simulation verification environment of the CBR traffic under the 3AP6STA topology. Figure 4(b) shows the serial simulation, uniformly divided and non-uniformly divided throughputs vary with the preset simulation time consumption threshold, and the packet loss rate is consistent with serial simulation.

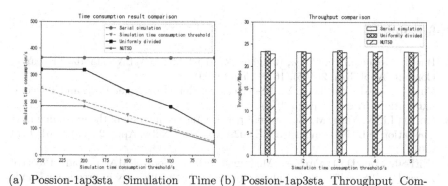

(a) Possion-1ap3sta Simulation Time Consumption Comparison Result (b) Possion-1ap3sta Throughput Comparison Result

Fig. 5. Possion-1ap3sta Comparison Result

Figure 5(a) shows the results of the serial simulation, uniform division, and non-uniform division simulation time consumption changes with the preset simulation time consumption threshold in the downlink simulation verification environment of the poisson traffic under the 1AP3STA topology. Figure 5(b) shows the serial simulation, uniformly divided and non-uniformly divided throughputs vary with the preset simulation time consumption threshold, and the packet loss rate is consistent with serial simulation.

From the above three sets of simulation results, it can be seen that for different traffic rates and different topologies, the simulation task which was proposed in Sect. 2.2 can be solved within the time consumption threshold through the time consumption factor and NUTSD algorithm. The throughput and packet loss rate are consistent with serial simulation. Compared with serial simulation and uniform time slice parallel simulation, non-uniform time slice parallel simulation can greatly reduce the simulation time consumption.

6   Conclusion

To solve the time consumption problem of traditional serial simulation in WLAN, this paper proposes a parallel simulation method based on offline learning with non-uniform time slice division. Through the modeling and analysis of the problem and the implementation of the NUTSD algorithm, the simulation verification is carried out on the IEEE 802.11ax simulation platform. The results show that the method can effectively reduce the simulation time consumption, and has a strong application prospect and value in WLAN simulation.

Acknowledgement. This work was supported in part by the National Natural Science Foundations of CHINA (Grant No. 61771392, No. 61871322 and No. 61771390), and Science and Technology on Avionics Integration Laboratory and the Aeronautical Science Foundation of China (Grant No. 201955053002 and No. 20185553035).

References

1. Hao, L., Zehua, G., Feng, G., Ronghua, Z.: IEEE 802.11 WLAN standard research. Comput. Appl. Res. **26**(05), 1616–1620 (2009)
2. Chunguang, M., Jiansheng, Y.: NS-3 Network Simulator. Name Posts and Telecommunications Press, Beijing (2014)
3. Qu, Q., Li, B., Yang, M.: Survey and performance evaluation of the upcoming next generation WLANs standard-IEEE 802.11ax. Mob. Netw. Appl. **24**(03), 1461–1474 (2019)
4. IEEE802.11ax/D5.1.Wireless Medium Access Control(MAC) and Physical Layer(PHY) Specifications: Enhancements for High Efficiency in Frequency Bands between 1 GHz and 6 GHz. (2019)
5. Fujimoto, R.M.: Parallel and Distributed Simulation Systems. Canada (2000)
6. Xioayan, W., MIngchun, Z.: Research and Application of Network Simulation Based on NS2. Comput. Simul. (2004)
7. Xinyu, R., Yuan, L.: Analysis and exploration of network simulation NS3. Comput. Technol. Dev. (2018)
8. Zhihong, Z.: Parallel computing based on MPI. China University of Geosciences, Beijing (2006)
9. Jin, Y.: Research on network parallel simulation method based on NS3. University of Electronic Science and Technology (2017)

10. Lei, W.: Research and implementation of parallel network simulation task optimization method. The Harbin University of Technology (2006)
11. Qian, W.: Design and implementation of NS2 multi-machine parallel simulation scheduler. Nanjing University of Posts and Telecommunications (2016)
12. Yu, H., Guangmin, H.: Development of computer parallel simulation platform for backbone communication network. Microcomput. Inf. **26**(16) (2010)
13. Yang, M., Li, B., Yan, Z.: MAC technology of IEEE 802.11ax: progress and tutorial. Mob. Netw Appl. **26**, 1122–1136 (2021)

A Joint Optimization Method for Scheduling and Random Access Based on the Idea of Particle-Based Access in IEEE 802.11ax

Ke Sun, Bo Li, Zhongjiang Yan[✉], and Mao Yang

School of Electronics and Information, Northwestern Polytechnical University, Xi'an, China
{libo.npu,zhjyan,yangmao}@nwpu.edu.cn

Abstract. At present, there are some problems in the mechnism of guarantee for the delay of uplink service in IEEE 802.11, 1) Many studies have optimized the expectation of delay of random access, but cannot privide deterministic guarantee of delay. 2) Scheduling access can effiectively provides guarantee for the performance of the delay of service, but there are some very urgent packets that cannot tolerate the waiting time required by scheduling. 3) There are few studies that consider optimal the delay of both scheduling and random access. To solve these problems, this paper proposes a joint optimization method of scheduling and random access, based on the idea of minimum access bandwidth in the theory of particle access and the corresponding access strategy: EDF (Early Deadline First). As a result, the packets created by scheduling users are in the minimum access bandwidth range at each time, and the idle time-frequency resources are distributed as evenly as possible in time. Therefore, the probability of collision between random access users and the resulting long waiting time can be reduced. The simulation results show that under the condition of moderate total traffic, the joint optimization method proposed in this paper can significantly reduce the access delay of random users on the premise of ensuring the delay requirements of scheduling users. The research result of this paper provides a new idea for further optimizing the delay of the scheduling and random users.

Keywords: Particle access · IEEE 802.11ax · Joint optimization of scheduling and random access · Guarantee of delay

1 Introduce

In recent years, with the rapid development of intelligent applications, the number of nodes in the network continues to expand, and users are more and more sensitive to the delay of wireless communication. However, the traditional access

© ICST Institute for Computer Sciences, Social Informatics and Telecommunications Engineering 2023
Published by Springer Nature Switzerland AG 2023. All Rights Reserved
D.-J. Deng et al. (Eds.): SGIoT 2022, LNICST 497, pp. 172–185, 2023.
https://doi.org/10.1007/978-3-031-31275-5_18

method of WiFi is CSMA/CA, which will cause a lot of collisions when there are a large number of nodes or a large amount of traffic. It will make the delay impossible to guarantee. Therefore, it is necessary to design a MAC protocol that can guarantee the requirement of delay. The research on service delay is mainly divided into two aspects, namely, optimizing random access and optimizing scheduling access. Both scheduling and random access, when scheduling access, AP allocates RU to STAs by sending Trigger Frame (TF); when random access, STA performs random access through Uplink-OFDMA Random Access (UORA). The main content of the research on optimizing random access is to optimize the delay through reservation, adaptive adjustment of parameters and other methods on the basis of the traditional CSMA/CA of IEEE 802.11. In [1], a Probabilistic Complementary Transmission Scheme (PCTS) is proposed to allow nodes to perform backoff retransmission with a certain probability after transmission failure to alleviate the retransmission delay and reduce unnecessary backoff window expansion. Reference [2] proposes a Multi-dimensional Busy Tone Arbitration (MBTA) mechanism, the arbitration phase is added before the node sends in UORA, which greatly reduces the probability of collision. References [3,4] use NOMA and beamforming mechanisms respectively to achieve simultaneous transmission by multiple STAs on the same RU to reduce collisions. However, the optimization of random access is still full of uncertainty and cannot provide a deterministic guarantee for delay.

The core idea of optimal scheduling access is to use AP to reasonably schedule the associated nodes to avoid collisions and meet the requirements of QoS for data packets. References [5,6] make adjustments on the basis of traditional polling to achieve guarantee of delay, Reference [5] analyzed the uplink delay performance of HCCA, and proposed a method to adaptively adjust the time of TXOP and other stages to ensure the delay. Reference [6] proposes that before data polling, an additional round of information transmission is added to report whether each node has packets to send, and nodes without packets will be skipped during data polling. Reference [7] also adopts the idea of separation of contral information and data transmission, based on the BSR of IEEE 802.11ax, it designs a buffer reporting technology that transmits information and data in two segments. Cooperating with the energy-saving mechanism it can improve efficiency. Reference [8] proposed a fair scheduling algorithm based on the Hungarian algorithm to solve the resource allocation problem of various real-time services in the context of LTE. Reference [9] uses the LTE scheduler to adapt to IEEE 802.11ax and uses the Hungarian algorithm to perform a thorough search with the utility function to get the best RU configuration. Optimized scheduling access can effectively guarantee the delay of general services, however some services' delay requirements are very strict, and the delay brought by scheduling cannot be tolerated, so it is more suitable to use random access to shorten the delay of access.

In the actual scenario, random access and scheduling access must exist at the same time. So these two aspects need to be considered at the same time when designing the MAC protocol for the guarantee of delay. References [10] and [2] research from the perspective of user selection of sending methods. Reference [10] studies the optimal distribution ratio of nodes choosing random access and scheduling access in the system to maximize the total throughput. Reference [2] found that random access is more suitable for short frames, and scheduled access is more suitable for long frames, so the optimal frame duration boundary can be calculated, and the DAMS algorithm is then proposed to let the AP estimate the optimal boundary, and send it to STAs to help select optimal method of access. References [11] studies from the perspective of AP scheduling, it proposes the concept of access capacity entropy, and designs a greedy algorithm Hybrid Access Strategy (HAS), which allocates RU to the user with the largest capacity entropy, However, it only considers throughput maximization and does not consider the guarantee of delay.

Based on the idea of particle access, this paper granulates the uplink service flow into information particles. and proposed a scheduling algorithm based on EDF. It can minimize the access bandwidth of the scheduled users and reduce the random access delay at the same time, and it is called the joint optimization algorithm of scheduling and random access. Then, with the OFDMA technology of IEEE 802.11ax, TF is used to complete the scheduling of subsequent T ms time-frequency resources. The joint optimization algorithm proposed in this paper minimizes the peak access bandwidth under the condition of meeting the requirements of delay for the scheduling user. In this way, more sufficient bandwidth resources are provided to random access packets at each time, so as to meet the requirements of delay for two types of access services (scheduling access and random access) to the limit.

2   Main Idea

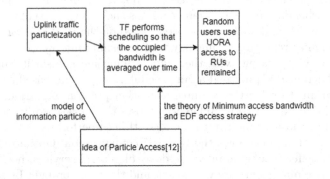

Fig. 1. Schematic diagram of the core idea of a joint optimization method for scheduling and random access based on the idea of particle access based on IEEE 802.11ax

As shown in Fig. 1, the core idea of this paper is based on the idea of particle access, including the flow model based on the information particle, the minimum bandwidth of particle access and its corresponding EDF access strategy. The core idea of this paper can be divided into the following parts:

1. Apply the model of particle access to granulate the uplink service flow into information particles. The end-to-end service flow can be modeled as a group of information particles, in which each information particle is a packet with the attributes of carrying information, creation time and deadline.
2. AP uses the TF to schedule the time-frequency space in the Tms after that, and uses the EDF strategy that can achieve the minimum access bandwidth with the idea of patticle access, so that the bandwidth occupied by the scheduling users is averaged as much as possible in time. Thus, this strategy reserves as much bandwidth resources as possible for random users to compete for access at each time.
3. The random user arrives randomly in the time domain and uses UORA for access [13], that is, the random user generates a random integer within the backoff window. If the positive number is less than the number of idle RUs, it randomly selects a RU for access. Else, the number of idle RUs will be subtracted from the backoff value. If two random users choose the same RU at the same time, it means a collision occuring, the backoff window of both nodes need to be doubled, and the random backoff value is regenerated, and the backoff starts.

3   Introduction to the Theory of Particle Access

In this section, the definitions of information particles, the group of information particles and their attrubutes are given. The sorting operation in the group of information particles is given. The reachable access bandwidth and the minimum reachable access bandwidth are defined. And a theorem proved that EDF is an access transmission strategy that can achieve the minimum accessible access bandwidth is given (the specific proof analysis can be found in Reference [12]).

Definition 1. *Information Particle: Information blocks to be transmitted with specific basic properties (including: carrying capacity I_i, initial time $t_{b,i}$, deadline $t_{e,i}$, etc.) are called information particles,which are used n_i to identify. The following are its main attributes: Its effective survival interval is $D_i = [t_{b,i}, t_{e,i}]$ (this paper only considers the particles that have arrived, that is, $t_{b,i} = 0$), The length of time covered T_{D_i} is the effective life span of the particle, that is $T_{D_i} = t_{e,i} - t_{b,i}$. The instantaneous transmission rate of the information particle at time t is recorded as $r_i(t)$, If n_i completes transmission within time interval D_i, it is called effiective transmission.*

Definition 2. *the Group of Information Particles: A non empty set containing $N(\geq 1)$ meaningful information particles, recorded as Q. Its carrying capacity is the sum of the carrying capacity of all information particles contained,that is $I_Q = \sum_{i \in Q} I_i$. Effective survival space D_Q of Q is the union of the effective survival intervals of all its information particles, that is $D_Q = \bigcup_{i \in Q} D_i$, and the total length of time covered T_{D_Q} is the effective survival span of Q.*

Definition 3. *Ascending sort operation $Op_{Inc}(Q)$ to the group of information particles Q: As given group of information particles Q, sort the information particles from small to large according to the their deadline, and give the ith information particle a serial number of "i", (its deadline is $t_{e,i}$)*

Definition 4. *Reachable Access Bandwidth $B_{re,Q}$ of the Information Particles Q: If there is a transmission strategy that can make all information particles in Qtransmit effectively, and the total instantaneous transmission rate meets $\sum_{i \in Q} r_i(t) \leq B_{re,Q}, (B_{re,Q} > 0, t \in D_Q)$, Then the access bandwidth $B_{re,Q}$ is reachable for Q.*

Definition 5. *Minimun Reachable Bandwidth $B_{re,Q}^{min}$ of the Group of Information Particles Q: the minimum value among all reachable access bandwidths within the effective survival space D_Q of the group of information particles Q.*

Theorem 1. *As for given group of information particles Q, using EDF strategy can achieve effective transmission under the minimum access bandwidth.*

This theorem gives the requirements of minimum bandwidth to send the entire group of information particles effectively, and the EDF strategy just meet all requirements, that is, it proves that EDF strategy can effectively send the whole group of information particles under the minimum reachable access bandwidth (refer to [12] Lemma 2 for a detail proof).

Lemma 1. *In the case of adopting the EDF transmission strategy, as the information particles are transmitted, the required minimum reachable access bandwidth will decrease or remain unchanged.*

This lemma gives the variation of the minimum reachable access bandwidth of a given group of information particles under the EDF transmission strategy. According to this lemma, this paper designs a scheduling algorithm to maintain the bandwidth occupied by information particles with the minimum access bandwidth at every moment. (refer to [12] Corollary 5 of Theorem 4 for a detail proof)

4 Joint Optimization Method of Scheduling and Random Access Based on the Idea of Particle Access

In this section, an access method based on the idea of particle, which is called the joint optimization algorithm of scheduling and random access. It realizes that the bandwidth occupied by the group of information particles of scheduling usrs is down to minimum access bandwidth at every time. The detailed algorithm flow of this method will be introduced below.

As shown in Fig. 2, the AP accesses the channel and enters the preparation phase. Firstly, AP obtains the transmission buffer information of the associated STAs through the technology of BSR, and obtains the deadline and carrying information of each packet which is ready to send in each STA. Then AP maps

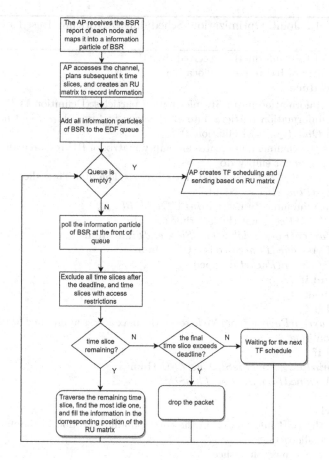

Fig. 2. Flowchart of joint optimization method of scheduling

the information of transmission buffers to the information particles of BSR with the attributes of carrying information and deadline. Finaly, AP adds these information particles of BSR to the EDF queue. At the same time, AP create a empty matrix(number of time slice · number of RU) of RU resource allocation. At this point, the AP perparation stage is over and the scheduling phase begins.

In the scheduling phase, the AP needs to allocate RU to the information particles of BSR in the EDF queue. When the EDF queue is not empty, the AP will get the information particle of BSR from the head of EDF queue. That is, this particle's deadline is the closest among the EDF queue. And then AP will exclude time slices that can not be accessed(including: the time slice is beyond the deadline of the information particle, the RU resources in the time slice are fully occupied, the source STA of this information particle has reached the limit of access ability). If there are still time slice available, then select the time slice, where RU occupies the least, and choose an idle RU to access. That is, fill this information particles of BSR into the matrix of RU resource allocation; If

---

Algorithm 1. Joint Optimization Scheduling Algorithm Based on Particle Theory

---

Input: List of BSR information received by AP
Output: Matrix of RU resource allocation
Begin proceduce
1: Map BSR information into BSR information particles (Definition 1)
2: Put BSR information particles into BSR queue to form Q_{BSR}, and perform the operation $Op_{inc}(Q_{BSR})$(Definition 3)
3: AP access the channel and creates an empty matrix of RU resource allocation
4: **while** Q_{BSR} is not empty **do**
5:     $CurrentPacket \Leftarrow Q_{BSR}.poll()$, $ThisSlice \Leftarrow$ The first Time slice
6:     $AssignedTimeSlice \Leftarrow$ NULL
7:     Current minimum Ru usage $minRU_{num} = RU_{num}$
8:     **while** $ThisSlice$ is not the last time slice **do**
9:       **if** $CurrentPacket.ddl > ThisSlice.endTime$ **then**
10:         **if** $AssignedTimeSlice$ is NULL **then**
11:           $CurrentPacket$ dropped
12:         **end if**
13:         break
14:       **end if**
15:       **if** $CurrentPacket.fromNode$ reach the max access ability in $ThisSlice$ **then**
16:         continue
17:       **end if**
18:       **if** $minRU_{num} > ThisSlice.usedRU$ **then**
19:         $AssignedTimeSlice \Leftarrow ThisSlice$
20:       **end if**
21:     **end while**
22:     Fill in the BSR information in the corresponding position in the matrix of RU resource allocation
23:     $ThisSlice \Leftarrow$ next time slice
24: **end while**
End proceduce

---

there is no time slice left, it is determined whether the last time slice is within its deadline. If it is, it means it has a chance to wait for the next TF to schedule, else, the information particle must be unable to effectively send, it will be discarded. After completing the traversal of all information particles in the EDF queue, the TF schedules according to the matrix of RU reasource allocation. At this point the AP schedululing phase ends, the specific algorithm is detailed in Algorithm 1, and the random access phase begins.

In random access phase, the packets arrival rule of random users satisfies the Poisson distribution. Random users will select a time slice with idle RU to access when they have packet need to be sent. If an RU is selected by one node, the access is successful; else, it is regared as collision. If the collision happens in more than half of RU after a node access, its backoff window will be doubled. Otherwise, the backoff window will remain the same for rebackoff and access. The detail algorithm can be found in Algorithm 2.

Algorithm 2. Joint optimization random access algorithm

Input: a random user access
Output: RU access
Begin proceduce
1: random user access the channel and create a random backoff value $OBO \in [0, OCW_{min}]$
2: $ThisSlice \Leftarrow$ next time slice recently
3: **if** $OBO \leq ThisSlice.remainRU_{num}$ **then**
4:    select $R\_STA.MaxAccessNum$ idle RUs randomly for access
5: **else**
6:    $OBO \Leftarrow OBO - ThisSlice.remainRU_{num}$
7: **end if**
8: **if** The number of RUs also selected by other R_STAs < $R\_STA.MaxAccessNum/2$ **then**
9:    this random user access success
10:    $R\_STA.collisionNum = 0$
11:    goto line 1
12: **else**
13:    collision occupies
14:    $R\_STA.collisionNum + +$
15:    **if** $R\_STA.collisionNum == MaxCollisionNum$ **then**
16:       currentPacket dropped, and goto line 1
17:    **else**
18:       $OCW \Leftarrow 2OCW$, and recreate a random backoff value $OBO \in [0, OCW]$
19:    **end if**
20: **end if**
End procedure

---

5   Simulation Verification

This section will introduce the simulation scenarios, related parameters, the simulation group scheme and the comparision group scheme. Finally it give the comparison of performance of following parameters: the average delay of the two groups of schemes in the simulation scenario (the average time taken from the creation of all sending packets to the completion of sending), the throughput (successful transmission per unit time) and the packet loss rate (packet loss: the number of random user collisions reaches the upper limit, and the scheduling user has not been allocated resources until the deadline).

5.1   Introduction to Simulation Platform

This paper uses C++ to build a simulation platform to simulate the uplink scenario. As shown in Fig. 3, in this paper the system is considered as single AP scenario, and there are n STAs associated with AP, among which there are n_s

S-STAs who uses scheduled access with the intensity of its service flow is λ_s, and there are n_r R-STAs who uses random access with the intensity of its service flow is λ_r.

In the IEEE 802.11ax environment, when the AP schedules the uplink service, STAs need to report the information of their transmission buffer through the BSR in advance, and then AP sends a TF to allocate the RU resource to the node. In this paper, the process of BSR is not the focus of consideration, so it is incorporated into the duration of TF.

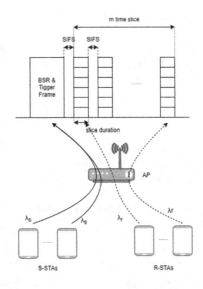

Fig. 3. Schematic diagram of joint access simulation scenario

As shown in Fig. 3, in this paper, the time-frequency resources scheduled by the AP to send TF are divided into m time slices, the length of each time slice (0.8 ms) and the interval between two time slice (16 μs). In addition, this paper limits the maximum RU that a S-STA can access in a single time slice, that is, the node access capacity. The specific simulation platform parameters are shown in Table 1.

Table 1. Table of simulation parameters.

Parameter Name	Value
number of timeslices	50
number of RUs	8
bandwidth of channel(MHz)	20
number of random users	5
number of scheduling users	8
random user traffic vs. scheduled user traffic	1:9
the ability of node access	1
length of a packet(bit)	2000
delay tolerance of packets(ms)	100
OCW_{min}	8
maximum retransmission times of random users	6
simulation duration(ms)	10000

5.2   Introduction to the Simulation Scheme

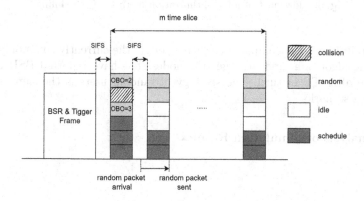

Fig. 4. Flowchart of joint optimization method of scheduling

As shown in Fig. 4, in the simulation scheme of this paper, the AP uses the scheduling access algorithm in the joint optimization method for scheduling and random access to allocate RU resources to the nodes that have reported the BSR. Then the AP sends TF to schedule the corresponding nodes to send in the allocated RU, so that the peak access bandwidth is minimized. In addition, the production packets of random users are completely random in time. Their packets select the nearest idle time slice, and use the UORA method to compete for access to the channel. If a collision occurs with two nodes, their OCWs will be doubled. And these nodes will join the competition of the UORA in the next idle time slice. random access packets will be dropped after their collision times reachs the maximum.

5.3   Introduction to the Comparision Scheme

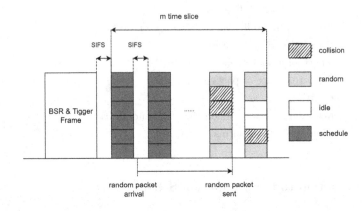

Fig. 5. Flowchart of joint optimization method of scheduling

As shown in Fig. 5, the comparison scheme adopts the currently commonly used scheduling algorithm, and arranges the nodes that have reported BSR in the time slice after TF in turn. The strategy of random users is the same as the simulation scenario.

5.4   Analysis of Simulation Results

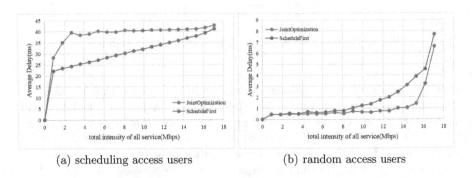

(a) scheduling access users   (b) random access users

Fig. 6. Figure of relationship between average delay and total traffic

As shown in Fig. 6, when the total traffic is small, the delay performance of the two methods is similar. The reason is that when the traffic is low, the random users who need to access in each time slice and the RU occupied by the scheduling users when accessing are less. Therefore, both methods can ensure the delay of random users. However, some scheduling users are allocated to a later time slice due to the minimum access bandwidth requirements of the scheduling algorithm, so the delay of scheduling users is larger. However, with the increase of user traffic, compared with the traditional scheduling first algorithm, random users gradually increase after the total traffic exceeds 8mbps. The joint optimization method can keep the random user delay at a very low level while ensuring the requirement for delay of scheduling users until the total traffic exceeds 14mbps. It can be seen that the joint optimization method can effectively ensure the service delay. As the traffic continues to increase, both scheduling schemes will make all RUs occupied by scheduling users' packets. Therefore, when the traffic is large enough, the performance of the two schemes will be close again.

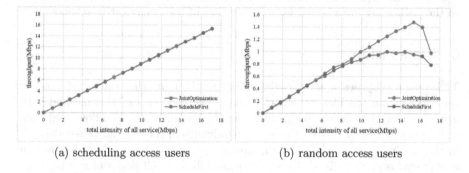

(a) scheduling access users   (b) random access users

Fig. 7. Figure of relationship between throughput and total traffic

As shown in Fig. 7, the scheduling user throughput performance of the two schemes is completely consistent. As for the random user performance, the throughput performance of the two schemes is similar when the total traffic is small or large. The reason for this phenomenon has been shown in the delay performance analysis. When the total traffic is in the range of 8–17 mbps, the Ru of the comparison scheme is concentrated in the later time slice, and a large number of random users compete in the same time slice. It leads to a high collision probability, which makes the channel utilization low. On the contrary, the experimental scheme makes the Ru distribution as average as possible in time, and it matches the distribution pattern of random users. As a result, the competition is more dispersed in the experimental scheme, which reduces the probability of collision, and thus produces better performance of throughput.

As shown in Fig. 8, the performance analysis of packet loss rate and through-put is similar. Both schemes can fully meet the needs of scheduling users without packet loss. For random users, when the total traffic is large or small, the per-formance of the two schemes is similar. When the total traffic is in the range

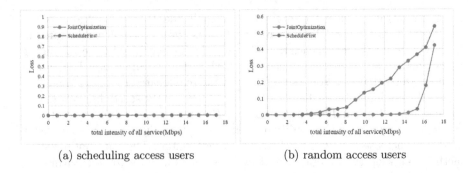

(a) scheduling access users   (b) random access users

Fig. 8. Figure of relationship between throughput and total traffic

of 5–17mbps, referring to the performance analysis of throughput, due to the different distribution of idle Ru in time of the two schemes, the collision probability of the experimental scheme is less than that of the comparative scheme, so the packet loss rate is also better than that of the comparative scheme.

6 Conclusion

This paper proposes a joint optimization method of scheduling and random access based on the idea of particleization. The core idea of this method is to use the theory of particle access to granulate the uplink service flow, and then use an EDF strategy to keep the access bandwidth of the scheduled users always in the minimum access bandwidth, so that the distribution of idle bandwidth is averaged over time, in this way, the probability of collision and waiting time of random user access can be reduced. For random users, the UORA method of IEEE 802.11ax can still be used for random access. The simulation results show that when the traffic flow is suitable, the joint optimization method proposed in this paper can significantly reduce the access delay of random users on the premise of guarantee the requirements for delay of scheduling users. The work in this paper only considers the optimization of uplink hybrid access (scheduling and random access). In the future, we will further study the uplink and downlink access methods based on the idea of particle access to guarantee the requirements for the latency performance of various services.

Acknowledgments. This work was supported in part by the National Natural Science Foundations of CHINA (Grant No. 61771390, No. 61771392 and No. 61871322), and Science and Technology on Avionics Integration Laboratory and the Aeronautical Science Foundation of China (Grant No. 201955053002 and No. 20185553035).

References

1. Wang, J., Wu, M., Chen, Q., Zheng, Y., Zhu, Y.-H.: Probability complementary transmission scheme for uplink OFDMA-based random access in 802.11ax WLAN. In: 2019 IEEE Wireless Communications and Networking Conference (WCNC), pp. 1–7 (2019). https://doi.org/10.1109/WCNC.2019.8885789
2. Xie, D., Zhang, J., Tang, A., Wang, X.: Multi-dimensional busy-tone arbitration for OFDMA random access in IEEE 802.11ax. IEEE Trans. Wirel. Commun. **19**(6), 4080–4094 (2020). https://doi.org/10.1109/TWC.2020.2979852
3. Lee, W.-J., Shin, W., Ruiz-de-Azua, J.A., Capon, L.F., Park, H., Kim, J.-H.: NOMA-based uplink OFDMA collision reduction in 802.11ax networks. In: 2021 International Conference on Information and Communication Technology Convergence (ICTC), 2021, pp. 212–214 (2021). https://doi.org/10.1109/ICTC52510.2021.9621014
4. Lee, Y.-H., Wu, W.-R.: A WLAN uplink collision-resolving scheme using multi-user beamforming technique. IEEE Trans. Veh. Technol. **69**(10), 11042–11054 (2020). https://doi.org/10.1109/TVT.2020.3007085
5. Feng, Y., Jayasundara, C., Nirmalathas, A., Wong, E.: A feasibility study of IEEE 802.11 HCCA for low-latency applications. IEEE Trans. Commun. **67**(7), 4928–4938 (2019). https://doi.org/10.1109/TCOMM.2019.2910055
6. Lv, Y., et al.: Request-based polling access: investigation of novel wireless LAN MAC scheme for low-latency E-health applications. IEEE Commun. Lett. **23**(5), 896–899 (2019). https://doi.org/10.1109/LCOMM.2019.2903801
7. Bai, J., Fang, H., Suh, J., Aboul-Magd, O., Au, E., Wang, X.: An adaptive grouping scheme in ultra-dense IEEE 802.11ax network using buffer state report based two-stage mechanism. China Commun. **16**(9), 31–44 (2019). https://doi.org/10.23919/JCC.2019.09.003
8. Mukhopadhyay, A., Das, G.: Low complexity fair scheduling in LTE/LTE-A uplink involving multiple traffic classes. IEEE Syst. J. **15**(2), 1616–1627 (2021). https://doi.org/10.1109/JSYST.2020.2991325
9. Bankov, D., Didenko, A., Khorov, E., Lyakhov, A.: OFDMA uplink scheduling in IEEE 802.11ax networks. In: 2018 IEEE International Conference on Communications (ICC), 2018, pp. 1–6 (2018). https://doi.org/10.1109/ICC.2018.8422767
10. Bhattarai, S., Naik, G., Park, J.-M.J.: Uplink resource allocation in IEEE 802.11ax. In: ICC 2019–2019 IEEE International Conference on Communications (ICC), 2019, pp. 1–6 (2019). https://doi.org/10.1109/ICC.2019.8761594
11. Yang, A., Li, B., Yang, M., et al.: Concept and analysis of capacity entropy for uplink multi-user media access control for the next-generation WLANs. Mob. Netw. Appl. **24**, 1572–1586 (2019)
12. Li, B., Sun, K., Yan, Z., et al.: Idea and Theory of Particle Access (2022). arXiv preprint arXiv:2203.15191
13. IEEE Standard for Information Technology-Telecommunications and Information Exchange between Systems Local and Metropolitan Area Networks-Specific Requirements Part 11: Wireless LAN Medium Access Control (MAC) and Physical Layer (PHY) Specifications Amendment 1: Enhancements for High-Efficiency WLAN, In: IEEE Std 802.11ax-2021 (Amendment to IEEE Std 802.11-2020), pp. 1–767, 19 May 2021. https://doi.org/10.1109/IEEESTD.2021.9442429

A Two-Level Adaptive Resource Allocation Algorithm for Quality of Service Guarantee in Home WiFi Networks

ZhanYu Zhang, Bo Li, Zhongjiang Yan[✉], and Mao Yang

School of Electronics and Information, Northwestern Polytechnical University,
Xi'an, China
wjiu@mail.nwpu.edu.cn, {libo.npu,zhjyan,yangmao}@nwpu.edu.cn

Abstract. Aiming at the problem that the service quality of audio and video, large file transmission and other services is difficult to guarantee in the home Wireless Fidelity (WiFi) network, this paper proposes a two-level adaptive resource allocation algorithm for quality of service guarantee (TRAQ), which can effectively avoid the starvation of large file transmission, to improve the success rate of audio and video service establishment and the fairness of multiple large file transmissions. Firstly, the quality-of-service guarantee problem of audio and video, large file transmission is modeled as the resource allocation problem in the scheduling period, with the goal of minimizing the Gini coefficient of multiple large file transmission rates and the constraint of ensuring the average transmission rate of all large files and the call loss rate of audio and video. Then, the arrival and service process of audio and video services is modeled as a M/M/m/m queuing model, and the first-level resource allocation ratio between the audio and video services and the large files services is obtained. Secondly, the second-level resource allocation ratio minimizing the Gini coefficient of large file transmission services is derived. Finally, the simulation results show that the proposed TRAQ not only balances the service requirements between the two types of services, but also achieves a certain transmission fairness within the large file transmission services.

Keywords: Home WiFi Network · TRAQ · Call Loss Rate · Services Starved

1 Introduction

In recent years, Wireless Local Area Network (WLAN) has penetrated into all aspects of life. Institute of Electrical and Electronics Engineers (IEEE) 802.11 WLAN is one of the most deployed wireless networks, and it has developed to IEEE 802.11 ax [2]. In the home network, this wireless network is also the most common one. In the current home WiFi network, there are various of network

D.-J. Deng et al. (Eds.): SGIoT 2022, LNICST 497, pp. 186–199, 2023.
https://doi.org/10.1007/978-3-031-31275-5_19

services, such as video, games, file transfer, etc. They can be divided into two categories according to their characteristics, namely audio and video services and large file transfer services. Among them, the characteristics of audio and video services are that the data transmission bandwidth needs to be guaranteed within a certain period of time. As for the large file transmission services, although they can tolerate the transmission for a period of time, they still need to ensure the transmission rates. Although 802.11 has proposed a scheduling access transmission mode, which characterized by the overall planning of the central control node. But it does not consider the fact that large file transfer services' transmission drops sharply and starves to death as the equipment becomes denser, and the traffic gradually increases.

The current research and related works on scheduling and transmission in 802.11 are as follows. Reference [3] proposed a utility optimization algorithm based on resource migration for the lack of efficient resource allocation methods for scheduling and random hybrid access with IEEE 802.11ax in a single-cell environment. Reference [4–8] analyzed the throughput and other performance of IEEE 802.11 wireless network scenarios in random access mode. Reference [9] designed an enhanced wait-for-select access method based on the access point (AP) scheduling-based framework of the IEEE 802.11ax draft. In reference [10], aiming at the related problems of uplink scheduling in IEEE 802.11ax, it optimized the research method in traditional cellular network and integrated it with the resource allocation of 802.11ax. In order to maximize the uplink transmission throughput, reference [11] combined the uplink transmission demand reporting and the uplink scheduling data transmission, and proposed a related maximization algorithm. References [12–14] studied the related technologies of hybrid access with coexistence of scheduled access and random access in the case of IEEE 802.11ax and 5G.

At present, there are still some problems related to scheduling access in IEEE 802.11ax. The problems to be solved are: 1. Various types of services have different characteristics, and there is no distinction between access services. Therefore, the current resource allocation plan is not targeted for different types of services. 2. There is also an unfair problem between multiple large file transfers. Because different services have different arrival times, varied sizes of files to be transferred, and relative priorities. So the bandwidth allocation between different file transfers is also a very important part.

Aiming at the above problems, this paper proposes a two-level adaptive resource allocation algorithm for quality of service guarantee. This algorithm effectively solves the problem that the completion time of large file transmission services cannot be guaranteed with the increase of audio and video services. This paper's core contributions are as follows: 1. The service guarantee problem of each service in the home WiFi network is modeled as the resource allocation problem in the scheduling period in IEEE 802.11ax. 2. A two-level resource allocation algorithm is proposed. The first level optimizes the ratio between audio and video services and large file transmission services, and the second level makes the allocation between large file services fairer. 3. The two-level resource allocation algorithm is simulated and verified. The results show that the first-level resource allocation algorithm can effectively prevent large file transmission services from being starved to death, and can ensure the access congestion probability of audio and video services. And the second-level resource allocation algorithm has balanced transmission fairness between the various services of large file transmission services.

The structure of the remaining chapters of this paper is arranged as follows. In the second section the composition of the network is first introduced, and the system model of scheduling and transmission under the IEEE 802.11ax architecture is established. In the third Section, a two-level resource allocation algorithm is introduced. Section 4 carries out simulation verification and performance analysis of the proposed two-level resource allocation method. The fifth Section summarizes the full text.

2   System Overview

2.1   Home WiFi Networks

In a wireless home WiFi network, there is often only one router, namely the AP, which is an integral part of the entire network. It is not only responsible for forwarding data, but also needs to download data from the supplier and deliver it to the device according to the needs of the device. Figure 1 shows a basic wireless home WiFi network.

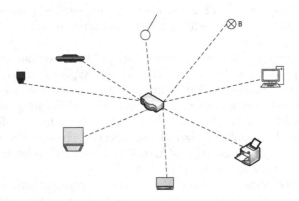

Fig. 1. Home WiFi network

Each wireless devices in the home network sends or receives numerous services through the AP. Currently, according to the characteristics, in the scheduling stage, there are two categories, audio and video services and large file transmission services. Here, the audio and video services is set as a type A service flow, and the large file transmission services is set as a type B service flow. Obviously, type A services need to guarantee their transmission bandwidth. They often have an apply bandwidth to indicate the size of the application. If the AP agrees, it must meet the apply bandwidth size, and reserve the corresponding bandwidth resources on the time-frequency. The type B services does not have such a rigid requirement, and its priority is lower than the type A service. For example, when the device version is updated, the size of the update file is generally above several hundred MBytes.

At present, there are N_A type A services and N_B type B services in the network with the total amount of resources D, all of which are single-hop services. The network channel is ideal, that is, there is no hidden terminal. There is only one AP in the network, and other nodes are called stations (STAs). The services of these STAs are all uplink services. The apply bandwidth of the type A service flow is W, the duration is μ. The size of the packet that needs to be transmitted for the type B service is S_B. The arrivals of the two types of service flows obey the Poisson distribution, and their mean values are λ_A and λ_B respectively. At the same time, the priority of type A is higher than that of type B, so with the addition of type A service flow, the resources transmitted by type B service flow will be compressed step by step until starved to death.

Factors such as different arrival times, data sizes, and priorities of type B services will also lead to greatly different completion times of type B services. According to this parameters, a Gini coefficient G will be used to represent the fairness between the type B service transmissions.

2.2 Transmission Mode of IEEE 802.11ax

With the development of IEEE 802.11, the related content of the 802.11ax protocol has been increasingly improved in recent years. Its representative innovative technology is that IEEE 802.11ax comprehensively enhances the multi-user medium access control (MAC) at the MAC layer. Figure 2 is the architecture of 802.11ax new technologies.

In WLAN, from the perspective of MAC, the current access methods are two types, including scheduling access and random access. In this paper, the access mode is the scheduling access. The scheduling access is that the central control node coordinates the overall situation, controls the access of all subordinate STAs, and allocates resources to the services that agree to access.

With the arrival of services, the AP performs resource scheduling and allocation according to the collected uplink transmission requirements of STAs. For type A service, if the current network resources are still free enough, it will be allowed to transmit data. As for the type B service, it can only use the remaining idle resources for transmission. Therefore, as the service flow increases gradually, the resources obtained by the type B service under the scheduling access are very scarce, the transmission rate R_B cannot be guaranteed, and the completion time becomes indefinite.

Since network resources are limited, and each type A service requires a certain bandwidth. The network resources are divided, and only m type A services can be accessed at the same time. Therefore, the subsequent access of type A will also be rejected due to insufficient resource allocation. The proportion of type

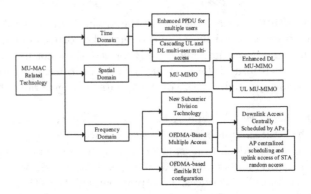

Fig. 2. Architecture of 802.11ax

A service that is denied access within a period of time is the call loss rate, that is, the congestion probability H_A. In this period, the proportion of resources occupied by the type A service is the type A channel utilization rate η.

2.3   Modeling Analysis

According to the analysis in the previous two sections, it is modeled as the resource allocation problem in the scheduling phase in IEEE 802.11ax to analyze and solve it.

The AP notifies each STA of the allocation result of each service in the next period of time in the form of a super frame. With the arrival of type A services, there are n_A services and n_B type B services that need to be scheduled and allocated. According to the priority and the arrival time, resources are allocated to the type A services in sequence. If there is still free time after the allocation, the remaining resources are allocated to the type B services. Figure 3 is a schematic diagram of resource allocation within a super frame in this case.

At this time, the channel utilization rate of type A service can be obtained $\eta = \frac{n_A \times W}{D}, (n_A < m)$, the average transmission rate of type B service $R_B = \frac{(1-\eta) \times D}{n_B}$.

Obviously, when a large number of type A services are accessed, the transmission rate of type B services tends to 0, which leads to the phenomenon of starvation.

The expression of the Gini coefficient G is designed according to its allocation ratio X_i in the remaining resources and the remaining packet size S_i, as well as the priority r_{ij} between each type B according to the priority:

$$G = \frac{\sum_{i,j}^{N} r_{ij}|k_i - k_j|}{\sum_{i,j}^{N} r_{ij}(k_i + k_j)} \tag{1}$$

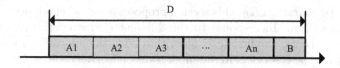

Fig. 3. Resource allocation

The sequence r_{ij} represents the difference in priority of the two types of B services. The priority of type B services is divided into four categories: 0, 1, 2, and 3. The smaller the value, the higher the priority. Its sequence is expressed as the following formula:

$$r_{ij} = \begin{cases} 0, i = j \\ \frac{|priority_i - priority_j|}{3}, i \neq j \end{cases} \tag{2}$$

Among them, k_i represents the time when the ith type B service flow is in this segment of resource Y and the remaining data is sent. Its expression is:

$$k_i = \frac{S_i}{Y \times X_i} \tag{3}$$

The value of Gini coefficient is the goal of algorithm design, G is as low as possible under the condition of ensuring R_B and H_A. As follows, where SET_{max}, SET_{min} are the maximum value of blocking probability and the minimum value of type B transmission rate respectively:

$$\min G = \frac{\sum_{i,j}^{N} r_{ij} |k_i - k_j|}{\sum_{i,j}^{N} r_{ij} (k_i + k_j)}, (i = 0, 1, 2 \cdots n_B, j = 0, 1, 2 \cdots n_B) \tag{4}$$

$$s.t. \quad \begin{aligned} H_A &\leq SET_{max} \\ R_B &\geq SET_{min} \end{aligned} \tag{5}$$

3 Algorithm

3.1 Algorithm Overview

In the second section, we introduced the model of allocating the service under 802.11ax scheduling access. At the same time, it is found that with the gradual increase of type A services, R_B is decreasing, and the phenomenon of starvation occurs.

In order to guarantee R_B, this section proposes a two-level adaptive resource allocation algorithm. In response to the different characteristics and different quality requirements, the first-level algorithm adds the allocation ratio of type A services and type B services in the super frame, effectively solves the starvation problem of type B services. The second-level is to reasonably allocate the total resources of type B according to the parameters such as priority and packet size, so that G is as small as possible. The two-level resource allocation algorithm effectively not only solves the problem of starvation of type B services, but also makes each type B service as fair as possible. It effectively balances the service requirements between type AB services and improves the overall service quality of the network.

3.2   First-Level Algorithm

As can be seen from the above, because the network has the maximum available bandwidth D, the service flow will be scheduled according to the access time. And each accessed service flow will occupy a certain bandwidth W. In terms of the two types of services flow, the occupied size of type A service is determined according to W, while type B services share the remaining idle resources. When the network is busy, it will reject subsequent service flows that want to access. Therefore, the system can be regarded as M/M/m/m queuing system [1], which is a call loss system.

The idea of the first-level algorithm is to change the resource m that provides services for type A and free up space to allocate resources for type B. This algorithm can not only meet the hard transmission requirements of type A services, but also enable type B services to be transmitted as much as possible, to reach a balance. Next, we will analyze the performance of the queuing system without modifying the m value.

Since the network resources only support the access of m type A service flows at most. The state probability p of the current number of type A service services in the network can be calculated. First, the state transition diagram of the M/M/m/m system can be represented as Fig. 4.

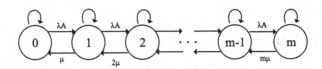

Fig. 4. State transition diagram

We can write the equilibrium equation for this state transition graph.

$$\begin{cases} \lambda_A p_{n-1} = n\mu p_n, n = 0, 1, \cdots, m \\ p_n = p_0 \left(\frac{\lambda_A}{\mu}\right)^n \frac{1}{n!}, n = 0, 1, \cdots, m \end{cases} \tag{6}$$

In this way, the congestion probability H_A is the probability that the subsequent type A access is rejected, that is, the probability that the access type A service flow is equal to m.

$$H_A = p_m = \frac{\frac{(\frac{\lambda_A}{\mu})^m}{m!}}{\sum_{n=0}^{m} \frac{(\frac{\lambda_A}{\mu})^n}{n!}} \tag{7}$$

And using Eq. 7, the busyness of each service time slot, that is, the resource utilization rate η, can be calculated. The formula is:

$$\eta_A = \frac{(1 - H_A) \times \lambda_A}{m \times \mu} \tag{8}$$

Then the bandwidth that can be used by type B is very simple to get from Eq. 9:

$$D_B = (1 - \eta_A) \times m \times W \tag{9}$$

With the increase of λ_A, H_A gradually increases, and R_B decreases greatly. In order to ensure the transmission rate, H_A is not less than the required value, and H_A must be not greater than the required value. Therefore, the first-level algorithm is proposed, which reserves a certain proportion of bandwidth resources to ensure the transmission of type B services, so that the number of resources serving type A services decreases from m to $m*$. New congestion probability H_A* and type B service transmission rate R_B*.

$$H_A* = p_{m*} = \frac{\frac{(\frac{\lambda_A}{\mu})^{m*}}{m*!}}{\sum_{n=0}^{m*} \frac{(\frac{\lambda_A}{\mu})^n}{n!}} \tag{10}$$

$$R_B* = R_{BControl} + R_{BIdle} = \frac{(D - m* \times W) + D_B*}{n_B} \tag{11}$$

From Eq. 11, it is easy to obtain that R_B* will no longer tend to zero. And although H_A* has increased, as long as H_A* is not greater than the limit value, the service quality of the type A service can still be guaranteed. Therefore, the first-level algorithm effectively allocates the proportion of type A and type B services in theory, avoiding the situation that type B services are starved to death.

3.3   Second-Level Algorithm

After coordinating the ratio between the type A services and the type B services to ensure a certain service quality of the two types of services, the average rate of the type B services is guaranteed. However, this method cannot average the completion time of each type B services. If a large file and a small file equally divide the type B services resources during this period, there will be a huge difference in the completion time. It will result in an unfairness between the two type B files.

The second-level resource allocation algorithm effectively solves the unfair problem of each type B business, and its derivation process is as follows.

According to the Gini coefficient given above, in order to make G as small as possible, the allocation ratios of different type B services in the resources are calculated.

To make G as small as possible, first calculate the minimum value in a super frame. First extract the molecular part $k_i - k_j$ in Eq. 1. Analyzing it, we get:

$$|k_i - k_j| = \left| \frac{S_i}{Y \times X_i} - \frac{S_j}{Y \times X_j} \right| \geq 0 \tag{12}$$

After merging it becomes:

$$|S_i \times X_j - S_j \times X_i| \geq 0 \tag{13}$$

Equation 13 can be equal to zero. When it is equal to zero, the denominator and the sequence can be ignored, indicating that the remaining resources are allocated according to the size ratio of the remaining data among the type B service flows. After such allocation, G in the super frame is zero, which achieves a certain degree of fairness.

Then the allocation ratio of type B services in type B resources is as follows:

$$\frac{S_1}{X_1} = \frac{S_2}{X_2} = \cdots = \frac{S_{n_B}}{X_{n_B}} = k \tag{14}$$

When assigned as Eq. 14, the Gini coefficient is equal to:

$$G = \frac{\sum_{i,j}^{N} r_{ij} |k_i - k_j|}{\sum_{i,j}^{N} r_{ij} (k_i + k_j)} = \frac{\sum_{i,j}^{N} r_{ij} |\frac{k}{Y} - \frac{k}{Y}|}{\sum_{i,j}^{N} r_{ij} (k_i + k_j)} = 0 \tag{15}$$

At this time, in each superframe, G reaches the minimum value.

The second-level algorithm achieves the fairness of the completion time of each type B service flow in general by achieving the fairness of different type B services in a single superframe.

Algorithm 1 Two-level Resource Allocation Algorithm.

Input:

    Total resources, D

    Established type A service, $Est_A = E_{A1}, E_{A2}, \cdots, E_{An}$;

    Established type B service, $Est_B = E_{B1}, E_{B2}, \cdots, E_{Bn}$;

    New arrival type A service, $New_A = C_{A1}, C_{A2}, \cdots, C_{Am}$;

    New arrival type B service, $New_B = C_{B1}, C_{B2}, \cdots, C_{Bm}$;

    Resource allocation result, $R = 0, 0, \cdots, 0$;

    Type B service size, $Size_B = S_{B1}, S_{B2}, \cdots, S_{Bm+n}$;

    Maximum number of type A after guarantee, $m*$;

Output:

    Resource allocation result, R;

1: BEGIN
2: Reserve type B service resources according to $m*$
3:   FOR each $i \in [1, m*]$ DO
4:       FOR each $j \in Est_A$ DO
5:          IF $(i \leq m*)$ THEN
6:             $R(i) = Est_{Aj}$
7:             $i++$
8:          ELSE
9:             BREAK
10:        ENDIF
11:      ENDFOR
12:     New_A is the same as Est_A
13:   ENDFOR
14: Set B ratio according to size
15: $Size = S_{B1} + S_{B2} \cdots + S_{Bm+n}$
16: FOR each $i \in Size_B$ DO
17:     $R(Bi) = S_{Bi} \div Size \times (D - m*)$
18: ENDFOR
19: **return** R;

3.4 Two-Level Resource Allocation Algorithm

With the arrival of the service in the network, the central control node allocates resources according to the rules of the two-level resource allocation algorithm, and allocates the resources in a superframe to the established and newly established AB type service flows in the service table in an orderly manner. The specific algorithm pseudocode is in this page.

4 Simulation

4.1 Simulation Platform Construction

Simulation tests are carried out in C++ software to verify the relevant performance optimization of the above two-level algorithm. Set the AP as the central control node. If there is a service request, it will directly check the busyness of the allocated time slot. If it is all busy, it means that the service is rejected. And at the same time, it will allocate resources to the accessed service. After this setting, the effect of simulating service flow scheduling access is achieved.

4.2   Simulation Results

In order to verify the relative performance improvement of the two-level resource allocation algorithm, test verification is carried out under a Basic Service Set (BSS). It is verified that under the same resources, the average rate of the type B service gradually decreases with the access intensity of the type A service λ_A.

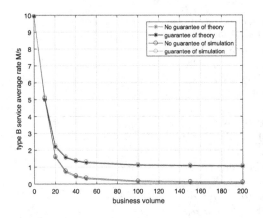

Fig. 5. Whether to guarantee the type B rate change

The abscissa in Fig. 5 is the product of the access intensity of type A services λ_A and the service time. The ordinate is the average transmission rate of type B services. It can be clearly seen from the figure that in theory and simulation, under the circumstance that type B service resources are guaranteed, as the service intensity increases, the rate can be guaranteed, and it will not tend to zero and cause starvation.

After ensuring R_B and H_A, the service quality between the two types of services is guaranteed. The second-level resource allocation algorithm makes the completion time of individual type B services as fair as possible. By changing the access intensity λ_B of type B services, the change of the total G under different λ_B is verified.

As can be seen from Fig. 6, under different type B guaranteed resource values, the difference between the Gini coefficients under the ratio of the remaining size of the package and the uniform distribution is obtained. It can be clearly seen from the curve that this algorithm effectively reduces the Gini coefficient, indicating that the transmission of each type B service is more fair.

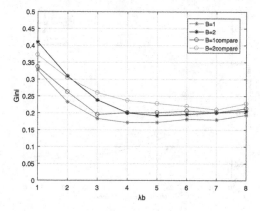

Fig. 6. Variation of Gini coefficient with type B service intensity

With the change of type B guaranteed resources, H_A will change to a certain extent, and according to the requirements, H_A should not be greater than the set value, and H_A under different guaranteed bandwidths is simulated and verified. The result is shown in Fig. 7.

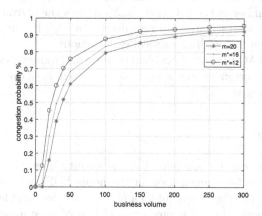

Fig. 7. Variation of congestion probability under different B service guarantees

It can be seen from Fig. 7 that the increase of type B guaranteed resources will indeed increase the congestion probability H_A. Therefore, while ensuring the transmission rate of type B services, the congestion probability of access to type A services should be reduced as much as possible, to achieve a certain balance between the two types of business.

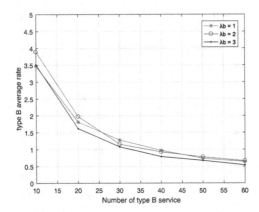

Fig. 8. Variation of type B average rate with type B service intensity

The optimization of the Gini coefficient has been verified and tested, and the overall Gini coefficient is made as small as possible. But the specific performance of different type B services cannot be seen in the Gini coefficient. Next, the transmission completion time of different type B services is simulated.

It can be seen from Fig. 8 that under different λ_B, R_B changes with the increase of the number of type B services. λ_B affects the arrival time of type B services. It can be seen the average rate decreases with the increase of type B services, which is in line with theoretical expectations.

To sum up, TRAQ solves the problem of more and more services in the home WiFi network to a certain extent, and effectively guarantees the different quality of service requirements.

5   Conclusion

This paper focuses on the problem that the quality of services such as audio and video and large file transmission in the home WiFi network is difficult to guarantee. Firstly, the distinctive audio and video services and large file services are divided. Subsequently, the queuing model is used to systematically analyze the performance of two types of services in scenarios. Next, the core ideas of TRAQ are introduced respectively.

Finally, the simulation verifies the performance optimization of the proposed TRAQ. The simulation results show that the first-level ensures the access of the audio and video service. At the same time, the average transmission rate of the large file transmission service will not be lower than the minimum value. The second-level algorithm effectively ensures the fairness between different large file transmission services. To sum up, the proposed TRAQ guarantees the service quality requirements of the business from two aspects, and effectively alleviates the starvation phenomenon of the large file transmission services.

Acknowledgement. This work was supported in part by the National Natural Science Foundations of CHINA (Grant No. 61771392, No. 61771390 and No. 61871322), and Science and Technology on Avionics Integration Laboratory and the Aeronautical Science Foundation of China (Grant No. 201955053002 and No. 20185553035).

References

1. Li, J., Sheng, M.: Fundamental of Communication Networks, 1st edn. Higher Education Press, Beijing (2004)
2. Lin, W., Li, B., Yang, M.: Integrated link-system level simulation platform for the next generation WLAN-IEEE 802.11 ax. In: 2016 IEEE Global Communications Conference (GLOBECOM), pp. 1–7. IEEE (2016)
3. Yang, A., Li, B.: Research on multiple access control technology for maximizing multi-user joint carrying capacity in unlicensed band. Northwestern Polytechnical University, PhD dissertation (2020)
4. Bianchi, G.: Performance analysis of the IEEE 802.11 distributed coordination function. IEEE J. Sel. Areas Commun. **18**(3), 535–547 (2000)
5. Li, B., Battiti, R.: Analysis of the IEEE 802.11 DCF with service differentiation support in non-saturation conditions. In: Solé-Pareta, J., et al. (eds.) ICQT/QofIS/WQoSR -2004. LNCS, vol. 3266, pp. 64–73. Springer, Heidelberg (2004). https://doi.org/10.1007/978-3-540-30193-6_7
6. Prakash, G., Thangaraj, P.: Throughput analysis of IEEE 802.11e EDCA under non saturation condition. In: 2011 3rd International Conference on Electronics Computer Technology, pp. 117–121 (2011)
7. Shafiul Kabir Chowdhury, N.M., Hussain, M.S., Ahmed, F.: Theoretical maximum throughput of IEEE 802.11e EDCA mechanism. In: 2010 13th International Conference on Computer and Information Technology (ICCIT), pp. 606–611 (2010)
8. Yazid, M., Ksentini, A., Bouallouche-Medjkoune, L., Aïssani, D.: Performance analysis of the TXOP sharing mechanism in the VHT IEEE 802.11ac WLANs. IEEE Commun. Lett. **18**(9), 1599–1602 (2014)
9. Er-Rahmadi, B., Ksentini, A., Meddour, D.E.: Enhanced uplink multi-users scheduling for future 802.11ax networks: wait-to-pick-as-available enhanced. In: Wireless Communications and Mobile Computing, pp. 3104–3122 (2016)
10. Bankov, D., Khorov, E., Lyakhov, A.: OFDMA uplink scheduling in IEEE 802.11ax networks. In: IEEE International Conference on Communications (ICC), pp. 1–6 (2018)
11. Bhattarai, S., Naik, G., Park, J.: Uplink resource allocation in IEEE 802.11ax. In: IEEE International Conference on Communications (ICC), pp. 1–6 (2019)
12. Ding, Z., Member, S., Fan, P., et al.: Simple semi-grant-free transmission strategies assisted by non-orthogonal multiple access. IEEE Trans. Commun. **67**(6), 4464–4478 (2019)
13. Choi, J., Seo, J.B.: Evolutionary game for hybrid uplink NOMA with truncated channel inversion power control. IEEE Trans. Commun. **67**(12), 8655–8665 (2019)
14. Yang, M., Li, B., Bai, Z., et al.: SGMA: semi-granted multiple access for non-orthogonal multiple access (NOMA) in 5G networking. J. Netw. Comput. Appl. **112**, 115–125 (2018)

Joint Energy Detection and Transmission Power Adjustment for FIM Problem in High Density WLANs

Yujie Wang, Qi Yang, Mao Yang$^{(\boxtimes)}$, Zhongjiang Yan, and Bo Li

School of Electronics and Information, Northwestern Polytechnical University, Xi'an, China
wwangyujie@mail.nwpu.edu.cn, {yangqi,yangmao,zhjyan,libo.npu}@nwpu.edu.cn

Abstract. With the rapid development of mobile internet services, the intensive deployment of wireless local area network (WLAN) is inevitable. Traditional WLAN uses carrier sense/collision avoidance (CSMA/CA) mechanism to avoid interference between links as much as possible. In the multi access points (APs) scenario, the traditional CSMA/CA may lead to the flow in the middle (FIM) problem, resulting in a sharp reduction in the throughput of the intermediate nodes and affecting the fairness of the whole network. Existing researches have shown that the FIM problem is more serious in the high density WLAN network. The existing researches on the FIM problem mainly focus on the dynamic optimization of a single parameter, the fairness and performance of the network cannot be well guaranteed. Therefore, this paper proposes a FIM oriented down link (DL) multi-parameter joint dynamic control scheme. AP as a centralized controller, regularly obtains the transmission status of the whole network, reduces the transmission opportunities of the strong AP through adaptive dynamic power and energy detection threshold control (A-DPEC) algorithm, and improves the transmission opportunities of the starvation AP, so as to achieve the performance and fair balance of the whole network. The simulation results show that the proposed scheme outperforms the comparing schemes.

Keywords: Wireless Local Area Networks · CSMA/CA · FIM · Dynamic Control

1 Introduction

With the rapid development of mobile internet services, the intensive deployment of WLAN network [1] has become inevitable. The high density deployment scenario is the main scenario faced by the next generation WLAN [2], and the intensive deployment of network will inevitably produce a variety of conflicts and interference [3,4]. Therefore, how to improve and effectively solve the problems of conflicts and interference under the high density WLAN deployment scenario has become particularly important.

D.-J. Deng et al. (Eds.): SGIoT 2022, LNICST 497, pp. 200–213, 2023.
https://doi.org/10.1007/978-3-031-31275-5_20

In high density WLAN networks, the overlapping basic service set (OBSS) [5] areas formed by overlapping multiple APs have increased significantly. Unfair competition and conflicts among OBSS users may lead to a decline in network throughput [6], which directly affects the quality of service (QoS) of users [7]. Among them, FIM problem is a typical interference problem in high density WLAN networks. It is mainly because when the network is dense, some intermediate nodes lack transmission opportunities, resulting in insufficient throughput, while their neighbor nodes obtain higher throughput, which affects the fairness of the whole network. Therefore, the core research of this paper is to improve the interference caused by FIM problem, develop appropriate solutions to improve the fairness of high density WLAN network and ensure network performance.

For FIM problem, the existing researches have the following solutions: Yin et al. [8] and Shimizu et al. [9] take the game theory as the core to ensure that different APs use different channels for information transmission, so as to improve the fairness between nodes and alleviate the FIM problem. Stojanova et al. [10] combines Markov chain to conduct theoretical analysis and simulation verification on the FIM problem. Potti et al. [11] combines genetic algorithm and gravitational search algorithm to find the optimal solution to adjust the contention window(CW) to ensure throughput and improve fairness. Fitzgerald et al. [12] improves the fairness of the whole network by classifying MAC queues and adjusting CW. Jang et al. [13] and Masri et al. [14] adopts rate control method to reduce the rate of strong nodes, increase the rate of starvation nodes, and improve the transmission opportunities of starvation nodes to improve the FIM problem. The existing researches have shown that dynamic optimization of parameters through algorithms can significantly improve the throughput of starvation nodes in high density scenarios, but there are still two problems: 1) existing algorithms for FIM problem mainly focus on the dynamic optimization of a single parameter in the network, and do not fully guarantee the performance and fairness of the network. 2) few researches have considered the adaptive dynamic adjustment of parameters from the FIM problem.

Thus, this paper proposes a dynamic management and control scheme based on tranmission power control and ED threshold adjustment. Starting from the technical root causes, combined with multi-parameter dynamic adjustment, this scheme solves and improves the FIM problem. The core idea of this scheme is that each AP regularly collects its own information and summarizes it to the centralized controller. The centralized controller makes a decision through comprehensive judgment of FIM index, and adjusts the dynamic tranmission power and ED threshold of the corresponding AP. The simulation results show that changing the node power and ED threshold dynamically can effectively solve the unfair problem between users caused by FIM problem, and improve the throughput and fairness of the whole network.

The sections of this paper are arranged as follows: Sect. 1 introduces the research background, research content and section arrangement of this paper. Section 2 briefly analyzes the FIM problem from the technical root causes and introduces the current research status of the FIM problem in detail. Section 3 introduces the joint energy detection and transmission power adjustment scheme in detail. In the Sect. 4, the performance of the proposed scheme is analyzed. Section 5 summarizes this paper.

2   FIM Problem Analysis and Related Work

2.1   FIM Problem Analysis

The FIM problem is that in high Density WLAN networks, due to the different perceptions of intermediate nodes and neighbor nodes, neighbor nodes continuously send packets to suppress intermediate node packets, so that the current node lacks transmission opportunities, resulting in the current node starvation.

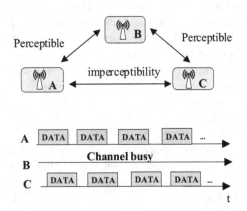

Fig. 1. FIM problem scenario

The specific scenario is shown in Fig. 1. Node A, node B and node C all use the same transmission power and clear channel assessment (CCA) threshold [15], in which node B, node A and node C can perceive, That is, the received signal strength indicator (RSSI) is greater than the ED threshold, but node A and node C cannot perceive it, that is, the RSSI is less than the CCA threshold, so node A and node C can simultaneously back off from the competitive channel to transmit data. However, for node B, if one of the neighboring nodes transmits data, node C will perceive that the channel is busy, It waits until the channel is idle. This situation causes node A and node C to preempt the channel with a high probability, and node B is difficult to preempt the channel, resulting in "starvation" of node B.

2.2 Related Work

At present, there have been many researches on FIM problem in the academic world. Figure 2 shows the existing researches structure of FIM. This section discusses the five aspects of Channel and Bandwidth selection, CW adjustment, Upper layer rate control, Power adjustment and CCA adjustment.

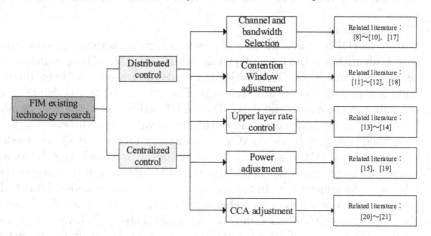

Fig. 2. Structure chart of existing technology research on FIM

(1) Channel and Bandwidth Selection

Yin et al. [8] proposes a distributed channel allocation scheme based on the idea of game theory, which mainly builds the system into a game model and uses spatial adaptive play (SAP) to find the Nash equilibrium point. In this scheme, each AP, as a decision-maker, randomly finds a channel, collects the working channels of two adjacent nodes, and randomly selects a user in each round. The selected users calculate their own benefits according to the benefit function, so as to update their channels based on the benefits. The newly updated channels make the "three-point interference unit" corresponding to the FIM problem as few as possible, so as to improve the FIM problem. Shimizu et al. [9] is still based on the idea of game theory. By designing an exact potential game (EPG), AP and STA as participants, collect channel conditions and CCA values, and calculate the gains. Participants adjust channel and spatial reuse capabilities according to the gains to alleviate node starvation. In the aspect of channel allocation, most of the existing researches are based on game theory to make decisions to obtain benefits and then optimize channel allocation. Stojanova et al. [10] proposed a Markov chain model to predict the throughput of each AP in WLAN according to the performance of the network topology of FIM problem and the throughput requirements of the AP. The model can be used for channel allocation. After the topology is given, it is concluded that large bandwidth is beneficial to throughput and small bandwidth is beneficial to fairness.

Xue et al. [17] allocates channels by setting thresholds and combining the queue conditions of nodes. It mainly calculates the weight according to the size of the queue and compares it with the set threshold. Only nodes higher than the threshold can be arranged for channels. When the queue length is reduced below the threshold, the algorithm ensures that the channel is switched in a very short time, so as to dynamically alleviate starvation nodes.

(2) CW Adjustment

Potti et al. [11] combines the hybrid genetic algorithm with the gravitational search algorithm (GSA) to adaptively adjust the CW. The population is generated through the GSA, multiple rounds of crossover, and continuous mutation to seek the optimal solution. The fitness function is determined according to the end-to-end delay. During CW adjustment, the best cwmin is selected for the node according to the fitness value of the fitness function. Fitzgerald et al. [12] divides MAC queues into control queue (CQ) and media access queue (MAQ). The main adjustment idea is that the longer the MAQ queue, the larger the CW, the shorter the MAQ queue, and the smaller the CW, so as to achieve the purpose of improving starvation nodes. Lim et al. [18] proposes a new detection technology for FIM problem, mainly through the physical energy detection mechanism implemented in WLAN to identify whether the node is in FIM state. If the node is in FIM state, it can intervene by adjusting CW within the set time to improve the channel access rate of starvation nodes.

(3) Upper Layer Rate Control

Jang et al. [13] classifies the states of a single STA, constructs a Markov model, obtains the steady-state probability, and calculates the throughput. On the basis of theoretical analysis, an upper layer rate control algorithm is proposed. The main idea is to set appropriate throughput threshold and rate threshold, reduce the speed of strong nodes through upper layer rate control, and increase the speed of starvation nodes, so as to improve the transmission opportunities of starvation nodes. Masri et al. [14] proposes an overhead free congestion control scheme (NICC), which generates no additional overhead so that nodes can inform each other of the congestion degree, and then the source node uses the enhanced additive increase multiplicative decrease (AIMD) algorithm to perform rate control. The rate control algorithm adjusts the congestion information received by the source node, The higher the degree of congestion, the greater the rate adjustment. However, the adjustment is not a blind adjustment, but is subject to the time limit set in NICC to avoid unnecessary rate adjustment, so as to alleviate FIM problem.

(4) Power Control

Mhatre et al. [15] proposed a power control algorithm based on Gibbs sampler. The core idea of the algorithm is to collect the throughput and CCA threshold values of each node, obtain the solution that minimizes the potential delay in combination with Gibbs sampler, and determine the optimal transmission power of each node. Akella et al. [19] analyzes the impact of power adjustment on the network in detail, and adjusts each node according to the network state. If the node state is bad, it will increase the power, otherwise it will reduce the power, so as to eliminate the starvation nodes.

(5) CCA Adjustment

Li et al. [20] considers that in IEEE 802.11, when a node detects a sensing range (SR) frame on the medium, it will delay the transmission for a fixed duration, which is unfair to the node. To solve this problem, the reference proposes an enhanced carrier sensing scheme, which distinguishes based on the length of the SR frame and then carries out the corresponding delayed transmission. Zaheeruddin et al. [21] analyzes in detail the impact of CCA adjustment on network throughput. The literature proves that it is necessary to consider the MAC layer and CCA across layers to optimize the network.

The channel and bandwidth selection method can reasonably allocate the channel to some extent, but the convergence time in the game theory model is long, and the improvement effect is not obvious. The upper layer rate control method directly regulates the nodes by obtaining the network status. The control effect is obvious, but it is difficult to implement due to the design of cross layer processing. Starting from the access mechanism, the CW adjustment method can alleviate the problem of node starvation. However, due to the randomness of the selection of the CW, the effect is difficult to guarantee. The power adjustment method can improve the performance of starvation nodes, but a single power adjustment can not guarantee the performance of the whole network. For the FIM problem, there is only a single theoretical research on CCA adjustment at present, and no technical implementation has been carried out by scholars.

3 FIM Joint Multi-parameter Adjustment Scheme

This paper mainly studies the downlink FIM problem. The proposed A dynamic scheme of multi-parameter joint adjustment which is mainly divided into three parts, namely, Data statistics and collection stage, FIM problem Recognition stage and A-DPEC adjustment algorithm stage. The specific scheme is described as follows:

3.1 Data Statistics and Collection Stage

Each AP regularly statistics its own network status information and completes data collection. The set is represented by A, $A = \{t, \bar{T}, R_{rssi}\}$, which contains the channel contention time, average rate and RSSI of the previous time period. The channel contention time is expressed in t, and the calculation formula is as follows:

$$t = \frac{\sum_{j=1}^{N} t_j}{N} \tag{1}$$

where N is the total number of retreats of the current node. t_j is the duration of the j-th retreat.

The average rate is expressed as $\bar{T}$. The unit is Mbps and the calculation formula is as follows:

$$\bar{T} = \frac{rxbytes}{T_{period}} \tag{2}$$

where $rxbytes$ is the total number of bytes successfully received by the node, and T_{period} is the set time period.

After the collection, each AP is summarized to the centralized manager through the control frame. AP1, as the centralized manager, is responsible for data collection and calculation. The control frame designed in the scheme is modified based on the frame format proposed in IEEE 802.11ax draft. The specific frame structure is shown in Fig. 3. Data is filled in the user information of the control frame, in which the channel contention time accounts for 2 bits, the average rate accounts for 1 bit, and RSSI is filled according to the number of APs.

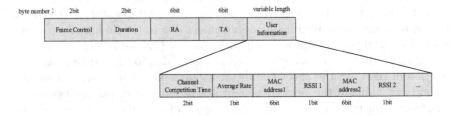

Fig. 3. Control Frame Structure

3.2   FIM Problem Recognition Stage

After obtaining the transmission information of APs. Using the average rate index and the improved Kuznets index to recognize the FIM problem nodes.

Based on the maximum average rate of the current node, $\bar{T}_h$ of 0.5 as the threshold, using $\bar{T}_f$ to represent, lower than $\bar{T}_f$ node, is judged as starvation node.

The Kuznets ratio is an index reflecting the overall income inequality. Combining RSSI and channel contention time, the improved recognitionn index formula of FIM problem based on Kuznets ratio is as follows:

$$R_i = \sum_{i=1}^{n} r_{ij} (t_i - t_j) \tag{3}$$

where i represents the i-th node. Where n represents the number of nodes.t_i and t_j are channel contention time for nodes i and j, r_{ij} Related factors for node i and node j. $r_{ij} \in [0,1]$. It represents whether the nodes need to compare. 0

represents no correlation between nodes, without comparison. 1 represents strong correlation between nodes, must be compared. r_{ij} defined as follows:

$$r_{ij} = \begin{cases} 0, R_{rssi} < C_{cca} \\ \frac{R_{rssi}+C_{cca}}{E_{ed}-C_{cca}}, C_{cca} \leq R_{rssi} \leq E_{ed} \\ 1, R_{rssi} > C_{cca} \end{cases} \tag{4}$$

where E_{ed} is the energy detection threshold, and C_{cca} is the carrier sensing threshold. Specific FIM recognition algorithm are as follows:

Algorithm 1. FIM Recognition Algorithm.

Input:
   Average rate,$\bar{T}_i$;
   Average rate threshold, $\bar{T}_f$;
   The number of node, n;
   Kuznets inex,R_i;
   Minimum Kuznets index,R_l;
Output:
   The states of node, n_i;
1: BEGIN
2: FOR each $i \in [1, n]$ DO
3:     IF $(\bar{T}_i < \bar{T}_f)$ THEN
4:         IF $(\bar{R}_i - \bar{R}_l > \bar{R}_t)$ THEN
5:             $n_i = 1$
6:         ELSE
7:             $n_i = 0$
8:         ENDIF
9:     ELSE
10:        $n_i = 0$
11:    ENDIF
12: ENDFOR
13: **return** n_i;

$\bar{R}_t$ is taken as the empirical value of 0.4. If the difference of the node is greater than $\bar{R}_t$, the node is considered to be a starvation node. Nodes meeting average rate index and Kuznets ratio index are determined as starvation nodes.

3.3   A-DPEC Adjustment Algorithm

Adaptive Dynamic Power and ED Control (A-DPEC) algorithm is based on the operation status of each AP to adaptively adjust the corresponding AP transmission power and ED threshold. T_p represents the original transmit power, E_d represents the original energy detection threshold. i represents the AP index. n_i represents the node state. If $n_i = 0$, it means that there is no FIM problem with node i. If $n_i = 1$, it means that there is FIM problem with node i. d is adjustment parameters, which value is 10.

Algorithm 2. A - DPEC Adjustment Algorithm.

Input:
    The time of slot,t_i;
    The time of simulation,t;
Output:
    The Adjustment of power value, tp_c;
    The Adjustment of Energy Detection Threshold ,ed_c;
1: BEGIN
2: FOR $t = t_j, j = 1, 2...n_{slot}$ DO
3:      IF $n_i = 0$ THEN
4:          $ed_c = d \times abs(R_t - R_i)$
5:      the current node is saturated and the power Adjusted
6:             IF $tp_i > tp$ THEN
7:               $tp_i = tp$
8:      ELSE
9:          $tp_c = d \times abs(R_t - R_i)$
10:     the current node is starvation and the ED Adjusted
11:          IF $ed_i < ed$ THEN
12:             $ed_i = ed$
13:    ENDIF
14: ENDFOR
15: **return** ed_c, tp_c;
16: $ed_i - > ed_i - ed_c$ Update ED value
17: $tp_i - > tp_i + tp_c$ Update the power value

The specific steps of the algorithm are as follows:

In the A-DPEC algorithm, it is proposed to adjust the parameter of starving nodes in the whole network according to the Kuznets index, which not only improves the throughput performance of nodes with high starving degree, but also ensures the throughput of other nodes. Because the algorithm is adjusted and improved according to the operation state of the whole network. In order to avoid the ED threshold and power of nodes that cannot be restored after adjustment, the check mechanism is added to the algorithm to ensure fairness.

4   Performance Evaluation

4.1   Simulation Scenario and Parameter Setting

In this paper, the protocol standard built on the basis of NS-3 [22,23] is used as the integrated system & link level simulation platformof [24,25] the next generation WLAN [22]. The cell radius is 10 m and STA nodes are randomly distributed. The specific scenario is shown in Fig. 4. Figure 4(a) is 3AP simulation scenario, and the distance between each AP and its neighbor AP is 40 m. Figure 4(b) shows the 6AP simulation scenario, and the circles with the same color are cells with the same frequency.

The simulation parameters are shown in Table 1.

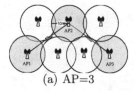
(a) AP=3

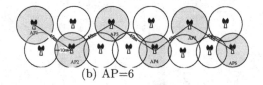
(b) AP=6

Fig. 4. Simulation Scenario

Table 1. Simulation Parameter.

Simulation Parameter	Parameter Setting
Tx Power	15 dBm
Channel bandwidth	40 MHz
RTS/CTS	open
SIFS	16us
DIFS	34us
Channel Position	36
Business Rate	1e8Mbps
Business Type	DL
MCS	9
Maximum frame aggregation length	65535
MPDU Frame Aggregation Number	21
NSS	2
CCA Threshold	−82 dBm
ED Threshold	−62 dBm

4.2   Simulation Results and Analysis

In this simulation, IEEE 802.11ax [2,20] and O-DCF scheme [12] of DL are used as comparison schemes respectively.

Figure 5 shows the performance comparison of 802.11ax, O-DCF scheme and FIM scheme when the number of AP is 3. When the number of AP is 3, the throughput of starvation AP is 405.23% higher than that of 802.11ax after using O-DCF scheme. The throughput of starvation AP is 330.65% higher than that of 802.11ax after using FIM scheme, and the total throughput of FIM scheme is 4.76% higher than that of O-DCF scheme. The channel contention time of starvation AP in O-DCF scheme is 250 times lower than that of 802.11 ax, and the channel contention time of starvation AP in FIM scheme is 2.8 times lower than that of 802.11 ax. The range of channel contention time of O-DCF scheme is 6.48, and the range of channel contention time of FIM scheme is 1.06. Compared with the fairness index of FIM, compared with 802.11ax and O-DCF, the gap of all node indexes of FIM scheme is smaller, and the whole network tends to be more equitable.

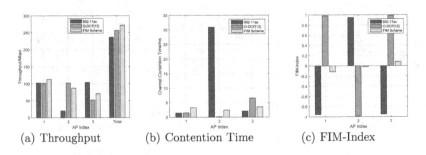

(a) Throughput   (b) Contention Time   (c) FIM-Index

Fig. 5. AP = 3 Performance comparison diagram

Figure 6 shows the performance comparison of 802.11ax, O-DCF scheme and FIM scheme when the AP number is 6. When the AP number is 6, the throughput of O-DCF scheme for starvation AP in 802.11ax increases by 178.9%, the throughput of FIM scheme for starvation AP increases by 162.3%, and the total throughput of FIM scheme increases by 5.9% compared with that of O-DCF scheme. The channel contention time of starvation AP in O-DCF scheme is 28 times lower than that of 802.11 ax, and the channel contention time of starvation AP in FIM scheme is 15 times lower than that of 802.11 ax. The range of channel contention time of O-DCF scheme is 4.56, and the range of channel contention time of FIM scheme is 2.59. Compared with the fairness index of FIM, compared with 802.11ax and O-DCF, the gap of all node indexes of FIM scheme is smaller, and the whole network tends to be more equitable.

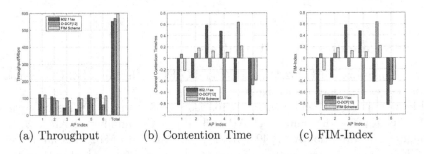

(a) Throughput   (b) Contention Time   (c) FIM-Index

Fig. 6. AP = 6 Performance comparison diagram

Figure 7 shows the performance comparison of 802.11ax, O-DCF scheme and FIM scheme when the AP number is 9. When the AP number is 9, the throughput of O-DCF scheme increases by 314.12% compared with that of 802.11ax starvation AP, the throughput of FIM scheme increases by 268.72% compared with that of 802.11ax, the total throughput of FIM scheme increases by 19.73% compared with that of O-DCF scheme, and the total throughput of O-DCF scheme decreases by 0.35% compared with that of 802.11ax. Compared with the fairness index of FIM, compared with 802.11ax and O-DCF, the gap of all node indexes of FIM scheme is smaller, and the whole network tends to be more equitable. Compared with the channel contention time, O-DCF scheme can greatly reduce the waiting time of starvation AP in the channel and greatly improve the transmission probability of the node. Compared with the FIM scheme, the O-DCF scheme has a great effect on the performance improvement of starvation AP in FIM problem. The main reason is that the O-DCF scheme adopts the method of adjusting the CW to dynamically adjust the CW. The selection of the CW is random and the result is unstable. With the increase of the cell number, the O-DCF scheme is difficult to guarantee the whole network throughput performance.

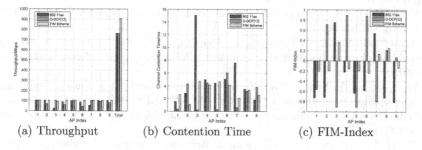

(a) Throughput   (b) Contention Time   (c) FIM-Index

Fig. 7. AP = 9 Performance comparison diagram

Compared with the O-DCF scheme, the FIM scheme in this paper can not only improve the throughput of starvation AP, but also ensure that the performance of other AP in the whole network will not be greatly affected. The main reason is that the FIM dynamic control scheme continuously controls AP with a short time slot, and can flexibly adjust the access probability of AP to ensure the performance of the whole network.

5   Conclusion

In order to solve the problem of FIM in high density WLAN network and improve the fairness and performance of WLAN network, this paper proposes a scheme based on power control and ED threshold adjustment. By recognizing starvation nodes and other nodes, the ED threshold and transmission power of corresponding nodes are dynamically adjusted to weaken the ability of strong nodes and enhance the performance of weak nodes. Through simulation, it is found that the throughput of the FIM scheme is increased by 19.73% compared with that of the O-DCF scheme, and the throughput of the total throughput of the network is increased by 330.65% compared with that of the 802.11ax, which effectively improves the performance of the starvation nodes and ensures the fairness of the whole network. This design is simple and easy to implement, and has good application prospect and value in high density WLAN network.

Acknowledgement. This work was supported in part by the National Natural Science Foundations of CHINA (Grant No. 61871322, No. 61771392, and No. 61771390), and Science and Technology on Avionics Integration Laboratory and the Aeronautical Science Foundation of China (Grant No. 20185553035, and No. 201955053002).

References

1. López-Raventós, Á., Bellalta, B.: Concurrent decentralized channel allocation and access point selection using multi-armed bandits in multi BSS WLANs. Comput. Netw. (2020)
2. Qu, Q., Li, B., Yang, M., Yan, Z., Yang, A., Yu, J., et al.: Survey and Performance Evaluation of the Upcoming Next Generation WLAN Standard - IEEE 802.11ax (2018)
3. Yang, M., Li, B.: Survey and perspective on extremely high throughput (EHT) WLAN—IEEE 802.11be. Mob. Netw. Appl. **25**(2) (2020)
4. Barrachina-Munoz, S., Wilhelmi, F., Bellalta, B.: To overlap or not to overlap: enabling channel bonding in high-density WLANs. Comput. Netw. **152**, 40–53 (2018)
5. Yang, M., Li, B., Yan, Z., Yan, Y.: AP coordination and full-duplex enabled multi-band operation for the next generation WLAN: IEEE 802.11be (EHT). In: 2019 11th International Conference on Wireless Communications and Signal Processing (WCSP). IEEE (2019)
6. Zhong, Z., Kulkarni, P., Cao, F., Fan, Z., Armour, S.: Issues and challenges in dense WiFi networks. In: Wireless Communications & Mobile Computing Conference IEEE (2015)
7. Nj, M., Sahib, S., Suryana, N., Hussin, B.: RTS/CTS Framework Paradigm and WLAN Qos provisioning methods. Int. J. Adv. Comput. Sci. Appl. **8**(2) (2017)
8. Bo, Y., Kamiya, S., Yamamoto, K., Nishio, T., Abeysekera, H.: Starvation mitigation for dense WLANs through distributed channel selection: potential game approach. In: 2017 14th IEEE Annual Consumer Communications & Networking Conference (CCNC). IEEE (2017)
9. Shimizu, H., Yin, B., Yamamoto, K., Iwata, M., Abeysekera, H.: Joint channel selection and spatial reuse for starvation mitigation in IEEE 802.11ax WLANs. In: 2019 IEEE 90th Vehicular Technology Conference (VTC2019-Fall). IEEE (2019)
10. Stojanova, M., Begin, T., Busson, A.: A Markov model for performance evaluation of channel bonding in IEEE 802.11, p. 102449 (2021)
11. Potti, B., Subramanyam, M.V., Prasad, K.S.: Hybrid Genetic Optimization to Mitigate Starvation in Wireless Mesh Networks (2015)
12. Fitzgerald, E., Körner, U., Landfeldt, B.: An analytic model for throughput optimal distributed coordination function (TO-DCF). Telecommun. Syst. **66**(2), 197–215 (2017). https://doi.org/10.1007/s11235-017-0275-6
13. Jang, H., Yun, S.Y., Shin, J., Yi, Y.: Game theoretic perspective of optimal CSMA. IEEE Trans. Wirel. Commun. 1 (2018)
14. Masri, A.E., Sardouk, A., Khoukhi, L., Hafid, A., Gaiti, D.: Neighborhood-aware and overhead-free congestion control for IEEE 802.11 wireless mesh networks. Wirel. Commun. IEEE Trans. **13**(10), 5878–5892 (2014)
15. Mhatre, V.P., Papagiannaki, K., Baccelli, F.: Interference mitigation through power control in high density 802.11 WLANs. In: IEEE Infocom-IEEE International Conference on Computer Communications. IEEE (2007)

16. Iwai, K., Ohnuma, T., Shigeno, H., Tanaka, Y.: Improving of fairness by dynamic sensitivity control and transmission power control with access point cooperation in dense WLAN. In: 2019 16th IEEE Annual Consumer Communications & Networking Conference (CCNC). IEEE (2019)
17. Xue, D., Ekici, E.: On reducing delay and temporal starvation of queue-length-based CSMA algorithms. In: Communication, Control, and Computing (Allerton), 2012 50th Annual Allerton Conference on IEEE (2012)
18. Lim, Y.S., Choi, J., Kim, C.K.: Practical application of physical energy detection to recognize starvation in 802.11 wireless networks. In: 2009 International Conference on Information Networking IEEE (2009)
19. Akella, A., Judd, G., Seshan, S., Steenkiste, P.: Self-management in chaotic wireless deployments. Wirel. Netw. **13**(6), 737–755 (2007)
20. Li, Z., Nandi, S., Gupta, A.K.: Improving fairness in IEEE 802.11 using enhanced carrier sensing. IEE Proc. Commun. **151**(5), 467–472 (2004)
21. Mahajan, P.: Optimized handoff algorithm for heterogeneous networks. IETE Tech. Rev. **3** (2020)
22. Wilhelmi, F., Muoz, S.B., Cano, C., Selinis, I., Bellalta, B.: Spatial reuse in IEEE 802.11ax WLANs. Comput. Commun. **170**(1) (2021)
23. Lin, W., Bo, L., Mao, Y., Qiao, Q., Bo, Y.: Integrated link-system level simulation platform for the next generation WLAN - IEEE 802.11ax. In: Global Communications Conference IEEE (2017)
24. Zhang, K.: The Research and Simulation of Channel Modeling and Interference Abstraction for the Next Generation WLAN (2020)
25. Cai, X.W.: Research and Implementation of MAC Technology and Integrated Simulation Platform for the Next Generation WLAN (2020)

An Uplink OFDMA Access Method for Low Latency in Next-Generation WLANs

Qingsong Gao, Ding Wang, Mao Yang$^{(\boxtimes)}$, Bo Li, and Zhongjiang Yan

School of Electronics and Information, Northwestern Polytechnical University, Xi'an, China
{wangd,yangmao}@nwpu.edu.cn

Abstract. The next generation of wireless local area network (WLAN) standard: IEEE 802.11be takes ultra-high-definition video and ultra-low latency services as its core service bearer targets. Orthogonal frequency division multiple access (OFDMA) technology can improve the efficiency of multi-access, but the OFDMA protocol of the existing WLAN can only serve one user per resource unit in a transmission process, and the data between different users needs to be filled with invalid information bits (padding) to ensure the alignment of the transmission time. Padding creates a waste of resources and affects the latency characteristics of the business. This paper proposes an uplink OFDMA access method for low latency in the next generation of WLANs, allowing the wireless access point (AP) to divide OFDMA resource unit into multiple periods from time and assign each period to a station (STA) to transmit. The scheme can avoid the waste of resources and improve the response speed of user services. In this paper, the protocol flow and frame structure of this method are designed in detail to make scheme have good compatibility with IEEE 802.11ax. Simulation results show that the proposed scheme can significantly improve latency performance compared with IEEE 802.11ax.

Keywords: Wireless local area network (WLAN) · Orthogonal frequency division multiple access(OFDMA) · IEEE 802.11ax · Throughput

1 Introduction

With the demand of customer consecutively increasing, ultra-high-definition video services and real-time applications (RTAs) will be important parts in future wireless networks. IEEE 802.11be which is next-generation WLAN standard will guarantee ultra-high throuthput and low-latency streams and make it to core service goals, which is the most important purpose of IEEE 802.11be [1]. IEEE 802.11be stands in a critical period for technical research supported, and the user's quality of service (QoS) is one of the important wireless key performance indicators(KPIs). IEEE 802.11be emphasizes ultra-high throughput and

D.-J. Deng et al. (Eds.): SGIoT 2022, LNICST 497, pp. 214–226, 2023.
https://doi.org/10.1007/978-3-031-31275-5_21

ultra-low latency. The requirements for QoS and user experience have large-scale improvement. It adopts a larger bandwidth up to 320MHz, and allows non-continuous channels to be aggregated and coordinated work between multiple APs. Emergency preparedness communications service (EPCS) and restricted target wake-up time mechanism (r-TWT) guarantees low latency for the service [2,3]. At the same time, large-scale networking of overlapping basic set service (OBSS) [4] is an important trend for next-generation WLAN. OBSS will cause a lot of conflicts [5,6]. So how to improve QoS and ensure more STAs to access is the key research direction of next generation of WLAN multi-access technology [7,8].

Since AP is a unified source node to initiate transmission for downlink transmission, AP can ensure low latency characteristics relying on its strong channel access capabilities and scheduling capabilities. However the uplink transmission chance needs to be competed by each STA, thus uplink transmission delay protection is a challenging topic of vital importance. OFDMA can improve multiple access efficiency which is introduced in IEEE 802.11ax standard [2] at 2021 for the first time. The uplink OFDMA process based on AP scheduling can improve the uplink access efficiency to a certain extent, and in multi-user scenarios AP will send trigger frame (TF) firstly which destinations are STAs of the cell to indicate the specific allocation of channel resources. Then STA will set the initial time, channel, and length of packet, to maintain alignment according to the TF.

In order to improve the performance of the uplink OFDMA, a number of studies and algorithms have been proposed. The authors of the paper [9] proposed that using algorithm based on non-orthogonal multiple access (NOMA) to increase the accessed number of STA, and dividing resource units (RUs) to different groups. The scheduled RU made two STA access by NOMA. Remain RUs were assigned to fixed STA for random access which can reduce the probability of collisions and increase throughput of the system. S. Bhattarai [10] proposed an optimal RU allocation algorithm, so AP need allocate as many scheduled RUs as possible to the STA in order to increase throughput. AP gave the optimal RU allocation scenarios based on the information in the Buffer State Report (BSR). Two kinds of up-link OFDMA random access (UORA) method were proposed by E. Avdotin and D. Bankov [11]. First algorithm allocated part of RUs to STAs by scheduling in the case of insufficient RUs, and the second scheduling was assigned to the subsequent STAs until all the STAs were fully allocated. The second algorithm grouped the STAs for loop in the Basic Service Set (BSS) and assigned RUs to each group. If a collision happened in an RU, STAs in the group would be round-robin again until no collision happened. Yang A. [12] proposed a grouping-based UORA algorithm. AP decided on grouping firstly, then AP calculated the utilization rate and maximized the utilization rate to achieve UORA improvement through the algorithm.

However, there is a common problem in existing research: the OFDMA protocol of the existing WLAN can only serve one user per RU during a transmission, and package needs to be filled with invalid information bits (padding) to ensure that the transmission time is aligned. S. Kim and J. Yun [13] made research on the setting of UpLinkLength. While dynamically adjusting the UpLinkLength can only allow a STA access in a RU, it still needs to fill package by padding quite a bit, which causes a waste of resources and affects latency performance of the stream.

Aiming at the problems of resource waste and poor latency guarantee of the existing WLAN uplink OFDMA protocol, this paper proposes an uplink OFDMA access method for low latency in the next generation of WLAN. The access method allows the wireless AP to divide OFDMA resource unit into multiple time periods of UpLinkLength, and each period is assigned to a STA for transmitting, which avoids the waste of resources and improves the response speed of STA services. In this paper, the protocol flow and frame structure of this method are designed in detail to make it have good compatibility. Simulation results show that the proposed method can significantly improve the latency performance and throughput performance compared with the resource allocation in 802.11ax.

The remainder of this paper is organized as follows. In Sect. 2, the traditional OFDMA access principle is analyzed and the possible problems are given. Section 3 builds a system model. Section 4 describes the protocol for low-latency OFDMA and gives several implementations. Mathematical analysis is given in the Sect. 5. The results are parsed and analyzed in Sect. 6. The paper is summarized in Sect. 7.

2   Uplink OFDMA Access Principle and Problem Analysis in WLAN

2.1   OFDMA Access Principle in IEEE 802.11ax

In the IEEE 802.11ax standard [2], MAC protocol allows multi-user to access simultaneously by OFDMA. The given bands 20 MHz, 40 MHz, 80 MHz and 160 MHz are divided into smaller frequency bands, these resource blocks are orthogonal to each other which is unified allocated by AP. User accesses channel according to the divided channel and subcarrier. OFDMA transmission can be divided into uplink and downlink. During the downlink transmission, AP knows all the buffered information and places this information in traffic indication message (TIM). STAs of the BSS are informed whether there are packets that need to be received through Beacon frames.

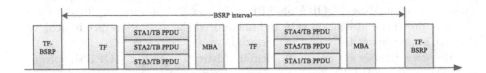

Fig. 1. Schematic diagram of the traditional OFDMA access principle.

During the uplink transmission, the AP doesn't get the specific cache information, thus AP can choose to send a buffer state report polling (BSRP) frame to require that STAs reply BSR frame to report all its cache information. As shown in Fig. 1, AP sends TF after collecting the cache packet informations, then STA1, STA2 and STA3 reply trigger-based PLCP protocol data unit (TB PPDU), AP responds multi-block ack (MBA) which marks that a scheduled transmission ends. STA is primarily based on two access methods, one of them is the AP's own scheduling algorithm, which allocates RU resource blocks to the STA. Since BSRP is sent periodically, AP can't get the buffer information in time for some low-latency stream. Thus there is an another access method that is random access by STA [14]. The AP will set the RU's association identifier (AID) to zero. At this time, the STA with low latency stream will selected the RU randomly which AID set to 0 to ensure transmission of low latency stream [15].

2.2   Analysis of OFDMA Access Problems

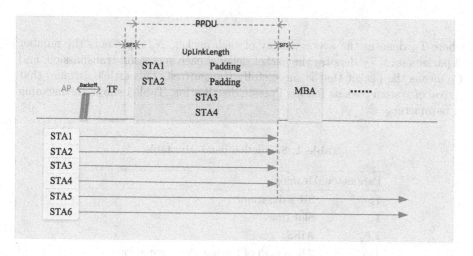

Fig. 2. Analysis of the 802.11ax uplink OFDMA.

In order to ensure the alignment of time in receiving terminal, AP will set transmit time (UpLinkLength) for each STA no matter which access method is adopted when using traditional OFDMA access scheme. Spec stipulates that STA must ensure that its duration is strictly aligned during the uplink transmission as shown in Fig. 2. STA3 and STA4 are scheduled to fill up the time for transmitting without padding during the scheduled transmission. Many STAs choose to take padding to supplement TB-PPDU beacuse of the different sizes of STAs' performed packets [13,16]. Due to packets of STA1 and STA2 can't fulfill the entire uplink length, it is necessary to use padding to make time aligned. Consequently STA5 and STA6 cannot get the transmission opportunity, and must wait for the next scheduled transmission at least. It will cause a larger delay. Therefore how to reasonably arrange the use of padding has become an important issue in the uplink OFDMA access scheme [17].

3 System Model

Without loss of generality, we consider the basic system model of the WLAN based on 1 AP and n STAs within a BSS:

$$N= \{N_1, N_2, N_3,......,N_n\} \tag{1}$$

To simplify the process, AP send TF to schedule STA directly, and the delay of system refers to the average delay per packet:

$$T_D = \frac{\sum_{1}^{N_p} T_T}{\sum_{1}^{n} P_T} \tag{2}$$

where T_D denotes the average delay of each packet, N_p represents the number of packets sent, T_T denotes the packet delay of each successful transmission, and P_T means the packet that is successfully transmitted. This article assumes that arrival of system packets follows Poisson distribution. Table 1 shows the meaning of parameters.

Table 1. Simulation parameter table.

Parameter	Meaning
T_s	SIFS duration.
T_{sl}	Slot time.
T_A	AIFS.
T_{UL}	The length of the uplink transmission.
T_{MBA}	Multi-Block ACK duration.
T_b	Backoff duration.
T_{TF}	TF duration.
S	Package size.
N_{ru}	Total number of RUs.
R_o	20M/40M RU number in IEEE 802.11ax.
R_s	Number of shared RUs.
P_s	Package production rate.

4 Description of the Uplink OFDMA Protocol for Low Latency

4.1 Protocol Overview

As shown in Fig. 2, it can be seen that the subsequent transmission packets are fulfilled with padding when the number of cache packets of STA1 and STA2 is in shortage in IEEE 802.11ax scheme. STA5 and STA6 cannot access channels in this TF transmission.

Therefore, we propose an enhanced RU allocation scheme as shown in Fig. 3. After AP got the buffer information of STA, we divide RUs into smaller resource blocks on partial RUs, allowing more STA to transmit compared with the resource division method in IEEE 802.11ax. At which point STA5 and SAT6 don't need to wait for the next TF scheduling which can effectively reduce the delay. AP scheduling algorithm is not covered by this article, whereas the AP scheduling should be reasonably arranged according to the urgency of STAs' packet. Thus we don't make more discussion here. In IEEE 802.11ax standard, bandwidth is devided dynamically. The allocation of shared RU and length of UpLinkLength can also be dynamically allocated.

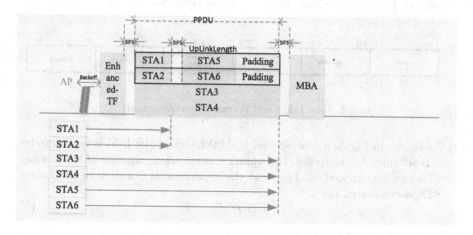

Fig. 3. Proposed uplink OFDMA protocol design.

4.2 Protocol Design

When designing the frame structure, it is necessary to specify the length of UpLinkLength for each STA and inform STA the beginning time. There are zero or more User Info Fields in Linked List Field. Each user has a separate information field followed by IEEE 802.11ax standard [2] where a User Info List Field exists. Therefore we use those fields to indicate that the STA is sent firstly (Former STA) in a RU during the uplink transmission, or sent secondly (Later STA), or occupies the entire RU block without sharing.

Considering specific operation and less payload, two implementations are given as following:

(1) As shown in Fig. 4, the UpLinkLength of Former STA and Later STA are specified under this scenario. The transmission duration of former STA is $\frac{1}{2}T_{UL}$, and the transmission duration of Later STA is calculated by:

$$T_L = \frac{1}{2}T_{UL} - T_s \qquad (3)$$

Starting time of Later STA is given as:

$$T_{ST} = \frac{1}{2}T_{UL} + T_s \qquad (4)$$

The time of entire orthogonal RU block is aligned. Implementation1 modifies the original B39 field to Shared RU, indicating that the RU is a shared RU. Then STA reads B40 field. It means that the STA is a Former STA if Station Location field is set to 1. Or else, it means that the STA is a Later STA. In which case STA can determine its duration and beginning time of sending according to above provisions. STA don't need to modify subfield supposed that it's allocated a monopoly RU. The overhead is 8 bits in this scenario.

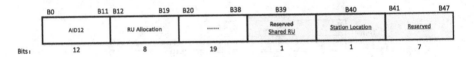

Fig. 4. User Info Field Format implementation1.

(2) As shown in Fig. 5, a new Special UpLinkLength (SU) field is added under this scheme. At this point, the uplink transmission duration of the Former STA can be denoted by T_{SU}, and the transmission duration of the Latter STA is calculated by:

$$T_L = T_{UL} - T_{SU} - T_s \qquad (5)$$

Starting time of Later STA is given as:

$$T_{ST} = T_{SU} + T_s \qquad (6)$$

This implementation has greater flexibility, which facilitates the scheduling of AP more reasonably in duration. The additional overhead for this scenario is 16bits.

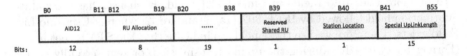

Fig. 5. User Info Field Format implementation2.

5 Theoretical Performance Analysis

The first STA position st for which no transmission opportunity was obtained in the mth transmission can be calculated as:

$$st = 1 + (mN_{ru}) \bmod (n), \qquad n < N_{ru} < 2n \qquad (7)$$

where the number of RUs is N_{ru}.

The STA set R that don't get a transmitting opportunity in the mth transmission can be formulated as:

$$R = \begin{cases} \{N_{st}, \cdots, N_{st+n-N_{ru}}\}, & st + n - N_{ru} \le n \\ \{N_{st}, \cdots, N_n, N_1, \cdots, N_{st-N_{ru}}\}, & st + n - N_{ru} > n \end{cases} \qquad (8)$$

In conjunction (1)(8), it can be known that the STA set B that gets the transmission opportunity is as following:

$$B = N - R \qquad (9)$$

According to the M/M/s queuing model [18], it can be known that:

$$\rho = \frac{\lambda}{\mu} \qquad (10)$$

$$\rho_s = \frac{\lambda}{s\mu} \qquad (11)$$

$$p_k = \begin{cases} \frac{\rho^k}{k!}p_0, & k = 1, \cdots, s-1, \\ \frac{\rho^k}{s!s^{k-s}}p_0, & k \ge s, \end{cases} \qquad (12)$$

$$ES = \frac{p_0 \rho \rho_s}{s!(1-\rho_s)^2} + \frac{1}{\mu} \qquad (13)$$

where λ means the rate of user arrival. μ denotes the rate of service for service desk. s means the number of service desks, namely N_{ru} in this system. ρ indicates the utilization rate of system single service desk. ρ_s manifests the total utilization rate of the system multi-service desk. p_k represents the number of customers in system. The user's remain time in system is ES, namely, average latency per packet.

Implementation1 is used for analysis for simplifying calculation. Packets arrive in bulk and batch out under this model. Combined (7)(8)(9), and the service rate of system's service desk μ is obtained by:

$$\mu = \frac{1}{\frac{2n-2N_{ru}}{n} \times 2T + \frac{2N_{ru}-n}{n} \times T} \qquad (14)$$

where T is the total duration of a service and is calculated as follows:

$$T = T_b + T_{TF} + 2T_s + T_A + T_{UL} + T_{MBA} \qquad (15)$$

where the calculation of T_A is shown in Eq. (16).

$$T_A = T_s + 2T_{sl} \tag{16}$$

Packets are batch in, batch out. We introduce the aggregation of degree A, the number of packets that can be served per transmission is calculated as:

$$A = \frac{\frac{P_s}{8S} \times n}{\mu N_{ru}} = \frac{nP_s}{8\mu S N_{ru}} \tag{17}$$

The rate of packet arrival can be expressed as the degree of aggregation of the total number of packages, as shown in formula (18):

$$\lambda = \frac{\frac{P_s}{8S} \times n}{A} = \mu N_{ru} \tag{18}$$

Combined formula (13)(14)(18), the average packet latency ES of the system T_D can be calculated as:

$$ES = \frac{1}{\mu} + T_f - T_a \tag{19}$$

where T_f denotes the average arrival time in a transmission before aggregation, T_a denotes the average arrival time in a transmission after aggregation which can be calculated by formula (17).

The total throughput Q of the system can be expressed as:

$$Q = \frac{N_p S}{T} \tag{20}$$

6   Performance Evaluation

6.1   Simulation Environment and Parameter Settings

We take integrated system & link level simulation platform [19,20] to build IEEE 802.11ax simulation platform, which is performed in one BSS simulation scenario, and the position of the STA is random. The simulation parameters are shown in Table 2.

6.2   Simulation Results and Analysis

The simulation results shows the comparison of throughput and latency between different scenarios at 20 MHz and 40 MHz, respectively.

(1) The package production rate increases

The number of shared RU is fixed to 5, the number of STA is fixed to 18, and the package rate of each STA increasing gradually from 1 to 6 in units of 500 kbps at this time. All useful RUs can be calculated as follows:

$$N_{ru} = R_o + R_s \tag{21}$$

Table 2. Simulation parameter value table.

Parameter	Value
T_s	16 ms
T_{sl}	9 μs
T_A	SIFS + 2*Slot time
T_{UL}	4 ms
T_{MBA}	84 μs
T_b	15 μs
T_{TF}	64 μs
S	200Bytes
N_{ru}	9/10(20M/40M)
R_o	20M/40M RU number in IEEE 802.11ax
R_s	5
P_s	2 Mbps

By looking up the table [2], the limiting throughput $Q_{h26-tone}$ of 26-tone is 10.0 Mbps at an MCS rate of nine and an NSS rate of one. Because of interaction of control frames in the system, and preamble packet size which is 36 bytes, limit throughput can be calculated of the system in 20 M bandwidth:

$$Q_h = R_o Q_{h26-tone} \frac{T_{UL}S}{T(S+S_p)} \tag{22}$$

The maximum throughput Q_h is 73.5 Mbps, thus BSS has not reached the full payload through comparison in simulation scene.

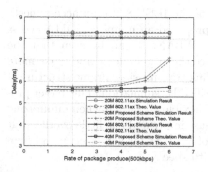

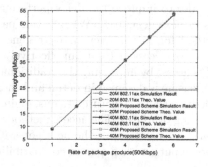

Fig. 6. Impact of different rate on delay performance

Fig. 7. Impact of different rate on throughput performance

The simulation results are shown in Fig. 6 and Fig. 7, and in the case of the same bandwidth of 20M or 40M, the improvement of delay performance is more

224 Q. Gao et al.

obvious after using proposed scheme compared with IEEE 802.11ax scheduling scheme [2]. When there are more STAs, the implementation of this scheme can significantly improve performance of delay. So that more stations can access the transmission in time without waiting for the next TF schedule.

(2) STA increases

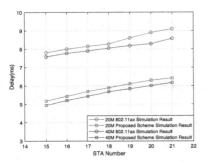 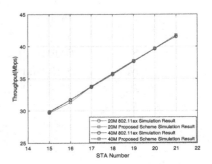

Fig. 8. Impact of STA number on delay performance

Fig. 9. Impact of STA number on throughput performance

It can be seen that this solution make more STAs access from Fig. 8 and Fig. 9, which can effectively reduce the delay of packet and ensure low latency transmission of the STA with the change of number of STAs.

7 Conclusion

In order to improve the delay performance of the IEEE 802.11ax access methods in next generation WLAN, this paper proposed an uplink OFDMA access method for low latency in next generation WLAN. It can be seen that the enhanced access method can effectively reduce the system delay and make more STAs access by improving the traditional uplink transmission. Frame structure of the scheme is designed in detail and then verified by simulation. This paper provides two frame structure designs, giving AP flexible allocation when minimizing signaling overhead. The access method designs simply and has little overhead, it provides a solution for the next generation of WLANs for low latency and high throughput and has a good compatibility with spec.

Acknowledgments. This work was supported in part by the National Natural Science Foundations of CHINA (Grant No. 61871322, No. 61771392, and No. 61771390), and Science and Technology on Avionics Integration Laboratory and the Aeronautical Science Foundation of China (Grant No. 20185553035 and No. 201955053002).

References

1. Levitsky, I., Okatev, Y., Khorov, E.: Study on simultaneous transmission and reception on multiple links in IEEE 802.11be networks. In: 2020 International Conference Engineering and Telecommunication (En & T), pp. 1–4 (2020). https://doi.org/10.1109/EnT50437.2020.9431275

2. IEEE standard for information technology-telecommunications and information exchange between systems local and metropolitan area networks-specific requirements part 11: wireless LAN Medium Access Control (MAC) and Physical Layer (PHY) specifications amendment 1: enhancements for high-efficiency WLAN. In: IEEE Std 802.11ax-2021 (Amendment to IEEE Std 802.11-2020), pp. 1–767 (2021). https://doi.org/10.1109/IEEESTD.2021.9442429

3. Chen, Q., Weng, Z., Xu, X., Chen, G.: A target wake time scheduling scheme for uplink multiuser transmission in IEEE 802.11ax-based next generation WLANs. In: IEEE Access, vol. 7, pp. 158207–158222 (2019). https://doi.org/10.1109/ACCESS.2019.2950464

4. Lanante, L., Roy, S.: Performance analysis of the IEEE 802.11ax OBSS_PD-Based Spatial Reuse. In: IEEE/ACM Transactions on Networking. https://doi.org/10.1109/TNET.2021.3117816

5. Zhong, Z., Kulkarni, P., Cao, F., Fan, Z., Armour, S.: Issues and challenges in dense WiFi networks. In: International Wireless Communications and Mobile Computing Conference (IWCMC), vol. 2015, pp. 947–951 (2015). https://doi.org/10.1109/IWCMC.2015.7289210

6. Yin, B., Kamiya, S., Yamamoto, K., Nishio, T., Morikura, M., Abeysekera, H.: Starvation mitigation for dense WLANs through distributed channel selection: potential game approach. In: 2017 14th IEEE Annual Consumer Communications & Networking Conference (CCNC) (2017), pp. 548–553. https://doi.org/10.1109/CCNC.2017.7983166

7. Zhao, X., Lei, L., Li, Z.: Modeling and analyzing per-flow saturation throughput for wireless Ad Hoc networks with directional antennas. In: 2018 IEEE 3rd International Conference on Cloud Computing and Internet of Things (CCIOT), pp. 94–97 (2018). https://doi.org/10.1109/CCIOT45285.2018.9032679

8. Lee, J., Lee, H., Yi, Y., Chong, S., Knightly, E.W., Chiang, M.: Making 802.11 DCF near-optimal: design, implementation, and evaluation. IEEE/ACM Trans. Networking 24(3), 1745–1758 (2016). https://doi.org/10.1109/TNET.2015.2432053

9. Lee, W.-J., Shin, W., Ruiz-de-Azua, J.A., Capon, L.F., Park, H., Kim, J.-H.: NOMA-based uplink OFDMA collision reduction in 802.11ax networks. In: 2021 International Conference on Information and Communication Technology Convergence (ICTC), pp. 212–214 (2021). https://doi.org/10.1109/ICTC52510.2021.9621014

10. Bhattarai, S., Naik, G., Park, J.-M.J.: Uplink resource allocation in IEEE 802.11ax. In: ICC 2019–2019 IEEE International Conference on Communications (ICC), pp. 1–6 (2019). https://doi.org/10.1109/ICC.2019.8761594

11. Avdotin, E., Bankov, D., Khorov, E., Lyakhov, A.: Enabling massive real-time applications in IEEE 802.11be networks. In: 2019 IEEE 30th Annual International Symposium on Personal, Indoor and Mobile Radio Communications (PIMRC), pp. 1-6 (2019). https://doi.org/10.1109/PIMRC.2019.8904271

12. Yang, A., Li, B., Yang, M., Yan, Z., Xie, Y.: Utility optimization of grouping-based uplink OFDMA random access for the next generation WLANs. Wireless Netw. 27(1), 809–823 (2020). https://doi.org/10.1007/s11276-020-02489-8

13. Kim, S., Yun, J.: efficient frame construction for multi-user transmission in IEEE 802.11 WLANs. IEEE Trans. Veh. Technol. **68**(6), 5859–5870 (2019). https://doi.org/10.1109/TVT.2019.2907281

14. Yang, A., Li, B., Yang, M., Yan, Z.: Group-based uplink OFDMA random access algorithm for next-generation WLANs. JNWPU **38**(1), 155–161 (2020). https://doi.org/10.1051/jnwpu/20203810155

15. Kosek-Szott, K., Domino, K.: An efficient backoff procedure for IEEE 802.11ax uplink OFDMA-based random access. IEEE Access **10**, 8855–8863 (2022). https://doi.org/10.1109/ACCESS.2022.3140560

16. Lin, C.-H., Chen, Y.-T., Lin, K. C.-J., Chen, W.-T.: acPad: enhancing channel utilization for 802.11ac using packet padding. In: IEEE INFOCOM 2017 - IEEE Conference on Computer Communications, pp. 1–9 (2017). https://doi.org/10.1109/INFOCOM.2017.8057127

17. Dutta, A., Gupta, N., Das, S., Maity, M.: MMRU-ALLOC: an optimal resource allocation framework for OFDMA in IEEE 802.11ax. In: 2020 IEEE 31st Annual International Symposium on Personal, Indoor and Mobile Radio Communications, pp. 1-6 (2020). https://doi.org/10.1109/PIMRC48278.2020.9217154

18. Tang, J.S.: Queuing Theory and Its Applications. Science Press, Beijing (2016)

19. Qu, Q., et al.: Survey and performance evaluation of the upcoming next generation WLANs standard - IEEE 802.11ax. Mobile Netw. Appl. **24**(5), 1461–1474 (2019). https://doi.org/10.1007/s11036-019-01277-9

20. Zhang, K.: Research on channel modeling and interference abstract simulation for next-generation WLANs. Master's thesis of Northwestern Polytechnical University. 2020.04

Edge Station Throughput Enhancement Method Based on Energy Detection Threshold and Transmission Power Joint Dynamic Adjustment

Fenglian Lan, Bo Li, Mao Yang[✉], and Zhongjiang Yan

School of Electronics and Information, Northwestern Polytechnical University,
Xi'an, China
lfl863779@mail.nwpu.edu.cn, {libo.npu,yangmao,zhjyan}@nwpu.edu.cn

Abstract. With the surge in demand for wireless traffic and network quality of service, wireless local area network (WLAN) has developed into one of the most important wireless networks affecting human life. In high density scenarios, large numbers of Access Point (APs) and Stations(STAs) will be deployed in a limited area, means large amount of signals will be overlapped and coverage between Basic Service Sets (BSSs), interference and collisions will become more severe, and if the sensitivity of edge STA detection channel is not enough, such as the energy detection (ED) threshold and reception sensitivity mismatch of STAs, edge STA's throughput may slow down seriously. So in this paper, we propose an edge STA throughput enhancement method based on ED threshold and TXPower joint dynamic adjustment to solve the problem of edge STA deceleration caused by ED threshold and reception sensitivity mismatch. By appropriately adjusting the ED threshold and TXPower of the BSSs with deceleration edge STAs, improving the sensitivity of edge STAs detection channel, and opportunity of edge STA's transmission packet is not greatly affected. Through the method of establishing mathematical model and simulation verification, it has great practical significance.

Keywords: ED threshold · TXPower · Joint dynamic adjustmented · Edge STA · Throughput enhancement

1 Introduction

WLAN and cellular network have become the dominant type of wireless networks [1]. Ericsson's latest mobility report shows that the compound annual growth rate (CAGR) of mobile traffic will grow by 30% from 2020 to 2024 [2]. Therefore, the high-density scenario will be the main deployment scenario for the next generation of WLAN [3–5] with the surge in data demand and rapid rise in WLAN deployment scale and density, requiring higher wireless network throughput to ensure network transmission quality [6,7]. Large bandwidth is the main feature

D.-J. Deng et al. (Eds.): SGIoT 2022, LNICST 497, pp. 227–240, 2023.
https://doi.org/10.1007/978-3-031-31275-5_22

of next-generation wireless networks [8], such as IEEE 802.11ax, 802.11be. But in high dense deployment, large numbers of APs and STAs will be deployed in a limited area, means large amount of signals will be overlapped and coverage between BSSs, interference and collisions will become more severe serious [9], some STAs are difficult to compete for channel by intra-BSSs interference, coupled with inter-BSSs's interference, the probability of receiving success will be greatly reduced. The next generation of WLAN random competition channel will aggravate the interference in multi-BSSs, and then cause station's throughput, BSS's throughput, and even the whole network's throughput decreases. So how to solve the BSSs's interference and ensure station's transmission quality is a key factor to improve network service and quality.

Inter stations interference is the main reason for limiting transmission efficiency and throughput of WLAN systems in high dense environments [10]. For the interference between WLAN stations, researchers have proposed many interference management methods, mainly including power control mechanism, distributed MIMO, dynamic distribution channel and other methods [11–19]. In [11–15], the authors proposed power control mechanism, such as M. Michalski et al. considered AP can estimate the interference plus noise ratio (SINR) of STA by the received signal strength indicator (RSSI) of STA, and then adjust the transmitting power according to the set minimum SINR limit [11], Y. Cai and J. Luo provided a network traffic power control method [12], A. Tsakmalis et al. considered that the power control can be performed adaptively according to the interference situation by adding a centralized controller for channel measurement and adjusting AP power to the system in the dense WLAN network [13–15]. The interference elimination technology and interference alignment method were adopted to eliminate BSS interference problem [16,17]. R. Akl proposed a method of using AP interchannel interference state through the dynamic channel allocation algorithm of WLAN system to minimize AP interference to allocate channels [18]. S. Jang studied the problem of channel assignment in AP coexistence networks and proposed heuristic algorithms for channel assignment [19]. Partial frequency multiplexing technology was used to improved edge STA throughput, but a certain spectral efficiency would be sacrificed [20]. Huawei considered that we could enable each BSS to share all spectrum resources through soft frequency multiplexing technology to improve the average BSS throughput and reduce interference to edge STA [21].

The existing researches on edge STA's interference mainly focused on intra-BSS, or inter-BSSs when channel state can be well detected by stations. However, there are few studies on interference of edge STA when stations channel detection is not sensitive, such as when station deceleration caused by the mismatch between ED threshold and reception sensitivity which is a common problem of multi-BSSs interference in highly dense scenarios, and will cause a typical edge STA throughput deceleration phenomenon. This paper aims at the problem of edge STAs throughput reduction caused by the mismatch of ED threshold and reception sensitivity between multi-BSSs in highly dense scenarios, analyzes and points out that the mismatch of ED threshold and reception sensitivity caused by inherent CSMA/CA mechanism of WLAN is an important reason for the continuous intensification of multi-BSSs interference in highly dense scenarios, proposes an edge STA throughput enhancement protocol based on ED threshold and TXPower joint dynamic adjustment, improve the sensitivity of edge STA detection channel and ensure that the edge STA's delivery opportunities are not greatly affected to improve the throughput performance of edge STA. Simulation results show that this protocol can improve the throughput performance of edge STAs, especially the edge STA with severe throughput reduction in high density scenarios.

The rest of this article is organized as follows. In Sect. 2, a problem-solving model is proposed to solve the problem of edge STA deceleration caused by the mismatch between ED threshold and reception sensitivity. In Sect. 3, we will analyze the problem of mismatch between ED threshold and receiver sensitivity in detail. The fourth section designs a protocol of the above proposed. Simulation results are shown in Sect. 5. The last Section concludes this paper.

2   System Model

Aiming at edge STA throughput reduction problem caused by mismatch between ED threshold and reception sensitivity of stations, this paper proposes an edge STA throughput promotion model based on the joint dynamic adjustment of ED threshold and TXPower in Fig. 1. For the convenience of describing system model and following description, relevant symbols are described in Table 1.

In this system model, STA periodically statistics some related information, which meets certain conditions, such as the RSSI value of packets from inter-BSS, the number of inter-BSS stations, the number of packets from inter-BSSs and so on, calculates itself throughput, and then feedback the relevant information to its AP. AP integrates the received information, and then gets the maximum STA throughput value of intra-BSS, the total number of stations of inter-BSS, the total number value of packets from inter-BSS, the minimum RSSI value of packets from inter-BSS and other information, then feeds back to centralized controller C. After receiving the information from each AP, C will evaluate the speed reduction problem and severity of edge STA, and then send the evaluation results to each AP. AP will adjust and optimize the ED threshold, TXPower and other relevant parameters of intra-BSS according to the evaluation results, and sends optimized parameters to its STAs. STA will adjust ED threshold and TXPower according to the received parameters.

3   Analysis of the Mismatch Between ED Threshold and Reception Sensitivity

The mismatch between ED threshold and reception sensitivity means that the received intra-BSS packet's RSSI value of a station is between ED threshold and carrier sense (CS) threshold, so it can not well perceive the channel is busy or idle, sometimes will mistake the channel idle when channel is busying actually, then constantly sends packets, resulting in collision and station throughput

Table 1. Symbol description.

Symbol	Symbolic meaning
C	Centralized controller.
A_i	The ith AP in this network.
S_{ij}	The jth STA of the ith AP.
e_{ij}	The ED threshold set by the jth STA to inter-BSS.
e_{ij}'	The optimized ED threshold set by the jth STA to inter-BSS.
p_{ij}	TXpower set by the jth STA in the current time period.
p_{ij}'	The optimized TXpower of the jth STA of the ith AP.
c_{ij}	CS threshold set by the jth STA to inter-BSS.
r_{ij}^o	The RSSI value of received packets of the jth STA from inter-BSS, value r_{ij}^o in (c_{ij}, e_{ij}).
r_{ij}^s	The minimum RSSI value of received inter-BSS packets of the jth STA, value r_{ij}^s is equal to $min\left(r_{ij}^o\right)$.
n_{ij}^o	The number of the inter-BSS stations of the jth STA phase mutual inductance packet, when the RSSI value of the packet in (c_{ij}, e_{ij}).
n_{ij}^r	The number of packets received from inter-BSS by the jth STA within the specified time period. The RSSI value of packets in (c_{ij}, e_{ij}).
t_{ij}^s	Throughput of the jth STA within the specified time period.
a_{ij}^o	The recorded inter-BSS station address of the jth STA, when the RSSI value of packets received from the inter-BSS in (c_{ij}, e_{ij}).
r_i^a	The minimum RSSI value r_i^a of inter-BSS packets received by all the STAs of the ith AP, value r_i^a is equal to $min\left(r_{ij}^s\right)$.
N_i^o	The total number of inter-BSS stations of the ith AP when the RSSI value of its STAs received packets from these stations in (c_{ij}, e_{ij}), value is equal to $\sum n_{ij}^o$.
N_i^r	The total number of inter-BSS packets received by all STAs of the ith AP, value N_i^r is equal to $\sum n_{ij}^r$.
T_i^s	The maximum STA throughput in the specified time period of ith AP, value T_i^s is equal to $min\left(r_{ij}^o\right)$.
M_i^a	Stores the information of ith AP about received inter-BSS packet number n_{ij}^r, throughput t_{ij}^s, and inter-station address a_{ij}^o.
T_{m^s}	The maximum throughput of STA in the time period in this network, value T_{m^s} is equal to $max\left(T_i^s\right)$.
N_{m^o}	The maximum number value of statistical inter-BSS stations of each BSS in the network, value N_{m^o} is equal to $max\left(N_i^o\right)$.
N_{m^r}	The maximum number value of statistical inter-BSS packets of each BSS in the network, value N_{m^r} is equal to $max\left(N_i^r\right)$.
D	Information about whether the edge STA deceleration occurs in each BSS.
S	Information about whether each BSS have serious edge STA throughput deceleration problem.

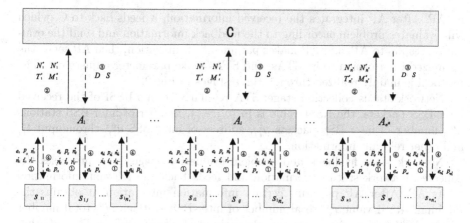

Fig. 1. System Model

decline, especially edge STA's throughput reduction. This paper mainly studies the mismatch between ED threshold and reception sensitivity between multi-BSSs.

IEEE 802.11 adopts CSMA/CA mechanism for signal transmission. CSMA/CA mainly judges the channel is busy or idle through physical carrier sense. The physical carrier sense function is realized through ED threshold and CS threshold. ED is that a station uses the energy received by physical layer to judge whether there is a signal for access. When the signal strength is greater than or equal to ED threshold, the channel will be considered busy; otherwise, the channel will be considered idle. In IEEE 802.11, CS is mainly used to identify the preamble of physical layer convergence protocol header of a data frame. If a received frame's energy is greater than or equal to CS threshold, which is considered that a signal is detected; otherwise, no signal is detected. In short, the CS threshold is the basis for judging whether a signal is received, ED threshold is the basis for a station to judge the channel busy or idle. Therefore, when the ED threshold of a station is mismatched with reception sensitivity, that is, a station detects that the energy of channel is less than ED threshold, will consider the channel idle and then sends packet. However, at this time, the destination station may be parsing the preamble in the header of corresponding physical layer for receiving inter-BSS packet (the RSSI of inter-BSS packet is greater than CS threshold but less than ED threshold), thus missing the preamble parsing of the packet actually sent to it, resulting in the packet being discarded.

4   Protocol Design

4.1   Basic Idea

This protocol monitors network transmission status through regular collecting network status information by STAs, and feed back the related information to its AP. After AP integrates the received information, it feeds back to C, which will evaluates problem according to the feedback information and send the evaluation results to AP, and AP makes parameter optimization, then AP sends the optimized information to its STAs, and STAs make parameter adjustment. The protocol is mainly realized through three stages in Fig. 2.

Network status collection stage: STA regularly counts RSSI of the received inter-BSS packets, the RSSI value is in (c_{ij}, e_{ij}), number of inter-BSS stations n_{ij}^o, number of inter-BSS packets n_{ij}^r, address of inter-BSS a_{ij}^o, throughput t_{ij}^s and other relevant information.

Network state feedback and problem evaluation stage: STA processes the collected network status information and feeds back the relevant information to its AP. After AP performs certain information integration, it obtains the minimum RSSI value r_i^a, total number of inter-BSS stations N_i^o, total number of inter-BSS packets N_i^r, maximum throughput of intra-BSS STA T_i^s, and other information such as M_i^s, and feeds back to C.

Parameter optimization, adjustment and release stage: C judges the deceleration of edge STA according to the feedback network state information, and sends the judgment results to each AP. AP will optimize ED threshold, TXPower and other related parameters according to the judgment results, and send the optimized results to its STAs. Upon receipt, STA will adjust parameters such as ED threshold and TXPower.

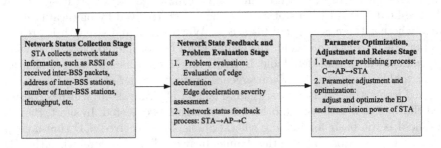

Fig. 2. Basic protocol process

4.2   Detailed Design

The basic process of this protocol is to collect, feed back, evaluate problems, optimize and adjust parameters on a regular basis. The follows is specific process.

(1) Network status collection stage.

Basic process of network state collection as in Fig. 3. STA (S_{ik}) statistics RSSI value (r_{ik}^o) of received packets come from STA (S_{jl}) of inter-BSS and get the minimum RSSI value (r_{ik}^s) of received inter-BSS packets according to the statistics of r_{ik}^o, records the address of inter-BSS STA (a_{ik}^o), counts the number of inter-BSS stations (n_{ik}^o), statistics the number of the received inter-BSS packets (n_{ik}^r), calculates throughput (t_{ik}^s) in the time period T and other network status related information.

(2) Network state feedback and problem evaluation stage.

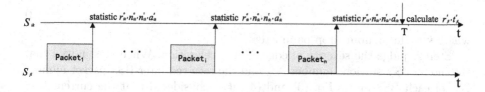

Fig. 3. Basic protocol process

1) Network state feedback phase.

Basic process of network state feedback in Fig. 4. STA sends station network state report (SNSR) frame to its AP after processing the collected network state related information at time of nT. The SNSR frame carries network state related information such as the minimum RSSI value r_{ik}^s, the calculated throughput t_{ik}^s, the statistics inter-BSS stations number n_{ik}^o, the received inter-BSS packets number n_{ik}^r, the ED threshold e_{ik} and TXPower p_{ik} set to inter-BSS in the current time period of STA and other information. AP performs the received information processing to obtain the minimum RSSI value r_i^a, the inter-BSS's stations number N_i^o, the received inter-BSS packets number N_i^r, the maximum STA throughput T_i^s, and other information M_i^a, then send an access point network state report (ANSR) frame, which carries the related network state information, to C. And C will get the maximum STA throughput value T_{m^s}, the maximum inter-BSS stations number N_{m^o}, the maximum value of received inter-BSS packets number N_{m^r}, then enters to the problem evaluation stage.

2) Problem evaluation stage.

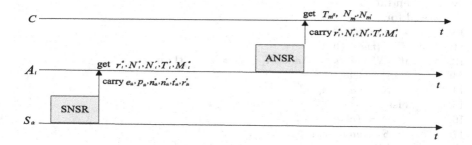

Fig. 4. Basic protocol process

Step 1: Judge STA deceleration. Judge whether the counted inter-BSS stations number n_{ik}^o and calculated STA throughput t_{ik}^s meet the Eq. (1) and (2) respectively. If so, it is considered that the current STA has an edge deceleration problem, and proceed to step 2; Otherwise, it is considered that no edge deceleration problem.

$$n_{ik}^o > R \tag{1}$$

where R is the edge deceleration parameter.

$$t_{ik}^s < k * T_m^s \tag{2}$$

where k is throughput drop parameters.

Step 2: judge the severity of edge STA deceleration. When it is judged that the inter-BSS's stations number N_{ik}^o and the received inter-BSS packet number N_{ik}^r of each BSS meets Eq. (3) and (4), it is considered that the current BSS edge reduction problem is serious.

$$N_i^o > k_1 * N_m^o \tag{3}$$

where k_1 is the edge deceleration severity parameter.

$$N_i^s > k_2 * N_m^s \tag{4}$$

where k_2 is the edge deceleration severity parameter.

The specific process of problem evaluation is shown in Algorithm 1.

Algorithm 1. Problem evaluation

Input: $t_{ik}^s; n_{ik}^o; T_{m^s}; N_i^o; N_i^r; d_{ik}; d_i^a; s_i^a; s_{ik}^s; a_i^a; n^a; n_i^s;$

      Initialize: $d_{ik} = false; d_i^a = false; s_i^a = false;$

      output: $D = map < a_i^a, d_i^a >; S = map < a_i^a, s_i^a > ;$

 1: **for** int $i = 1$ to n^a **do**

 2:    **for** int $k = 1$ to n_s^k **do**

 3:       **if** $(n_{ik}^o > R) \, and \, (t_{ik}^s < k * T_{m^s})$ **then**

 4:          $d_i^a = true$

 5:          $d_{ik}^s = true$

 6:       **else**

 7:          $d_{ik}^s = false$

 8:       **end if**

 9:    **end for**

10:    $D = map < a_i^a, d_i^a >$

11:    **if** $(d_i^a = true)$ **then**

12:       **if** $(N_i^o > k_1 * N_{m_o}) \, and \, (N_i^r > k_2 * N_{m^r})$ **then**

13:          $s_i^a = true$

14:          $S = map < a_i^a, s_i^a >$

15:       **else**

16:          $s_i^a = false$

17:          $S = map < a_i^a, s_i^a >$

18:       **end if**

19:    **end if**

20: **end for**

---

(3) Parameter optimization, adjustment and release stage.

According to the above evaluation results, C sends it to each AP, stations for corresponding parameter optimization and adjustment. The adjustment and optimization process of specific parameters is as follows:

Step 1: after receiving the parameters issued by C, the AP determines whether the edge deceleration problem occurs in BSS. If it does, execute step 2; Otherwise, proceed to step 6.

Step 2: judge the severity of edge deceleration problem in BSS. If the problem is serious, proceed to step 3; Otherwise, go to step 4;

Step 3: optimize the TXPower and inter-BSS ED threshold parameters of each STA, send the optimization results to each STA, and execute step 5;

Step 4: optimize the inter-BSS ED threshold parameters of each STA in BSS, send them to each STA, and execute step 5.

Step 5: STA adjusts the parameters according to the optimized parameters distributed by its AP.

Step 6: STA does not make any parameter adjustments.

ED threshold and TXPower optimization meet Eq. (5) and (6). Specific parameter optimization process, such as Algorithm 2.

$$e'_{ik} = r_i^a \tag{5}$$

$$p'_{ik} = p_{ik} + e_{ik} - e'_{ik} + P \tag{6}$$

where P is a TXPower optimization parameter.

Algorithm 2. Parameter optimization

Input: $d_i^a; s_i^a; e_{ik}; p_{ik}; r_i^a; n_s^i;$
        Initialize: $d_{ik} = false; d_i^a = false; s_i^a = false;$
        output: $e'_{ik}; p'_{ik};$
1: **if** $(d_i^a = true)$ **then**
2:     **for** int $k = 1$ to n_s^k **do**
3:        $e'_{ik} = r_i^a$
4:     **end for**
5: **end if**
6: **if** $(s_i^a = true)$ **then**
7:     **for** int $k = 1$ to n_s^k **do**
8:        $p'_{ik} = p_{ik} + e_{ik} - e'_{ik} + P$
9:     **end for**
10: **end if**

---

5 Performance Evaluation

In this paper, we adopt integrated system & link level simulation platform [22, 23], and set two simulation scenarios, four simulation verifications in total.

5.1   Basic Simulation Parameter Settings

The location of BSS main channel is 36, and STA number is 3 in each AP. The transmission bandwidth is 40 MHz in Fig. 5, and 80 MHz in Fig. 7. The traffic is saturated. Other simulation parameters are shown in Table 2.

Table 2. Simulation parameter

Simulation Parameter	Value	Simulation Parameter	Value
Protocol mode	IEEE 802.11ax [24]	UL/DL	UL
Transmission Mode	SU	AMSDU	7
TX Power (initial)	15dBm	AMPDU	21
TXOP(Yes/No)	Yes	CW_{min}	15
RTS/CTS(Yes/No)	Yes	CW_{max}	1023
NSS Number	2	SIFS	16us
Traffic Type	BE	DIFS	43us
ED (initial)	40 MHz: -72 dBm 80 MHz: -62 dBm	Data Rate(DL)	0
CS (initial)	40 MHz:-79 dBm 80 MHz: -76 dBm	Data Rate(UL)	1e9

5.2   Simulation Scenario Setting and Analysis

(1) 40 MHz-3AP simulation scenario

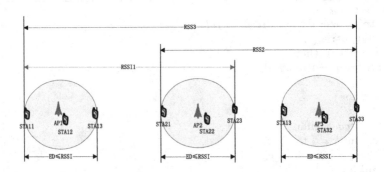

Fig. 5. 40 MHz-3AP Simulation scenario

In Fig. 5, two different AP distance and BSS radius are set to make RSSI perceived by stations between BSSs different in Table 3 and 4. In Table 3 and (a) of Fig. 6, BSS radius is 6 meters (m), and AP's distance is from about 26 m to 60 m. In Table 4 and (b) of Fig. 6, BSS radius is 8 m, and AP's distance is from about 40 m to 90 m. The simulation results as shown in Fig. 6.

Table 3. 3AP-Radius(6m)-RSSI.

RSSI	Pre-adjustment	Adjusted
RSSI1	ED ≤ RSSI1; CS<RSSI1<ED	ED ≤ RSSI1
RSSI2	ED ≤ RSSI2	ED ≤ RSSI2
RSSI3	CS<RSSI3< ED	ED ≤ RSSI3

Table 4. 3AP-Radius(8m)-RSSI.

RSSI	Pre-adjustment	Adjusted
RSSI1	CS<RSSI1<ED	ED ≤ RSSI1
RSSI2	ED ≤ RSSI2; CS<RSSI2 <ED	ED ≤ RSSI2
RSSI3	RSSI3 < CS	ED ≤ RSSI3

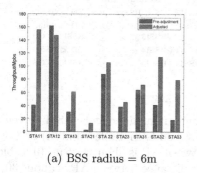

(a) BSS radius = 6m

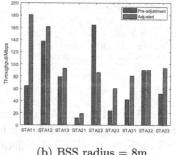

(b) BSS radius = 8m

Fig. 6. 40 MHz-3AP-Throughput Comparison

In Fig. 6, the overall throughput of each BSS has increased after adjustment, especially the throughput of edge BSSs. In (a) of Fig. 6, the throughput of each STA in the BSS is increased by from 12.4% to 438%, except STA12. Each STA's throughput in edge BSS is obvious (increased by 18.0% to 438%). The number of STA with decreased throughput decreases from 7 to 4, a decrease of 42.86%. In (b) of Fig. 6, each STA's throughput is increased by from 2.75% to 276%, except STA22. Each STA's throughput in edge BSS is obvious (increased by from 17.24% to 276%). The number of STA with decreased throughput decreases from 6 to 4, a decrease of 33.3%. And whether in (a) or (b) of Fig. 6, the number of edge STA with reduction throughput decreased from 6 to 4, a decrease of 33.3%.

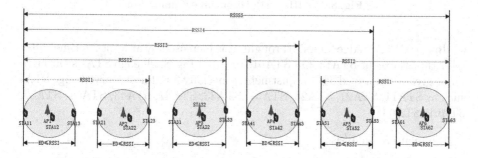

Fig. 7. 80 MHz-6AP Simulation scenario

(2) 80 MHz-6AP simulation scenario

Table 5. 6AP-Radius(6m)-RSSI.

RSSI	Pre-adjustment	Adjusted
RSSI1	RSSI1 ≤ CS	ED ≤ RSSI1
RSSI2	RSSI2 ≤ CS; CS<RSSI2<ED	ED ≤ RSSI2
RSSI3	CS < RSSI3 <ED	ED ≤ RSSI3
RSSI4	CS < RSSI4 <ED	ED ≤ RSSI4
RSSI5	CS<RSSI5 <ED; RSSI5 < CS	ED≤RSSI5; RSSI5≤CS

Table 6. 6AP-Radius(8m)-RSSI.

RSSI	Pre-adjustment	Adjusted
RSSI1	ED ≤ RSSI1; CS<RSSI< ED	ED ≤ RSSI1
RSSI2	CS < RSSI2 <ED	ED ≤ RSSI2
RSSI3	CS<RSSI3<ED; RSSI3 < CS	ED≤RSSI3; RSSI3 < CS
RSSI4	RSSI4 < CS	ED < RSSI4
RSSI5	RSSI5 < CS	RSSI5 ≤ CS

In Fig. 7, two different AP distance settings are made to make RSSI perceived by stations between BSSs different in Table 5 and 6. In Table 5 and (a) of Fig. 8, the BSS radius is 6 m, and the distance between AP is about 17.5 m. In Table 6 and (b) of Fig. 8, BSS radius is 8 m, and the distance between AP is about 30 m. The simulation results as shown in Fig. 8.

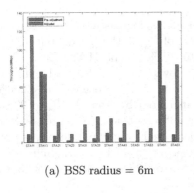
(a) BSS radius = 6m

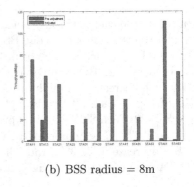
(b) BSS radius = 8m

Fig. 8. 80 MHz-6AP-Throughput Comparison

In (a) of Fig. 8, edge STAs's throughput is increased by at least 2.6 times after adjustment, except STA13 and STA61. In (b) of Fig. 8, all edge STAs's throughput is greatly improved after adjustment, especially for almost starved edge STAs such as STA11, STA21, STA23, STA31, STA33, STA41, STA43, STA51, STA53, STA61, STA63.

(3) Simulation Analysis

After the ED threshold of the throughput reduction of edge STAs is lowered, the detection channel is more sensitive, which reduces the collision probability between the packets sent by the edge STAs and inter-BSS's STA, and improves the throughput. However, when the ED threshold of a STA is lowered, the STA's sending opportunities will decrease, which may lead to a decrease of STA's throughput. Therefore properly increasing the transmission power of the BSS can ensure that the sending opportunities of the BSS's edge STA will not decrease as much as possible, so as to improve the edge STA's throughput.

6 Conclusion

Aiming at the edge STA's throughput serious reduction caused by mismatch between ED threshold and reception sensitivity of multi-BSSs in highly dense scenes, this paper proposes a throughput increase protocol and method for edge STAs based on the joint dynamic adjustment of ED threshold and TXPower. Through the adjustment and optimization of the inter-BSS ED threshold and TXPower of some BSSs, edge STA's throughput is improved. According to the above simulation results, it can be seen that this method can better improve the serious throughput reduction edge STAs. The design of this protocol is simple. It can greatly improve the throughput degradation of edge STAs caused by mismatch between ED threshold and reception sensitivity in BSSs. It has a strong application prospect and value.

Acknowledgements. This work was supported in part by the National Natural Science Foundations of CHINA (Grant No. 61871322, No. 61771390, and No. 61771392), and Science and Technology on Avionics Integration Laboratory and the Aeronautical Science Foundation of China (Grant No. 20185553035, and No. 201955053002).

References

1. Cisco. Global mobile data traffic forecast update. Cisco Visual Networking Index: White PAPer (2019)
2. Ericsson. The power of 5G is here and will continue to spread across the globe in the coming years. Ericsson Mobility Report (2019)
3. Wireless LAN medium access control (MAC) and physical layer (PHY) specifications amendment 6: Enhancements for high efficiency WLAN. IEEE Draft 802.11ax/D2.0 (2017)
4. Deng, C., et al.: IEEE 802.11be-Wi-Fi 7: new challenges and opportunities. (4) (2020)
5. Kim, S., Yun, J.H.: Wider-bandwidth operation of IEEE 802.11 for extremely high throughput: challenges and solutions for flexible puncturing. IEEE Access **8**, 213840–213853 (2020)
6. Fan, Q., et al.: Video delivery networks: challenges, solutions and future directions. Comput. Electr. Eng. **66**, 332–341 (2018). http://www.sciencedirect.com/science/article/pii/S0045790617308972
7. Qiao, J., He, Y., Shen, X.S.: Improving video streaming quality in 5genabled vehicular networks. IEEE Wirel. Commun. **25**(2), 133–139 (2018)
8. Yang, M., Li, B.: Survey and perspective on extremely high throughput (EHT) WLAN - IEEE 802.11be. Mob. Netw. Appl. **25**(2) (2020)

9. Yang, M., et al.: AP coordination and full-duplex enabled multi-band operation for the next generation WLAN: IEEE 802.11be (EHT). In: 2019 11th International Conference on Wireless Communications and Signal Processing (WCSP). IEEE (2019)

10. Zhong, Z., et al.: Issues and challenges in dense WiFi networks. In: Wireless Communications & Mobile Computing Conference. IEEE (2015)

11. Michalski, M., Staniec, K.: A simple performance-boosting algorithm for transmit power control in WLAN access points. In: 2016 21st International Conference on Microwave, Radar and Wireless Communications (MIKON). IEEE (2016)

12. Cai, Y., Luo, J.: A dynamic power control scheme based on NetFlow for reducing WLAN interference. In: 2012 8th International Conference on IEEE Wireless Communications, Networking and Mobile Computing (WiCOM) (2012)

13. Xu, Y.-J., Yan, X.D., Xu, H.-M.: Research on TPC algorithm in a dense WLAN environment. Microelectron. Comput. **25**, 19–21 (2007)

14. Tsakmalis, A., Chatzinotas, S., Ottersten, B.: Power control in cognitive radio networks using cooperative modulation and coding classification. In: Weichold, M., Hamdi, M., Shakir, M.Z., Abdallah, M., Karagiannidis, G.K., Ismail, M. (eds.) CrownCom 2015. LNICST, vol. 156, pp. 358–369. Springer, Cham (2015). https://doi.org/10.1007/978-3-319-24540-9_29

15. Silva, E., et al.: A new centralized active and reactive power control strategy for voltage regulation in power distribution networks with high penetration of photovoltaic generation. In: International Conference on Harmonics & Quality of Power. IEEE (2016)

16. Dai, H., et al.: Downlink capacity of interference-limited MIMO systems with joint detection. IEEE Trans. Wirel. Comm. **3**, 442–452 (2003)

17. YetiS, C., Gou, T., Jafar, S., Kayran, A.: On feasibility of interference alignment in MIMO interference networks. IEEE Trans. Signal Process. **58**(9), 4771–4782 (2010)

18. Akl, R., Arepally, A.: Dynamic channel assignment in IEEE 802.11 networks. In: IEEE International Conference on Portable Information Devices. IEEE (2007)

19. Jang, S., Bahk, S.: A channel allocation algorithm for reducing the channel sensing/reserving asymmetry in 802.11ac networks. IEEE Trans. Mob. Comput. **14**(3), 458–472 (2015)

20. Elayoubi, et al.: Performance evaluation of frequency planning schemes in OFDMA-based networks. IEEE Trans. Wirel. Commun. **7**, 1623–1633 (2008)

21. Huawei. Soft frequency reuse scheme for UTRAN LTE. TSG RAN WG1 Meeting #41, Athens, Greece, May 2005 (2005)

22. Lin, W., et al.: Integrated link-system level simulation platform for the next generation WLAN - IEEE 802.11ax. In: Global Communications Conference. IEEE (2017)

23. Qiao, Q., et al.: Survey and performance evaluation of the upcoming next generation WLANs standard - IEEE 802.11ax. Mob. Netw. Appl. **24**(3) (2019)

24. IEEE Standard for Information Technology-Telecommunications and Information Exchange between Systems Local and Metropolitan Area Networks-Specific Requirements Part 11: Wireless LAN Medium Access Control (MAC) and Physical Layer (PHY) Specifications Amendment 1: Enhancements for High-Efficiency WLAN, in IEEE Std 802.11ax-2021 (Amendment to IEEE Std 802.11-2020), pp. 1–767 (2021). https://doi.org/10.1109/IEEESTD.2021.9442429

A Channel Reservation Mechanism in IEEE 802.11be for Multi-cell Scenarios

Siyuan Liu, Ding Wang, Mao Yang$^{(\boxtimes)}$, Zhongjiang Yan, and Bo Li

School of Electronics and Information, Northwestern Polytechnical University,
Xi'an, China
{wangd,yangmao}@nwpu.edu.cn

Abstract. With the surge in demand for latency-sensitive traffic, the next-generation Wireless Local Area Network (WLAN) standard IEEE 802.11be has recognized the improvement of worst-case latency and jitter as one of its core objectives. Reservation-based contention-free channel access scheme achieves lower latency. Nevertheless, the channel reservation still has some limitations. In a multi-cell scenario, the Access Point (AP) is not capable of managing external cell users, which will cause interference to the reserved users during the reservation period, resulting in deteriorating channel conditions and increasing latency. Hence, in this paper, we propose a channel reservation mechanism with multi-cell coordination capability, enabling the sharing of channel reservation information among different cell APs and restricting the corresponding users to remain in silence during the reservation period, to avoid interference from internal and external cell users on the reserved users. Moreover, we propose a management frame protection scheme based on channel reservation mechanism that reduces the probability of management frame loss by offering channel reservation to the management frames. The effectiveness of the channel reservation mechanism and the management frame protection scheme is verified by simulations. It is demonstrated that the latency of latency-sensitive traffic in a multi-cell scenario using the proposed mechanism is significantly improved over the existing works.

Keywords: Wireless local area network (WLAN) · IEEE 802.11be · Channel Reservation · Multi-Cell Coordination · Low Latency

1 Introduction

Recently, latency-sensitive traffic has emerged for various sectors, such as cloud gaming and remote medical monitoring. This traffic usually requires low latency and high reliability to meet the demands of their application scenarios, whereas the widely used Wireless Local Area Network (WLAN) standard IEEE 802.11ax [1] has efficient network performance, but it cannot guarantee timely data delivery due to the uncertainty of the CSMA/CA channel access mechanism, and thus cannot meet the requirements of latency-sensitive traffic.

D.-J. Deng et al. (Eds.): SGIoT 2022, LNICST 497, pp. 241–253, 2023.
https://doi.org/10.1007/978-3-031-31275-5_23

As a result, the next-generation WLAN standard IEEE 802.11be [2] has listed the worst-case latency and jitter improvement as one of the core objectives, and new technologies and features will be introduced in the Physical layer (PHY) and Medium Access Control layer (MAC) to improve the latency.

The traditional IEEE 802.11 standard defines the Distributed Coordination Function (DCF) and the Point Coordination Function (PCF). DCF uses contention-based CSMA/CA mechanism to access the channel and simultaneously uses binary exponential backoff algorithm to defer channel access time to reduce the probability of collision. The standard also proposes Enhanced Distributed Channel Access (EDCA) mechanism based on DCF to meet QoS requirements. EDCA classifies traffic into four categories, each with different priorities and backoff parameters. High-priority traffic has more optimal backoff parameters, like smaller maximum contention window size. PCF uses contention-free point coordinators to manage channel access and schedules node transmissions by polling. This method introduces significantly more cost and complexity, plus the loss of scheduling information due to uncertainty in unlicensed bands. In contrast, DCF has higher reliability, lower cost, and simpler implementation. Therefore, DCF has been more widely used. But DCF still has a higher probability of collision when the number of users is large, and channel access becomes more difficult, resulting in increased latency. Accordingly, the contention-based channel access mechanism may not meet the low latency and high-reliability requirements of latency-sensitive traffic.

The IEEE 802.11ax standard introduces Orthogonal Frequency Division Multiple Access (OFDMA) technology and Multi-User Multi-Input Multi-Output (MU-MIMO) technology to strengthen the concurrency capability. Based on these two technologies, the multi-user uplink transmission scheduling scheme allows users to access the channel free of competition for latency reduction. The IEEE 802.11ax standard enhances the Target Wake Time (TWT) technique introduced by the IEEE 802.11ah standard [3] as well as introduces broadcast TWT, which utilizes reservation-based channel access to enable users to transmit data during the reserved period with less contention, thereby reducing latency. The next generation WLAN standard, IEEE 802.11be, introduces Restricted TWT (R-TWT) technology derived from broadcast TWT technology, a mechanism that reduces latency by providing additional channel protection to channel reservation period to further reduce contention. These scheduling or reservation-based channel access methods are more appropriate for transmitting latency-sensitive traffic than competition-based access methods.

A few limitations exist, however, in the use of the above techniques. One of the very critical limitations is the interference from OBSSs. In multi-cell scenarios, whether using scheduling-based or reservation-based channel access, the Access Point (AP) cannot effectively coordinate external cell users. While the channel is idle, the external cell users may transmit data at any time and even transmit without contention when they have TXOP. Channel conditions deteriorate due to the uncertainty of the access channel for external cell users, and users with low latency demand who are scheduled or have reservation periods may not be able to access the channel rapidly, and thus latency-sensitive traffic cannot be transmitted in time. Therefore, in multi-cell scenarios, APs need to coordinate with external cell users in an effective way to reduce the competition from external cell users. Besides, in the multi-cell high-density scenario, when the AP performs channel reservation or schedule, the relevant management frames could be lost due to collision, and since the retransmission mechanism does not apply to such management frames, the users cannot establish communication with the AP in the period following and thus cannot provide rapid channel access to the latency-sensitive traffic, which results in increased latency. Therefore, in multi-cell high-density scenarios, APs need to minimize management frame transmission loss effectively.

In light of this, this paper investigates the solution to the problem of interference from OBSSs for channel reservation and management frame loss in a multi-cell scenario. The contributions of this paper are mainly as follows:

1) A channel reservation mechanism in a multi-cell scenario is proposed. It reduces the competition by coordinating the channel access of different BSS users through APs and Wireless Access Point Controller (AC). In the multi-cell scenario, before the AP allocates reservation periods to users, the channel reservation information is first forwarded to the external cell AP through the AC so that it can coordinate the external cell users. With multi-cell coordination, APs can eliminate interference from external cell users, and users with low latency demand can rapidly access the channel for data transmission during the reservation period, consequently reducing latency.

2) In addition, this paper proposes a scheme to transmit management frames using channel reservation, where the AP can transmit management frames during a regular channel reservation period, while the user remains in silence during that period, which reduces the probability of management frame loss and allows the user to receive the channel reservation information correctly, thereby preventing the latency increase due to channel reservation information loss.

The remainder of this paper is organized as follows: In Sect. 2, the related work is introduced. Section 3 presents the channel reservation mechanism in the multi-cell scenario and the scheme of utilizing channel reservation to protect the management frame transmission in the multi-cell high-density scenario. The performance is simulated and analyzed in Sect. 4. Section 5 concludes the whole paper.

2 Related Work

Many researchers have investigated in recent years for MAC protocol performance enhancement. Paper [4] proposed a distributed reservation MAC protocol called EBA. The node sends information about future backoff values to other nodes through data frames, and other nodes select backoff values avoiding the already selected values. A centralized channel reservation MAC mechanism is proposed in the paper [5]. Nodes transmit data during reserved periods and compete to obtain channel reservations during unreserved periods. The paper [6] proposes a competition-based distributed channel reservation MAC protocol. Nodes compete during the competitive periods and the nodes that succeed in the competition broadcast their reservation information of the channel using RTS/CTS like mechanism before transmitting the data. Nodes reserving channels send data during the reservation period. A multi-hop distributed channel reservation mechanism has been proposed in the papers [7,8]. The node sends multiple future channel reservation information to other nodes through data frames, so that the reservation information can be sent multiple times. A collision-free backoff mechanism is proposed in the paper [9]. Nodes can reserve or release the backoff value by managing frames. In paper [10], a distributed channel reservation mechanism is proposed. When a node sends data, the channel is reserved in the form of NAV and the node can send data again after successful data delivery. Extensive research on TWT has been carried out in academia in recent years. The paper [11] investigated the effect of clock drift on TWT and compared two channel access modes under TWT uplink transmission: random contention access and AP scheduling access, and found that the former provides lower transmission time, while the latter provides lower power consumption. The paper [12] investigates the performance gain of TWT and finds that it brings significant throughput gains when combined with the uplink multi-user feature of IEEE 802.11ax, despite the additional management overhead required, along with almost constant average latency when the traffic load varies. The paper [13] combines the MU-based orthogonal frequency division multiple access (OFDMA) function of IEEE 802.11ax with TWT scheduling to improve throughput by negotiating the appropriate target beacon transmission time and staggering the wake time of nodes to reduce competition. In the paper [14], the MU function of IEEE 802.11ax is combined with broadcast TWT to improve throughput by scheduling the suitable number of nodes through AP to maximize their parallel transmission without collision using the channel resources. The paper [15] proposes a machine learning-based traffic category detection model and an adaptive TWT wake interval configuration scheme so that the TWT parameters can be adjusted according to the traffic category of real-time data to reduce competition and power consumption. A time-aware scheduling scheme based on TWT is proposed in the paper [16]. The paper [17] treats as a graph coloring problem by grouping nodes to find the minimum chromatic number enabling as many nodes as possible to transmit in parallel at the same time, thus improving throughput and energy efficiency. Although the above research has improved the MAC protocol performance, it has not paid much attention to the OBSSs interference. Hence, this paper proposes a channel reservation mechanism in a multi-cell scenario to solve the OBSSs interference by multi-cell coordination, as well as to solve the management frame loss problem by using channel reservation to transmit management frames.

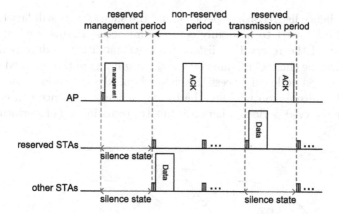

Fig. 1. Period classification of channel reservation mechanism and operation of various types STAs during different period.

3 A Channel Reservation Mechanism in a Multi-cell Scenario

3.1 Basic Idea

In the channel reservation mechanism, the period is classified into reserved period and non-reserved period, as shown in Fig. 1. Among them, the reserved period is further classified into reserved management period and reserved transmission period, which will be referred to as management period and transmission period respectively. During the transmission period, the reserved Station (STA) transmits latency-sensitive traffic through randomly contention access channels, while other STAs enter silence state. During the management period, APs transmit reservation information over randomly contention access channels, and other STAs enter silence state. During non-reserved period, all STAs transmit data over random contention access channels. Benefits from the above classification, AP can exclude contention of STAs during the management period, thus reducing the probability of losing management frames and their reservation information due to collision. The reserved STAs can rapidly access the channel without contention during the transmission period, thus eliminating the contention and conflicts caused by other STAs and thereby reducing latency.

To implement period classification, all nodes will maintain two period lists, reservation list and silence list. For STAs, the reservation list records the transmission period information allocated to itself, and the silence list records the reserved period (including transmission period and management period) information allocated to other nodes. For APs, the reservation list records the transmission periods allocated to internal cell STAs, and the silence list records the transmission periods allocated to external cell STAs. Besides, AP maintains an additional management list to record management period information. STAs enter the silence state when the Time Synchronization Function (TSF) matches any of the silence list recording periods, and the silence state will last for a fixed duration. Nodes start to randomly compete for access channels when the TSF matches any of the reservation list or management list recording periods. For ensuring that the channel remains idle at the beginning of the reserved period so that the reserved node can access the channel quickly, the node must determine before each transmission whether the frame exchange sequence can end before the nearest reserved period, otherwise, this transmission is not performed.

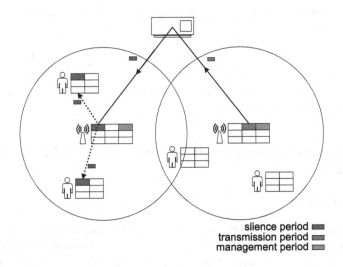

slience period ▰
transmission period ▰
management period ▰

Fig. 2. Multi-cell coordination operation of channel reservation mechanism.

To eliminate the interference of OBSSs, AP needs to notify the reservation list to the adjacent external cell nodes for multi-cell coordination, as shown in Fig. 2. AP forwards its reservation list to the adjacent AP through AC, and the adjacent AP adds the list to its silence list and then broadcasts the silence list to all STAs in the belonging BSS through management frames, and STAs add the list to their silence list. As a result of the above operation, the transmission period information can be shared among the cell nodes, thus excluding the interference of OBSSs. In addition, the management period should occur cyclically and each reserved period included in the management frame shouldn't exceed the next management period.

3.2   Channel Reservation Mechanism Algorithm

We use the following notation to describe the channel reservation algorithm:

1) Node: A denotes AP1, $a_n(n \geq 1)$ denotes the n-th STA associated with A; B denotes AP2, $b_n(n \geq 1)$ denotes the n-th STA associated with B. etc.

2) Period: T denotes the current time, TP denotes the transmission period, and MP denotes the management period. TP_i denotes the i-th transmission period and the same as the management period.

3) List: RL denotes the reservation list, SL denotes the silence list, and ML denotes the management list. $RL_i(i \geq 0)$ denotes the i-th period in the reservation list and the same for the other lists. We assume that the list is always in ascending order and there is no invalid period (an invalid period is a period whose beginning time is less than the current time), so RL_0 denotes the nearest valid reservation period to the current time and the same for other periods.

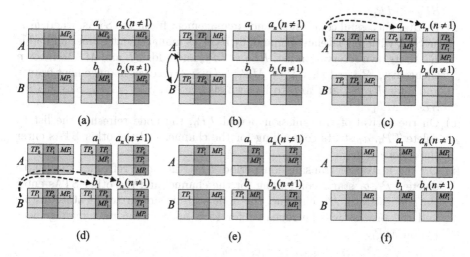

Fig. 3. Illustration of node operation and list status at different periods of channel reservation mechanism in two cell network topologies. (a) Node operation and list status before management period MP_0. (b) Node operation and list status after AP allocation and exchange transmission period in management period MP_0. (c) Node operation and list status after A sends a management frame in management period MP_0. (d) Node operation and list status after B sends a management frame in management period MP_0. (e) Node operation and list status in the first transmission period TP_0. (f) Node operation and list status in the second transmission period TP_1.

The channel reservation algorithm is described in Fig. 3. The green list represents the reservation list, the red list represents the silence list, the orange list represents the management list, and the periods in the list are sorted in ascending order from top to bottom:

(a) Before the management period MP_0 is about to arrive, there are no other periods recorded in the node list except MP_0. In the STAs silence list, $SL_0 = MP_0$; in the APs management list, $ML_0 = MP_0$.

(b) On the arrival of management period MP_0, the node refreshes the list to delete MP_0. APs update the management period, and in the management list,$ML_0 = MP_1$. A allocates transmission period TP_0, and in the reservation list, $RL_0 = TP_0$; B allocates transmission period TP_1, and in the reservation list, $RL_0 = TP_1$; After the allocation, A and B exchange RL information and add each other RL to their own SL, and in the A silence list, $SL_0 = TP_1$;In the B silence list, $SL_0 = TP_0$.

(c) After the above operation, APs start to contend for channels, and A successfully contends and sends management frames to STAs, where a_1 is an STA with low latency demand. a_1 receives management frames and adds RL to its own reservation list, $RL_0 = TP_0$, and adds SL and ML to its own silence list, $SL_0 = TP_1$, $SL_1 = MP_1$; $a_n(n \geq 2)$ receives management frames and adds RL,SL and ML to own silence list, $SL_0 = TP_0$, $SL_1 = TP_1$, $SL_2 = MP_1$.

(d) B After successful contention sends management frames to STAs, where b_1 is an STA with low latency demand. b_1 receives management frames and adds RL to its own reservation list, $RL_0 = TP_1$, and adds SL and ML to its own silence list, $SL_0 = TP_0$, $SL_1 = MP_1$; $b_n(n \geq 2)$ receives management frames and adds RL,SL and ML to its own silence list, $SL_0 = TP_0$, $SL_1 = TP_1$, $SL_2 = MP_1$.

(e) On the arrival of transmission period TP_0, the node refreshes the list to delete TP_0. a_1 starts contending for the channel and the other STAs enter the silence state.

(f) On the arrival of transmission period TP_1, the node refreshes the list to delete TP_1. b_1 starts contending for the channel and the other STAs enter the silence state. At this time, the node state is similar to the state in (a), and the process will be repeated for each node in the next management period MP_1.

4   Performance Evaluation

4.1   Simulation Environment and Parameter Settings

In this paper, we use the NS-3-based IEEE 802.11be network simulation platform for simulation. We validate the performance of the scheme by comparing the latency and throughput of users with low latency demand and other users respectively in four scenarios: EDCA scenario, R-TWT scenario, channel reservation scenario, and channel reservation scenario combined with management frame protection scheme (hereafter referred to as enhanced channel reservation scenario). The simulation parameters are shown in Table 1.

4.2   Simulation Results and Analysis

Figure 4 and Fig. 5 show the trend of the average latency of users with low latency demand and the average latency of users without low latency demand in different scenarios when the number of STAs increases in the 2×2 multi-cell network topology, respectively. From Fig. 4 and Fig. 5 we can observe that:

Table 1. Simulation parameter value table.

Parameter	Value
Management period cycle	100 ms
Reserved period duration	1 ms
Number of transmission periods in the management period cycle	5
Traffic rate	1e8bps
BSS size	15×15 m
network topology	2×2
Number of AP in BSS	1
Number of user with low latency demand in BSS	1
Latency sensitive traffic access category	VI
other traffic access category	BE
VI min/max contention window	15/31
BE min/max contention window	15/1023

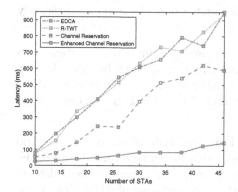

Fig. 4. Average latency of users with low latency demand in four scenarios of 2×2 network topology

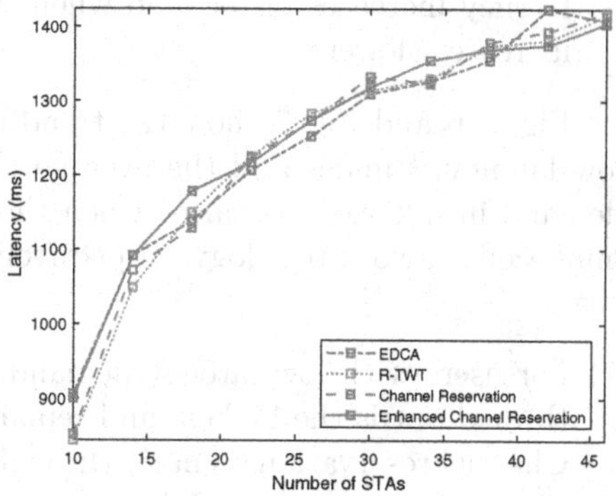

Fig. 5. Average latency of users without low latency demand in four scenarios of 2×2 network topology

1) For users with low latency demand. Enhanced channel reservation scenario latency is the lowest and increases slowly with a larger number of STAs. Channel reservation scenario latency is only higher than enhanced channel reservation scenario and increases faster with a larger number of STAs. EDCA scenario latency and R-TWT scenario latency are the highest, and there is no significant difference between them, both of which increase rapidly with a larger number of STAs. Therefore, when the number of STAs becomes larger, the difference between the latency of the enhanced channel reservation scenario and the other three scenarios gradually expands.

2) For users without low latency demand. There is no significant difference between the latency of the four scenarios. The latency increases with a larger

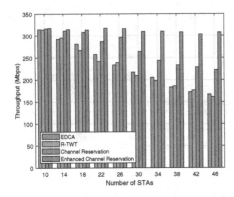

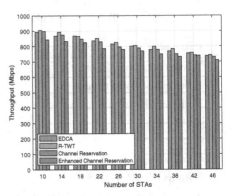

Fig. 6. Average throughput of users with low latency demand in four scenarios of 2×2 network topology

Fig. 7. Average throughput of users without low latency demand in four scenarios of 2×2 network topology

number of STAs for all four scenarios. When the number of STAs is less, the latency increases faster, and when the number of STAs is more, the latency increases slower.

Figure 6 and Fig. 7 show the trend of the average throughput of users with low latency demand and the average throughput of users without low latency demand in different scenarios when the number of STAs increases in the 2×2 multi-cell network topology, respectively. From Fig. 6 and Fig. 7 we can observe that:

1) For users with low latency demand. Enhanced channel reservation scenario throughput is the highest and remains stable with a larger number of STAs. Channel reservation scenario throughput is only lower than enhanced channel reservation scenario and decreases with a larger number of STAs. EDCA scenario throughput and R-TWT scenario throughput are the lowest and there is no significant difference between them, both decrease with a larger number of STAs. Therefore, when the number of STAs becomes larger, the difference between the throughput of the enhanced channel reservation scenario and the other three scenarios gradually expands.

2) For users without low latency demand. The enhanced channel reservation scenario has the lowest throughput, and the channel reservation scenario throughput is only higher than the enhanced channel reservation scenario. The R-TWT scenario has the highest throughput, followed by the EDCA scenario. However, there is no significant difference between them. The throughput of all four scenarios decreases slowly as the number of STAs becomes larger.

The main reasons for the trends in Fig. 4, 5, 6 and Fig. 7 are:

1) For users with low latency demand, when the number of STAs becomes larger, the network environment deteriorates, leading to an increase in latency as well as a decrease in throughput. In the EDCA scenario, although users with

low latency demand enjoy the backoff parameter for easier access to the channel, they still have difficulty accessing the channel when the number of STAs is larger and are prone to conflicts, resulting in higher latency and lower throughput; in the R-TWT scenario, although it is possible to keep other users in the cell in silence during the reservation period to provide channel protection for users with low latency demand, it is incapable of managing users from external cells. Therefore, when the number of external cell users is large, channel protection is ineffective, resulting in high latency and low throughput; the channel reservation mechanism, with multi-cell coordination capability, can silence other users including external cell users during the reservation period, providing channel protection for users with low latency demand. However, when the number of STAs is large, the management frames carrying reservation information are easily lost, resulting in better delay and throughput than the above two mechanisms, but the improvement is not significant; the enhanced channel reservation mechanism, with multi-cell collaboration and management frame protection capability, can effectively avoid the loss of management frames and make users with low delay demand free from interference by other users including external cell users during the reservation period. Therefore, the latency is minimized and the throughput is maximized.

2) For users without low latency demand, when the number of STAs becomes larger, the network environment deteriorates, leading to an increase in latency as well as a decrease in throughput. When the number of STAs is less, the network environment is better, and the increment in the number of STAs leads to a sudden deterioration of the network environment and an intensified trend of latency increase, but the throughput decreases slowly due to the high number of STAs. When the number of STAs is more, the network environment is poor, the increment in the number of STAs only leads to a gradual deterioration of the network environment, the trend of increasing delay slows down, and the throughput still keeps decreasing slowly. In the EDCA scenario, users without low delay demand are not restricted, the throughput is higher, but the impact on delay is smaller. The R-TWT scenario silences other users in this cell during the reservation period, and the overall network conflict is reduced. For users without low latency demand, throughput is improved, but the impact on latency is smaller. In the channel reservation scenario and the enhanced channel reservation scenario, users without low latency demand cannot transmit during the reservation period, resulting in a decrease in throughput, but with a small impact on latency.

We can see from the above analysis that the proposed channel reservation mechanism combining the management frame protection scheme as compared to the EDCA mechanism, and R-TWT mechanism, can significantly improve the latency and throughput of users with low latency demand without sacrificing too much the latency and throughput of users without low latency demand.

5   Conclusion

To solve the interference problem of OBSSs to channel reservation in multi-cell scenarios, this paper proposes a novel channel reservation mechanism, and a management frame protection scheme to solve the management frame loss problem in multi-cell high-density scenarios. It is demonstrated through simulation that the proposed channel reservation mechanism and management frame protection scheme can effectively solve the interference problem of OBSSs and management frame loss, thus improving the latency and throughput of users with low latency demand.

Acknowledgments. This work was supported in part by the National Natural Science Foundations of CHINA (Grant No. 61871322, No. 61771392, and No. 61771390), and Science and Technology on Avionics Integration Laboratory and the Aeronautical Science Foundation of China (Grant No. 20185553035 and No. 201955053002).

References

1. IEEE. IEEE 802.11ax Draft Standard for Information technology Telecommunications and information exchange between systems Local and metropolitan area networks Specific requirements-Part 11: Wireless LAN Medium Access Control (MAC) and Physical Layer (PHY) Specifications (2021)
2. IEEE. IEEE 802.11be (D2.0) Draft Standard for Information technology Telecommunications and information exchange between systems Local and metropolitan area networks Specific requirements-Part 11: Wireless LAN Medium Access Control (MAC) and Physical Layer (PHY) Specifications (2022)
3. IEEE. IEEE 802.11ah Draft Standard for Information technology Telecommunications and information exchange between systems Local and metropolitan area networks Specific requirements-Part 11: Wireless LAN Medium Access Control (MAC) and Physical Layer (PHY) Specifications (2016)
4. Choi, J., Yoo, J., Choi, S., Kim, C.: EBA: an enhancement of the IEEE 802.11 DCF via distributed reservation. IEEE Trans. Mob. Comput. 4(4), 378–390 (2005). https://doi.org/10.1109/TMC.2005.57
5. Chao, I., Lai, C., Chung, Y.: A reservation-based distributed MAC scheme for infrastructure wireless networks. In: 2018 3rd International Conference on Intelligent Green Building and Smart Grid (IGBSG), pp. 1–4 (2018). https://doi.org/10.1109/IGBSG.2018.8393531
6. Ma, M., Yang, Y.: A novel contention-based MAC protocol with channel reservation for wireless LANs. IEEE Trans. Wirel. Commun. 7(10), 3748 (2008). https://doi.org/10.1109/T-WC.2008.08885
7. Bo, L., Wenzhao, T., Hu, Z., Hui, Z.: m-DIBCR: MAC protocol with multiple-step distributed in-band channel reservation. IEEE Commun. Lett. 12(1), 23–25 (2008). https://doi.org/10.1109/LCOMM.2008.071561
8. Li, B., Li, W., Valois, F., Ubeda, S., Zhou, H., Chen, Y.: Performance analysis of an efficient MAC protocol with multiple-step distributed in-band channel reservation. IEEE Trans. Veh. Technol. 59(1), 368–382 (2010). https://doi.org/10.1109/TVT.2009.2028029

9. Lei, X., Rhee, S.H.: Design of a collision-free backoff method to improve the IEEE 802.11 DCF. In: 2016 Eighth International Conference on Ubiquitous and Future Networks (ICUFN), pp. 395–397 (2016). https://doi.org/10.1109/ICUFN.2016.7537057

10. Lei, X.Y., Rhee, S.H.: Sender-initiated reservations for reducing collisions in 802.11 MAC. In: 2013 Fifth International Conference on Ubiquitous and Future Networks (ICUFN), pp. 288–291 (2013). https://doi.org/10.1109/ICUFN.2013.6614827

11. Bankov, D., Khorov, E., Lyakhov, A., Stepanova, E.: Clock drift impact on target wake time in IEEE 802.11ax/ah networks. In: 2018 Engineering and Telecommunication (EnT-MIPT), pp. 30–34 (2018). https://doi.org/10.1109/EnT-MIPT.2018.00014

12. Nurchis, M., Bellalta, B.: Target wake time: scheduled access in IEEE 802.11ax WLANs. IEEE Wirel. Commun. **26**(2), 142–150 (2019). https://doi.org/10.1109/MWC.2019.1800163

13. Chen, Q., Liang, G., Weng, Z.: A target wake time based power conservation scheme for maximizing throughput in IEEE 802.11ax WLANs. In: 2019 IEEE 25th International Conference on Parallel and Distributed Systems (ICPADS), pp. 217–224 (2019). https://doi.org/10.1109/ICPADS47876.2019.00040

14. Chen, Q., Zhu, Y.-H.: Scheduling channel access based on target wake time mechanism in 802.11ax WLANs. IEEE Trans. Wirel. Commun. **20**(3), 1529–1543 (2021). https://doi.org/10.1109/TWC.2020.3034173

15. Qiu, W., Chen, G., Nguyen, K.N., Sehgal, A., Nayak, P., Choi, J.: Category-based 802.11ax target wake time solution. IEEE Access **9**, 100154–100172 (2021). https://doi.org/10.1109/ACCESS.2021.3096940

16. Schneider, B., Sofia, R.C., Kovatsch, M.: A proposal for time-aware scheduling in wireless industrial IoT environments. In: 2022 IEEE/IFIP Network Operations and Management Symposium, NOMS 2022, pp. 1–6 (2022). https://doi.org/10.1109/NOMS54207.2022.9789864

17. Chen, Q.: An energy efficient channel access with target wake time scheduling for overlapping 802.11ax basic service sets. IEEE Internet Things J. https://doi.org/10.1109/JIOT.2022.316333

An Adaptive Beamtracking Method for the Next Generation mmWave WLAN

Qingkun Li, Mao Yang$^{(\boxtimes)}$, Zhongjiang Yan, and Bo Li

School of Electronics and Information, Northwestern Polytechnical University,
Xi'an, China
liqingkun01@mail.nwpu.edu.cn, yangmao@nwpu.edu.cn

Abstract. With the development of next generation mobile communication and short distance communication, mmWave is becoming more and more critical. The transmission rate and bandwidth of mmWave are greater than that of low frequency band. mmWave can effectively provide large-flow and low-latency service over short distances. Next generation WLAN, such as 802.11ad/ay, already uses mmWave. mmWave uses the directional gain antenna, and beamtracking is performed to determine the new working beam when one end of the communication is displaced. The beamtracking method is designed in detail in 802.11ad /ay: beamtracking is performed after data is sent. This method takes the delay into account, but it is easy to lose packets when nodes move quickly. To address this issue, we design an adaptive beamtracking method (ABT), which adjusts the order of sending data and performing beamtracking according to the number of consecutive beamtracking request. It can take both throughput and delay into account. The simulation results show that the adaptive beamtracking method can achieve the same delay as the beamtracking method in 802.11ad/ay, and the throughput is greater than the beamtracking method in 802.11ad/ay.

Keywords: Next generation WLAN · mmWave · Beamtracking · 802.11ad/ay

1 Introduction

In recent years, with the development of automatic driving, industrial Internet and virtual reality, people's demand for large bandwidth services and low latency services has gradually increased [1]. WLAN such as 802.11ax works in 2.4 GHz and 5 GHz frequency band, with a maximum bandwidth of 160 MHz and a theoretical rate of 9.6 Gbps. This frequency band is also the operating frequency of Bluetooth and Radar, so the channel is very crowded. In order to avoid the disadvantages of low frequency band, in 2013, the WIFI Alliance launched 802.11ad, which operates at 60 GHz, has a maximum bandwidth of more than 1 GHz and a maximum rate of 8 Gbps. It uses mmWave to greatly improve the bandwidth

© ICST Institute for Computer Sciences, Social Informatics and Telecommunications Engineering 2023
Published by Springer Nature Switzerland AG 2023. All Rights Reserved
D.-J. Deng et al. (Eds.): SGIoT 2022, LNICST 497, pp. 254–265, 2023.
https://doi.org/10.1007/978-3-031-31275-5_24

and rate of short distance communication. The next generation mmWave WLAN 802.11ay is improved on the basis of 802.11ad. By introducing MIMO, channel bonding and other technologies, the maximum bandwidth is 8.64 GHz and the theoretical rate is 100 Gbps [2].

mmWave is easy to fade and the communication distance is short. Directional antenna is needed to improve the gain. Because the beam has direction, the beam alignment should be carried out first in mmWave communication. When displacement or occlusion occurs in the communication process, the communication quality will be affected or even communication cannot be achieved. Therefore, beamforming (BF) and beamtracking (BT) are very important processes in mmWave communication. In future communication scenarios, such as autonomous driving and virtual reality, etc. [3], mobility becomes an important feature, and communication with directional transmission is more sensitive to movement. Therefore, Beamtracking has become the focus of academia and industry. It means that when one end of the communication is moving, the other end can find in timely and perform beamtracking, determine the new work beam pair and notify the other side.

The beamtracking process specified in 802.11ad/ay is as follows [4]: If the RSSI (Received Signal Strength Indication) of the data packet is lower than a certain threshold, beamtracking will be performed. In the next transmission, beamtracking is performed after data is sent, and the beam pair with the largest RSSI is selected as the new working beam pair and notified to the other side. However, there is a certain lag in this way. Beamtracking is performed after the packet is sent, when the move speed of node is very fast, the packet will often fail to be transmitted. If the node moves continuously and uses this beamtracking method every time, each data packet will be lost.

For a long time, people are trying to reduce the overhead of beamtracking from MAC layer, physical layer and channel. In reference [5], starting from the channel and aiming at the problem that the channel model of the current beamtracking algorithm is too simplified, Markov multi-beamtracking algorithm is introduced to maintain multiple beams for tracking at the same time. In reference [6], starting from the physical layer, Extended Kalman Filter is used to track the channel on the static antenna, the error variance estimated by Extended Kalman Filter is used to calculate the array vector error, and the minimum mean square error beamformer is used to update the beamforming weights. Reference [7] proposed a multi base station cooperative beamforming method to improve the communication quality at the cell boundary. Although these papers improve the efficiency of beamtracking from the physical layer and channel, they do not analyze it from the MAC layer. By changing the order of sending data and performing beamtracking, we can reduce the packet loss rate when node moves fastly.

To reduce the lag of beamtracking method in 802.11ad/ay, we design an adaptive beamtracking method (ABT), which adjusts the order of sending data and performing beamtracking according to the number of consecutive beamtracking request. It can take both throughput and delay into account. Post-beamtracking means sending data before performing beamtracking. Pre-beamtracking means sending data after performing beamtracking. Record the number of consecutive post-beamtracking. If the number reaches the threshold, it indicates that the current movement of the node is intense and the post-beamtracking method is likely to fail. In this case, we should switch to pre-beamtracking. In the pre-beamtracking period, the change value of beam before and after beamtracking is recorded. If it is less than a certain threshold for n consecutive times, it indicates that the node is moving slowly and can be converted to post-beamtracking. Simulation results show that the throughput and delay of the proposed scheme are better than beamtracking method in 802.11ad/Ay, and no extra overhead is introduced.

The remainder of this paper is structured as follows: Sect. 2 introduces the beamtracking method in 802.11ad and the problem of post-beamtracking. Section 3 introduces the detailed design of adaptive beamtracking. In Sect. 4, the performance of beamtracking method in 802.11ad/ay and adaptive beamtracking is verified by simulation, and the difference in throughput and delay between them is analyzed.

2   Related Works and Problem Analysis

2.1   The Beamtracking in IEEE 802.11ad/ay

mmWave uses the directional antenna. According to the width of the directional beam, the horizontal plane of the device is divided into different sectors, and each sector has a specific sector ID. The best transmitting beam and the best receiving beam are required for transmission. In this paper, we assume that each sector contains only one beam, and one sector ID corresponds to one beam. In 802.11ad/ay, the transmission is made up of beacon interval one by one. The following figure shows the structure of a beacon interval (see Fig. 1). The BHI is used for beam training at the beginning of each beacon interval, and the DTI is used for data transmission [4].

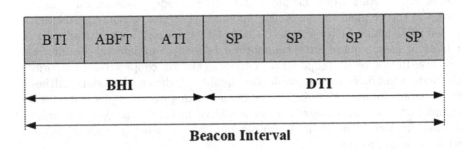

Fig. 1. The structure of a beacon interval.

In BHI, the best transmitting beam TX_1 and the best receiving beam RX_1 to be used in this superframe are determined. If no movement or occlusion occurs in the DTI phase, TX_1 and RX_1 can be used in this beacon interval all the time. Otherwise, the beamtracking is triggered, which is used to find the best transmitting beam TX_2 and the best receiving beam RX_2. The figure below shows the beamtracking process (see Fig. 2).

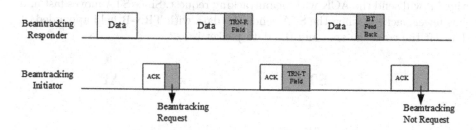

Fig. 2. The beamtracking process in 802.11ad/ay.

The beamtracking process is divided into the following steps:

Step1: If a station receives a data which RSSI is higher than -68 dBm and less than -60 dBm, it will carry a beamtracking request when it sends an ACK. The station that sends the beamtracking request is called the beamtracking initiator.

Step2: The station that receives an ACK carrying the beamtracking request is called the beamtracking responder. When beamtracking responder sends data, TRN-R field is appended. The TRN-R field is used to perform a responder sector sweep after data is sent. When the sweep is complete, the initiator will know the best send sector of responder.

Step3: The initiator receives data, replies with an ACK, TRN-T field is appended. The TRN-T field is used to perform a initiator sector sweep after ACK is sent. Each sector sweep frame carries the result of the best send sector of responder in step2.

Step4: The responder receives the ACK and knows its best send sector. We can also know the best send sector of initiator after TRN-T. When responder sends data again, Beamtracking Feed Back field is appended, which contains the best send sector of initiator.

Step5: The initiator receives the Beamtracking Feed Back, changes its sector and sends an ACK using the new sector. This ACK will finish a beamtracking process.

2.2 Problem Analysis

The beamtracking in 802.11ad/ay has the following problems. Firstly, the beamtracking is triggered by the RX. Secondly, beamtracking is performed after the data is sent. Thirdly, when node moves fast, beamtracking in 802.11ad/ay will lose packets.

As shown in the following figure (see Fig. 3), the blue area is the coverage area of the current beam pair, the purple area is the coverage area of the next beam pair. The STA moves fast and the AP is fixed. When the STA is about to leave the coverage area, one data packet is sent and received by the AP. We assume that RSSI is greater than -68 dBm and less than -60 dBm. As mentioned above, the AP will send the ACK with beamtracking request. Since STA moves fast and has fewer packets, when the STA sends the data with TRN-R field appended, it has left the coverage area and the data packet is lost.

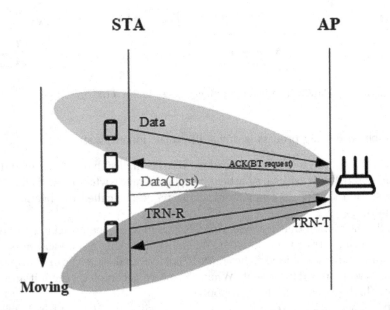

Fig. 3. The scenario that beamtracking process in 802.11ad/ay will drop packet.

3 Adaptive Beamtracking Process

3.1 Basic Idea

The order of sending data packet and performing beamtracking affects packet delay and throughput. If beamtracking is performed after data packet is sent, the packet delay is not affected by beamtracking, but the probability of packet loss is increased. If beamtracking is performed before data packet is sent, data packet will be sent successfully, however, the beamtracking takes time, and packet is affected by the beamtracking, which increases the packet delay. The following figure compares the post-beamtracking with the pre-beamtracking (see Fig. 4). It can be found that the pre-beamtracking avoids packet loss but also introduces certain delay. If we can take two methods into account, the packet loss rate of beamtracking in 802.11ad/ay can be reduced while the packet delay is guaranteed.

802.11ad/ay Beamtracking

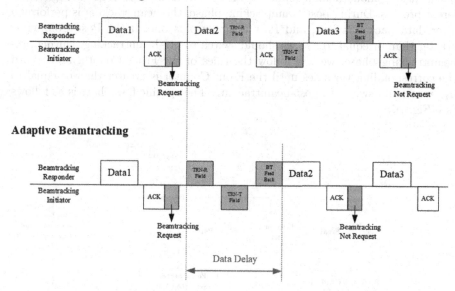

Adaptive Beamtracking

Fig. 4. The difference between 802.11ad/ay beamtracking and adaptive beamtracking in packet Delay.

The adaptive beamtracking follows the frame structure of ACK and DATA in 802.11ad/ay, and only changes the process. After beamtracking is triggered, the order of sending data packet and performing beamtracking is adjusted according to the number of consecutive beamtracking request. The specific process is as follows.

3.2 Detail Design

Firstly, two counters are introduced:

Post Counter: During the post-beamtracking phase, the number of consecutive post-beamtracking is recorded. This counter sets to 0 if the RSSI received is greater than −60 dBm. When this counter is greater than or equal to n_P, we should switch to pre-beamtracking.

Front Counter: During the pre-beamtracking phase, we should record the times that the beam difference before and after the beamtracking is less than or equal to Δ. If the beam difference is greater than Δ, this counter sets to 0. When this counter is greater than or equal to n_F, we should switch to post-beamtracking.

By maintaining these two counters, adaptive beamtracking can be achieved. The process is as follows. When sending data, the station should check whether the beamtracking is requested. If beamtracking is not required, sets Post Counter and Front Counter to 0. If beamtracking is required, according to the current beamtracking mode(default mode is post-beamtracking), we'll go through a different process. During post-beamtracking phase, the beamtracking is performed after data packet is sent, and Post Counter plus one. If the Post Counter is greater than or equal to n_P, we should switch to pre-beamtracking. During pre-beamtracking phase, we will follow the rules of the Front Counter and record the corresponding variables until the Front Counter is greater than or equal to n_F, we should switch to post-beamtracking. The specific flow chart is as follows (see Fig. 5).

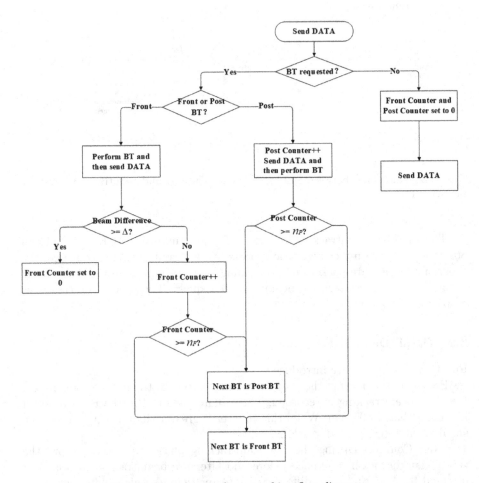

Fig. 5. The adaptive beamtracking flow diagram.

4   Performance Evaluation

4.1   Simulation Scenario and Parameter Configuration

The simulation platform of this paper is designed according to TCP/IP model
(Table 1).

Table 1. Parameter configuration.

Parameter	Value
BSS Number	1
STA Number	1
AP Number	1
Traffic Rate	400 Mbps to 4000 Mbps
Packet Size	80000 bytes
AMPDU Size	1, 2, 4, 8, 16, 32
BI Duration	0.1 s
CCA threshold	−68 dBm
BT threshold	(−68 dBm, 60 dBm)
Simulator Duration	200 s

4.2   Simulation Results

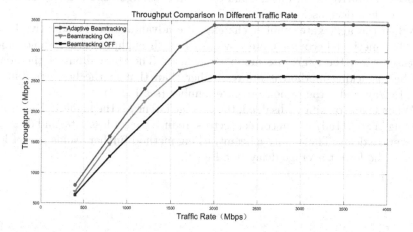

Fig. 6. Throughput comparison between ABT & beamtracking in 802.11ad/ay in different traffic rate.

When beamtracking is disabled, the throughput is the lowest. The beamtracking in 802.11ad/ay can correct sectors, reduce packet loss rate, and improve the throughput. The adaptive beamtracking method further avoids packet loss and has the highest throughput (see Fig. 6).

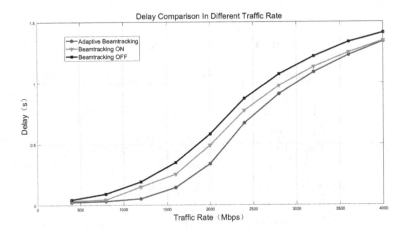

Fig. 7. Delay comparison between ABT & beamtracking in 802.11ad/ay in different traffic rate.

When beamtracking is disabled, the average latency is the highest. The beamtracking in 802.11ad/ay can correct sectors, reduce packet loss rate, and decrease the average delay. The adaptive beamtracking method further avoids packet loss and has the lowest average delay. With the increase of traffic rate, the delay difference of adaptive beamtracking and the beamtracking in 802.11ad/ay increases first and then decreases (see Fig. 7).

When the aggregate number changes, the advantage of the adaptive beam Tracking method becomes more obvious. The throughput of the same mode increases when the aggregate number increases. The throughput of the adaptive beamtracking method is always higher than that of the beamtracking in 802.11ad/ay under the same aggregate number (see Fig. 8).

When beamtracking is disabled, the average latency is the highest. The beamtracking in 802.11ad/ay can correct sectors, reduce packet loss rate, and decrease the average delay. The adaptive beamtracking method further avoids packet loss and has the lowest average delay (see Fig. 9).

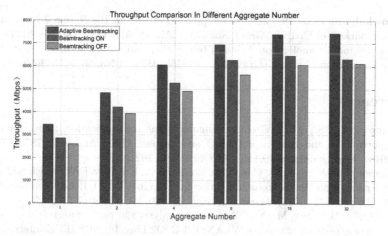

Fig. 8. Throughput comparison between ABT & beamtracking in 802.11ad/ay in different aggregate number.

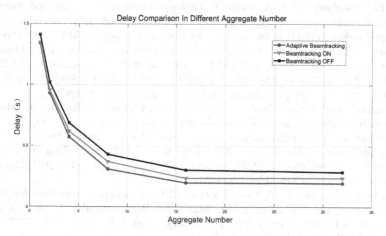

Fig. 9. Delay comparison between ABT & beamtracking in 802.11ad/ay in different aggregate number.

5   Conclusion

In this paper, aiming at the lag of beamtracking in 802.11ad/ay, we design an adaptive beamtracking method. According to the number of consecutive beamtracking request, the order of sending data packet and performing beamtracking is adjusted. In this way, both throughput and packet delay can be taken into account. Simulation results show that adaptive beamtracking method improves the throughput compared with the beamtracking in 802.11ad/ay, and the packet delay of the two methods is similar. In different traffic rate and different aggregate number, the throughput of adaptive beamtracking is higher than the beamtracking in 802.11ad/ay.

Acknowledgements. This work was supported in part by the National Natural Science Foundations of CHINA (Grant No. 61871322, No. 61771392, and No. 61771390), and Science and Technology on Avionics Integration Laboratory and the Aeronautical Science Foundation of China (Grant No. 20185553035 and No. 201955053002).

References

1. Rappaport, T.S., et al.: Wireless communications and applications above 100 GHz: opportunities and challenges for 6G and beyond. IEEE Access **7**, 78729–78757 (2019). https://doi.org/10.1109/ACCESS.2019.2921522
2. Ghasempour, Y., da Silva, C.R.C.M., Cordeiro, C., Knightly, E.W.: IEEE 802.11ay: next-generation 60 GHz communication for 100 Gb/s Wi-Fi. IEEE Commun. Mag. **55**(12), 186–192 (2017). https://doi.org/10.1109/MCOM.2017.1700393
3. Lei, L., Li, B., Yang, M., Yan, Z.: System analysis and performance evaluation for the next generation mmWave WLAN: IEEE 802.11ay. In: 2018 IEEE International Conference on Signal Processing, Communications and Computing (ICSPCC), pp. 1–6 (2018). https://doi.org/10.1109/ICSPCC.2018.8567616
4. IEEE Standard for Information technology-Telecommunications and information exchange between systems-Local and metropolitan area networks-Specific requirements-Part 11: Wireless LAN Medium Access Control (MAC) and Physical Layer (PHY) Specifications Amendment 3: Enhancements for Very High Throughput in the 60 GHz Band, in IEEE Std 802.11ad-2012 (Amendment to IEEE Std 802.11-2012, as amended by IEEE Std 802.11ae-2012 and IEEE Std 802.11aa-2012), pp. 1–628 (2012). https://doi.org/10.1109/IEEESTD.2012.6392842
5. Blandino, S., Senic, J., Gentile, C., Caudill, D., Chuang, J., Kayani, A.: Markov multi-beamtracking on 60 GHz mobile channel measurements. IEEE Open J. Veh. Technol. **3**, 26–39 (2022). https://doi.org/10.1109/OJVT.2021.3138697
6. Jayaprakasam, S., Ma, X., Choi, J.W., Kim, S.: Robust beam-tracking for mmWave mobile communications. IEEE Commun. Lett. **21**(12), 2654–2657 (2017). https://doi.org/10.1109/LCOMM.2017.2748938
7. Hoshino, K., Fujii, T.: A study on optimal beam selection algorithm for multi-cell coordinated beamforming. In: 2021 IEEE 93rd Vehicular Technology Conference (VTC2021-Spring), pp. 1–5 (2021). https://doi.org/10.1109/VTC2021-Spring51267.2021.9448840
8. Da Silva, C.R.C.M., Kosloff, J., Chen, C., Lomayev, A., Cordeiro, C.: Beamforming training for IEEE 802.11 ay MmWave systems. In: 2018 Information Theory and Applications Workshop (ITA), pp. 1–9 (2018). https://doi.org/10.1109/ITA.2018.8503112
9. Nitsche, T., Cordeiro, C., Flores, A.B., Knightly, E.W., Perahia, E., Widmer, J.C.: IEEE 802.11ad: directional 60 GHz communication for multi-Gigabit-per-second Wi-Fi [Invited Paper]. IEEE Commun. Mag. **52**(12), 132–141 (2014). https://doi.org/10.1109/MCOM.2014.6979964
10. Nitsche, T., Flores, A.B., Knightly, E.W., Widmer, J.: Steering with eyes closed: Mm-Wave beam steering without in-band measurement. In: 2015 IEEE Conference on Computer Communications (INFOCOM), pp. 2416–2424 (2015). https://doi.org/10.1109/INFOCOM.2015.7218630
11. Zhou, P., Fang, X., Fang, Y., Long, Y., He, R., Han, X.: Enhanced random access and beam training for MmWave wireless local networks with high user density. IEEE Trans. Wirel. Commun. **16**(12), 7760–7773 (2017). https://doi.org/10.1109/TWC.2017.2753779

12. Zhang, D., Chen, H., Kokshoorn, M., Li, Y., Wei, N., Vucetic, B.: A probe-then-refine beam tracking algorithm for MmWave MISO systems. In: 2018 IEEE International Conference on Communications Workshops (ICC Workshops), pp. 1–6 (2018). https://doi.org/10.1109/ICCW.2018.8403590

13. Ismayilov, R., Kaneko, M., Hiraguri, T., Nishimori, K.: Adaptive beam-frequency allocation algorithm with position uncertainty for millimeter-wave MIMO systems. In: 2018 IEEE 87th Vehicular Technology Conference (VTC Spring), pp. 1–5 (2018). https://doi.org/10.1109/VTCSpring.2018.8417622

A Collision Aware Multi-link Operation for Next Generation WLAN

Disheng An, Bo Li, Mao Yang$^{(\boxtimes)}$, and Zhongjiang Yan

School of Electronics and Information, Northwestern Polytechnical University, Xi'an, China
andisheng@mail.nwpu.edu.cn, {libo.npu,yangmao,zhjyan}@nwpu.edu.cn

Abstract. In a wireless local area network (WLAN), when the contention is fierce, most of the frames are collided and backoff windows are doubled, resulting in a low channel efficiency. 802.11 be introduces multi-link opertaions (MLO) but faces nonsimultaneous transmit and receive (NSTR) problem which limits the prospects of multi-links. In this paper a new multi-link operation scheme is proposed. When a link is transmitting, antennas from the other link usually suffer huge inteference and can't receive properly. In the proposed scheme the interfered antennas are switched to the transmitting link to monitor collisions. If collisions are detected, one of the colliders stops transmitting. Collisions are thus eliminated at the early stage. Simulation shows that using this scheme, the channel efficiency of a highly competitive network stays at a high level compared to traditional solutions. Simulation also shows that the proposed scheme offers better QoS.

Keywords: Multi-link Operation · 802.11be · WLAN · NSTR

1 Introduction

With its simplicity in setting up and high mobility, WLAN has been widely adopted in households, factories and enterprises as LAN solutions. The prevalence of 802.11n/ac/ax in the marketplace has proved its success [1,3]. In 2019, the project of 802.11be was initiated. As a next generation WLAN protocol, 802.11be has adopted MCS of 4096QAM, bandwidth of 320 MHz and up to 16 spatial streams which work together to achieve a bit rate as high as 46.1184 Gbps, leading to a 30 Gbps MAC layer throughput and better quality of service [2]. A paradigm shift made by 802.11be in its protocol family is multi-link operation (MLO) [4]. Before 802.11be, a device has only one radio. Devices in a pre-802.11be BSS work on either 5 GHz or 2.4 GHz frequency band. In 802.11be, multi-link devices (MLD) are introduced which has two or more radios working independently on different frequency bands.

The new generation of WLAN comes with two problems. Firstly, as the bit rate is becoming higher, the time used for transmitting MPDUs in a frame

D.-J. Deng et al. (Eds.): SGIoT 2022, LNICST 497, pp. 266–276, 2023.
https://doi.org/10.1007/978-3-031-31275-5_25

exchange is becoming smaller. However, the time used in backoff procedure, the time used to transmit preamble and the time used to transmit control frames remain constant, which reduces the marginal benefit brought by high bit rate. Secondly, AP MLDs are often considered to have well isolation among their antennas that the antennas of each link in an AP MLD are placed far enough that transmission on one link will not interfere the reception on other links. However, because STA MLDs have higher mobility and smaller volume and sometimes cheaper in cost, they have weak isolation between links. When a STA MLD is transmitting on a link, antennas on other links of the MLD will suffer huge in-device coexistence (IDC) interference [5], resulting a failure of reception.

The IDC interference makes it impossible for links to work independently. If a link just waits for the other to finish before working, it will be a waste of multi-link capability. With the assumption that MLDs have the ability to perform link switching and the ability to detect jitter of energy in the existence of IDC interference, this paper proposed a scheme using the idle link to detect collisions on the transmitting link, which not only reduces the use of control frames but also avoids failures caused by data collision.

The article is organized as follows. In Sect. 2, we review the operation of multi-link and have a brief introduction to existing multi-link operation schemes. Existing problems are analyzed in Sect. 3. In Sect. 4 and 5, the proposed scheme is described. We will see how the proposed scheme keeps the network from congestion even when contention is fierce. Simulation results and analysis are presented in Sect. 6. In Sect. 7 we will discuss more details about implementation and pending work.

2   Review of Multi-link Operation

The standard has offered many types of Multi-Link Operation. For example enhanced multi-link single-radio (EMLSR), Simultaneous Transmit and Receive (STR), and Non-Simultaneous Transmit and Receive (NSTR) including PPDU(PHY protocol data unit) alignment and Wait-Slot. In the mode of EMLSR [4], antennas switch from one link to another to perform MIMO transmission and MIMO reception. In the mode of STR, MLDs can transmit on one link while receiving on the other link. Because the number of links are doubled, the theoretical channel capacity are doubled as well. However, in the mode of NSTR, due to IDC interference mentioned above, MLDs can't transmit on one link while receiving on the other link. The transmission on one link will also affect carrier sensing and energy detection on other links. It's a challenge to coordinate all the links while make the largest use of them. PPDU Alignment aligns the end time of PPDUs on two links to prevent the solicited PPDU (for example block acknowledgment) from interfering the carrier sensing on the other link required by the trigger based PPDU process, if the other link is transmitting a PPDU with trigger [6]. Wait-Slot aligns the beginning of transmission on two links, by letting the link that firstly finished backoff to wait for the other link to finish. When both link reach zero [7], they transmit simultaneously, thus neither of the two links are interfered nor set idle. A threshold can be set for Wait-Slot process that if the remaining backoff slots of the lagging link is above the threshold, the preceding link can skip waiting. PPDU Alignment and Wait-Slot are illustrated in Fig. 1 and Fig. 2.

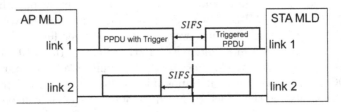

Fig. 1. NSTR PPDU alignment.

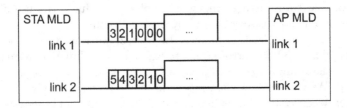

Fig. 2. NSTR wait slot.

3   Problem Analysis

Multi-link operations mentioned above avoid idling by transmitting on two links simultaneously, which do improve the channel efficiency. However, in a dense network where there are many STAs and big uplink traffics, the contention of channel will be fierce [9]. A traditional method may increase backoff windows to mitigate the contention, at the cost of a worse latency and throughput performance. When collision happens, STAs in conflict are not aware of the fact that they are transmitting useless bits, so they keep transmitting till the end, which makes the channel useless for a period of preamble time plus a data time. As the 802.11 protocol evolves, the duration of preamble is getting longer and longer [8,10]. The duration of data is also getting longer with elongated maximal MPDU aggregation. To reduce the span when channel is useless, RTS and CTS mechanism could be used in the contention. However, the frame exchange procedure of RTS and CTS brings an additional overhead of a RTS time plus a CTS time plus two SIFS time, which is comparable to data's length and can't be neglected [11] (Fig. 3).

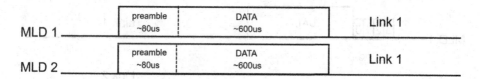

Fig. 3. Collisions make channel useless.

4 Basic Operation of the Proposed Scheme

MLDs using this method are assumed to have the ability to switch the working link of antennas from one to another within a link switching time of microseconds or instantly. After link switch, antennas working on the new link are assumed to have the ability to detect interference from other devices with the presence of self interference from transmitting antennas of this device. The ability to demodulate and receive packages is not required.

The procedure begins when a STD MLD having packages in buffer has updated its backoff counters on both links, and a DIFS or an AIFS of clear channel has been waited (Fig. 4):

Step 1. The MLD performs backfoff on both links. If one of the link is busy, as shown in Fig. 5, only one link needs to backoff.

Step 2. If one link finishes backoff firstly, antennas from the other link should be switched to this link. The bakcoff on the latter link should be paused.

Step 3. MLD begins transmission on the link that firstly finished backoff, while antennas from the other link begins to detect interference.

Step 4. If no interference is detected during a certain period of time, antennas should be switched back to original link.

Step 5. If interference is detected during the detection span, this MLD should stop transmission immediately. And antennas should be switched back to original link. And wait for the channel to be clear to backoff again.

Step 6. When the transmission is finished, go to Step 1.

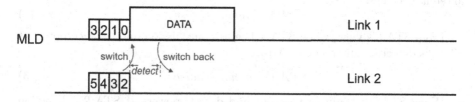

Fig. 4. Basic operation of the proposed scheme, when both links are idle.

The duration of detection should be long enough that other STA MLDs in the same BSS are aware of this transmission.

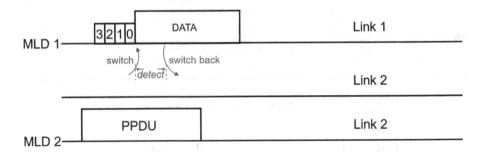

Fig. 5. Basic operation of the proposed scheme, when one link is busy.

5   Collision Awareness Mechanism

Collision happens when two or more devices in the BSS have the same number of backoff slots which is the smallest among all devices. They begein to transmit at almost the same time. Because when they are transmitting, their antennas are set to the receiving state, they can't perceive each other. They don't stop until the end of transmission. Because other devices can't do anything during the collison, the channel is deemed to be wasted.

With the proposed scheme, devices are able to perceive each other in the early stage of a collision. One of the colliders can stop its transmission to avoid interfering the other. In this way, there is always a PPDU being transmitted and decoded correctly, and channel is not wasted.

It's necessary to figure out which device should stop transmission when collision is detected. See Fig 6 and Fig 7. Assume both STA 1 and STA 2 reach the last backoff slot but STA 1 is a bit (microseconds or within a microsecond) earlier STA 2. When STA 1 is transmitting and using the other link detecting, STA 2 hasn't sent a bit. So interference power at STA 1's detection antenna equals to

$$noise \tag{1}$$

Soon STA 2 begins to transmit, and the interference at STA 1's detection antenna becomes:

$$STA\ 2's\ signal + noise \tag{2}$$

From STA 2's view, when STA 1 begins transmission, interference power at STA 2's detection antenna equals to:

$$STA\ 1's\ signal + noise \tag{3}$$

When STA 2's begin to transmit and detect, powers at STA 2's detection antenna is still:

$$STA\ 1's\ signal + noise \tag{4}$$

STA 1 experiences a rise of interference while STA 2 doesn't. We let the device that experiences a rise of interference to stop transmission. In this way, among all the devices that has the same number of backoff slots, the last one wins.

Power sensed by STA1

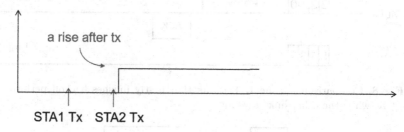

Fig. 6. Channel power sensed at STA 1.

Power sensed by STA2

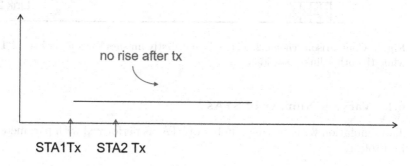

Fig. 7. Channel power sensed at STA2.

6   Simulation Results

The simulation results are carried out with a system-level discrete-event network simulation program. In this program, packages are generated by application layer in a uniform arrival which is dependent on the traffic rate. Upper MAC are designed to coordinates lower MACs and manages a package queue that is shared by its lower MACs. Lower MACs are designed to perform AMPDU assembling and perform frame exchange with peers. Each low MAC works on a link. PHY is in charge of determining packages' durations and energy, and simulate the decoding process by calculating the overlap of PPDUs at the time of receiving. Existence of overlapping PPDUs means happening of collision, then the package is dropped instead of decoded.

This proposed scheme is compared with two basic opeariton and RTS/CTS aided basic operation illustrated in Fig. 8 and Fig 9. In the comparison scheme, the link that firstly finishes backoff transmits, with no coordination with the other link. The other link just stay being interfered.

All devices in the simulation are multi-link devices. STA MLDs are evenly placed as a circle with the AP MLD at center. Power and distance are adequate for devices to listen to each other and hidden-node problem is not considered.

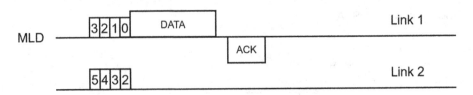

Fig. 8. Comparison scheme 1. The link that firstly finishes backoff performs DATA/ACK, while the other link stays idle.

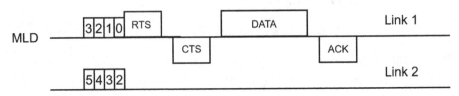

Fig. 9. Comparison scheme 2. The link that firstly finishes backoff performs RTS/CTS, while the other link stays idle.

6.1   Varying Number of STAs

The simulation with varying number of STAs is performed with parameters show in Table 1.

Table 1. Simulation Parameters.

Parameter	Value
Traffic Direction	up link signal user
Traffic Rate (Mbps)	500
Band Width (MHz)	320
MCS (802.11be)	13
Maximal MPDU Aggregation	1024
Package Size (Bytes)	1500
Number of AP	1
Number of STA	1–29
Backoff Window	(7, 15)
Number of Link	2

The simulation results in Fig. 10 show how throughput changes as the number of STA increases. And Fig 11 shows how latency changes as the number of STA increases. As the number of STA increases, the contention becomes fierce. In all cases, throughput firstly increases and then falls, latency keeps increasing. In the case of bare DATA/ACK, the throughput reached a maximum of 2 Gbps, then drops as the number of STAs increases. The RTS/CTS aided case reached a maximum throughput of 5.5 Gbps. The congestion didn't show its effect until the number of STA goes around 15, the maximal backoff window slots. It also suffers a throughput drop because much of the channel time is wasted at collided RTS frames.

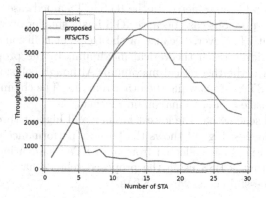

Fig. 10. Throughput performance of proposed scheme and comparison scheme. Varying number of STAs.

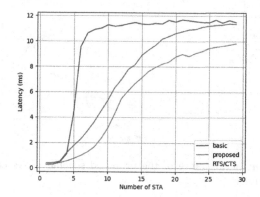

Fig. 11. Delay performance of proposed scheme and comparison scheme. Varying number of STAs.

In the proposed case, the throughput reached theoretical maximum then drops slowly. The comparison cases wasted most of the channel time at the collision of PPDUs, so their throughput is low and latency is high compared to the proposed scheme.

6.2 Varying Traffics

The simulation with varying traffics is performed with parameters show in Table 1 besides that the number of STA is fixed at 25 and the traffic rate varies from 1 Mbps to 1 Gbps. The simulation results are shown in Fig. 12 and Fig. 13 in a log scale.

In all cases the throughput increases as traffic rate increases, then saturated at a certain value. While latency keeps increasing. In the bare DATA/ACK case, as traffic rate increases, the frequency of contention goes up. The throughput drops as contention becomes fierce. In the RTS/CTS aided case, the throughput is higher than the previous case because RTS has a smaller overhead compared with DATA PPDU. However, because of the frequent collision of RTS frames, the throughput didn't reach theoretical maximum. In the proposed case, the throughput reached the theoretical maximum. Although collision happens, one of the conflicting STAs stops while the other remains. The channel is not wasted by transmitting useless bits, so maximum reached.

The proposed scheme has the lowest latency and highest throughput among the compared schemes. Fig. 14 shows the fairness performance of the proposed scheme. Data of Fig. 14 is collected from a 10 STAs simulation. From the pie plot we can see that a BSS using the proposed scheme have nearly the same possibility of successful access for its STAs.

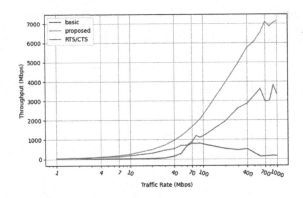

Fig. 12. Throughput performance of the proposed scheme verses comparison. while the other link stay idle.

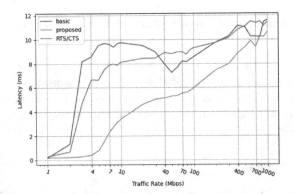

Fig. 13. Delay performance of the proposed scheme verses comparison scheme

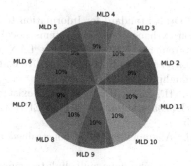

Fig. 14. The percentage of transmitted data of each MLD during the simulation, of all transmitted data during the simulation. The pie plot shows the fairness of the proposed scheme.

7 Conclusion and Future Works

We have proposed a multi-link operation scheme which detects collision at the early stage with the help of antennas from other links. Due to in-device coexistence interference, antennas of a link couldn't receive when other link is transmitting, and couldn't transmit if there are other devices transmitting on current link. We put the interfered link into use by using it to detect power changes on other links. The simulation results shows the proposed scheme has a near theoretical throughput in a dense single BSS, and a relative good latency performance compared with traditional schemes.

There are studies on self interference cancellation showing that dozens of dB of self interference can be suppressed [14, 15]. Implementations of full duplex also shows it is possible for antennas to detect power change with the presence of self interference [13]. The detection works at the initial period of preamble. To facilitate power detection, different structures and coding schemes for preamble need to be evaluated.

Fairness with the presence of legacy devices remains to be studied.

Acknowledgment. This work was supported in part by the National Natural Science Foundations of CHINA (Grant No. 61871322, No. 61771390, and No. 61771392), and Science and Technology on Avionics Integration Laboratory and the Aeronautical Science Foundation of China (Grant No. 20185553035 and No. 201955053002).

References

1. Deng, C., et al.: IEEE 802.11be Wi-Fi 7: new challenges and opportunities. IEEE Commun. Surv. Tutorials, **22**(4), 2136–2166 (2020)
2. Cariou, L.: 802.11 EHT proposed PAR. IEEE 802.11-18/1231r6 (2019)
3. Yang, M., Li, B.: Survey and perspective on extremely high throughput (EHT) WLAN — IEEE 802.11be. Mobile Netw. Appl. **25**(5), 1765–1780 (2020). https://doi.org/10.1007/s11036-020-01567-7

4. IEEE P802.11be/D2.0 Draft Standard for Information technology- Telecommunications and information exchange between systems Local and metropolitan area networks- Specific requirements. Part 11: Wireless LAN Medium Access Control (MAC) and Physical Layer (PHY) Specifications. Amendment 8: Enhancements for extremely high throughput (EHT) (2021)

5. Wang, W., Lu, Y., Xu, H., Zhou, H.: In-device coexistence interference evaluation and detection in LTE-a system. In: 2012 IEEE 75th Vehicular Technology Conference (VTC Spring)

6. Li, Y., Guo, Y., et al.: Alignment in STR constrained mulSti-link. doc.: IEEE 802.11-20/0433r5

7. Seok, Y., Lu, K., Yee, J.: Synchronous multi-link transmission of Non-STR MLD. doc.: IEEE 802.11-20/1053r0

8. Shrivastava, S., Ribeiro, V.J.: Overhearing packet transmissions to reduce preamble overhead and improve throughput in IEEE 802.11 networks. In: 6th International Conference on Communication Systems and Networks (COMSNETS), pp. 1–8 (2014)

9. Baba, Y., Matsumoto, A., Shao, P., Davis, P.: Wireless LAN rate control with frame collision classification. In: International Conference on Wireless Communications, Signal Processing and Networking (WiSPNET), pp. 2448–2453 (2016)

10. Morino, Y., Hiraguri, T., Yoshino, H., Nishimori, K.: Proposal of overhead-less access control scheme for multi-beam massive MIMO transmission in WLAN systems. In: 16th Annual Mediterranean Ad Hoc Networking Workshop (Med-Hoc-Net), pp. 1–5 (2017)

11. Kaneko, M.: Throughput analysis of csma with imperfect collision detection in full duplex-enabled WLAN. IEEE Wireless Commun. Lett. 6(4), 490–493 (2017)

12. Jibukumar, M.G., Shajahan, S., Preetha, P., Sethulekshmi, G.: Impact of capture effect on receiver initiated collision detection with sequential resolution in WLAN. Int. Comput. Sci. Eng. Conf. (ICSEC), pp. 1–6 (2015)

13. Xin, Y., et al.: Technical report on full duplex for 802.11 IEEE 802.11-18/0498r6 (2018)

14. Fang-jing, S.H.I., Yang-yu, F.A.N., Xin-yuan, W.A.N.G., Yong-sheng, G.A.O.: Photonic radio frequency self-interference cancellation system based on phase modulators. Acta Electron. Sin. 10, 1900–1907 (2021)

15. Higuchi, K., Benjebbour, A.: Non-orthogonal multiple access (NOMA) with successive interference cancellation for future radio access. IEICE Trans. Commun. 98(3), 403–414 (2015)

Protocol, Algorithm, Services
and Applications

Angular Position Estimation
for Human-Following and Robot Navigation

Isaac Asante$^{(\boxtimes)}$ ⓘ, Lau Bee Theng ⓘ, and Mark Tee Kit Tsun ⓘ

Faculty of Engineering, Computing and Science, Swinburne University of Technology, Kuching, Sarawak, Malaysia
iasante@swinburne.edu.my

Abstract. Mobile robot navigation and human following are two related areas under the field of robotics that have garnered a lot of interest over the years, due to their advantages in the real world, in various settings. Modern techniques depending exclusively on computer vision for environmental data input commonly rely on state-of-the-art object detection methods to obtain data about the location of detected objects in a scene. However, these detection frameworks do not directly provide the angular position of obstacles and human targets in images. In this research project, the Mask R-CNN instance segmentation framework detects static objects and humans in an environment. A chain of algorithms is then used to transform the image's content and pixel information into a one-dimensional array that can be mapped to the robot's field of view. The findings show that the result can aid a mobile robot in estimating the angular position of obstacles and a human in a scene, which is necessary for collision-free navigation and robot-human following in an unknown environment. The proposed method also shows adaptivity as it works outdoors and indoors under poor lighting conditions. It can be used as a standalone algorithm in robotics simulations with webcams and static images.

Keywords: Robot Navigation · Instance Segmentation · Object Detection

1 Introduction

The research topics associated with developing an autonomous companion robot can be subcategorized for a direct appreciation of the dilemmas that pervade the subdomains of this area of interest. Locomotion, perception, path planning [1], and continuous target tracking [2] all constitute the fundamentals of robot-human following activities, regardless of the nature of the environment. This research focuses on perception, which consists of obtaining environmental data to aid the robot in building knowledge of its surroundings. This perception involves the robot sensing entities around itself – be it a human target or objects posing as dynamic or static obstacles – along with their position relative to itself [3].

© ICST Institute for Computer Sciences, Social Informatics and Telecommunications Engineering 2023
Published by Springer Nature Switzerland AG 2023. All Rights Reserved
D.-J. Deng et al. (Eds.): SGIoT 2022, LNICST 497, pp. 279–290, 2023.
https://doi.org/10.1007/978-3-031-31275-5_26

2 Background

Cameras have been utilized for many years in mobile robot navigation projects to receive visual input and build algorithms to help a wheeled robot navigate unguided while avoiding collisions indoors or outdoors. Monocular and stereo cameras have served well for such objectives [4, 5], and depth cameras have also been a common choice for modern techniques [6–11]. Knowing who to track and where to navigate to avoid collisions is indispensable for a human-following mobile robot. This means that the distinction between a human and an object is vital. This implies that object detection is at the core of the activity, and state-of-the-art machine learning models, such as those made available via the TensorFlow Object Detection API [12], offer viable solutions for this very challenge.

Nonetheless, robust open-source detection models such as CenterNet [13], EfficientDet [14], SSD MobileNet [15], SSD ResNet [16], and Faster R-CNN [17] typically output bounding boxes [18], for which the coordinates normally provide information as to where the classified objects are detected in an image. Thus, in an uncontrolled environment where objects may not necessarily be shaped as cubes or cuboids, it becomes theoretically unreliable for a robot to base its estimation of an obstacle's angular position relative to its camera solely on the object's bounding box upon detection by a trained model. Image segmentation appears to be practical in addressing this shortcoming. In recent years, it has become common to employ segmentation techniques as part of systems developed for person or object tracking. Facebook AI Research's Mask R-CNN framework has been a recurrent choice in such studies. It extends from Faster R-CNN and can generate instance segmentation masks at considerable speeds running at five frames per second and achieving mask AP of 35.7 when tested on the COCO dataset with a ResNet-101 backbone [19]. This makes it efficient for general video segmentation and real-time segmentation on a live camera feed, such as in the case of a navigating mobile robot equipped with a visual sensor. In [20], Mask R-CNN is used for classification on Video Instance Segmentation (VIS), along with an adaptation of the network by [21]. The framework can further be extended to improve its various components, as shown in [22], where an enhanced information propagation method is built on top of Mask R-CNN.

The diversity of robust detectors and low-power sensors today suggests that end-to-end lightweight robot navigation and human tracking systems can be developed using state-of-the-art frameworks and techniques, and existing ones can be improved. With cameras being mainstream in robotics as input sensors, it is worth exploring new ways of pairing instance segmentation methods with computer vision algorithms to achieve high-performance object classification, human tracking, and collision-free navigation.

Table 1 presents the results of evaluations of the proposed angular position estimation algorithm for different RGBD cameras commonly used in the robotics industry [23]. The results indicate that at lower resolutions on a machine equipped with a Tesla T4 graphics processing unit, the algorithm can match Mask R-CNN's execution speed of 5 fps [19].

Table 1. Angular position estimation algorithm evaluation

Camera	RGB Resolution	FOV	Total New Feature Maps	1D Matrix Data Points	Execution Time (In Milliseconds)
Microsoft® Kinect™ 2.0	1920x1080	70°H, 60°V	3	60	842
ASUS® XtionPro™ Live	640x480	58°H, 45°V	3	80	171
Intel® RealSense™ Camera D455	1280x800	90°H, 65°V	3	80	439
Orbbec® Astra Mini™	640x480	60°H, 49.5°V	3	80	185
roboception® rc_visard™	1280x960	61°H, 48°V	3	80	517
MYNT EYE	752x480	146°D, 122°H, 76°V	3	94	201

3 Proposed Solution

This paper presents a fast way of processing two-dimensional image data from a camera to estimate the angular positions of objects and a target human in a scene relative to a robot's camera. The proposed method is designed in a simulated environment, which therefore eliminates the need for a real human subject, or additional elements such as active markers [24]. The results connote a strong relationship between the contents of an input image obtainable through instance segmentation masks, the image's original shape, and the camera's field of view (FOV). Computing the data from this triad of information using this paper's chain of algorithms makes it possible to estimate the angular position of elements in a scene relative to the mobile robot's central field of vision.

The proposed solution uses the TensorFlow backend with Keras and Python 3 and employs the Mask R-CNN framework. The latter is suitable for the project's objective, as the required model output for the expected result is a set of instance segmentation masks corresponding to regions containing persons or static objects in the input image. Here, the input images are assumed to be frames captured by a camera mounted on a mobile robot at specific intervals. The goal of this phase is not to implement an end-to-end mobile robot navigation system but to demonstrate how two-dimensional information from an image is enough to control a robot's rotation angle as it navigates without substantial computational overhead. As the eventual human-following system is set to be fully implemented in the Robot Operating System (ROS), this can be achieved by accurately estimating the yaw value that should be published to the mobile robot's odometry topic subscribed. Though odometry messages representing a robot's orientation in free space generally use quaternions [25], it is possible to obtain Euler angles from quaternions in

ROS using the Transformations library [26]. During the image processing part of this project, inferences are run on one image at a time per GPU. With a single GPU, the batch size is set to 1. A pre-trained model is used instead because training an object detection or segmentation model on a standard collection such as the Microsoft COCO dataset can be time-consuming [27]. For efficacy, the solution relies on the pre-trained weights from the Mask R-CNN 2.1 release [28] and functions from the source code files available on the GitHub repository [29]. The backbone utilized is ResNet-101, which has been measured with higher mean average precision than other renowned convnet architectures such as VGG-16 [30] in benchmark tests involving both the PASCAL VOC 2007 and 2012 and COCO datasets. The class names for the detections list include labels of several objects commonly found in indoor spaces. Ensuring that labels for indoor items such as furniture are included among the set of classes recognizable by the model is vital. This is because the proposed solution explained is meant to be part of an indoor robot navigation model in subsequent phases of this research.

3.1 Merging Segmentation Masks

The predictions from the model contain the segmentation masks for every classification in its matrix, grouped in a container of shape (h, w, n), where h is the height of the original input image, w is the image's width, and n is the total number of masks returned by the prediction. Visualizing the results clarifies how the various instances can be depicted in a single two-dimensional matrix.

The solution's objective is to yield knowledge about a scene during robot-human following—specifically obtaining knowledge about the presence of a human and obstacles in a scene. Therefore, the segmentation masks must be consolidated. Because the masks' matrices initially consist of boolean values, converting them to integers restricts them to two equivalent possibilities: 1 or 0. Any value in the converted matrix that reads 0 points to an area in the original image where the pixel did not belong to the mask class. Conversely, a value of 1 denotes a pixel belonging to the mask in question—or put differently, it indicates that it corresponds to a recognizable class in that region of the original image. However, this is not enough to distinguish between a person and an obstacle during robot navigation. The next step to address this drawback is to re-assign the numerical values for each mask based on their class, per the class names from the COCO dataset used to train the Mask R-CNN model.

Where the value is currently one after the switch in data type from boolean values to integers, a higher positive value is assigned if the name of the class associated with the mask is 'person'. Otherwise, a large negative value is assigned because the mask refers to a static object or obstacle the mobile robot must avoid during navigation. The value is left intact for other areas where the pixel value is 0. This methodology uses default values $\{-4, 0, 4\}$ to update each mask from the prediction results per the mentioned conditions (Table 2). Upon updating the integers for all masks, any matrix corresponding to an obstacle's mask is expected to comprise only the unique values $\{-4, 0\}$. On the other hand, a human's mask would have the unique values $\{0, 4\}$. This pixel re-assignment step is indispensable to the pooling operation illustrated in Fig. 1.

The subsequent step consists of matrix additions to consolidate all instance segmentation masks into one 2D matrix. The latter aims to hold pixel information about the

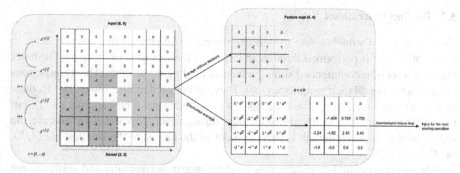

Fig. 1. Illustration for the average pooling algorithm. The discount factor d gets raised to a new power (incremented by 1) at every vertical stride. This sample uses an input matrix of shape (8, 8) and a kernel of shape (2, 2) to generate a down-sampled featured map of discounted averages of shape (4, 4). In practice, input images would be much larger, and dynamic kernel selection would be required to optimize the downsampling process.

three derived groups of object detections of interest for collision-free robot navigation: Obstacle, Void, and Human. This information was retained in the previous step through the pixel values $\{-4, 0, 4\}$ used in the re-assignment function. In a project with different conditions, the length and values in the set of pixels would have to be different to reflect the main objectives.

Here, the sum of all masks results in a new matrix of shape *(h, w)*, where h is the height of the original input image, and w is the original width, just as before. For clarification, all masks in the prediction results had the same shape. It is not uncommon for generated masks to have overlapping pixels [20], and although this may be an inconsequential phenomenon in some ways, it is to be anticipated. Whenever this happens, the sum of matrix elements may produce values lower than -4 or higher than 4. For example, despite each mask having either $\{-4, 0\}$ or $\{0, 4\}$ as a set of unique values, as explained before, the resulting matrix may be composed of the set $\{-8, -4, 0, 4, 8\}$, due to overlapping pixels.

Table 2. Assigning pixel values in masks

New Values	Purpose
-4	A pixel belongs to a static object or obstacle in the current mask's matrix
0	A pixel that does not belong to any detection in the current mask's matrix. It may indicate free space, belong to other masks in the prediction results, or refer to objects not detectable by the Mask R-CNN model in the original image
4	Pixels that belong to a human detection in the current mask's matrix

3.2 Pooling Operations

The extraction of valuable data to estimate the angles of entities in a scene relative to the mobile robot is performed through an indefinite number of pooling steps. The latter relies on a set of recommended sliding windows holding no weights. This is analogous to kernels having all their weights set to 0. They are not used as filters to extract features from the matrix sum as it would be done with a traditional CNN approach [31], but they still produce down-sampled feature maps through average pooling. In this case, the shapes of the proposed default kernels in order of the largest to the smallest are (8, 8), (4, 4), and (2, 2).

The strides required to slide across an input matrix horizontally and vertically are calculated using integer divisions. The input's height is divided by the kernel's height, whereas the input's width is divided by the kernel's width, as illustrated in Fig. 1 above. Nevertheless, to adapt the algorithm to the problem at hand, collision-free robot navigation and human following, the pooling operations start on the input's bottom left side. The vertically-reversed pooling operation is to get a discounted average for the fitting patches of the input feature map. The discount factor introduced here gradually lessens the pixel averages in different map regions. At every stride in an upward direction, the discount is amplified. Theoretically, this pooling technique lets objects closer to the mobile robot's base take precedence over those farther away or positioned higher off the ground. The rationale behind this averaging method is that, as a wheeled agent without the ability to fly, the mobile robot is bound to maintain ground contact at all times. Obstacles on the floor at a near distance pose a much higher risk of collision than those that are either further away or high enough for the robot to pass underneath them.

Figure 1 presents a sample matrix sum conveying obstacles represented as red cells with negative values; a human represented as green cells with positive values; and free space as white cells with zeros. The pooling operation starts from the matrix's bottom-left corner using a kernel of shape (2, 2) and moves towards the right before making an upward stride to calculate the averages from left to the right. This step is repeated until the sliding window reaches the input matrix's top right corner. As the matrix is of shape (8, 8), the kernel can slide four times to the right and four times upward without any overlap for a total of 16 average values stored correspondingly in a smaller shape matrix (4, 4). In this illustration, the array v denotes the sequence of vertical strides possible, from 1 to n, starting from the bottom. Each value in the sequence is referenced as $v[i]$ in Fig. 1, with i representing each value's index inside the array v. The discount factor's default value is initialized to 0.9. Any time the kernel makes a stride up, the discount factor is raised to the power of $v[i]$. In this case, the discount value goes from 0.9^1 to 0.9^4; that is, from 0.9 to 0.6561. Therefore, all the average values calculated by the sliding window in the bottom row are multiplied by a discount factor of 0.9.

In contrast, the values in the topmost sliding row are multiplied by a discount factor of 0.6561. In practice, this algorithm takes a feature map. It provides a down-sampled version of it to use as input for further processing, as visualized in Fig. 2. Nonetheless, performance must be considered, and it must be noted that excessive down-sampling may occur in two ways, as explained below.

Firstly, relying on the larger default kernel of shape (8, 8) alone may produce smaller feature maps rapidly, but this is bound to cause significant information loss. Secondly,

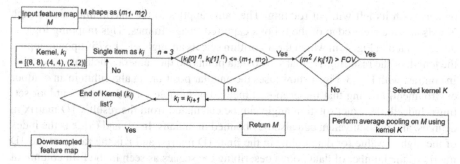

Fig. 2. A breakdown of the kernel selection algorithm, which ensures that the best kernel is used at every step to recursively perform the discounted average pooling operation. The processing stops once the feature map gets smaller than the field of view of the robot's camera. Here, the exponent n in the first condition is recommended to be set to 3.

relying solely on the smaller kernel of shape (2, 2) may retain a lot of useful information but may require too many iterations, thus becoming impractical. Consequently, the proposed technique introduces a kernel selection algorithm for each iteration. As explained in Fig. 2, the aim is to maintain a balance between rapid downsampling and information retention at every step. Once no more kernel can be fitted into the returned feature map, the column-wise sum is calculated and used to determine which part of the captured scene must be avoided from left to right. The logic is that the final 1D matrix generated by the column-wise addition represents the robot's rotation range r in degrees, as noted in (1). The middle of the range ($0°$) represents the robot's central field of vision.

$$r = [-1 * (FOV/2), FOV/2] \tag{1}$$

Nevertheless, to further speed up the downsampling process and retain more information, a coefficient n is introduced, and the robot's camera's field of view FOV is added to the kernel selection algorithm. The recommendation for this method which yielded the most desirable performance results in early tests was $n = 3$, and the field of view of the camera used in this case was 58 degrees. In the final step, the 1D matrix is normalized and plotted in a graph for visualization purposes. As seen in Fig. 3, the high data points in the graph indicate areas from the original image that contain the strongest human presence, whereas the low points imply the presence of obstacles to avoid. The lower the point, the likelier it is to refer to an object close to the robot or an obstacle perceived as relatively large. In an indoor environment with only one human target and no other person, the single highest data point would indicate their angular position in the scene relative to the robot's camera. This can be seen in Fig. 3, where the human in the dark office room is detected by the model and assigned high data points in the graph (constituting a peak), as opposed to the detected office chairs causing dips in the plotted line. The aim is to map the length of the 1D matrix—its count of elements or the maximum value on the plot's X-axis—to the field of view of the robot's camera. This way, the middle coordinate on the X-axis becomes the 0-degree angle in the real world or the default rotation angle when the robot is fixated on a direction and not rotating. The actual 0 coordinate on the X-axis thus represents the far edge of what the robot perceives on its left without rotating. The same applies to the maximum value on the X-axis and the right edge of the robot's captured image frames. This mapping logic is demonstrated in Fig. 4, in which the algorithm selects an angle of 21.375° upon mapping the length of the resulting 1D matrix (80 data points) to the camera's field of view (57°). In contrast with Fig. 3, Fig. 4 showcases the angular positioning algorithm in an outdoor environment, proving that the proposed method is suitable for indoor and outdoor settings. Indeed, the exact rotation angle can be calculated from the result's 1D matrix in degrees, and the equivalent can also be obtained in radians. In (2) and (3), x is the index of the highest value (or data point) in the final 1D matrix, and r is the range of the 1D matrix or the number of data points describing the scenes as seen in the fifth column of Table 1. FOV is the camera's field of view. Below is the mapping formula to obtain the angle of rotation in degrees:

$$deg = (x * (FOV/2))/(r/2) - FOV/2 \qquad (2)$$

To obtain the equivalent value in radians, the value of π is introduced. This is useful, considering angles are typically computed in radians in ROS.

$$rad = ((x * (FOV/2))/(r/2)) * (\pi/180) - (FOV/2) * (\pi/180) \qquad (3)$$

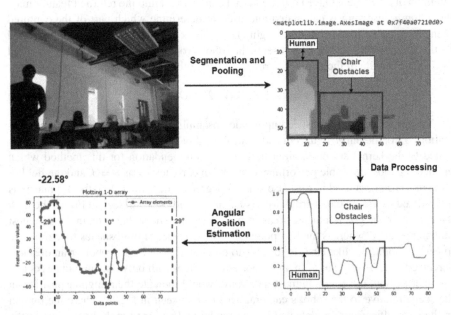

Fig. 3. Live snapshot from a test carried out in an indoor office under poor lighting conditions. The high data points are assigned to the human target. In contrast, the three detected chairs force three noticeable dips in the graph, providing the robot with information about areas to avoid. Here, the angular position estimation algorithm recommends that the robot rotate 22.58° to the left to get the human target in its central field of vision.

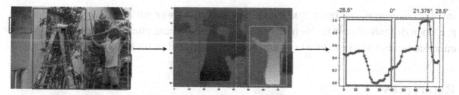

Fig. 4. Illustration of the angular position estimation algorithm on a static image portraying an outdoor environment. The segmentation data gets processed, and the results are fed to the mapping algorithm, which outputs the most suitable degree angle the robot has to turn to face the target. Here, the output is 21.375° to the right.

4 Conclusion and Future Work

The significance of this research work can be linked to the lack of vision-based scene perception techniques that can be employed in different settings, especially indoor robot navigation. Self-driving cars and assistive technology for the visually impaired are two notable domains that share many requirements that an autonomous wheeled robot would need to track a human target without collision. The relevance has to do with the sightless nature of the main agents involved, despite the scenes being prone to various elements to identify, avoid, and track [32–39]. Restricting a robot's perception strictly to a specific set of recognizable items limits the efficacy of the robot's model in the real world, as the robot is bound to encounter elements and situations it has not seen before. This could require the entire technique to be re-engineered multiple times. Treating scene perception as a general problem for which the solution does not technically depend on the exact modules used is the key to rethinking what it means for a robot to perceive entities and changes in its environment in real-time. The focus is on determining the position of objects and a human target relative to the robot's central field of view. However, the proposed method can theoretically be extended to include depth information for path planning. The segmentation framework used could be replaced with a more efficient one. The default set of values for pixel re-assignment could be extended to include various groups of objects based on their importance or danger levels. The default list of kernels proposed could be expanded to include larger kernels for higher-resolution images. The coefficient from the dynamic kernel selection algorithm could be tweaked based on the level of pixel information required to retain. The possibilities to amend, improve and scale the proposed technique are endless. The essential takeaway from this paper is that it demonstrates a novel yet simple approach for performing scene understanding using pixel information without extensive training time. It does so primarily by using image segmentation and applying fundamental matrix mathematics to aid a robot in perceiving the angular position of entities in its surroundings. Moreover, it works irrespective of the camera's RGB resolution (Table 1) and input image size and is invariant to poor lighting conditions – indoors or outdoors. It is also functional as a standalone system that can be used as part of a vision-based surveillance system without restrictions on what can be tracked. It may be used directly on a webcam like in Fig. 3, which means it can be ported onto different platforms to be integrated with other software and algorithms.

Future work for this research includes implementing this logic into a ROS package and performing extensive evaluations for real-time robot-human following. It also involves assessing the technique's accuracy regarding navigation in free space and the presence of multiple obstacles in the real world. In the next phase of this research, these enhancements shall be carried out and reported in detail, with supporting evidence.

References

1. Alatise, M.B., Hancke, G.P.: A review on challenges of autonomous mobile robot and sensor fusion methods. IEEE Access **8**, 39830–39846 (2020). https://doi.org/10.1109/ACCESS.2020.2975643
2. Lau, B.T.: An Improved indoor robot human-following navigation model using depth camera, active IR marker and proximity sensors fusion. Robotics **7**(1), 4 (2018). https://doi.org/10.3390/robotics7010004
3. Barber, R., Crespo, J., Gómez, C., Hernámdez, A.C., Galli, M.: Mobile robot navigation in indoor environments: geometric, topological, and semantic navigation. Appl. Mob. Robot. (2018). https://doi.org/10.5772/INTECHOPEN.79842
4. Wang, M., Su, D., Shi, L., Liu, Y., Miro, J.V.: Real-time 3D human tracking for mobile robots with multisensors. In: 2017 IEEE International Conference on Robotics and Automation, pp. 5081–5087 (2017). https://doi.org/10.1109/ICRA.2017.7989593
5. Chen, B.X., Sahdev, R., Tsotsos, J.K.: Integrating stereo vision with a CNN tracker for a person-following robot. In: Liu, M., Chen, H., Vincze, M. (eds.) ICVS 2017. LNCS, vol. 10528, pp. 300–313. Springer, Cham (2017). https://doi.org/10.1007/978-3-319-68345-4_27
6. Liu, H., Luo, J., Wu, P., Xie, S., Li, H.: People detection and tracking using RGB-D cameras for mobile robots. Int. J. Adv. Robot. Syst. **13**(5), 172988141665774 (2016). https://doi.org/10.1177/1729881416657746
7. Condés, I., Cañas, J.M.: Person following robot behavior using deep learning. In: Fuentetaja Pizán, R., García Olaya, Á., Sesmero Lorente, M.P., Iglesias Martínez, J.A., Ledezma Espino, A. (eds.) WAF 2018. AISC, vol. 855, pp. 147–161. Springer, Cham (2019). https://doi.org/10.1007/978-3-319-99885-5_11
8. Chen, E.: lFOLOr: a vision-based human-following robot, pp. 224–232 (2018). https://doi.org/10.2991/amcce-18.2018.40
9. Condés, I., Cañas, J.-M., Perdices, E.: Embedded deep learning solution for person identification and following with a robot. In: Bergasa, L.M., Ocaña, M., Barea, R., López-Guillén, E., Revenga, P. (eds.) WAF 2020. AISC, vol. 1285, pp. 291–304. Springer, Cham (2021). https://doi.org/10.1007/978-3-030-62579-5_20
10. Nguyen, A., Tran, Q.: Autonomous navigation with mobile robots using deep learning and the robot operating system (2020). http://arxiv.org/abs/2012.02417. Accessed 18 June 2021
11. Chan, W.P., Radmard, S., Hew, Z.Q., Morris, J., Croft, E., Van der Loos, H.F.M.: Autonomous person-specific following robot (2020). http://arxiv.org/abs/2010.08017. Accessed 09 July 2021
12. Tensorflow: models/research/object_detection at master · tensorflow/models. GitHub (2021). https://github.com/tensorflow/models/tree/master/research/object_detection. Accessed 26 July 2021
13. Duan, K., Bai, S., Xie, L., Qi, H., Huang, Q., Tian, Q.: CenterNet: keypoint triplets for object detection. In: Proceedings of IEEE International Conference on Computer Vision, vol. 2019-Octob, pp. 6568–6577 (2019). https://doi.org/10.48550/arxiv.1904.08189
14. Tan, M., Pang, R., Le, Q.V.: EfficientDet: scalable and efficient object detection. In: Proceedings of IEEE Computer Society Conference on Computer Vision and Pattern Recognition, pp. 10778–10787 (2019). https://doi.org/10.48550/arxiv.1911.09070

15. Liu, W., et al.: SSD: single shot multibox detector. In: Leibe, B., Matas, J., Sebe, N., Welling, M. (eds.) ECCV 2016. LNCS, vol. 9905, pp. 21–37. Springer, Cham (2016). https://doi.org/10.1007/978-3-319-46448-0_2

16. Lu, X., Kang, X., Nishide, S., Ren, F.: Object detection based on SSD-ResNet. In: Proceedings of 2019 6th IEEE International Conference on Cloud Computing and Intelligence Systems, CCIS 2019, pp. 89–92 (2019). https://doi.org/10.1109/CCIS48116.2019.9073753

17. Ren, S., He, K., Girshick, R., Sun, J.: Faster R-CNN: towards real-time object detection with region proposal networks. IEEE Trans. Pattern Anal. Mach. Intell. **39**(6), 1137–1149 (2017). https://doi.org/10.1109/TPAMI.2016.2577031

18. Padilla, R., Passos, W.L., Dias, T.L.B., Netto, S.L., Da Silva, E.A.B.: A comparative analysis of object detection metrics with a companion open-source toolkit. Electron **10**(3), 279 (2021). https://doi.org/10.3390/ELECTRONICS10030279

19. He, K., Gkioxari, G., Dollar, P., Girshick, R.: Mask R-CNN, pp. 2961–2969 (2017)

20. Luiten, J., Torr, P., Leibe, B.: Video instance segmentation 2019: a winning approach for combined detection, segmentation, classification and tracking. In: 2019 IEEE/CVF International Conference on Computer Vision Workshop (ICCVW), pp. 709–712 (2019). https://doi.org/10.1109/ICCVW.2019.00088

21. Luiten, J., Voigtlaender, P., Leibe, B.: PReMVOS: proposal-generation, refinement and merging for video object segmentation. In: Jawahar, C., Li, H., Mori, G., Schindler, K. (eds.) ACCV 2018. LNCS (LNAI and LNB), vol. 11364, pp. 565–580. Springer, Cham (2018). https://doi.org/10.1007/978-3-030-20870-7_35

22. Liu, S., Qi, L., Qin, H., Shi, J., Jia, J.: Path aggregation network for instance segmentation. In: Proceedings of IEEE Computer Society Conference on Computer Vision and Pattern recognition, pp. 8759–8768 (2018). https://doi.org/10.1109/CVPR.2018.00913

23. 3D Camera Survey. ROS-Industrial (2022). https://rosindustrial.org/3d-camera-survey. Accessed 12 July 2022

24. Tee Kit Tsun, M., Bee Theng, L., Siswoyo Jo, H., Lun Lau, S.: Proposing a sensor fusion technique utilizing depth and ranging sensors for combined human following and indoor robot navigation (2016). http://dx.doi.org/10.1145/3033288.3033345. Accessed 17 May 2021

25. Quaternion Message. ROS Documentation (2022). http://docs.ros.org/en/noetic/api/geometry_msgs/html/msg/Quaternion.html. Accessed 16 May 2022

26. Gohlke, C.: Homogeneous transformation matrices and quaternions. Laboratory for Fluorescence Dynamics. University of California, Irvine, California (2021). https://github.com/cgohlke/transformations/. Accessed 16 May 2022

27. Bharati, P., Pramanik, A.: deep learning techniques—R-CNN to mask R-CNN: a survey. In: Das, A., Nayak, J., Naik, B., Pati, S., Pelusi, D. (eds.) Computational Intelligence in Pattern Recognition. Advances in Intelligent Systems and Computing, vol. 999, pp.657–668. Springer, Singapore (2020). https://doi.org/10.1007/978-981-13-9042-5_56

28. Release Mask R-CNN 2.1 · matterport/Mask_RCNN. https://github.com/matterport/Mask_RCNN/releases/tag/v2.1. Accessed 15 May 2022

29. Abdulla, W.: Mask R-CNN for object detection and instance segmentation on Keras and TensorFlow. GitHub (2017). https://github.com/matterport/Mask_RCNN. Accessed 15 May 2022

30. He, K., Zhang, X., Ren, S., Sun, J.: Deep residual learning for image recognition. In: Proceedings of IEEE Computer Society Conference on Computer Vision and Pattern Recognition, vol. 2016-Decem, pp. 770–778 (2015). https://arxiv.org/abs/1512.03385v1. Accessed 22 July 2021

31. Chauhan, R., Ghanshala, K.K., Joshi, R.: Convolutional neural network (CNN) for image detection and recognition. In: 2018 First International Conference on Secure Cyber Computing and Communication (ICSCCC), pp. 278–282 (2018). https://doi.org/10.1109/ICSCCC.2018.8703316

32. Ran, T., Yuan, L., Zhang, J.B.: Scene perception based visual navigation of mobile robot in indoor environment. ISA Trans. **109**, 389 (2021). https://doi.org/10.1016/J.ISATRA.2020.10.023

33. A. Uçar, Y. Demir, and C. Güzeliş: Object recognition and detection with deep learning for autonomous driving applications, vol. 93, no. 9, pp. 759–769 (2017). https://doi.org/10.1177/0037549717709932

34. Gupta, A., Anpalagan, A., Guan, L., Khwaja, A.S.: Deep learning for object detection and scene perception in self-driving cars: survey, challenges, and open issues. Array **10**, 100057 (2021). https://doi.org/10.1016/J.ARRAY.2021.100057

35. Du, Q., et al.: Deep learning-based object detection and scene perception under bad weather conditions. Electron. **11**(4), 563 (2022). https://doi.org/10.3390/ELECTRONICS11040563

36. Wang, L., et al.: Multi-view fusion-based 3D object detection for robot indoor scene perception. Sensors **19**(19), 4092 (2019). https://doi.org/10.3390/S19194092

37. Chen, L., Yang, Z., Ma, J., Luo, Z.: Driving scene perception network: real-time joint detection, depth estimation and semantic segmentation. In: 2018 IEEE Winter Conference on Applications of Computer Vision, vol. 2018-Janua, pp. 1283–1291 (2018). https://doi.org/10.1109/WACV.2018.00145

38. Kaur, B., Bhattacharya, J.: Scene perception system for visually impaired based on object detection and classification using multimodal deep convolutional neural network. J. Electron. Imaging **28**(01), 1 (2019). https://doi.org/10.1117/1.JEI.28.1.013031

39. Brunetti, A., Buongiorno, D., Trotta, G.F., Bevilacqua, V.: Computer vision and deep learning techniques for pedestrian detection and tracking: a survey. Neurocomputing **300**, 17–33 (2018). https://doi.org/10.1016/j.neucom.2018.01.092

Social Risk Analysis of Smart Grid Based on Emerging Technologies in the Chinese Context: A Review Based on CiteSpace

Ziyi Chen and Yingsi Zhao[✉]

School of Economics and Management, Beijing Jiaotong University, Beijing, China
yszhao@bjtu.edu.cn

Abstract. Social risk is one of the important topics in the world today. It is constantly being discussed by scholars. As the largest developing country, China's analysis of the social risks brought about by the development of smart grids is worth learning from. However, few Chinese scholars have explored the social risks involved in the emerging concept of the Smart Grid (SG). Due to the close integration of smart grids with emerging technologies such as artificial intelligence, this paper intends to provide a general direction and logic for the social risks of SGs by discussing the social risks brought by emerging technologies. Therefore, this paper uses CiteSpace to conduct author cooperation network analysis, keyword co-occurrence analysis, and keyword clustering analysis on Chinese social risk literature based on the CNKI database. The keywords are sorted into five categories, namely risk categories, risk sources, governance tools or means, results or purposes, and related terms. The risk sources are further subdivided into three categories: technical, social issues, and events. Then the technical part is carried out, combined with the characteristics of the SG to explore its impact mechanism on social risks and put forward corresponding countermeasures.

Keywords: Smart Grid · Social Risk · CiteSpace

1 Introduction

Social risk is the possibility of threats and uncertainties arising from social modernization, which will cause irreversible harm to all individuals [1]. In a narrow sense, it can be considered that social risk refers to the possibility that the behavior of individuals or groups will cause the destruction of social order [2]. With the acceleration of the modernization process and the continuous improvement of the level of science and technology, the possibility of social disorder and social chaos caused by a trivial incident of an individual or group has increased sharply with the blessing of high technology and advanced communication technology. Few Chinese scholars have explored the social risks involved in the emerging concept of the smart grid. Since the smart grid is closely integrated with emerging technologies such as artificial intelligence, this paper provides

D.-J. Deng et al. (Eds.): SGIoT 2022, LNICST 497, pp. 291–308, 2023.
https://doi.org/10.1007/978-3-031-31275-5_27

a general direction and logic for the social risks of smart grids by discussing the social risks brought by emerging technologies.

Smart grids are grid systems that are upgraded with the development of emerging technologies. As defined by the U.S. Department of Energy, a Smart Grid (SG) uses digital technology to improve reliability, security, and efficiency (both economic and energy) of the electric system from large generation, through the delivery systems to electricity consumers and a growing number of distributed-generation and storage resources [3]. With the increase of the interaction between the external environment and the power system, under the background of the continuous increase of the scale of the power grid system, the enhancement of system nonlinearity, and the constant increase of operating modes, the data source, and data volume are constantly increasing. The analysis and control of the power grid are becoming more and more difficult. Challenges are also increasing. With the development of emerging technologies such as artificial intelligence, the four aspects of "source network load storage" have been greatly improved, and then the power grid can realize the transformation process from the passive control of the traditional power grid to the active response of the SG so that to a large extent avoid risk. Because the smart grid has the characteristics of large-scale distribution, strong system integration, and obvious intelligence, the social risks it brings are worth discussing by scholars. As in the case of the cyberattack on the Venezuelan national grid in 2020, which resulted in the malignant consequences of a massive national power outage.

Exploring the research status of social risks in SG is helpful to empower risk management from a theoretical level. However, in developing countries, including China, the development of the SG is later than that of European and American countries, and there are few studies on SGs and social risks. Exploring the social risks of China's smart grid is conducive to providing theoretical and practical references for other developing countries. Since less research has been done on the social risks associated with SGs, which are closely integrated with emerging technologies such as artificial intelligence, this paper focuses on exploring the possible social risks associated with the emerging technologies behind SGs to provide a general direction and logic for the study of social risks associated with SGs. Therefore, this paper selects the CSSCI social risk research literature based on CNKI, uses CiteSpace for visual literature analysis, sorts out the research status and research hotspots of China's social risk, and explores the social risk source and formation mechanism of the SG based on emerging technologies.

2 Literature Review

According to the US Department of Energy, "A Smart Grid uses digital technology to improve reliability, security, and efficiency (both economic and energy) of the electric system from large generation, through the delivery systems to electricity consumers and a growing number of distributed-generation and storage resources" [3]. The application of new technologies aims to help the traditional grid improve efficiency and reliability, making the whole power system more economical [4]. However, with the interaction of more elements, the Smart Grid (SG), as a new generation of grid system, is bound to bring more forms and complex risks on top of the traditional grid system, including risks from digital communication and computer systems, in addition to human, policy, and political risks [5]. Scholars have also mentioned the social nature of these risks in their research. Gunduz and Das argue that disruption of the communication system of the SG can lead to social disorder and national security issues [6]. In the Chinese context, "strong SG" is the choice for development. A strong SG is one of the characteristics of a secure, high-quality, and reliable power supply [7].

Social risk has different definitions in several professional fields such as sociology, geography, psychology, law and social security, economy and public policy [8]. The reason why there are different definitions of social risk in various fields is that the concept of social risk itself is formed by combining the concepts of several different fields [9]. The term "risk" itself is the definition of insurance, while "social risk" can be understood as the social dimension of "risk", thus reflecting the multidisciplinary intersection of social risk. In addition, a series of concepts closely related to "social risk", such as "risk society", "social governance", "social security", and "emergency management" is defined in the field of sociology and even public administration. The interconnection of terms from multiple disciplines has resulted in the broad concept of "social risk. In brief, social risk in sociology refers to the uncertainty of social loss, which is narrowly defined as a system alongside politics, economy, culture, etc.; social loss accordingly refers to a loss alongside politics, economy, culture, etc., which can be considered as a disruption of social order; furthermore, social risk in a narrow sense is defined as a risk alongside politics, economy, culture, etc. cultural risk, etc., rather than a risk in a broad sense, involving multiple disciplines; meanwhile, the social risk here differs from political risk, economic risk, cultural risk, etc., but under certain conditions, political risk, economic risk, cultural risk, etc., may be transformed into social risk [2].

As one of the theories closely related to the study of social risk, there are three major theoretical orientations of risk society, namely the institutionalist school, the realist school, and the culturalist school. The representatives of the institutionalist school are Ulrich Beck and Giddens, who believe that the current globalized society, with the continuous development of modernity and science and technology, has become a risk society and that none of the individuals in the society is immune to the risks it contains; and that with the development of science and technology, the prevalence of globalization, and the rapid evolution of modernization, risks and their potential destructiveness have become unparalleled. Further, Beck defines social risk as to the possibility of threats and uncertainties arising from the modernization of society, which will cause irreversible harm to all individuals [1]. In contrast to Beck, who is more concerned with technological risks, Giddens prefers to emphasize the social risks posed by institutions. Giddens argues that human interventions in society and nature have continuously shaped social risks, of which the four institutional pillars of modernity, namely the world nation-state system, the world capitalist economy, the international division of labor system, and military totalitarianism, are the source of the risks [10]. Further, Giddens divides risks in modern societies into two categories, "external risks" and "man-made risks", based on the sources of risk generation. External risks consist of emergency contingencies that occur frequently and are usually planned for, such as natural disasters and social conflicts in the traditional sense. Man-made risks, on the other hand, refer to the risks that arise from the growing knowledge that human beings acquire through their continued exploration of the world through knowledge and practice, especially the risks that arise from the constant changes in science and technology.

Social problems and emergencies, as a source of social risk, have led to many studies and discussions on their impact on social risk. In addition, technology, as one of the sources of social risk according to Beck, and also as one of the sources of man-made risk, its impact on social risk has also triggered many scholars' studies and discussions. George S. Day and Paul J.H. Schoemaker define emerging technologies as "having the potential to remake entire industries and obsolete established strategies" and characterize them as "traumatic" [11]. Scholars have discussed the multiple forms of societal risks associated with new mining technologies that bring efficiency and economic benefits, such as the enhancement of existing risks, the expansion of the scope of existing risks, and the possible emergence of entirely new risks [12]. The possible social risks perceived by researchers of Genetically Modified (GM) food have also been explored, and it is suggested in the article that the ethical and moral risks associated with GM food first affect consumers' attitudes towards the technology, which in turn has an indirect effect on social risk perceptions, i.e. how audiences perceive the ethical and moral risks of GM food affects their perceptions of GM technology, which further affects their risk perceptions of GM food [13].

In the world's smart grid construction as well as the construction of a strong SG in the Chinese context, AI technology exists as a supporting technology for the smart grid, helping to upgrade the power system in terms of data processing [14, 15]. In the Chinese context, some scholars have explored the impact of AI technologies on social risks, and the study concluded that AI technologies can trigger ethical and moral aberrations, the polarization of social structures, alienation of technological development, high difficulty in regulation caused by algorithmic black boxes, and difficulty in determining responsibility for accidents caused by the unknown status of AI as a status [16]. Some scholars have also discussed the possible social risks brought by the virtual reality-based immersive platform "metaverse" and given aspects that need attention; on the one hand, attention should be paid to the negative effects of the highly addictive nature of the "metaverse"; on the other hand, attention should be paid to. On the other hand, it is important to pay attention to the oppression of employees due to the telecommuting property of the "metaverse", i.e., the invisible violation of employees' labor rights [17].

The focus on the social risks associated with the SG can be focused on the paths of social risks associated with high technologies such as artificial intelligence. Summarizing how Chinese scholars view the social risks associated with various types of high technologies, including artificial intelligence technologies, can help inform the study of social risks associated with the development of the SGs based on high technologies. The framework and focus of Chinese research on social risks, as well as the sources and mechanisms of social risks in China, can provide a reference for research in other countries and for developing countries to deal with social risks brought about by high technologies.

3 Research Methodology and Data Sources

This paper uses CiteSpace 5.8.R3 (Expires June 30, 2022) to conduct a visual literature analysis to capture the overall research on "social risk". CiteSpace is an information visualization literature analysis software developed by Professor Chaomei Chen of
Drexel University. The software is able to find some hidden connections among a large
amount of related literature based on keywords, citations, authors and institutions, and
present the connections in a visual way. Further, the software can sort out the research
lines, research hotspots in different time periods, and key literature connecting different
research directions based on the literature data, simplifying the process of searching and
filtering important literature and reducing the difficulty of overviewing the current status
of research [18].

In order to sort out the sources and formation mechanisms of "social risk" in China,
the CNKI (National Knowledge Infrastructure) database is used as the source of literature
data in this paper. In order to collect the literature on "social risk" as accurately and
comprehensively as possible, the statement "(SU = "social risk" OR TI = "social risk")
AND KY = "social risk" was entered into Professional Search, where "SU" means
"Subject", "TI "SU" means "Subject", "TI" means "Title", "KY" means "Keyword",
and select "Synonym Search", "Dates" select "All", select "Academic Journals", and
limit the "Source Type" to "CSSCI" (Chinese Social Sciences Citation Index), in order
to collect as much authoritative literature on the topic of "social risk" as possible. The
search yielded a total of 442 articles, with a publication year range of 1998–2022 and a
total of 20 disciplines.

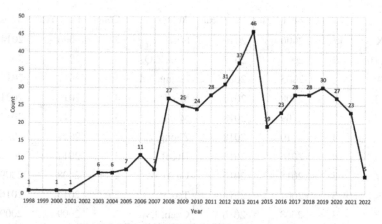

Fig. 1. China Social Risk Annual Posting Data.

Since 1998, the research intensity of "social risk" has been increasing year by year,
reaching a peak in 2014, when 46 papers were published, and then In 2015, the popularity
dropped, and although it rebounded, there are still fluctuations (see Fig. 1). In other
words, despite the decline in research enthusiasm, there are still scholars in China who
are concerned with the research on "social risk".

4 Visualization Analysis

CiteSpace was used to analyze the literature data samples visually. The literature data downloaded from the CNKI database was imported into CiteSpace for format conversion, and 442 valid data were obtained. The time span of the literature data was from 1998 to 2022, so the "Time Slicing" was set to "From 1998 JAN To 2022 DEC". In the panel, the settings related to "Text Processing" were kept as default, and "Author" and "Keyword" were selected in the "Node Type" section according to the type of analysis. In the "Links" section, select "Strength" as "Cosine" and "Scope" as "Within Slices" by default. In the "Selection Criteria" section, "g-index" is selected by default, and the default k value is 25. "Pruning" is selected differently according to different node types.

In the visualization part, this paper analyzes the literature samples item by item, because CiteSpace for CNKI literature data source only supports the analysis of author and institution cooperation network and keyword co-occurrence analysis, because the cooperation between institutions is less, so only present the visualization analysis about author cooperation network and keyword co-occurrence. In the keyword analysis section, in addition to keyword co-occurrence analysis, keyword clustering analysis was also conducted to obtain the general direction of social risk research.

4.1 Author Collaboration Network Analysis

Table 1. Author Posting Data.

Author	Count	First Year	Last Year	Author	Count	First Year	Last Year
Tong, X.	15	2006	2016	Liu, Y.	3	2006	2014
Zhang, H.B.	9	2006	2022	Wen, Z.Q.	3	2016	2019
Wu, Z.M.	8	2005	2020	Zhang, X.L.	3	2017	2018
Zhang, L.	6	2008	2016	Mo, H.L.	3	2019	2021
Bai, W.J.	5	2009	2018	Mo, F.	3	2012	2013
Li, S.Z.	4	2010	2018	Zhong, Z.J.	3	2021	2022
Xie, J.G.	4	2016	2019	Hu, B.	3	2012	2012
Chen, Y.H.	3	2015	2015	Lu, H.W.	2	2008	2009
Chen, S.J.	3	2001	2014	Tao, P.	2	2013	2016
Xia, Y.Z.	3	2008	2016	Chen, J.W.	2	2009	2009

The analysis of research collaboration networks can help to understand the collaboration between authors over time and the intensity of collaboration. The analysis of the authors' publications in the original literature data are summarized in Table 1, which lists the publications on "social risk" since 1998, including the names of scholars, the number of publications, their affiliation, and the year of the first and last publication. It can be observed that Tong X. has published the most articles, with 14 articles related to "social risk" since he first published them in 2006. Zhang H.B., who shares the same affiliation with Nanjing University, has also published 9 articles on the topic of "social risk" since 2006. Compared with Tong X., whose last article on "social risk" was published in 2016, Zhang H.B. has been studying "social risk" for a longer period of time and is still publishing in the field of "social risk" in 2022. The last article on "social risk" was published in 2016. In addition to these two scholars, there are other scholars who focus on the topic of "social risk", such as Wu Z.M. (8 articles), Zhang L. (6 articles), and Bai W.J. (5 articles).

Using CiteSpace software, the nodes were set as authors based on the default threshold to explore the collaborative relationships among authors. Software calculations yielded the number of critical nodes 403 (N = 403), 167 critical paths (E = 167), and the largest CC: 8. Figure 2 shows the analysis of the author collaboration network formed by CiteSpace, in which all Chinese characters are marked with English translations below the Chinese, and synonyms may be used to refer to the original academic terms due to translation problems. The visual analysis of the collaboration network shows that there are mostly collaborative relationships among authors who publish more articles.

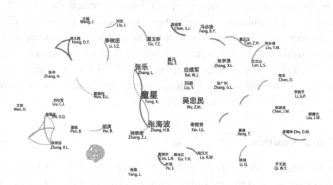

Fig. 2. Author Collaboration Network.

For example, Tong X. collaborated with Zhang H.B. and Zhang L., respectively. In addition, Zhang H.B. and Zhong Z.J., who had three publications, also had collaborative relationships. Based on the literature data, Zhong Z.J.'s first research paper on "social risk" was published in 2021, and he has published three articles in just over a year, which can be regarded as one of the more dedicated scholars in this field in China. It can also be seen that many scholars have conducted independent research, i.e., they have not collaborated with other scholars, such as Wu Z.M., Bai W.J., Xie J.G., Liu Y., Zhang X.L., and Mo F. In addition, there are also scholars who have made some collaboration with other scholars, such as Li S.Z., Chen S.J., Xia Y.Z., Mo H.L., Lu H.W., etc.

Specifically, Tong X. is the director of the Center for Societal Risk and Public Crisis Management Studies, Nanjing University, Jiangsu Province, China, and the director of Jiangsu Province Social Risk Research Base. He has published many papers on "social risk". "As one of his main research areas, he has conducted many collaborative studies with other scholars in the field, such as Zhang H.B., Nanjing University, Zhang L., Shandong.

University, and Tao P., Among them, Tong X. and Zhang H.B.'s paper on the governance of the mass unexpected incidents is widely recognized by the academic community. They discussed the classification and nature of mass unexpected incidents and conducted a case study of the more iconic mass unexpected incidents in China, summarized the dynamic model of Unorganized mass unexpected incidents, and proposed many new ideas related to mass unexpected incidents, which provided a theoretical basis for subsequent scholars to study mass unexpected incidents [19].

Zhang H.B. is a professor at the School of Government Administration, Nanjing University, and a researcher at the Center for Societal Risk and Public Crisis Management Studies, Nanjing University with Tong X. His research interests include social risk, emergency response, and emergency management. His research areas include social risk, emergency management, crisis management, and public safety. He has collaborated with Tong X., Zhong Z.J., and Yan J. In the area of social risk research, Zhang H.B. has co-authored many papers with Tong X. In addition to the above-mentioned research papers on mass unexpected incidents, many other studies have received attention from other scholars. For example, Zhang H.B. is the first author of a research paper exploring the structure of emergency management in China, in which Zhang H.B. and Tong X. focus on the internal structure of emergency management practice in China, based on the major disasters that have occurred in China in the past two decades, such as the 2003 atypical disaster. Disaster events in China in the last two decades such as atypical pneumonia in 2003 and the Lushan earthquake in 2013 for case analysis, summarizing the changes in the framework of emergency management practice in China and adding a theoretical basis for related research [20].

4.2 Keyword Analysis

By using CiteSpace to set the node type as "Keyword" for keyword co-occurrence analysis, we can observe the frequency of different keywords in the article and then discover the research hotspots. Figure 3 shows the keyword co-occurrence network formed by CiteSpace, in which all Chinese characters are marked with English translations below the Chinese, and due to translation problems, synonyms may be used to refer to the original academic terms. In addition, to make the visualization graph more concise and clear, the #Years Per Slice in Time Slicing was set to 3, Pruning was set to "Pathfinder" and "Pruning sliced network", and the number of key nodes in the visualization result was 321 ($N = 321$), and the key paths The size of the nodes or the Chinese font size represents the frequency of keywords, while the line between the nodes represents the presence of two keywords in the same paper at the same time. The font size shows that scholars focus on "social risk" as well as "risk society", "social governance", "public crisis", "risk governance", "risk", "social security", "social management", and "emergency management". "and "emergency management". In addition to the keywords related to "governance", "management" and "protection", we can observe the keywords of "artificial intelligence", "social transformation", and "social transformation"."., "social transformation", "migrant workers", "emerging technologies", "ethnic regions The keywords of "artificial intelligence", "social transformation", "migrant workers", "emerging technologies", "ethnic areas" and "globalization" have also received more attention from scholars. Among them, some scholars believe that the social risks caused by artificial intelligence should not be underestimated. Taking the highly cited paper of scholar Ma Changshan as an example, he argues that AI can trigger ethical and moral deformation, the polarization of social structure, alienation of technological development, high difficulty in regulation caused by an algorithmic black box, and high difficulty in determining the responsibility of accidents caused by the unknown status of AI as a status [16].

Fig. 3. Keyword Co-occurrence Network.

Further, keyword clustering analysis was conducted using CiteSpace based on the keyword co-occurrence network, as shown in Fig. 4, where all Chinese characters have English translations marked below the Chinese. In addition, different color blocks represent different categories formed after keyword clustering, and the ordinal number before the cluster indicates the size of the cluster, and the smaller ordinal number means the larger the cluster, i.e., the more keywords included. The CiteSpace visualization software formed a total of 41 clusters, of which only 25 clusters were shown, such as "#0 risk society", "#1 risk", "#2 social security", "#4 public crisis" and "#5 communication" "#6 Artificial Intelligence", "#16 Platform Economy", "#18 Genetic Weapons", "#19 Meta-Universe", "#20 Genetic Weapons", and "#21 Genetic Weapons". "#19 Meta-universe" and "#28 Simulation Prediction" are relatively small clusters.

From the keywords, we can analyze that scholars focus on four main areas. First, scholars focus their attention on the mechanisms that explain the sources of risk that lead to social risks, such as "artificial intelligence", "emergencies", "ethnic regions", "land conflicts", and "land conflicts. "land conflicts", "internet rumors", and "social transformation. Secondly, scholars focus on the factors that influence social risk, such as "communication", "media", "cold thinking", etc. Third, scholars focus on how to solve social risks, such as "state supervision", "big data", "criminal law regulation",

Fig. 4. Keyword Clustering.

"criminal law response" etc. Fourth, scholars have focused on the adverse consequences of social risks, such as "public crises" and so on. That is, scholars have explored the causes, influencing factors means to resolve, and adverse consequences of social risks based on different perspectives.

5   Analysis of Social Risk Generation Mechanisms

5.1   Identification of Social Risk Sources

In the part of identifying risk sources, first, based on the keywords identified by CiteSpace for manual classification, further, in the classification of risk sources to filter out technology-related keywords, such as "artificial intelligence", "network", "genetic technology", "big data", etc. Next, back to the original article to check whether it is a risk source or an important antecedent, rather than a category such as governance tools. Finally, the keyword-based classification, based on the specific content of the original article, reclassifies the screened keywords related to technology while being a source of risk to obtain specific technologies, such as classifying "gene editing", "gene products", "gene technology", "gene technology", "gene weapon" were combined into "gene technology", and the terms "universal era" and "Internet of Everything" into "Internet of Everything", or "IoE"; "Meta-universe" and "Virtual Reality" into "Virtual Reality Technology"; "Artificial Intelligence" and "AI Face Changing" into "Artificial Intelligence". The "artificial intelligence" and "AI face-swapping" are classified as "artificial intelligence", etc. At the same time, the keywords in the category of governance tools were also filtered, and technology-related keywords such as "big data", "algorithmic governance" and "simulation prediction" were selected. The keywords in the category of governance tools were filtered to identify technology-related keywords, such as "big data", "algorithmic governance" and "simulation prediction". Further, when the keywords were retrieved from the original article, the differences in the roles of the keywords in some articles were also filtered. For example, "artificial intelligence" is considered by most scholars as a source or important antecedent of risk, but some scholars categorize it as a governance tool for social risk.

Table 2. Keyword Classification.

	Keywords
Risk Categories	Social Risk; Economic Risk; Environmental Risk; Political Risk; Technological Risk; Ethical Risk; Cost Risk; Operational Risk; Revenue and Expenditure Risk
Source of Risk	Artificial Intelligence; Urbanization; Emergencies; Migrant Workers; Modernization; Ethnic Areas; Individualization; Gender Imbalance; Rural; Internet Rumors
Governance Tools	Government; Collaborative Governance; Technical Decision Making; Indicator Systems; Government Responsibility; Public Policy; Legal Regulation; Early Warning; Public Participation; Social Control
Results or Purpose	Public Crisis; Harmonious Society; Social Stability; Equality; Crisis Events; Social Justice; Social Crisis; Equity and Justice; Balance of Interests; Balance of Interests
Related Terms	Risk Society; Social Governance; Risk Governance; Risk; Social Security; Social Management; Emergency Management; Governance; Public Governance; Contemporary China

Based on the four research directions derived from the keywords, the 321 keywords summarized by CiteSpace were manually classified into five categories: risk category, risk source (or important antecedent), governance tool or instrument, outcome or purpose, and related terms. Among them, Table 2 shows the classification of the 10 keywords with the highest word frequency in each of the above five categories, and due to translation issues, synonyms may be used to refer to the original academic terms. In Table 2, the keywords are ranked in order of their frequency, i.e., the keywords ranked first to have the highest number of occurrences. The analysis shows that in the risk category section, except for social risk, scholars discuss economic risk and environmental risk most often together with social risk, followed by political risk and technological risk. Many Chinese scholars also focus on the impact of AI on social risks, including the types of social risks it may cause or how to use AI to mitigate social risks. In the process of urbanization, various types of social conflicts, such as land disputes and labor disputes, occur from time to time, and thus social risks emerge [21]. Emergencies as antecedents of social risks have also received much scholarly attention. Further, migrant workers as one of the highly Chinese-specific phenomena have also received attention from scholars.

In the part of governance tools or instruments, the role of government is clearly one of the most concerned and trusted instruments by Chinese scholars. The government-led risk regulation system is the top priority to counteract a large number of social risks [22]. In addition, a collaborative multi-subject governance mechanism is also quite recognized by Chinese scholars. How to start from the grassroots and form multi-subject collaborative governance to further effectively resolve social risks has been discussed by many scholars [23]. In the result or purpose part, a public crisis as a crisis event that threatens public safety and normal social order after the disruption of social club order is one of the malignant consequences of uncontrolled social risk, and every individual in society will be negatively affected by the public crisis, which may further cause panic to intensify the malignant consequences. The transformation of a social risk into a public crisis is only necessary if the overall system is vulnerable and the risk factors meet the disaster-causing conditions [24]. On the other hand, in contrast to the malignant consequences of the public crisis category, building a harmonious society and maintaining social stability is one of the many purposes of controlling social risks.

Overall, the sources of social risk can be divided into two broad categories, namely technology, social problems, and emergencies. Since the latter two belong to external risks as defined by Giddens, they usually possess preplanned plans to control and reduce social risks after they occur. And in the current era of various science and technology blowouts, more and more emerging technologies are constantly impacting daily life. While technology facilitates people's daily life and contributes to industrial development and even innovation, the consequences are also worth considering. Therefore, this paper focuses on the mechanism of the impact of science and technology on social risks.

5.2 Identification of Social Risk Sources

Types of Technologies Influencing Social Risks. Table 3 shows the keywords belonging to the technology category obtained after filtering based on the keywords categorized as risk sources, and the technologies to which they belong. The technology categories are divided into eight categories: artificial intelligence, Internet technology, genetic technology, virtual reality technology, nanotechnology, Internet of everything, information technology, and communication technology, based on the general categories of technology.

Based on the frequency of keywords, the impact of AI technology on social risk is more concerned by Chinese scholars. And scholars focus not only on the technology itself but also on the technology derived from AI algorithms. Taking face recognition technology supported by AI algorithms as an example, Sun D.R. focuses on the possible spoofing attack and the alienation of face recognition technology into the composite technology Leviathan, the former is the act of people with ulterior motives using fake identification information to deceive the face recognition technology system and gain access to it, which breaks the trusted access system and causes social risks. The latter represents the rapid development of technology that can develop uncontrollably without proper control, thus causing social risks [25].

In addition, gene technology is also of great interest to Chinese scholars, and the direction is not limited to genetic weapons, genetic products, gene editing, and gene technology. In the context of gene technology, scholars have also mentioned the risk of

Table 3. Technical Keywords.

Technology	Keyword
Artificial Intelligence	Artificial Intelligence
	AI Face Replacement
Internet Technology	Cyber
Gene Technology	Genetic Weapons
	Genetic Products
	Gene Editing
	Gene Technology
Virtual Reality Technology	Metaverse
	Virtual Reality
Nanotechnology	Nanotechnology
Internet of Everything	Internet of Everything Era
	Internet of Everything
Information Technology	Information Technology
Communication Technology	Communication Technology

alienation when discussing its social risks. For example, Yang J. discusses the inevitable off-target effect in gene editing, i.e., the risk of alienation that is difficult to control due to the inevitable mistakes in implementation [26]. In addition, Zhang J. argues that the risk posed by human gene editing is not only brought by uncontrollable technology but also poses a serious threat to the current stable and peaceful situation of human beings, i.e., the problem arises from the technical level to the social level [27].

In general, scholars have focused on the double-edged sword effect of technology, especially the social risks that may be brought by the alienation of technology. And as technology develops, the social risks it poses will continue to change in terms of content, form, and intensity [28].

Keywords Characteristics of Technologies that Pose Social Risks. First, there is the potential to reshape the industry and even benefit humanity. Artificial intelligence refers to a system in which machines can demonstrate intelligence to perceive the environment, make judgments, and take actions to achieve goals like humans. It can help humans to deal with problems and predict future trends to a certain extent, and in the process, without human assistance, artificial intelligence can analyze information from different sources through various sensors or data inputs and make real-time feedback. Currently, AI has been applied to many industries, including healthcare, smart transportation, smart city, finance and trade, etc. It contains a variety of application scenarios, including search engines, personalized recommendations for advertising, intelligent voice assistants, intelligent customer service, intelligent translation, driverless, etc., to achieve empowerment for many traditional industries and add vitality to emerging industries. Nanotechnology also has this same characteristic. Nanotechnology is a technology that uses a single atom or molecule, a substance between 1 and 100 nm in size. As the basic science and technology of many advanced technologies, it empowers physics and computer technology and then gives rise to many scientific fields, such as nanophysics, nanobiology, nanochemistry, nanofabrication technology, etc. Nanotechnology is widely used in medicine, energy, aerospace, and even daily use of clothing fabrics, displays, etc. are all applied to some extent. Gene technology has also changed people's perceptions and is widely used in the pharmaceutical industry to achieve genetic identification of parentage, genetic diagnosis of genetic diseases, gene therapy for genetics, cloning technology, and various drugs, such as recombinant drugs and biological vaccines. The revolutionary disruption of these technologies has greatly improved people's lives.

Second, there are hidden dangers in the application process. These technologies, despite their long development time, still have many hidden dangers as of now. For example, artificial intelligence currently has problems such as data leakage, imperfect regulations, and technical defects that lead to abnormal work, such as driverless cars that cause traffic accidents for no reason. In 2018, researchers at the University of Oxford, the University of Cambridge, and the artificial intelligence organization Open AI published a study on the potential for AI to be manipulated for malicious purposes, enabling remote control of driverless cars, drones, and other AI-based devices, which in turn can carry out unlawful acts and create social risks [29]. The potential hazards of nanotechnology on human health and the environment are of concern to scholars. The human skin system can effectively prevent macroscopic particles from entering the human body to safeguard human health from the harsh external environment, however, the particles of nanomaterials are too small and can simply enter the human body in the form of diffusion or penetration through the skin, which can negatively affect human health [30]. Genetically modified food, for example, is a conservative food in many countries, and its entry into the market is subject to strict scrutiny by different agencies and levels, and the controversy caused by genetically modified food is constantly being discussed.

Third, what it can achieve is greater than people's ability to control it. Artificial intelligence, for example, is "technologically autonomous", meaning that artificial intelligence devices based on deep learning algorithms can "think" for themselves and generate corresponding behavior. In this case, it is difficult to judge the direction and size of the extension of its capabilities, which exceeds the expectations and cognition of the R&D personnel, so it is extremely difficult for the R&D personnel to effectively control the AI to prevent possible malignant results, which generates social risks; in addition, there is a possibility that the AI will evolve into Artificial Superintelligence, which will possess intelligence far beyond human imagination, which will inevitably generate corresponding social risks [31].

In general, the technologies that have received much attention in the study of social risks usually have the potential to change the status quo and reshape industries and even benefit humanity, but at the same time, there are still various hidden risks in their use, which involve every individual in society. As this technology develops further, it will become increasingly difficult for humans to control it. As a newly emerged power grid system, the application of artificial intelligence and other high technology is an important reason for the SG's realization. The presence of artificial intelligence and other technologies allows the grid system to move from passive control to active response. The application of new technologies in this process also corresponds to the reshaping of the industry, the existence of hidden dangers, and the inability to fully control the characteristics. Therefore, the SG may indeed pose social risks in the application of emerging technologies.

Mechanisms of Technology's Impact on Social Risks and Countermeasures. Risk is an inherent property of science and technology [32], while it adds convenience to human life and achieves breakthroughs to reduce the cost of living or working, its complexity and destructiveness cannot be underestimated. From the perspective of consumers or users of technology-based products, in the process of consumption and use, there are factors that may contribute to social risks, such as the consequences of malicious control of technology-based products by others, or the potential for malicious consequences of improper operation during use, which have the potential to disrupt the social order and therefore generate social risks.

From the perspective of the overall process, first of all, in the research and development stage, the technology itself may have certain hidden dangers but also can not exclude the possibility of researchers with malicious intentions using technology to design products or services [31]. At the stage of use, there is a possibility that the process of use may go wrong, be maliciously controlled, or be difficult to control its negative effects, etc. [16]. Once these situations occur, the wide audience and media dissemination increase the possibility of social order being disrupted, thus creating social risks. Further, from the perspective of future design or use, the ability of human beings to control the rapidly developing technology becomes a potential risk [33], i.e., whether the products produced by the technology itself can be controlled and whether the consequences of the things or even the human body transformed by the technology can be controlled.

Although the SG uses machine learning, deep learning, and artificial intelligence technologies to achieve the majority of known and unknown cyber threats [34], there are still some cyber security problems [35] since the system is not perfect and the mechanism is not flexible enough. In contrast, there are social risks in the application of science and technology to the SG in the research and development phase, the operational phase, and the prospective phase.

Overall, as shown in Fig. 5, there are seven components that contribute to the creation of social risks in the process of creating products with technology and their use, namely, hidden dangers or defects in the technology itself, problems with the initial intention of people using the technology, errors in the methods used by people when using the technology, malicious control of technology-related products when used by people, side effects in the product itself, future products that cannot be effectively controlled, and the Consequences brought about by things or human bodies, where these consequences also include the consequences of things that technology can accomplish that are greater than people's ability to control.

In terms of countermeasures, the first step is to continuously improve the laws and regulations that govern emerging technologies such as artificial intelligence. Legal regulation to prevent certain social risks, give full play to the advantages and convenience of emerging technologies, to curb their risks and malignant consequences. However, legal

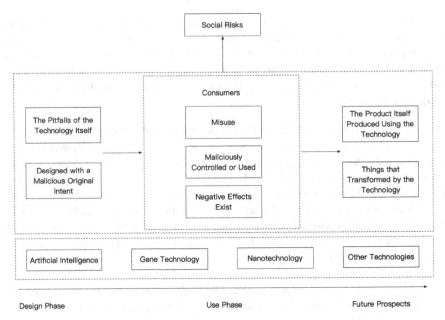

Fig. 5. Mechanisms by Which Technology Affects Social Risk.

regulation has lag and incompleteness, it is difficult to carry out prospective restraint, and there are also certain loopholes that cannot be completely covered, so it is necessary to constantly update the legal regulation, and play an active role in regulatory agencies, and constantly monitor the link of emerging technologies that may bring social risks, so as to control the social risks of emerging technologies at the national level. Secondly, at the enterprise level, especially the central enterprises involved in the national grid, they should actively fulfill their corporate social responsibility, adhere to corporate ethics, comprehensively examine and evaluate the social risks of applying various emerging technologies, continuously adhere to corporate values and principles, focus on the interests of corporate stakeholders, and reduce the possibility of malicious development at the R&D level. Third, in terms of scientific research institutions, we should continue to explore new technologies, study new technologies and new methods to reduce the hidden dangers of emerging technologies, continuously improve the theory and practice of emerging technologies, provide guidance for enterprise applications, and reduce the uncontrollability of future technological development. Fourth, from a network security perspective, it is important to adequately prevent external intrusions and, if they do occur, to use filing to reduce the negative impact on the grid system and thus reduce social risk.

6   Conclusion

This paper analyzed the main factors and countermeasures of social risk brought by the SG in China based on CiteSpace information visualization literature analysis software, including author analysis, keyword co-occurrence analysis, and keyword clustering analysis, and classified all designed keywords into five categories: risk category, risk source or important antecedent, management tool or instrument, result or purpose, and related terms, and extracted keywords related to technology by classifying the risk source. The risk formation mechanism is analyzed and corresponding countermeasures are proposed for the emerging technologies associated with the SG. In general, Chinese scholars' research on social risk focuses on the impact of various social problems, emergencies, and emerging technologies on social risk. In the technology-specific section, scholars give different understandings, with some scholars positively viewing the turnaround of big data technology for social risk control and others cautiously observing the various risks that may be brought by artificial intelligence technology. In the section of social risk formation mechanisms, the impact path of emerging technologies on social risk is analyzed in the context of the SG, and corresponding countermeasures are proposed for different aspects. In future research, the current status of social risk research can be explored for other aspects of the SG, and the impact of other categories of emerging technologies involved in the SG on social risk can be extended to explore the impact mechanism of social problems or emergencies brought about by the SG on social risk, in order to expand the research related to social risk.

References

1. Beck, U.: Risk Society: Towards a New Modernity. Sage Publications (1992)
2. Fung, B.Y.: Exploring the relationship between social risk and risk society. J. Jiangsu Adm. Coll. (05), 76–81 (2008)
3. U.S. Department of Energy., Office of Electricity Delivery and Energy Reliability: The Smart Grid: An Introduction. Litos Strategic Communication, East Providence, Rhode Island (2008)
4. Metke, A.R., Ekl, R.L.: Smart grid security technology. In: Innovative Smart Grid Technologies (ISGT), pp. 1–7. IEEE (2010)
5. Khurana, H., Hadley, M., Lu, N., Frincke, D.A.: Smart-grid security issues. IEEE Secur. Priv. **8**(1), 81–85 (2010)
6. Gunduz, M.Z., Das, R.: Cyber-security on smart grid: threats and potential solutions. Comput. Netw. **169**, 107094 (2020)
7. Liu, Z.Y.: Build strong smart grid as pillar of sound and rapid development. Power Syst. Clean Energy **9**, 1–3 (2009)
8. Lupu, L.: The concept of social risk: a geographical approach. Quaestiones Geogr. **38**(4), 5–13 (2008)
9. Zhang, H.B.: Paradigm of social risk research. J. Nanjing Univ. (Philos. Humanit. Soc. Sci. Edn.) (02), 136–144 (2008)
10. Giddens, A.: The Consequences of Modernity. Stanford University Press, Stanford (1990)
11. Day, G.S., Schoemaker, P.J.H.: Avoiding the pitfalls of emerging technologies. Calif. Manage. Rev. **42**(2), 8–33 (2000)
12. Keenan, J., Kemp, D., Owen, J.: Corporate responsibility and the social risk of new mining technologies. Corp. Soc. Responsib. Environ. Manag. **26**(4), 752–760 (2019)
13. Ghasemi, S., Ahmadvand, M., Karami, E., Karami, A.: Social risk perceptions of genetically modified foods of engineers in training: application of a comprehensive risk model. Sci. Eng. Ethics **26**(2), 641–665 (2020)
14. Li, B., Gao, Z.Y.: Analysis and prospect on the application of artificial intelligence technologies in smart grid. Electr. Power **50**(12), 136–140 (2017)

15. Omitaomu, O.A., Niu, H.: Artificial intelligence techniques in smart grid: a survey. Smart Cities **4**(2), 548–568 (2021)
16. Ma, C.S.: Social risks of artificial intelligence and its legal regulation. Legal Sci. (J. Northwestern Univ. Polit. Sci. Law) (06), 47–55 (2020)
17. Jian, S.Y.: "Meta-universe": a future concept in the stage of basic technology. J. Shanghai Univ. (Soc. Sci. Edn.) (02), 1–16 (2022
18. Chen, C.: Searching for intellectual turning points: progressive knowledge domain visualization. Proc. Natl. Acad. Sci. **101**(suppl 1), 5303–5310 (2004)
19. Tong, X., Zhang, H.B.: Mass emergencies and their governance - a reconsideration in the framework of integrated analysis of social risks and public crises. Academia (02), 35–45 (2008)
20. Zhang, H.B., Tong, X.: Changes in the structure of emergency management in china and a theoretical generalization. Soc. Sci. China (03), 58–84+206 (2008)
21. Li, G. P., Yi, L.: Embedded regulation: policy innovation of social organizations in the context of urbanization. Jiangxi Soc. Sci. (06), 234–239 (2018)
22. Huang, X.H.: Risk regulation research: building a knowledge system for social risk governance. Adm. Forum (02), 73–80 (2016)
23. Yang, D.: Path selection of collaborative governance of social risks at the grassroots based on SFIC model: an example of public deliberation on letter and petition matters by village (resident) councils in L city. Huxiang Forum (02), 107–118 (2022)
24. Xu, W.J., Liao, X.M.: Analysis of disaster-causing mechanisms of major social risks and construction of prevention and control mechanisms–a study based on risk prevention and control of the new crown pneumonia epidemic. Soft Sci. (06), 46–51 (2020)
25. Sun, D. R.: Social risks of face recognition technology and its legal regulation. Sci. Res. (01), 12–20+32 (2021)
26. Yang, J.: Regulation of social risk of gene editing. Sci. Technol. Law (03), 84–94 (2019)
27. Zhang, J.: On legal control of human gene editing. Henan Soc. Sci. **27**(08), 87–91 (2019)
28. Xie, J.G., Tan, M.Y.: Social well-being and social risk in the age of Wanlian. New Horiz. (06), 86–93 (2019)
29. Brundage, M., et al.: The malicious use of artificial intelligence: forecasting, prevention, and mitigation. arXiv preprint arXiv:1802.07228 (2018)
30. Fei, D. Y.: Gray sorrow - the social risks of nanotechnology. Philos. Dyn. (01), 23–26+36 (2004)
31. Tang, J.: Research on social risk response of artificial intelligence. Teach. Res. (04), 89–97 (2019)
32. Zhao, W. L.: Science and technology and social risk. Sci. Technol. Dialect. (03), 50–55 (1998)
33. Wan, P. J.: Artificial intelligence's historical debate, risk consideration and future prediction—take the influence on education as key point. Zhejiang Soc. Sci. (02), 148–154+147+160 (2021)
34. Zhou, L.M., Gu, Y.P.: Innovation of social risk governance in the era of artificial intelligence. J. Hohai Univ. (Philos. Soc. Sci.) **23**(3), 38–45 (2021)
35. Chehri, A., Fofana, I., Yang, X.: Security risk modeling in smart grid critical infrastructures in the era of big data and artificial intelligence. Sustainability **13**(6), 3196 (2021)

Using HTC Vive to Design a Virtual Reality Simulation Environment on Radiography

Lun-Ping Hung[1], Mine-Che Wu[2], Yu-Rang Jhang[3], and Wen-Lung Tsai[3]([✉])

[1] Department of Information Management, National Taipei University of Nursing and Health Sciences, Taipei 112, Taiwan
[2] Radiation Oncology Division, Far-Eastern Memorial Hospital, New Taipei 220, Taiwan
[3] Department of Information Management, Asia Eastern University of Science and Technology, New Taipei 220, Taiwan
wltsai@mail.aeust.edu.tw

Abstract. This study aims to design and develop a virtual reality situational simulation system for the radiation oncology unit in a hospital. This study applies HTC Vive, Autodesk 3ds Max and Unity 3D to develop a virtual reality simulation model, followed by programming in the C# language and Visual Studio compiler to create a virtual scene for the stereotactic radiography imaging verification process. The result of this study provides a prototype system.

Keywords: radiography · virtual reality · HTC Vive · simulation system

1 Introduction

In recent years, using virtual reality (VR) related technologies in various industries, particularly the medical, healthcare, and education sectors, has become increasingly popular. Integrating information and smart technologies in teaching and training can address additional challenges faced by traditional methods.

Featuring interactivity and real-time response, VR allows users to freely operate the computer and view the completed design from any angle and position [1]. VR technology has shown great promise in the research and development, training, and education of medical physiology, gastrointestinal endoscopy simulators, clinical anatomy simulators, among other applications. In addition, it is widely used in the field of medical imaging. According to foreign studies, VR simulation featuring dynamic interaction and feedback can help students in related medical imaging degrees cultivate their clinical skills.

By creating a scenario similar to the actual clinical situation, simulation teaching allows students to continuously practice skills in the virtual clinical scene, while the clinical supervisor observes their execution process and provides feedback [2]. In radiography, the integration of VR with the cultivation of radiography talents to perform online and offline theoretical and practical courses have the advantages of both high efficiency and convenience.

D.-J. Deng et al. (Eds.): SGIoT 2022, LNICST 497, pp. 309–314, 2023.
https://doi.org/10.1007/978-3-031-31275-5_28

2 Literature Reviews

In recent years, VR-related technologies have matured, with various VR products developed by different industries in response to the introduction of VR technology. VR refers to an emerging computer technology that combines multimedia and simulation techniques to create a virtual environment that integrates auditory, visual, and other senses, allowing users to be immersed and interact with it [3].

VR refers to the "simulation of reality." VR primarily uses real-time 3D rendering to present immediate, dynamic, and interactive scenes to shorten the gap in the user's cognition. When assisted by appropriate software and hardware human-machine interfaces, it allows users to interact with the virtual simulation and, as a result, increases their interest and learning effectiveness [4]. VR devices provide users with immersive experiences in three-dimensional virtual scenes. The most famous VR headsets at present include Oculus Rift, 3Glasses, HTC Vive, and PlayStation VR, with the HTC Vive being the most popular [5].

The HTC Vive is currently one of the most popular VR headsets. Through the "room-scale" technology, HTC Vive converts a room into a three-dimensional space using a locater, allowing users to navigate and move around naturally in the virtual world. In addition, the device allows users to dynamically manipulate objects using motion-tracked handheld controllers, providing a sophisticated interactive, communicative, and immersive experience [6]. This study uses HTC Vive as the VR hardware and combines it with auditory and visual VR technologies to provide users with a good VR experience. The visual part uses interactive question-and-answer and the operation simulation of virtual objects, whereas the auditory part incorporates objects related to the virtual ones. The combination of the two will bring a realistic virtual interactive experience.

Image-guided radiation therapy (IGRT) uses advanced imaging technology to better define the tumor target and is critical in reducing and ultimately eliminating uncertainties. [7] Currently, most radiologic technology programs teach students positioning and radiation dose techniques in a traditional X-ray laboratory. Virtual simulation provides a safe and convenient learning environment where students can practice techniques without the risk of irradiating patients. Instructors can foster deep learning in virtual simulation laboratory environments by designing the software around specific course outcomes (e.g., cognitive and psychomotor skills) and engaging in sound educational strategies and theory [8].

3 Method and System Design

This study aims to develop a VR-based system that can address the challenges and issues of existing training programs for radiography interns and staff. It is expected that this system can improve the professional ability of users and, as a result, increase radiography accuracy. In terms of system simulation, this study will first use Autodesk 3ds Max and Unity 3D to develop a VR simulation model, followed by programming in the C# language and Visual Studio compiler to create a virtual scene for the stereotactic radiography imaging verification process.

Figure 1 is the system architecture in this study. The VR terminal device (HTC Vive), shown on the right of the figure, communicates with Unity at the hardware layer together with Open VR API and Steam VR API. The system is supplemented with specific exoskeleton data and object configurations to create a complete set of VR interactive experiences after compilation by Unity.

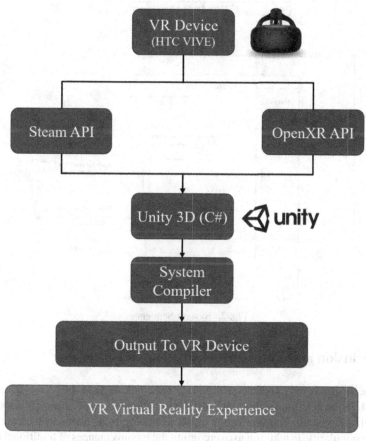

Fig. 1. System Architecture

This study sequentially models the pre-planned simulation scenes before importing the completed model into Unity. Considering compatibility issues, the attributes of the shader are set independently in Unity. The light source is subsequently adjusted to make the scene more realistic. Once the scene is constructed, the VR device is connected to Unity through the API. After the compilation is executed, the API will immediately judge and process the tracking information of the locator, output it as an image through operations in Unity, and send it back to the helmet to achieve the final visual feedback effects (Fig. 2).

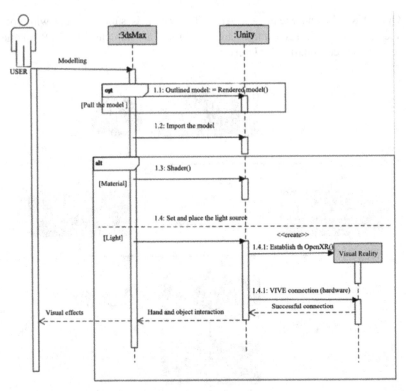

Fig. 2. System Sequence

4 Conclusion and Future Works

Currently, this study only presents preliminary system design and the prototype as Fig. 3 and Fig. 4. In the near future, this study will be used to develop a complete VR radiography simulation system. The application of VR technologies in the medical care industry is gaining popularity. In addition to overcoming the inconveniences of traditional healthcare practice and education, it is capable of significantly improving the working methods and execution efficiency of healthcare in the future. However, some technical challenges remain, including integration of medical and nursing information systems, clarity and resolution of screen presentation, accuracy of interaction, and durability of hardware equipment. Although numerous software-related and hardware-related technical problems need to be addressed, applications of VR in the medical field have bright future prospects.

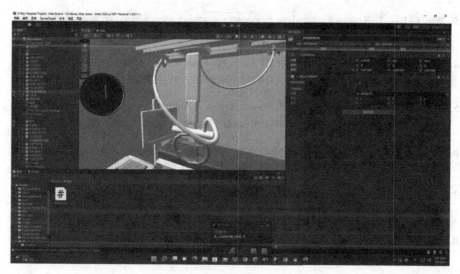

Fig. 3. Screenshot of X-Ray Machine

Fig. 4. Screenshot of System Instructions

References

1. Li, Z., Kiiveri, M., Rantala, J., Raisamo, R.: Evaluation of haptic virtual reality user interfaces for medical marking on 3D models. Int. J. Hum. Comput. Stud. **147**, 102561 (2021)
2. Lei, Y.Y., Zhu, L., Sa, Y.T.R., Cui, X.S.: Effects of high-fidelity simulation teaching on nursing nursing students' knowledge, professional skills and clinical ability: a meta-analysis and systematic review. Nurse Educ. Pract. **60**, 103306 (2022)

3. Wu, Y., Liu, J.: Research on college gymnastics teaching model based on multimedia image and image texture feature analysis. Discov. Internet Things **1**(1), 1–13 (2021). https://doi.org/10.1007/s43926-021-00015-6

4. Sung, B., Mergelsberg, E., Teah, M., D'Silva, B., Phau, I.: The effectiveness of a marketing virtual reality learning simulation: a quantitative survey with psychophysiological measures. Br. J. Edu. Technol. **52**(1), 196–213 (2021)

5. Borglund, F., Young, M., Eriksson, J., Rasmussen, A.: Feedback from HTC vive sensors results in transient performance enhancements on a juggling task in virtual reality. Sensors **21**(9), 2966 (2021)

6. Wang, Y., Grant, S., Grist, M.: Enhancing the learning of multi-level undergraduate Chinese language with a 3D immersive experience-an exploratory study. Comput. Assist. Lang. Learn. **34**(1–2), 114–132 (2021)

7. Chamunyonga, C., Rutledge, P., Caldwell, P.J., Burbery, J.: The implementation of MOSAIQ-based image-guided radiation therapy image matching within radiation therapy education. J. Med. Radiat. Sci. **68**(1), 86–90 (2021)

8. Little, J.: Using virtual simulation to increase deep learning in radiography students. Radiol. Technol. **92**(4), 324–330 (2021)

Bidirectional Scanning Based Medium Access Control Algorithm in Directional Aviation Relay Network with Multiple Air Nodes

Gaoxiang Ma, Zhongjiang Yan[✉], Mao Yang, and Bo Li

School of Electronics and Information, Northwestern Polytechnical University, Xi'an, China
{zhjyan,yangmao,libo.npu}@nwpu.edu.cn

Abstract. Directional aviation relay networks are widely used to improve the performance of ad hoc networks. Aiming at the disadvantage of large data packet delay of directional aviation relay network with single air node, this paper proposes a medium access control algorithm based on multiple air nodes and bidirectional scanning, which can effectively reduce the total delay of data packets. First, the algorithm divides multiple air nodes into two groups, using clockwise and counterclockwise scanning modes respectively, to provide data relay and forwarding services for ground nodes. According to the number of air nodes and their scanning mode, as well as the sector in which the destination node of the to-be-sent traffic is located, the ground nodes determine whether the to-be-sent traffic uses a single-aircraft relay two-hop transmission or a double-aircraft relay four-hop transmission link in a distributed manner. Secondly, the theoretical model of unidirectional scanning and bidirectional scanning algorithm is built, and the theoretical packet delay distribution law of the two algorithms as well as the optimal ratio of bidirectional scanning algorithm in reducing packet delay compared with unidirectional scanning algorithm is obtained. Finally, the performance of the proposed algorithm is verified by simulation. The simulation results are consistent with the theoretical analysis, which show that in the case of 4 to 8 air nodes, compared with unidirectional scanning algorithm, the total delay of packets in bidirectional scanning algorithm is reduced by 23.10%–28.81%.

Keywords: directional aviation relay network · multiple air nodes · MAC · data packet delay

This work was supported in part by the National Natural Science Foundations of CHINA (Grant No. 61771392, No. 61871322 and No. 61771390), and Science and Technology on Avionics Integration Laboratory and the Aeronautical Science Foundation of China (Grant No. 201955053002 and No. 20185553035).

1   Introduction

Due to the limitation of energy of nodes in network, wireless ad hoc networks have shortcomings in terms of transmission power and transmission distance, especially in long-distance networks and scenarios where the line of sight is blocked by terrain, so it is difficult to guarantee the quality of point-to-point communication between the source node and the destination node. Therefore, relay technology is widely used in wireless ad hoc networks to improve the link state between the source node and the destination node and expand the coverage of the network. A network that uses small unmanned aerial vehicles as a relay platform to carry directional wireless network communication equipment to assist ground nodes in data transmission in network scenarios with large spans, such as in articles [1,2], is called a directional aviation relay network (DARN). The drones in it are called air nodes.

The directional aviation relay network has the advantages of widening network coverage, improving network throughput, facilitating network management, reducing packet delay and being easy to deploy. However, its medium access control protocol design also faces severe challenges such as increased propagation delay and increased collision probability.

For the medium access control technology of directional aviation relay network, the existing research in [2–11] mainly focuses on reducing collision probability, avoiding channel competition, optimizing link distance and making full use of the interval between sending and receiving packets caused by propagation delay. In [2] Yan Z J et al. proposed a medium access control protocol that divides the network scene according to the link distance from the ground node to the air node. In order to solve the problem of the efficiency reduction of medium access control protocol caused by the increase of propagation delay, in [6–8] Zhou W L et al. designed an environment adaptive medium access control protocol using the TBAG protocol framework that is controlled and triggered by the air node in the scenario of deploying a single air node. In [9] Xiafei Bu et al. proposed to use orthogonal frequency division multiple access technology to improve network efficiency considering the power consumption of UAVs. In [10] Muhammad Farhan Sohail et al. applied non-orthogonal multiple access technology to UAV relay network to improve the total network transmission rate and energy utilization and expand the network coverage. In [11] Jiangbin Lyu et al. proposed a cyclic multiple access protocol by using the periodic change of the signal strength between the UAV and the ground nodes during the circular motion of the UAV.

Resource allocation is closely related to medium access control technology. Because the idea of competing for network resource used by traditional DCF technology will cause waste of time resources in large-scale directional aviation relay networks, scholars at home and abroad have also conducted in-depth research on resource allocation algorithms applied to large-scale directional aviation relay networks. In [8,9] Zhou W L et al. proposed an algorithm for time slot resource allocation based on the link distance based on TBAG protocol architecture. The air node uses the propagation delay of communication with the long-distance ground nodes to communicate with the short-range ground nodes opportunistically, and makes a unified arrangement for the packet sending sequence of all the nodes in the network in the data transmission stage in current time frame. In [12] Daniel T. Bennett et al. proposed a shortest path first method to reduce network overhead by optimizing beam switching sequence and improve the throughput of ground nodes by optimizing time allocation of beams. In [13] Jin Li et al. proposed a resource allocation algorithm to improve resource utilization for cellular networks with multiple UAVs.

The current medium access control technologies proposed for directional aviation relay networks mainly focus on reducing packet collisions, improving medium access control efficiency, shortening packet propagation delays, or solving the adverse effects caused by increased packet propagation delay. But few literatures mentioned the optimization of packet delay, or the application of multi-air nodes deployment mode in reducing packet delay. Aiming at the problem of packet delay optimization, this paper proposes a bidirectional scanning medium access control algorithm for multi-air nodes scenario. The ground nodes sense the number of air nodes and their scanning mode, and determines in a distributed manner whether the traffic to be sent uses a single-aircraft relay two-hop transmission or a double-aircraft relay four-hop transmission mode according to the sector where the destination node of the traffic to be sent is located. Theoretical analysis and simulation verification confirm the performance of the medium access control algorithm proposed in this paper in optimizing packet delay.

This paper consists of six chapters. The first chapter introduces the research background and research significance of DARN. The second chapter introduces the directional aviation relay network model. The third chapter proposes a bidirectional scanning medium access control algorithm for multi-air nodes scenario. The fourth chapter analyzes the packet delay performance of the proposed algorithm theoretically. The fifth chapter verifies the performance of the medium access control algorithm proposed by simulation. And the sixth chapter is the summary and conclusion of the whole paper.

2   Network Model

The network coverage is a circular area with a radius of RD_1. The ground nodes are evenly distributed in the network, and multiple air nodes that cannot communicate with each other directly do a uniform circular motion with a small radius of RD_2 around the center of the network. The air nodes can be regarded as stationary at the center of the network given that $RD_1 \gg RD_2$.

Fig. 1. Time frame structure.

In order to expand the coverage and reduce the interference range, the air nodes use directional antennas that can realize beam switching to cover the

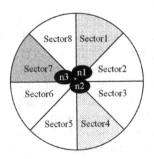

Fig. 2. Schematic diagram of multi-air nodes cover the network area.

ground network. There are N identical air nodes that can not communicate with each other in the network. The width of the directional beam divides the network into M sectors, and the time is divided into time frames of duration Δ as shown in Fig. 1. Each air node serves ground nodes in M sectors sequentially in a scanning manner, and each air node can only cover one sector in each time frame.

All nodes work in the same frequency band. Due to the problem of co-frequency interference, at most M air nodes can be deployed in the network, covering all the M sectors at the same time. And the beams of any two air nodes cannot cover the same sector at the same time.

Let $P(g,d)$ represents the data packet with ground node g as the source node and ground node d as the destination node. Let the sector where g is located be S_g, and the sector where d is located be S_d. Let each air node serve each sector for the same length of time, denoted as Δ. n represents the air node currently serving the sector where g is located. n' is the air node whose scanning mode is different from that of n and reaches the sector where g is located earlier than any other air nodes that has the same scanning mode with it. T_n^2 is the single-aircraft two-hop packet delay with air node n as the relay node, and $T_{n'}^2$ is the single-aircraft two-hop packet delay with air node n' as the relay node. Without loss of generality, assuming that the scanning mode of air node n is clockwise, while the scanning mode of air node n' is counterclockwise.

Figure 2 is a schematic diagram of a network scenario with 8 sectors and 3 air nodes, where $n1, n2, n3$ represents the 3 air nodes.

3   Bidirectional Scanning Medium Access Control Algorithm

3.1   Basic Idea

Because the destination nodes of the traffic flow of the source node are evenly distributed in all the sectors, the multi-air nodes medium access control algorithm proposed in this paper divides the air nodes equally into two groups. The first group performs counterclockwise beam scanning, and the second group performs clockwise beam scanning.

The medium access control algorithm proposed in this paper is called the bidirectional scanning algorithm. The medium access control algorithm using the traditional idea that all air nodes scan in the same direction and work independently without affecting each other is called the unidirectional scanning algorithm, and is used for performance comparison in this paper. On the basis of bidirectional scanning, this paper designs a four-hop relaying link where the data packet passes through source node, air node A, ground relay node, air node B and destination node in turn, to further reduce the packet delay.

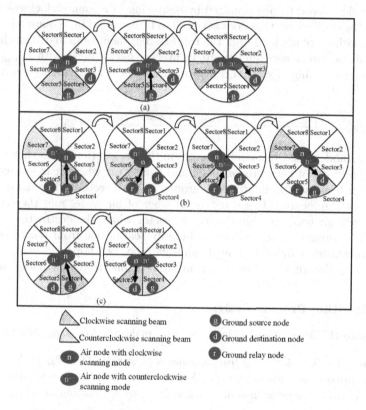

Fig. 3. Schematic diagram of packet delay optimization.

Figure 3 shows a schematic diagram of the idea of packet delay optimization. In scenario (a), if select the air node n' that scans counterclockwise for two-hop relay, only two beam rotations are needed to complete the packet transmission, which is better than selecting the air node n that scans clockwise. In scenario (b), a double-aircraft four-hop relay is used, node n receives the data packets from the source node, and sends them to the ground relay node when its beam rotates to sector 6, so that node n' can receive the data packets again when its beam rotates to sector 6 and send them to the destination node located in sector

5 when its beam rotates to sector 5. Only 3 beam rotations are required to deliver the packets to the destination node, which is better than the two-hop links that requires 8 beam rotations. In scenario (c), the data packet transmission delay can be minimized by directly passing the data packets through node n.

Because the air nodes cannot communicate with each other, each air node will serve M sectors in turn, instead of serving some of the sectors individually. Approximate analysis shows that the bidirectional scanning algorithm provides the source node with the option of transmitting data packets in the counterclockwise direction, thereby reducing the packet delay by half. If it is considered that the traffic flows need to be optimized by delivering in a counterclockwise direction, and the traffic flows that does not need to be delivered in a counterclockwise direction both accounts for $1/2$ of the total traffic, then compared with the unidirectional scanning algorithm (donate its average packet delay with T_{Delay}), the bidirectional scanning algorithm can obtain a packet delay optimization ratio of about 25%:

$$\frac{T_{Delay} - (0.5 \times T_{Delay} + 0.5 \times 0.5 T_{Delay})}{T_{Delay}} = 25\% \tag{1}$$

The air nodes need to maintain a ground node location table that records the MAC address of each ground node and the sector where it is located, and periodically broadcast to inform each ground node of sectors where all nodes in the network are located. Based on the number of air nodes and the scanning mode of each air node, combined with the sector where the destination node is located, the ground source node distributedly selects one from the three data packet transmission links, two single-aircraft relay two-hop transmission links and a double-aircraft relay four-hop transmission link, to reduce packet delay.

3.2   Algorithm Process Design

To facilitate the description of the algorithm, make the following definitions.

Definition 1. *Downlink data transmission request table (DL-REQ). The downlink data transmission request table with the air node n as source node and ground nodes as destination node, including the column of destination node.*

Definition 2. *Uplink traffic request table (UL-REQ). A table formed by air node n by collecting the uplink traffic request of all ground nodes, including the column of relay mode (four-hop or two-hop) of the traffic, whether the air node is the last hop and destination node.*

Definition 3. *Forwarding queue (FOR-QUE). A queue composed of data packets with ground node g as relay node instead of destination node.*

Definition 4. *Sending Queue (SEND-QUE). A queue consisting of data packets that are most suitable to be relayed and forwarded by the air node n that is serving the sector according to the relay link selection algorithm.*

Definition 5. *Downlink traffic response table (DL-RES). Air node n collects the downlink traffic response of all ground nodes into this table, which includes the column of destination node and whether to agree to receive downlink data.*

Algorithm 1. Bidirectional Scanning Multiple Access Algorithm.

Input:
    1. Number of air nodes (N) and their scanning mode, 2. S_d

1: **while** True **do**
2:    n serves sector m, sends its own scanning mode and DL-REQ to the sector
3:    Ground node g receives information
4:    **if** g is included in the DL-REQ **then**
5:        g replys downlink traffic response to n, ready to receive downlink traffic
6:    **end if**
7:    **if** (FOR-QUE of g is not empty) or (SEND-QUE of g is not empty) **then**
8:        g sends an uplink traffic transmission request to n
9:    **end if**
10:   n receives responses from all ground nodes
11:   **if** n has packets as the 2nd hop source node in four-hop relay link **then**
12:      **if** The DL-RES of n is not empty **then**
13:        n selects the nearest node in DL-RES as ground relay node of the four-hop relay link and inserts the traffic into the DL-RES
14:      **else**
15:        n abandons the four-hop relay for these packets
16:      **end if**
17:   **end if**
18:   n executes the resource allocation according to UL-REQ and DL-RES and broadcasts the time slot allocation result to ground nodes (the resource allocation algorithm described is not within the scope of this paper)
19:   Nodes transmit data according to resource allocation result
20:   $m = m + 1$ // Beam switching
21:   **if** $m > M$ **then**
22:      $m = m - M$
23:   **end if**
24: **end while**

To facilitate the theoretical analysis of packet delay, the following definitions are made:

Definition 6. *Waiting delay. The time required from the generation of the data packet by the ground node to the reception of the packet by an air node.*

Definition 7. *Forward delay. The time required form the data packet generated by a ground node is received by an air node to the time when the data packet is received by the destination node.*

Because the two processes do not overlap in time, the discrete probability distributions of packet waiting delay and forward delay are statistically independent.

The data transmission process of bidirectional scanning algorithm is shown in Algorithm 1.

In Algorithm 1, in rows 2–10 the air node performs uplink and downlink traffic collection, in rows 11–18 the air node performs resource allocation based on the traffic collection results, in row 19 nodes perform data transmission, and the air node in rows 20–23 performs beam switching.

The ground nodes determine the sending queue through a distributed relay link selection algorithm, and the algorithm procedure is shown in Algorithm 2.

Algorithm 2. Relay Link Selection Algorithm.

Input:
    Number of air nodes and their scanning mode
    The sector where the destination node d is located
Output:
    Selected relay link
1: **for** $P(g, d)$ in Data packet queue **do**
2:     Read packet destination address d
3:     **if** d and g are in the same sector **then**
4:         g selects air node n that currently serving the sector to perform double-aircraft four-hop relay
5:     **else**
6:         Calculate $T_n^2 = \Delta \times (S_g \to_{clk} S_d)$ // $S_g \to_{clk} S_d$ is the number of sectors went through by clockwise scanning from sector S_g to sector S_d
7:         Calculate $T_{n'}^2 = \Delta \times (S_{n'} \to_{aclk} S_g \to_{aclk} S_d)$ // $S_{n'} \to_{aclk} S_g$ is the number of sectors went throuht from $S_{n'}$, the current serving sector of n' to the sector where g is located. $S_g \to_{aclk} S_d$ is the number of sectors went through by counterclockwise scanning from sector S_g to sector S_d
8:         **if** $T_n^2 < T_{n'}^2$ **then**
9:             g selects n as the relay node for two-hop transmission and inserts the data packet $P(g, d)$ into the sending queue
10:        **else**
11:            g does not select n as the relay node
12:        **end if**
13:     **end if**
14: **end for**

---

4 Theoretical Analysis of Algorithm Performance

4.1 Performance Analysis of Unidirectional Scanning Algorithm with Multi-air Nodes

Waiting Delay. It can be proved that evenly distributing the beams scanning in the same direction can make the maximum and average waiting delay of each sector reach the minimum value at the same time. That is, when the number of sectors is divisible by the number of beams, the beams are equally spaced, or when the number of sectors is not divisible by the number of beams, the beams are approximately equally spaced. As shown in Fig. 2, the concept of unit is introduced, and N beams divide all sectors into N units, and the number of sectors in each unit is $\lfloor M/N \rfloor$ or $\lceil M/N \rceil$. The number of units containing $\lceil M/N \rceil$ sectors is $\left(M - N \lfloor M/N \rfloor \right)$, and the number of units containing $\lfloor M/N \rfloor$ sectors is $\left[N - \left(M - N \lfloor M/N \rfloor \right) \right]$. For example, in Fig. 2, 3 uniformly distributed beams divide 8 sectors into 3 units, and each unit has 3, 3 and 2 sectors respectively. The air nodes cannot communicate with each other, so each air node will serve M sectors in turn. Therefore, after M time frames, each sector is served N times, and after $\lceil M/N \rceil$ time frames, each sector will be served at least once. So $\lceil M/N \rceil$ is the upper limit of the waiting delay.

Because the ground nodes select the nearest air node to send the uplink data packets, and the source node needs at least one time frame to send the data packets to the air node, the value range of the waiting delay (in time frames) is $\left[1, \lceil M/N \rceil \right]$ and obey the uniform distribution. Its discrete probability distribution law is as follow.

$$P\left(T_{Wait}^{unidirectional} = t_{Wait}^{unidirectional}\right) = \begin{cases} \frac{N}{M}, & t_{Wait}^{unidirectional} = 1, 2, \cdots, \lfloor \frac{M}{N} \rfloor \\ \frac{M - N \lfloor M/N \rfloor}{M}, & t_{Wait}^{unidirectional} = \lceil \frac{M}{N} \rceil \end{cases} \tag{2}$$

Forward Delay. Because in the unidirectional scanning algorithm, each air node is exactly the same. The ground nodes do not need to select the air nodes, so the packet transmission delay is only related to the number of sectors between the two sectors where the source node and the destination node are located. And its probability distribution law is:

$$P\left(T_{Forward}^{unidirectional} = t_{Forward}^{unidirectional}\right) = \frac{1}{M}, t_{Forward}^{unidirectional} = 1, 2, \cdots, M \tag{3}$$

Total Delay. The probability distribution of the total delay of the data packet of the unidirectional scanning algorithm is equal to the distribution of the sum of the two independent random variables, the waiting delay and the forward delay. Its distribution and mathematical expectation of the total data packet delay of unidirectional scanning algorithm are as follow.

$$P\left(T_{Delay}^{unidirectional} = t_{Delay}^{unidirectional}\right)$$
$$= \begin{cases} \frac{N \times \left(t_{Delay}^{unidirectional} - 1\right)}{M^2}, & t_{Delay}^{unidirectional} = 2, \cdots, \lfloor \frac{M}{N} \rfloor + 1 \\ \frac{1}{M}, & t_{Delay}^{unidirectional} = \lceil \frac{M}{N} \rceil + 1, \cdots, M + 1 \\ \frac{1}{M} - \frac{N \times \left(t_{Delay}^{unidirectional} - M - 1\right)}{M^2}, & t_{Delay}^{unidirectional} = M + 2, \cdots, \lceil \frac{M}{N} \rceil + M \end{cases} \tag{4}$$

$$E\left(T_{Delay}^{unidirectional}\right) = \left(1 - \frac{N}{2M} \times \lfloor \frac{M}{N} \rfloor\right) \times \left(\lfloor \frac{M}{N} \rfloor + 1\right) + \frac{1 + M}{2} \tag{5}$$

4.2   Performance Analysis of Bidirectional Scanning Algorithm with Multi-air Nodes

Analytical Method. The situation of the multi-air nodes bidirectional scanning algorithm is more complicated and it is difficult to carry out accurate performance analysis. Therefore, the analysis of bidirectional scanning algorithm is estimated based on the theoretical analysis results of unidirectional scanning algorithm. And the optimal ratio that can be obtained by bidirectional scanning algorithm compared with the unidirection scanning algorithm in the average total delay of data packets is estimated. In two special scenarios, the 8-sector 4-air node scenario and the 8-sector 8-air node scenario, Matlab is used to enumerate all possible cases of the sector where the source node is located, the sector where the destination node is located, and the sector where the beam is located when the source node generates a packet in bidirectional scanning algorithm. All possible combinations of these three parameters are enumerated, the total packet delay of each case is obtained and the distribution law is calculated. The mathematical expectation is also obtained to test the estimation results.

Waiting Delay. Compared with the unidirectional scanning algorithm, the bidirectional scanning algorithm divides all air nodes into two groups, which provide relay services for ground nodes respectively. Since the destination nodes are evenly distributed in the network, the probability that the source node selects two groups of air nodes is considered equal. Therefore, the waiting delay of the bidirectional scanning algorithm is approximately twice that of the unidirectional scanning algorithm, and its distribution law is:

$$P\left(T_{Wait}^{bidirectional} = t_{Wait}^{bidirectional}\right) = \begin{cases} \frac{N}{2M}, & t_{Wait}^{bidirectional} = 1, 2, \cdots, \left\lfloor \frac{2M}{N} \right\rfloor \\ \frac{M - \frac{N}{2} \times \left\lfloor \frac{2M}{N} \right\rfloor}{M}, & t_{Wait}^{bidirectional} = \left\lceil \frac{2M}{N} \right\rceil \end{cases} \quad (6)$$

Forward Delay. When the delay T_{Delay} of selecting an air node that scans clockwise is more than $M/2$, selecting another air node that scans counterclockwise for relay may have a shorter forward delay of $(M - T_{Delay}) < M/2$. Therefore, it is approximated that the forward delay of the bidirectional scanning algorithm can be optimized to $1/2$ of the unidirectional scanning algorithm, and its distribution law is:

$$P\left(T_{Forward}^{bidirectional} = t_{Forward}^{bidirectional}\right) = \frac{2}{M}, t_{Forward}^{bidirectional} = 1, 2, \cdots, \frac{M}{2} \quad (7)$$

Total Delay. The distribution law of the total packet delay in the bidirectional scanning algorithm can also be obtained by calculating the distribution of the sum of two independent random variables, the waiting delay and the forward delay. Its distribution law and mathematical expectation are as follow.

$$P\left(T_{Delay}^{bidirectional} = t_{Delay}^{bidirectional}\right)$$

$$= \begin{cases} \frac{N \times \left(t_{Delay}^{bidirectional} - 1\right)}{M^2}, t_{Delay}^{bidirectional} = 2, \cdots, \left\lfloor \frac{2M}{N} \right\rfloor + 1 \\ \frac{2}{M}, t_{Delay}^{bidirectional} = \left\lceil \frac{2M}{N} \right\rceil + 1, \cdots, \frac{M}{2} + 1 \\ \frac{2}{M} - \frac{N \times \left(t_{Delay}^{bidirectional} - \frac{M}{2} - 1\right)}{M^2}, t_{Delay}^{bidirectional} = \frac{M}{2} + 2, \cdots, \left\lceil \frac{2M}{N} \right\rceil + \frac{M}{2} \end{cases} \tag{8}$$

$$E\left(T_{Delay}^{bidirectional}\right) = \left(1 - \frac{N}{4M} \times \left\lfloor \frac{2M}{N} \right\rfloor\right) \times \left(\left\lfloor \frac{2M}{N} \right\rfloor + 1\right) + \frac{1 + \frac{M}{2}}{2} \tag{9}$$

4.3 Performance Comparison of Unidirectional and Bidirectional Scanning Algorithms

For the mathematical expectation of the total packet delay, compared with the unidirectional scanning algorithm, the optimal ratio that the bidirectional scanning algorithm can achieve is:

$$\gamma = \frac{E\left(T_{Delay}^{unidirectional}\right) - E\left(T_{Delay}^{bidirectional}\right)}{E\left(T_{Delay}^{unidirectional}\right)} \tag{10}$$

In the 8-sector 4-air node scenario and the 8-sector 8-air node scenario, the estimated optimal ratios of bidirectional scanning algorithm are as follow.

$$\gamma|_{M=8,N=4} = [(3/2 + 9/2) - (5/2 + 5/2)]/(3/2 + 9/2) = 1/6 \approx 16.67\%$$
$$\gamma|_{M=8,N=8} = [(1 + 9/2) - (3/2 + 5/2)]/(1 + 9/2) = 3/11 \approx 27.27\% \tag{11}$$

It can be seen that compared with the unidirectional scanning algorithm, the bidirectional scanning algorithm can further optimize the packet delay. In the scenarios of 8 sectors and 4 air nodes, and 8 sectors and 8 air nodes, the optimal ratio of bidirectional scanning algorithm compared with unidirectional algorithm obtained by computer is 19.27% and 31.82% respectively, which is close to the estimated result.

5 Simulation and Verification

5.1 Simulation Scene Construction

The performance of the proposed medium access control algorithm is tested and verified by using the NS3 simulation platform in the Linux operating system, and the performance of the two kinds of medium access control algorithms in the multi-air nodes scenario is compared.

The network range is equally divided into 8 sectors according to the directional beamwidth. The number of ground nodes are set to 16, 32 and 64 in turn, which are evenly distributed in all the sectors. The data packet generation of each traffic flow obeys the periodic process, and the destination nodes are also evenly distributed in all the sectors. And there are 1, 4 and 8 air nodes in turn. Therefore, there are 9 simulation scenarios in total, and the specific parameters are shown in Table 1.

Table 1. Simulation parameter notation and configuration.

Notation	Parameter meaning	Value
M	Number of sectors	8
N	Number of air nodes	1, 4, 8
Δ	Duration of a time period	15 ms
RD_1	Radius of network coverage	150 km
RD_2	Radius of the circular motion of air nodes	1 km

5.2   Simulation Results

The average packet delay of all simulation scenarios is shown in Fig. 4. When there are 4 air nodes in the network, the theoretical analysis results and simulation results of the packet delay probability distribution of the two algorithms are shown in Fig. 5. When there are 8 air nodes in the network, the theoretical analysis results and simulation results of the packet delay probability distribution of the two algorithms are shown in Fig. 6.

The average packet delay decreases with the increase of the number of air nodes. Compared with the single air node deployment scheme, the multi-air nodes deployment scheme can significantly reduce the average data packet delay. When there are 4 and 8 air nodes, compared with scenario with only one air node, the average packet delay of the bidirectional scanning algorithm is reduced by 85.39% and 89.47%, and the delay of unidirectional scanning algorithm is reduced by 82.39% and 85.21%, respectively.

The bidirectional scanning algorithm can further optimize the packet delay based on the unidirectional scanning algorithm. When there are 4 air nodes, compared with the unidirectional scanning algorithm, the bidirectional scanning algorithm reduces the average packet delay by 23.10%. And when there are 8 air nodes, compared with the unidirectional scanning algorithm, the bidirectional scanning algorithm reduces the average packet delay by 28.81%. The simulation results are consistent with the theoretical optimization ratios of 19.27% and 31.82%. In this paper, the duration of a time frame is used as the delay interval, and the percentage of data packets in each delay interval is counted. It can be seen from Fig. 5 and Fig. 6 that the packet delay distribution obtained by the simulation is consistent with the results obtained by the theoretical analysis.

In terms of throughput, compared with the single-air node scheme, the throughput of the multi-air nodes scheme is significantly increased, while the throughput of the bidirectional scanning algorithm is similar to that of the unidirectional scanning algorithm.

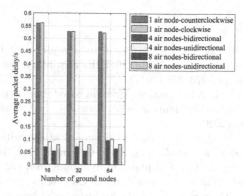

Fig. 4. Average data packet delay.

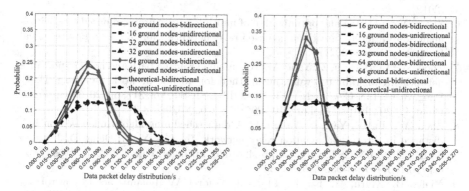

Fig. 5. Probability distribution of data packet delay with 4 air nodes.

Fig. 6. Probability distribution of data packet delay with 8 air nodes.

6   Conclusion

In this paper, a multi-air node-oriented bidirectional scanning medium access control algorithm is proposed for the directional aviation relay network. The distributed relay link selection algorithm enables the ground nodes to dynamically adjust the data packet transmission link according to the number and scanning mode of the air nodes, shortening the total delay of data packets from the source node to the destination node. Simulation results demonstrate that multi-air nodes can significantly reduce packet delay and increase network throughput. And compared with the traditional unidirectional scanning algorithm, the bidirectional scanning algorithm proposed in this paper can further reduce the delay of packets. When the number of air nodes is not less than 4, compared with unidirectional scanning algorithm, the packet delay can be reduced by about 23.10%–28.81%. In terms of average packet delay and delay probability distribution, the simulation results are in good agreement with theoretical analysis.

References

1. Shake, T., Amin, R.: Maximizing interconnectedness and availability in directional airborne range extension networks. In: 2017 IEEE Military Communications Conference, Baltimore, pp. 273–278 (2017)
2. Yan, Z.J., Li, Q., Li, B.: A link distance division based time division multiple access protocol for directional aeronautical relay networks. J. Northwest. Polytechnical Univ. **38**, 147–154 (2020)
3. Zeng, Y., Zhang, R., Lim, T.: Wireless communications with unmanned aerial vehicles: opportunities and challenges. IEEE Commun. Mag. **54**(5), 36–42 (2016)
4. Mehta, D., Ganguly, B.: Effect of platform dynamics on aerial layer network performance. In: IEEE Military Communications Conference, pp. 1704–1709 (2014)
5. Schug, T., Dee, C., Harshman, N., et al.: Air force aerial layer networking transformation initiatives. In: IEEE Military Communications Conference, pp. 1974–1978 (2012)
6. Zhou, W.L.: Design and optimization of multiple access protocol based on environment adaptation in directional aviation relay network. Northwestern Polytechnical University, Xi'an (2021)
7. Zhou, W., Li, B., Yan, Z., Yang, M.: A combined routing path and node importance network invulnerability evaluating method for ad hoc network. In: Deng, D.-J., Pang, A.-C., Lin, C.-C. (eds.) WiCON 2019. LNICST, vol. 317, pp. 20–33. Springer, Cham (2020). https://doi.org/10.1007/978-3-030-52988-8_3
8. Zhou, W., Li, B., Yan, Z., Yang, M.: A data scheduling algorithm based on link distance in directional aviation relay network. In: Lin, Y.-B., Deng, D.-J. (eds.) SGIoT 2020. LNICST, vol. 354, pp. 426–440. Springer, Cham (2021). https://doi.org/10.1007/978-3-030-69514-9_33
9. Xiafei, B., Xinru, M., Ru, D.: Flying LTE for UAV dynamic access control. In: IEEE/CIC International Conference on Communications in China (ICCC), pp. 9–11 (2020)
10. Sohail, M., Leow, C., Won, S.: Non-orthogonal multiple access for unmanned aerial vehicle assisted communication. IEEE Access **6**, 22716–22727 (2018)
11. Jiangbin, L., Yong, Z., Zhang, R.: Cyclical multiple access in UAV-aided communications: a throughput-delay tradeoff. IEEE Wireless Commun. Lett. **5**(6), 600–603 (2016)
12. Bennett, D., Brown, T.: Optimal data scheduling of mobile clients serviced using beamforming antennas. In: IEEE Military Communications Conference, pp. 1–10 (2012)
13. Li, J., Han, Y.: optimal resource allocation for packet delay minimization in multilayer UAV networks. IEEE Commun. Lett. **21**(3), 580–583 (2017)
14. Yang, A., Li, B., Yang, M., Yan, Z.: A bi-directional carrier sense collision avoidance neighbor discovery algorithm in directional wireless ad hoc sensor networks. Sensors **19**(9), 2120 (2019)

Research on Backbone Routing Protocol of Ad Hoc Network Based on SDN

Yiming Yang, Ding Wang, Mao Yang$^{(\boxtimes)}$, Zhongjiang Yan, and Bo Li

School of Electronics and Information, Northwestern Polytechnical University, Xi'an, China
yangmao@nwpu.edu.cn

Abstract. In recent years, with the development of Internet of Things and UAV network, Ad Hoc networks have increased the number of nodes, enhanced node mobility, and become more sensitive in delay. However, the existing Ad Hoc network routing protocols have some disadvantages, such as high signaling overhead, slow response speed and slow convergence speed. In order to improve the efficiency of routing protocols, we propose a backbone routing protocol based on SDN (software defined network). The core idea of the protocol is as follows. Firstly, there is a logical centralized controller to implement the control plane strategy such as backbone node selection algorithm, and the centralized controller can switch between deep control and shallow control flexibly according to the network state. Secondly, the backbone nodes exchange control signaling, and other nodes transmit data through the backbone nodes, which can reduce the signaling cost and ensure the response speed and convergence speed of routes. Simulation results in multiple topologies show that the centralized backbone routing protocol significantly reduces the overhead of establishing routes and improves the throughput.

Keywords: Backbone routing protocol · SDN · High efficiency · Ad hoc network

1 Introduction

Ad Hoc network is a wireless network that contains no infrastructure. In Ad Hoc network, each node has the routing function. Nodes exchange signaling to form the routing table. Because nodes in Ad Hoc networks can move freely and do not depend on infrastructure, Ad Hoc networks are widely used in scenarios with complex communication requirements such as emergency communications, military exercises, UAV communications, disaster relief, and intelligent communications [1].

Ad Hoc networks have the advantages of easy to deploy, unlimited topology, and fast to organize network. However, due to the lack of infrastructure, end-to-end transmission between nodes needs to be established based on routing

D.-J. Deng et al. (Eds.): SGIoT 2022, LNICST 497, pp. 329–341, 2023.
https://doi.org/10.1007/978-3-031-31275-5_30

protocols. Nowadays, routing protocols in Ad Hoc networks can be divided into two categories: proactive routing protocol (table driven routing protocol) and on-demand routing protocol. In recent years, with the development of the needs of the Internet of Things and UAV network, Ad Hoc networks have increased the number of nodes, enhanced node mobility, and become more sensitive to delay. Therefore, how to improve the efficiency of routing protocols has become the focus of academic research.

On-demand routing protocols only look for paths when nodes need to send data. The location-based anonymous routing proposed in literature [2] achieves the anonymity and security of nodes in Ad Hoc networks. The Ad Hoc on-demand distance vector routing proposed in literature [3] avoids the problem of DSDV, makes nodes store the required routes, minimizes broadcast demand, reduces memory demand and unnecessary duplication to save resources. Although the existing on-demand routing protocols have been improved in terms of network security and resource saving, they have not improved in terms of route response speed and convergence speed. This is because the on-demand routing method needs to find the path before sending data each time, and then sends the data packet after finding the path, which greatly increases packet delay. When the path fails to find, the resources and time of the protocol package will be wasted, and the network stability will be greatly reduced.

In the proactive routing protocol, the node broadcasts and forwards protocol packets to form a routing table regardless of whether it needs to send packets. The OLSR model based on security clustering proposed in reference [4] extends the network lifetime by motivating the normal behavior of nodes. The resource-aware OLSR routing mechanism in mobile Ad Hoc networks proposed in literature [5] relies on battery power and available bandwidth to select MPRs, which improves the availability of the network and prolongs the service time of the network. Although the existing proactive routing protocols have good availability, they still have the problem of excessive signaling. This is because whether the node sends packets or not, it will broadcast protocol packets periodically and forward these to form a routing table. A large number of protocol packets will cause congestion in the network, occupy channel resources, affect packet sending and receiving, and bring huge overhead to the node.

According to the survey, the existing studies on these two protocols are formed in a certain perspective, which cannot meet the Ad Hoc network scenario. In order to deal with the scenario of Ad Hoc network with increasing number of nodes and enhanced mobility, and solve the problems of large overhead and slow convergence rate of existing routing protocols, we design a backbone routing protocol based on SDN. The core idea of the protocol is as follows. There is a logical controller in the whole network, which is responsible for the selection of backbone nodes. The controller also uses the Dijkstra algorithm to select bridge nodes which will establish full connectivity between backbone nodes through the bridge nodes. The current network status is judged by collecting network information periodically. The shallow control function is used for networks with rapidly topology changes, and the deep control function is used for networks with slowly topology changes. Only backbone nodes need to forward routing control information, and the controller adjusts the policy based on the network status. In this way, the signaling overhead is effectively reduced, the network service life is prolonged, and the route response speed and convergence speed are improved to ensure the reliability of network.

The structure of this paper is as follows: Sect. 2 describes the backbone routing architecture based on SDN; Sect. 3 introduces the design of the protocol from the control plane and the data plane. Section 4 shows the simulation verification results in different scenarios. Section 5 gives the final conclusion.

2 Backbone Routing Architecture Based on SDN

In the traditional network layer, the control plane is combined with the data plane and deployed on each node in a distributed architecture. This architecture makes it difficult to update the version of the control plane and has few functions. SDN separates the data plane from the control plane. Data planes are deployed in distributed mode, and the control planes of all nodes are centralized. In this way, the network is easy to manage and can be programmed to meet special service requirements. In addition, routes can be allocated according to traffic to realize load balancing.

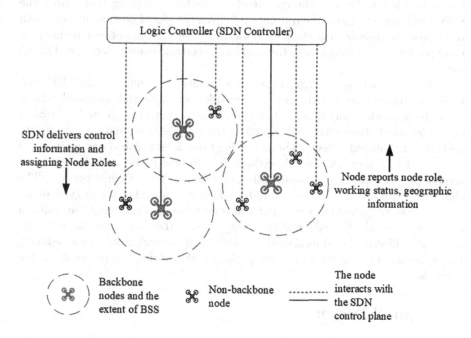

Fig. 1. Backbone routing architecture based on SDN.

Referring to the traditional SDN architecture, we design a backbone routing protocol based on SDN. The centralized control backbone routing architecture consists of two parts: the controller and the nodes in the network. The SDN controller obtains node information, link status, working status and other information reported by the nodes in the network through the interface. Based on the information, the SDN controller makes decisions and sends them to nodes to realize the configuration of network resources and the setting type of nodes. The above figure shows the specific architecture diagram (see Fig. 1).

The SDN controller in the centralized control backbone routing protocol designed in this paper has the function of adjusting the management network policy in real time. By collecting node information in the network regularly, the controller determines the network status and decides whether the shallow control strategy or the deep control strategy should be adopted.

When the topology changes slowly, the SDN controller will determine that the current network is stable and the position of nodes changes very little in a short time. In this case, deep control is adopted. SDN controller will collect the position, power, working status and other information of the nodes in the network, according to the selection algorithm of backbone node, selecting the backbone nodes and its corresponding non-backbone nodes in a BSS. At the same time, according to the topology information of the nodes in the network, the routing table of the backbone nodes is calculated and updated, and the information is delivered to each node in the network through the interface to complete the node role division and the update of the backbone routing table. Since the SDN controller calculates the routing table from the global perspective, the path result may be shorter than the path obtained by the method of exchanging protocol packets, which accelerates the response speed and convergence speed of the route.

When the topology changes rapidly and nodes move quickly, the SDN controller will determine that the current network is unstable and nodes will join or leave the network at any time. In this case, shallow control is adopted. The SDN controller selects backbone nodes based on the collected information to complete node role assignment. The backbone routing table is established and maintained by the Ad Hoc network through exchanging protocol packets. Nodes send and receive protocol packets automatically according to the specified process. The shallow control has more functions and can flexibly respond to topology changes.

In any scenes, the SDN controller will collect the information of the nodes in the network regularly, make real-time responses to the changes in the network, and make different decisions according to different network states, thus reducing the overhead of exchanging protocol packets and ensuring the reliability of the network.

3   Protocol Design

3.1   Control Plane

In this paper, nodes in Ad Hoc network are divided into different BSS (Basic Service Set). Backbone node refers to BSS header node and bridge node in each BSS. Non-backbone node refers to other nodes in the BSS. The most important

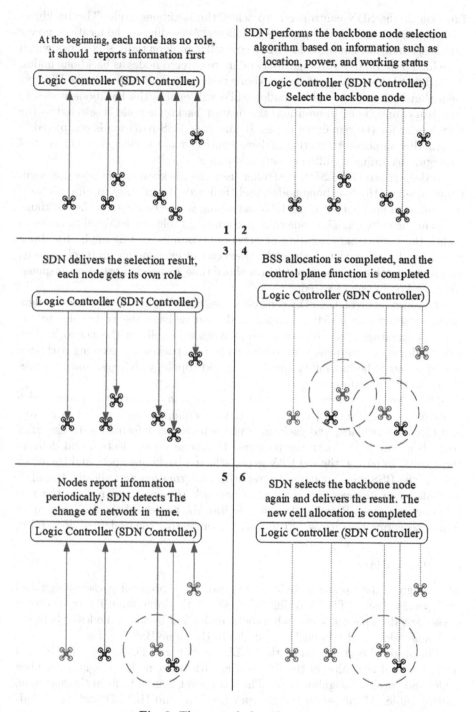

Fig. 2. The control plane functions.

function of the SDN controller is to select the backbone node. The backbone node algorithm used in this paper is as follows. According to the location, power and other information of nodes, SDN controller preferentially sets nodes which have high power, large coverage area and more covered nodes as backbone nodes. According to the coverage of the backbone nodes, the controller uses the Dijkstra algorithm to select the bridge nodes while will enable the backbone nodes to establish connections. In addition, the nearest backbone node is selected as the BSS header for the remaining nodes. In this way, BSS partition is completed.

Another important function of logic controller is to select different control strategies according to different network states.

In deep control, the SDN controller uses the backbone node selection algorithm to select the backbone nodes, and then uses the existing routing protocol to obtain the backbone routing table according to the topology of the backbone nodes in the network. The node roles and routing table are delivered to nodes to realize the reasonable allocation of network resources. In this mode, backbone nodes can be selected to reduce the overhead of exchanging protocol packets, and routing table can be formed in a short time to accelerates route response speed and convergence speed.

In shallow control, the SDN controller uses the backbone node selection algorithm to select the backbone nodes, and then delivers the node roles to the nodes to complete the division of node types and cells in the network. This mode reduces the overhead of exchanging protocol packets by selecting backbone nodes, reduces the instability caused by rapid topology changes, and improves the network throughput.

The following picture shows the function diagram of the control plane, which contains six UAV nodes (see Fig. 2). At the beginning, each node has no role and the color is black, and each node needs to report information to the SDN controller. The SDN controller performs backbone node selection and delivers the results. In part 4, the red UAV is the selected backbone node, and the black UAV is the BSS member node. By reporting information periodically, the SDN controller can discover the changes of network topology and update the role information timely. Part 5 to Part 6 describes the process of the SDN controller from discovering the change of topology to completing the update of node roles.

3.2   Data Plane

The design of data plane is divided into two parts: protocol packet design and data packet design. The following figure shows the interaction flow of protocol packet and data packet between backbone nodes and backbone nodes or between backbone nodes and non-backbone nodes in the same BSS (see Fig. 3).

The protocol packet includes the HELLO packet and TC packet. The HELLO packet is used to maintain the link status with other nodes, one-hop neighbor table, and two-hop neighbor table. The TC packet is used to form the backbone routing table. All nodes on the network need to send HELLO packets periodically. Only backbone nodes need to periodically send TC packets to generate the backbone routing table.

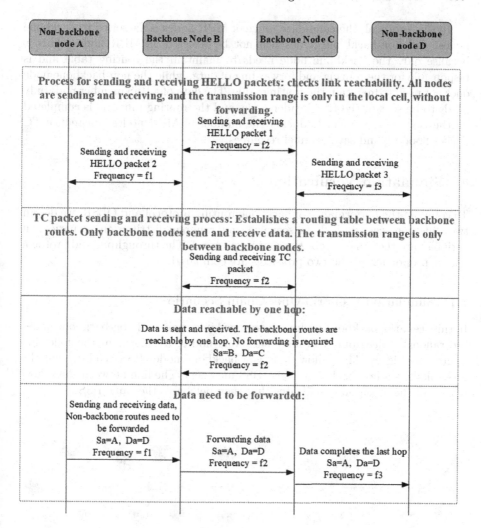

Fig. 3. The data plane functions.

For data packet, according to the different types of source nodes, the data forwarding process can be divided into two categories:

(1) If the source node is a non-backbone node, the data needs to be forwarded to the BSS header node of the same BSS. The BSS header node queries the next backbone node to be forwarded according to the backbone routing table, and the BSS header node of the destination BSS forwards the data to the destination node.

(2) If the source node is a backbone node, the next backbone node to be forwarded is queried according to the backbone routing table, and the BSS header node in the destination BSS is forwarded to the destination node.

In this protocol, the candidate range of MPR nodes is narrowed to backbone nodes, and non-backbone nodes will not be selected as MPR nodes. This is because only the backbone node needs to maintain the routing table and is responsible for the routing and forwarding of data, while the non-backbone node does not need to maintain the routing table. The data of a BSS member node only needs to be sent to the BSS header node, and the routing function is completed by the BSS header node. Reducing the number of MPR nodes can reduce TC packet flooding and save channel resources.

4 Simulation Verification

To compare the performance of backbone routing protocol and OLSR, we design two different scenarios: chain scenario and random distribution scenario. All variables are the same except the routing protocol. The throughput and protocol packet proportion of the two protocols are compared.

4.1 Simulation Scenario One: Chain Scenario

In this scenario, backbone nodes are arranged in a chain and non-backbone nodes are randomly distributed around backbone nodes, as shown in the following figure (see Fig. 4). The yellow node is a backbone node (BSS header), and the green node is a non-backbone node (BSS member). The line between the yellow node and the green node indicates that they belong to the same BSS.

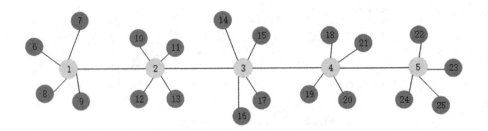

Fig. 4. Chain scenario.

4.2 Simulation Scenario One: Result Analysis

In different protocols, the throughput varies with the traffic rate. As can be seen from the figure (see Fig. 5), when the rate is less than 10 Mbps, the channel is not saturated, so the throughput of both protocols increases with the increase of the traffic rate. When the rate is 10 Mbps, the throughput reaches the maximum. When the rate is greater than 10 Mbps, the channel reaches saturation and the throughput remains stable. At different traffic rate, the throughput of the backbone routing protocol is always higher than that of OLSR (Table 1).

Table 1. Simulation parameters.

Parameter	Value
Traffic Rate	0.01 Mbps to 50 Mbps
Simulator Duration	10 s
Number of nodes	25

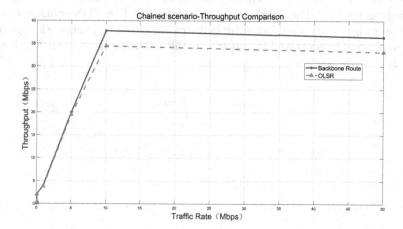

Fig. 5. The throughput of chain scenario.

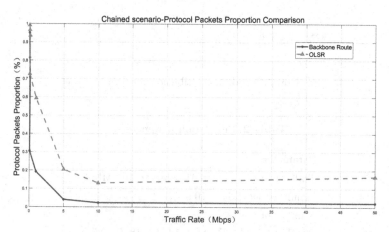

Fig. 6. The protocol packet proportion of chain scenario.

In different protocols, the protocol packet proportion varies with the traffic rate. As can be seen from the figure (see Fig. 6), protocol packet proportion decreases first and then tends to be flat. When the rate is less than 10 Mbps, the number of data packet increases with the rate, so the protocol packet proportion decreases gradually. When the rate is 10 Mbps, the number of packets tends to saturate. When the rate is greater than 10 Mbps, the proportion of protocol packets remains unchanged. At different traffic rate, the protocol packet proportion of the backbone routing protocol is always lower than that of OLSR.

4.3 Simulation Scenario Two: Random Distribution Scenario

In the random distribution scenario, the coordinates of twenty-five nodes are randomly generated. The backbone nodes are selected by SDN controller, and then the bridge nodes are selected by Dijkstra algorithm. The network topology of scenario two is generated, as shown in the following figure (see Fig. 7 and Table 2).

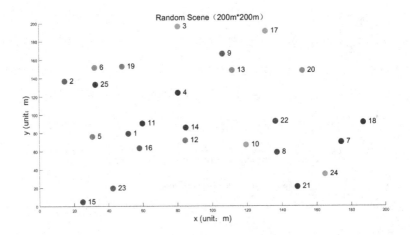

Fig. 7. Random distribution scenario.

Table 2. Simulation parameters.

Parameter	Value
Traffic Rate	0.01 Mbps to 100 Mbps
Simulator Duration	10 s
Number of nodes	25
Backbone Node ID	8, 9, 14, 16, 18, 23, 25
Bridge Node ID	4, 7, 10

4.4   Simulation Scenario Two: Result Analysis

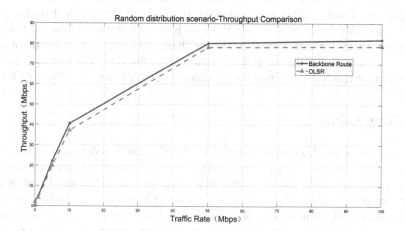

Fig. 8. The throughput of the random distribution scenario.

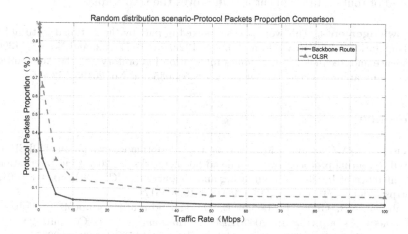

Fig. 9. The protocol packet proportion of the random distribution scenario.

In different protocols, the throughput varies with the traffic rate. As can be seen from the figure (see Fig. 8), when the rate is less than 50 Mbps, the channel is not saturated, so the throughput of both protocols increases with the increase of the traffic rate. When the rate is 50 Mbps, the throughput reaches the maximum. When the rate is greater than 50 Mbps, the channel reaches saturation and the throughput remains stable. At different traffic rate, the throughput of the backbone routing protocol is always higher than that of OLSR.

In different protocols, the protocol packet proportion varies with the traffic rate. As can be seen from the figure (see Fig. 9), protocol packet proportion decreases first and then tends to be flat. When the rate is less than 50 Mbps, the number of data packet increases with the rate, so the protocol packet proportion decreases gradually. When the rate is 50 Mbps, the number of packets tends to saturate. When the rate is greater than 50 Mbps, the proportion of protocol packets remains unchanged. At different traffic rate, the protocol packet proportion of the backbone routing protocol is always lower than that of OLSR.

5   Conclusion

In this paper, a backbone routing protocol based on SDN is designed to solve the problems of excessive signaling overhead, slow response speed and slow convergence speed of existing Ad Hoc network routing protocols. A logical centralized controller performs backbone node selection, switches control policy between deep control and shallow control according to the network status flexibly and timely, reduces signaling overhead, and ensures the response speed and convergence speed of routes. Simulation results in multiple topologies show that the proposed centralized control backbone routing protocol significantly reduces the overhead of route establishment and improves the throughput.

Acknowledgements. This work was supported in part by the National Natural Science Foundations of CHINA (Grant No. 61871322, No. 61771392, and No. 61771390), and Science and Technology on Avionics Integration Laboratory and the Aeronautical Science Foundation of China (Grant No. 20185553035 and No. 201955053002).

References

1. Hashim, A.-A., Farhan, M.M., Alshybani, S.: Performance evaluation of OLSR and AODV routing protocols over mobile ad-hoc networks. In: 2019 First International Conference of Intelligent Computing and Engineering (ICOICE), pp. 1–8 (2019). https://doi.org/10.1109/ICOICE48418.2019.9035171
2. Kulkarni, N.S., Gupta, I., Raman, B.: On demand routing protocols for mobile ad hoc networks: a review. In: 2009 IEEE International Advance Computing Conference, pp. 586–591 (2009). https://doi.org/10.1109/IADCC.2009.4809077
3. Perkins, C.E., Royer, E.M.: Ad-hoc on-demand distance vector routing. In: Proceedings WMCSA 1999. Second IEEE Workshop on Mobile Computing Systems and Applications, pp. 90–100 (1999). https://doi.org/10.1109/MCSA.1999.749281
4. Chriqi, A., Otrok, H., Robert, J.: SC-OLSR: secure clustering-based OLSR model for ad hoc networks. In: 2009 IEEE International Conference on Wireless and Mobile Computing, Networking and Communications, pp. 239–245 (2009). https://doi.org/10.1109/WiMob.2009.48
5. Romanik, J., Kraśniewski, A., Golan, E.: RESA-OLSR: resources-aware OLSR-based routing mechanism for mobile ad-hoc networks. In: 2016 International Conference on Military Communications and Information Systems (ICMCIS), pp. 1–6 (2016). https://doi.org/10.1109/ICMCIS.2016.7496549

6. Rahman, M., Mambo, M., Inomata, A., Okamoto, E.: An anonymous on-demand position-based routing in mobile Ad Hoc networks. In: International Symposium on Applications and the Internet (SAINT 2006), pp. 7, 306 (2006). https://doi.org/10.1109/SAINT.2006.13

7. Kreutz, D., Ramos, F.M., Veríssimo, P.E., Rothenberg, C.E., Azodolmolky, S., Uhlig, S.: Software-defined networking: a comprehensive survey. Proc. IEEE 103(1), 14–76 (2015). https://doi.org/10.1109/JPROC.2014.2371999

8. Gupta, L., Jain, R., Vaszkun, G.: Survey of important issues in UAV communication networks. IEEE Commun. Surv. Tutorials, 18(2), 1123–1152. Secondquarter (2016).https://doi.org/10.1109/COMST.2015.2495297

9. Xia, W., Wen, Y., Foh, C. H., Niyato, D., Xie, H.: A survey on software-defined networking. IEEE Commun. Surv. Tutorials, 17(1), 27–51. Firstquarter (2015). https://doi.org/10.1109/COMST.2014.2330903

10. Sharma, P.K., Chen, M.Y., Park, J.H.: A software defined fog node based distributed blockchain cloud architecture for IoT. IEEE Access 6, 115–124 (2018). https://doi.org/10.1109/ACCESS.2017.2757955

11. Perkins, C.E., Royer, E.M., Das, S.R., Marina, M.K.: Performance comparison of two on-demand routing protocols for ad hoc networks. IEEE Pers. Commun. 8(1), 16–28 (2001). https://doi.org/10.1109/98.904895

12. Zhang, H., Guo, J.: Application of manet routing protocol in vehicular ad hoc network based on NS3. In: 2017 7th IEEE International Conference on Electronics Information and Emergency Communication (ICEIEC), pp. 391–394 (2017). https://doi.org/10.1109/ICEIEC.2017.8076589

13. Hao, J., Duan, G., Zhang, B., Li, C.: An energy-efficient on-demand multicast routing protocol for wireless ad hoc and sensor networks. In: 2013 IEEE Global Communications Conference (GLOBECOM), pp. 4650–4655 (2013). https://doi.org/10.1109/GLOCOMW.2013.6855685

14. Zeng, Y., Zhang, R., Lim, T.J.: Wireless communications with unmanned aerial vehicles: opportunities and challenges. IEEE Commun. Mag. 54(5), 36–42 (2016). https://doi.org/10.1109/MCOM.2016.7470933

15. Shakhatreh, H., et al.: Unmanned aerial vehicles (UAVs): a survey on civil applications and key research challenges. IEEE Access 7, 48572–48634 (2019). https://doi.org/10.1109/ACCESS.2019.2909530

A Coexistence Method of Short-Range Heterogeneous Network Based on Cell Cooperation

Yunlong Wang, Bo Li, Mao Yang$^{(\boxtimes)}$, and Zhongjiang Yan

School of Electronics and Information, Northwestern Polytechnical University,
Xi'an, China
yangmao@nwpu.edu.cn

Abstract. The rapid economic development has promoted the rapid increase of mobile traffic and mobile devices. Short-range wireless networks working in unlicensed frequency bands have attracted widespread attention due to their advantages of openness, freeness and high rate. Therefore, there are many types of short-range wireless networks working in unlicensed frequency bands, such as WLAN, Bluetooth, ZigBee, etc. When the above two or more networks are arranged in the same place, serious interference between the networks will be caused by spectrum overlap. The hybrid MAC network can flexibly configure time slots of Time Division Multiple Access (TDMA) and Carrier Sense Multiple Access with Collision Avoid (CSMA/CA). Therefore, a coexistence method of short-range heterogeneous network based on cell cooperation (CM-HNCC) was proposed to solve the coexistence of hybrid MAC network and Wi-Fi. This algorithm can reduce the delay of high priority traffic and improve the throughput of hybrid MAC network under the premise of ensuring network fairness. Finally, the effectiveness of CM-HNCC is verified by establishing mathematical model and simulation.

Keywords: Short-range heterogeneous network · Unlicensed frequency band · High-priority traffic · Community collaboration

1 Introduction

The rapid development of global economy has promoted the rapid increase of communication traffic, but the spectrum resources are limited [1]. Therefore, WLAN (IEEE802.11be/IEEE802.11ax), Bluetooth, ZigBee and other networks working in ISM (Industrial Scientific Medical) band have been developed rapidly because of their advantages of openness, freeness and high rate [2].

Heterogeneous network refers to the network where multiple access networks and internet service provider (ISP) coexist, and is a common form of wireless network. The emergence of heterogeneous network makes the fusion and coexistence

D.-J. Deng et al. (Eds.): SGIoT 2022, LNICST 497, pp. 342–354, 2023.
https://doi.org/10.1007/978-3-031-31275-5_31

of heterogeneous network become the development trend of future communication. Scholars have done a lot of research on the coexistence of heterogeneous networks. Lin et al. [3] dynamically adjusted the value of the contention window (CW) to obtain the maximum throughput. In order to address the performance degradation of long term evolution (LTE)and wireless fidelity (Wi-Fi) heterogeneous networks in dense scenarios, S. Sagari et al. [4] proposed dynamically selecting access channels by sensing channel state. If the channel to be accessed is found to be idle, then the channel is accessed, otherwise, continue to find other channels. A. Dziedzic et al. [5] used machine learning to determine the number of current Wi-Fi cells, and adjusts the duty ratio of LTE according to the number of Wi-Fi cells. C. Chen et al. [6,8] discussed the coexistence performance of LTE and Wi-Fi under the condition of fixed CW length. Y. Song et al. [8] studied how to obtain the maximum system throughput by obtaining the optimal CW length.

However, there are few studies on the coexistence of hybrid MAC networks with other networks. In this paper, we introduce a hybrid MAC networks, and study its coexistence with Wi-Fi. Both the hybrid MAC network and Wi-Fi work in ISM band. When they work in the same area at the same time, they will interfere with each other. TDMA time slot in hybrid MAC network will be affected by Wi-Fi, which will cause collision and reduce the performance of hybrid MAC network. In CSMA/CA time slot, due to the addition of Wi-Fi, the number of competitive nodes increases, which further increases the collision probability and reduces the performance of hybrid MAC network and Wi-Fi.

A coexistence method of short-range heterogeneous network based on cell cooperation (CM-HNCC) is proposed to solve this problem. The main idea is that predict the high and low priority traffic (represented by LT) of hybrid Mac and the traffic of Wi-Fi, then calculate the TDMA duration according to the traffic. When the hybrid MAC network is in the time division multiple access (TDMA) time slot, Wi-Fi stops sending packets to ensure the transmission quality of hybrid MAC network. CW of LT traffic in the hybrid MAC network is appropriately adjusted, so as to increase the competitiveness of Wi-Fi in CSMA/CA time slot. Finally, the performance of Wi-Fi is guaranteed, the throughput of hybrid MAC high priority traffic (represented by HT) is improved, and the time delay is reduced.

The paper is outlined as follows. In the Sect. 2 we mainly introduce the frame structure of hybrid MAC network. In Sect. 3 CM-HNCC is introduced. In Sect. 4 the theoretical throughput calculation method is introduced. In Sect. 5 validates the effectiveness of CM-HNCC by simulation results. Concluding remarks are given in Sect. 6.

2   Architecture of Hybrid MAC Network

The time slot distribution of hybrid MAC network is shown in Fig. 1. T-s time slot uses TDMA communication technology. C-s time slot uses distributed coordination function (DCF) mechanism. Hybrid MAC network will send beacon frame at B time slot.

Fig. 1. Time slot distribution of hybrid MAC network.

In C-s time slot, DCF mechanism is adopted [9]. The DCF mechanism is a basic access method for nodes to access wireless channels. It combines CSMA/CA technology and acknowledge character (ACK) technology, and uses binary exponential backoff to avoid conflicts. The DCF mechanism is shown in Fig. 2. If the node senses that the channel is the state of ideal within a DIFS (distributed inter frame spacing) duration, it will select a random value in the initial contention window $(0, CW - 1)$ as the initial value of backoff counter. When the backoff counter decreases to 0, the data will be transmitted (as shown in Fig. 2(a)). Collision occurs if the backoff counter of two or more nodes decrease to 0 at the same time, that will double the contention window (as shown in Fig. 2(b)). Select a random value in the doubled CW to repeat the above process. When the CW reaches the maximum contention window ($CW_{\max}$), the size of the CW will remain unchange if a collision occurs again. The HT traffic and the LT traffic of the hybrid MAC network compete for the channel in C-s time slot. The initial CW of HT traffic is smaller than the initial CW of LT traffic. The $CW_{\max}$ of HT traffic is smaller than that of LT traffic. Therefore, the probability that the HT traffic successfully sends data in the C-s time slot is greater than that of LT traffic.

In T-s time slots, each node transmits data within the time period allocated by the center control node (CCN). There will be no packet collision and loss in T-s time slots if the channel is ideal. Priority delivery of HT traffic is ensured in T-s time slot. LT traffic can also be sent in T-s time slots when there is only LT traffic.

3   CM-HNCC

The CM-HNCC algorithm consists of three steps, as shown in Fig. 3: Step 1 - forecast the traffic of hybrid MAC network and Wi-Fi. Calculate the length of T-s time slot using Algorithm 1. Step 2 - update the CW of LT traffic using Algorithm 2. Step 3 - Wi-Fi keep silence in T-s time slot.

The hybrid MAC network has T-s and C-s time slots. Priority delivery of HT traffic is ensured in T-s time slot. LT traffic can also be sent in T-s time slots when there is only LT traffic. In C-s time slot, HT and LT traffic access the channel using DCF mechanism. CM-HNCC algorithm requires Wi-Fi to keep silence when hybrid MAC network is in T-s time slot to ensure the quality of service (QoS) of HT traffic. The length of T-s time slot is very important. The longer the T-s time slot length, the less friendly it is to Wi-Fi. If T-s time slot length is too short, QoS of HT traffic cannot be guaranteed. This paper proposes

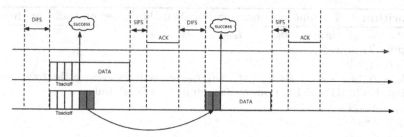

(a) Successful transmission.

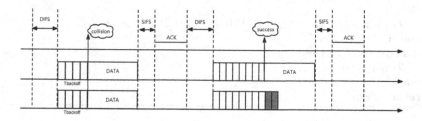

(b) The collision.

Fig. 2. DCF mechanism.

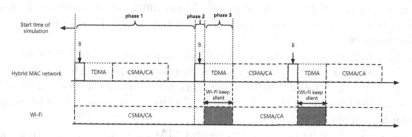

Fig. 3. CM-HNCC.

Algorithm 1 to solve this problem. The core idea of this algorithm is to confirm the length of T-s time slot according to the proportion of various traffic rate.

B_{vo} indicates the traffic rate of HT. B_{BE} indicates the traffic rate of LT. B_{be} indicates the rate of Wi-Fi. T_{min} indicates minimum value of T-s time slot duration. T_1 indicates the time duration needed for a successful transmission in hybrid MAC network. T_2 indicates the time duration needed for a successful transmission in Wi-Fi. T_{TDMA} indicates the length of T-s time slot.

Algorithm 1. T-s time slot confirmation algorithm based on traffic prediction.

Input: B_{vo} B_{BE} B_{be} T_{min} T_1 T_2

Output: T_{TDMA}.

1: $T_{TDMA} = 0$

2: $t_{vo} = 0$ $t_{BE} = 0$ $t_{be} = 0$ t_{vo} t_{BE} t_{be} respectively indicate the transmission duration of HT and LT, transmission duration of Wi-Fi traffic.

3: $t_{vo} = S_{vo}/T_1$

4: $t_{BE} = S_{BE}/T_1$

5: $t_{be} = S_{be}/T_2$

6: **if** $t_{vo} + t_{BE} + t_{be} < 1$ **then**

7:      $T_{TDMA} = t_{vo} \cdot (t_{vo} + t_{BE})/(t_{vo} + t_{BE} + t_{be})$

8: **else**

9:      $T_{TDMA} = t_{vo}/(t_{vo} + t_{BE} + t_{be}) \cdot (t_{vo} + t_{BE})/(t_{vo} + t_{BE} + t_{be})$

10: **end if**

11: **if** $T_{TDMA} < T_{min}$ **then**

12:      $T_{TDMA} = \min(T_{min}, t_{vo})$

13: **end if**

14: **return** T_{TDMA}

CM-HNCC algorithm requires Wi-Fi to keep silence when hybrid MAC network is in T-s time slot. The QoS of HT can be guaranteed by that way, but this method reduces the ability of Wi-Fi to compete for channel resources. To solve this problem, Algorithm 2 was proposed. Algorithm 2 can dynamically increase the CW of LT to increase the ability of Wi-Fi to compete for channel resources in C-s time slot.

CW_{old} indicates the initial value of contention window of LT business in hybrid MAC network . d indicates the adjustment step of contention window. CW_{new} indicates the initial value of contention window of LT after update. Pu represents the theoretical throughput of Wi-Fi after increasing CW of LT traffic. Pu can be calculated by formula 16.

Finally, Wi-Fi keep silence when hybrid MAC network is in T-s time slot. The hybrid MAC network first broadcasts beacon frame, which contains beacon interval, T-s time slot duration, T-s time slot duration and other information. After the STAs of hybrid MAC network receive the beacon frame, they set them own T-s time slot period and C-s time slot period according to the information from beacon frame.

Algorithm 2. competitive window adjustment algorithm.

Input: T_{TDMA} CW_{old} d

Output: CW_{new}

1: $CW_{new} = 0$

2: P_o represents the theoretical throughput of Wi-Fi at $T_{TDMA} = 0$

3: **while** $P_u \cdot (1 - T_{TDMA}) < P_o$ **do**

4:      $CW_{old} = CW_{old} + d$

5: **end while**

6: $CW_{new} = CW_{old}$

7: **return** CW_{new}

Nodes of Wi-Fi can also receive beacon frame sent by hybrid MAC network. AP of Wi-Fi puts T-s time slot duration into its own beacon frame (See Fig. 4). The beacon frame contains a quiet element field, and Wi-Fi silence can be realized through network allocation vector (NAV). The structure of quiet element field is shown in Fig. 5. Quiet element field contain 8 bytes in total. Quiet Count (QC) means that Quiet Period (QP) will start after the time of $TBTT \cdot QC$. QP is the silent period. Quiet Duration is the duration of silence. Quiet Offset (QO) is the time offset. In this paper. Quiet Duration is the length of T-s time slot of hybrid MAC network, QC is 0, QP is 1, QO is 0.

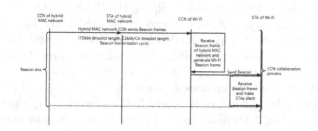

Fig. 4. Beacon frames interaction.

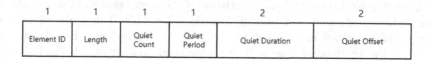

Fig. 5. Quiet element structure.

The silence time and duration of Wi-Fi are shown in Fig. 6. When the nodes of Wi-Fi receive the beacon frame sent by CNN, they obtain the corresponding silence time and duration from the beacon. Nodes of Wi-Fi keep silent for the corresponding period of time without sending any packets. After the end of silence, nodes of Wi-Fi normally compete for the channel to send packets.

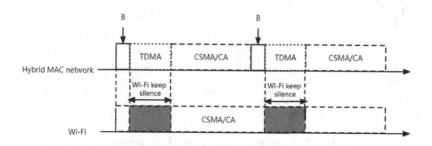

Fig. 6. Wi-Fi keep silence in TDMA time slot.

4   Analysis of Theoretical Throughput

G. Bianchi et al. [10] use a very simple method to analyze the saturated throughput of IEEE802.11 working in DCF mechanism. Ahmed N et al. [11] analyze the unsaturated throughput of IEEE802.11 with single traffic. In the case of hidden terminals, Fu-Yi Hung et al. [12] analyze the saturated and unsaturated throughput of Wi-Fi with single traffic. However, there is little research on the saturated throughput of heterogeneous network. Therefore, this paper proposes an analysis method to analyse the theoretical throughput of heterogeneous network, in the assumption of ideal channel conditions, no hidden terminal and finite number of terminals. This method can accurately obtain the throughput.

Theoretical analysis is divided into two parts. Firstly, the Markov model is used to study the backoff stage of a Wi-Fi node and a hybrid MAC network node, and further obtain the probability of nodes in each state. Then we analyze the behavior of each node and calculate the theoretical throughput.

Suppose that the maximum backoff stages of Wi-Fi is m_1 and the $CW_{\min}$ is w_1. The maximum backoff stages of hybrid MAC network is m_2 and the $CW_{\min}$ is w_2. As shown in Fig. 7, there are $(m_1 + 1) \cdot (m_2 + 1)$ states of the whole Markov chain. Each state is represented by $p(i,j)$. i indicates that the node of Wi-Fi has collided i times and j indicates that the node of hybrid MAC network has collided j times.

According to the knowledge of statistics, if the contention window is $(0, W)$, then the average number of backoff value is $(W + 1)/2$. The probability of a node sending a packet in a backoff slot is $2/(W + 1)$. Therefore, when the status is $p(i,j)$, the probability that a Wi-Fi node sends packet in a backoff slot is

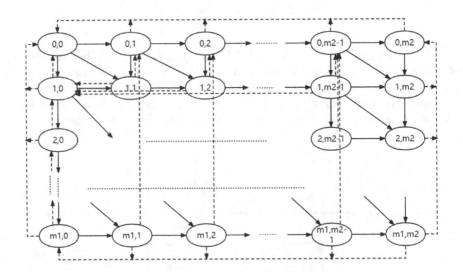

Fig. 7. Backoff stages markov chain model.

$P_{bi} = 2/(2^i \cdot (w_1 + 1))$. The probability that a hybrid MAC network node sends a packet in a backoff slot is $P_{uj} = 2/(2^j \cdot (w_2 + 1))$.

P indicates the average probability of each node sending packets in a backoff slot. n_1 indicates the number of nodes in hybrid MAC network. n_2 indicates the number of nodes in Wi-Fi network. $n = n_1 + n_2$ indicates the total number of nodes of heterogeneous network. $P_{ij-ideal}$ indicates the probability that the backoff slot is idle in state $p(i, j)$.

$$P_{ij-ideal} = (1 - P_{bi}) \cdot (1 - P_{uj}) \cdot (1 - P)^{n-2}. \tag{1}$$

P_{ij-sb} indicates the probability that a node of Wi-Fi successfully sends packets.

$$P_{ij-sb} = P_{bi} \cdot (1 - P_{uj}) \cdot (1 - P)^{n-2}. \tag{2}$$

P_{ij-su} indicates the probability that a node of hybrid MAC network node successfully sends packets.

$$P_{ij-su} = (1 - P_{bi}) \cdot P_{uj} \cdot (1 - P)^{n-2}. \tag{3}$$

P_{ij-cbu} indicates the collision probability between a node of Wi-Fi and a node of hybrid MAC network.

$$P_{ij-cbu} = P_{bi} \cdot P_{uj} \cdot (1 - P)^{n-2}. \tag{4}$$

P_{ij-sB} indicates the probability that the background traffic sends package successfully.

$$P_{ij-sB} = (1 - P_{bi}) \cdot (1 - P_{uj}) \cdot (1 - P)^{n-3} \cdot P. \tag{5}$$

P_{ij-cbB} indicates the collision probability between a Wi-Fi node and the background traffic flow.

$$P_{ij-cbB} = P_{bi} \cdot (1 - P_{uj}) \cdot \left[1 - (1 - P)^{n-2}\right]. \tag{6}$$

P_{ij-cuB} indicates the collision probability between a node of hybrid MAC network and the background traffic flow.

$$P_{ij-cuB} = (1 - P_{bi}) \cdot P_{uj} \cdot \left[1 - (1 - P)^{n-2}\right]. \tag{7}$$

$P_{ij-cbuB}$ indicates the collision probability between a node of hybrid MAC network , a node of Wi-Fi and the background traffic flow.

$$P_{ij-cbuB} = P_{bi} \cdot P_{uj} \cdot \left[1 - (1 - P)^{n-2}\right]. \tag{8}$$

When the markov chain reaches the steady state, the inflow probability of each state is equal to the outflow probability. According to this theorem, the steady-state probability P_{ij} of each state can be calculated by numerical method.

The throughput of system can be calculated by Eq. 9. T_{bs} indicates the successful transmission duration of Wi-Fi. T_{bc} indicates the collision duration of

Wi-Fi. T_{us} indicates the average successful transmission duration of hybrid MAC network. T_{uc} indicates the collision duration of hybrid MAC network. The successful transmission duration and collision duration of Wi-Fi and hybrid MAC network can be calculated by Eq. 10.

$$S = \frac{L_s(\text{payloadinformationtransmittedinaslottime})}{L_{sum}(\text{engthofaslottime})} \tag{9}$$

$$\left(\begin{array}{l} T_s = H + T_{payload} + SIFS + \delta + ACK + DIFS \\ T_c = H + T_{payload} + DIFS + \delta \end{array} \right. \tag{10}$$

where $H = MAC_{hdr} + PHY_{hdr}$ represents the transmission duration of package header. δ represents propagation delay. SIFS (short inter frame space) refers to short frame interval. DIFS (DCF inter frame space) indicates DCF frame interval. ACK indicates the transmission duration of ACK.

In state $p(i, j)$, the duration of idle time , duration of successful transmission time and duration of collision time can be calculated by Eq. (11–13).

$$T_{ij-ideal} = P_{ij-ideal} \cdot \sigma \cdot P_{ij} \tag{11}$$

$$T_{ij-s} = P_{ij-sb} \cdot T_{bs} + P_{ij-su} \cdot T_{us} \cdot P_{ij} + P_{ij-sB} \cdot \left[\frac{P_{ij-sb} \cdot T_{bs} \cdot n_1 + P_{ij-su} \cdot T_{us} \cdot n_2}{P_{ij-sb} \cdot n_1 + P_{ij-su} \cdot n_2} \right] \cdot P_{ij} \tag{12}$$

$$
\begin{aligned}
T_{ij-c} = {} & P_{ij-cbu} \cdot \max(i+1, j+1) \cdot T_{bc} + P_{ij-cbB} \cdot (i+1) \cdot T_{bc} \cdot P_{ij} \\
& + P_{ij-cuB} \cdot (j+1) \cdot T_{uc} \cdot P_{ij} \\
& + P_{ij-cbuB} \cdot \max(i+1, j+1) \cdot \max(T_{bc}, T_{uc}) \cdot P_{ij}
\end{aligned} \tag{13}
$$

where σ represents the length of a backoff slot. $T_{ij-ideal}$ indicates the idle time duration under the state of $p(i, j)$. T_{ij-s} indicates the successful transmission duration under the state of $p(i, j)$. T_{ij-c} indicates the collision duration under the state of $p(i, j)$.

In state $p(i, j)$, T_{ij-bs} indicates the successful transmission duration of Wi-Fi. T_{ij-us} indicates the successful transmission duration of hybrid MAC network.

$$T_{ij-bs} = P_{ij-su} \cdot T_{us} \cdot P_{ij} + P_{ij} \cdot P_{ij-sB} \cdot \left[\frac{P_{ij-su} \cdot T_{us} \cdot n_2}{P_{ij-sb} \cdot n_1 + P_{ij-su} \cdot n_2} \right] \tag{14}$$

$$T_{ij-us} = P_{ij-sb} \cdot T_{bs} \cdot P_{ij} + P_{ij} \cdot P_{ij-sB} \cdot \left[\frac{P_{ij-sb} \cdot T_{bs} \cdot n_1}{P_{ij-sb} \cdot n_1 + P_{ij-su} \cdot n_2} \right] \tag{15}$$

The theoretical throughput of Wi-Fi (S_{be}) can be calculated by Eq. 16. The theoretical throughput of hybrid MAC network (S_u) can be calculated by Eq. 17.

$$S_{be} = \frac{\sum\limits_{0}^{m_1}\sum\limits_{0}^{m_2} T_{ij-bs}}{\sum\limits_{0}^{m_1}\sum\limits_{0}^{m_2} T_{ij-ideal} + \sum\limits_{0}^{m_1}\sum\limits_{0}^{m_2} T_{ij-s} + \sum\limits_{0}^{m_1}\sum\limits_{0}^{m_2} T_{ij-c}} \tag{16}$$

$$S_{u} = \frac{\sum\limits_{0}^{m_1}\sum\limits_{0}^{m_2} T_{ij-us}}{\sum\limits_{0}^{m_1}\sum\limits_{0}^{m_2} T_{ij-ideal} + \sum\limits_{0}^{m_1}\sum\limits_{0}^{m_2} T_{ij-s} + \sum\limits_{0}^{m_1}\sum\limits_{0}^{m_2} T_{ij-c}} \tag{17}$$

Then the total throughput of Wi-Fi and hybrid MAC networks can be calculated by Eq. 18.

$$S_{sum} = \frac{\sum\limits_{0}^{m_1}\sum\limits_{0}^{m_2} T_{ij-s}}{\sum\limits_{0}^{m_1}\sum\limits_{0}^{m_2} T_{ij-ideal} + \sum\limits_{0}^{m_1}\sum\limits_{0}^{m_2} T_{ij-s} + \sum\limits_{0}^{m_1}\sum\limits_{0}^{m_2} T_{ij-c}} \tag{18}$$

5   Performance Evaluation

The simulation platform used is integrated System & Link Level Simulation Platform [13]. This simulation platform can simulate the short-range wireless network at system level and link level.

When $n_1 = 5$, $m_1 = 4$, $n_2 = 5$, $m_2 = 4$, the steady-state probability of each state in markove chain is shown in Table 2.

Figure 8 shows the variation of throughput of Wi-Fi, hybrid MAC network, and heterogeneous network with CW_{min} of hybrid MAC network. The CW_{min} of Wi-Fi is 31, and the number of STAs in both the hybrid MAC and Wi-Fi is 5. As can be seen from the Fig. 8, the theoretical throughput and simulation throughput of Wi-Fi are basically equal. The theoretical throughput of hybrid MAC network is approximately equal to the simulation throughput. The total simulation throughput is approximately equal to the theoretical throughput. The results show that the theoretical model is correct (Table 1).

The number of nodes in both Wi-Fi and hybrid MAC networks is 5. The CW_{min} of HT traffic is 7. Set the CW_{max} of HT traffic to 31. The CW_{min} of LT traffic is 31. The CW_{max} of LT traffic is 511. The C-s time slot is 20000 µs. The T-s time slot changes dynamically. The CW_{min} of Wi-Fi is 31 and the CW_{max} is 511. The change of the throughput of Wi-Fi and the total throughput of hybrid MAC with the HT traffic rate is shown in Fig. 9(a). The variation of HT traffic time delay with HT traffic rate is shown in Fig. 9(b).

As can be seen from Fig. 9(a), the throughput of Wi-Fi is basically unchanged after using CM-HNCC, which shows that this method can ensures the fairness between networks. The throughput of hybrid MAC is improved after using CM-HNCC. As can be seen from Fig. 9(b), CM-HNCC can significantly reduce the time delay of HT and ensure the real-time performance of HT.

Table 1. System parameters and additional parameters used in simulation.

Parameter names	Wi-Fi	hybrid MAC network
Propagation delay σ	1 μs	1 μs
Packet header H	8 μs	10 μs
Packet transmission duration	148 μs	179 μs
SIFS	16 μs	16 μs
DIFS	43 μs	43 μs
ACK transmission duration	32 μs	32 μs
Slot time	9 μs	9 μs

Table 2. Steady-state probability of markov chain.

$P(i,j)$	$j=0$	$j=1$	$j=2$	$j=3$	$j=4$
$i=0$	0.2747	0.1384	0.0741	0.0398	0.0030
$i=1$	0.1284	0.0724	0.0369	0.0190	0.0014
$i=2$	0.0634	0.0350	0.0181	0.0091	0.0009
$i=3$	0.0322	0.0165	0.0085	0.0043	0.0006

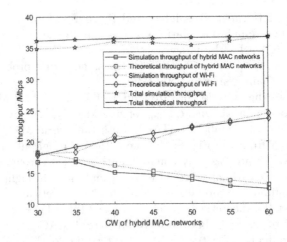

Fig. 8. Simulation and theoretical throughput vary with CW of hybrid MAC network.

The abscissa of Fig. 10(a) and Fig. 10(b) is the HT rate of the hybrid MAC network. The traffic rate of Wi-Fi, HT and LT are equal. Before and after using CM-HNCC algorithm, the throughput of Wi-Fi has no obvious change, which shows that CM-HNCC algorithm can ensure the fairness between networks. When the traffic rate is low, the total throughput of hybrid MAC network does not change significantly. However, with the increasing of traffic rate, the CM-

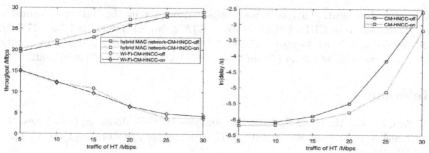

(a) Throughput changing with HT traffic rate. (b) HT delay changing with HT traffic rate.

Fig. 9. Throughput and HT time delay changing with HT traffic rate.

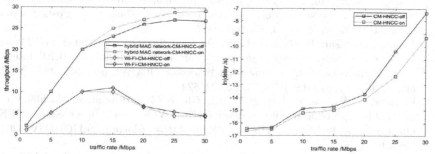

(a) Throughput changing with traffic rate. (b) HT time delay changing with traffic rate.

Fig. 10. Throughput and HT delay changing with traffic rate.

HNCC algorithm can significantly increase the total throughput of the hybrid MAC network. It can be seen from Fig. 10(b) that the CM-HNCC algorithm can significantly reduce the time delay of HT traffic.

6   Conclusion

In heterogeneous networks consisting of Wi-Fi and hybrid MAC network, CM-HNCC was proposed to solve the problem of coexistence of Wi-Fi networks and hybrid MAC network. CM-HNCC can ensure fairness between networks and improve network performance. The Wi-Fi network can be IEEE802.11be or IEEE802.11ax.

When the traffic rate of the heterogeneous network consisting of Wi-Fi and hybrid MAC network is low, the throughput of the hybrid MAC network is not significantly improved by using CM-HNCC algorithm, and the time delay of HT is not significantly decreased. With the increase of traffic rate, the throughput of hybrid MAC network is improved, while the time delay of HT is significantly reduced.

Acknowledgement. This work was supported in part by the National Natural Science Foundations of CHINA (Grant No. 61871322, No. 61771390, and No. 61771392), and Science and Technology on Avionics Integration Laboratory and the Aeronautical Science Foundation of China (Grant No. 20185553035, and No. 201955053002).

References

1. Suh, D., Ko, H., Pack, S.: Efficiency analysis of WiFi offloading techniques. IEEE Trans. Veh. Technol. **65**(5), 3813–3817 (2016). https://doi.org/10.1109/TVT.2015. 2437325
2. Paul, L.C., Ahmed Ankan, S.S., Lee, W.-S.: A slotted patch array antenna with a partial ground plane for WiFi/Bluetooth/Zigbee applications. In: 2021 IEEE Indian Conference on Antennas and Propagation (InCAP), pp. 560–563 (2021). https://doi.org/10.1109/InCAP52216.2021.9726451
3. Lin, S., Wen, X., Hu, Z., Lu, Z.: Improving throughput through dynamically tuning contention window size in dense wireless network. J. China Univ. Posts Telecommun. **24**(4), 27–33 (2017). ISSN 1005-8885
4. Sagari, S., Seskar, I., Raychaudhuri, D.: Modeling the coexistence of LTE and WiFi heterogeneous networks in dense deployment scenarios. In: IEEE International Conference on Communication Workshop (ICCW), pp. 2301–2306 (2015). https://doi.org/10.1109/ICCW.2015.7247524
5. Dziedzic, A., Sathya, V., Rochman, M.I., Ghosh, M., Krishnan, S.: Machine learning enabled spectrum sharing in dense LTE-U/Wi-Fi coexistence scenarios. IEEE Open J. Veh. Technol. **1**, 173–189 (2020). https://doi.org/10.1109/OJVT.2020. 2981519
6. Chen, C., Ratasuk, R., Ghosh, A.: Downlink performance analysis of LTE and WiFi coexistence in unlicensed bands with a simple listen-before-talk scheme. In: 2015 IEEE 81st Vehicular Technology Conference (VTC Spring), pp. 1–5 (2015). https://doi.org/10.1109/VTCSpring.2015.7145789
7. Jeon, J., Niu, H., Li, Q.C., Papathanassiou, A., Wu, G.: LTE in the unlicensed spectrum: evaluating coexistence mechanisms. In: 2014 IEEE Globecom Workshops (GC Wkshps), pp. 740–745 (2014). https://doi.org/10.1109/GLOCOMW. 2014.7063521
8. Song, Y., Sung, K.W., Han, Y.: Coexistence of Wi-Fi and cellular With listen-before-talk in unlicensed spectrum. IEEE Commun. Lett. **20**(1), 161–164 (2016). https://doi.org/10.1109/LCOMM.2015.2504509
9. Cheng, Y., Yang, D., Zhou, H., Wang, H.: Adopting IEEE 802.11 MAC for industrial delay-sensitive wireless control and monitoring applications: a survey. Comput. Netw. **157**, 41–67 (2019). ISSN 1389-1286
10. Bianchi, G.: Performance analysis of the IEEE 802.11 distributed coordination function. IEEE J. Sel. Areas Commun. **18**(3), 535–547 (2000). https://doi.org/10. 1109/49.840210
11. Zaki, A.N., El-Hadidi, M.T.: Performance evaluation of IEEE 802.11-based wireless LANs under finite-load conditions. AEU - Int. J. Electron. Commun. **62**(5), 327–337 (2008). ISSN 1434-8411
12. Hung, F.-Y., Marsic, I.: Performance analysis of the IEEE 802.11 DCF in the presence of the hidden stations. Comput. Netw. **54**(15), 2674–2687 (2010). ISSN 1389-1286
13. Survey and performance evaluation of the upcoming next generation WLANs standard-IEEE 802.11 ax. Mobile . Netw. Appl. **24**(5), 1461–1474 (2019)

Using Push Technology to Discover Factors Influencing Consumers' Intention to Purchase Greenwashed Products

Chia-Ling Ho[1]([envelope]), James Robert Forster[2], and Ling-Yun Yen[3]

[1] General Education Center, National Taipei University of Nursing and Health Sciences, Taipei, Taiwan, Republic of China
chialingho@ntunhs.edu.tw
[2] Tamkang University, New Taipei, Taiwan, Republic of China
[3] Department of Information Management, National Taipei University of Nursing and Health Sciences, Taipei, Taiwan, Republic of China

Abstract. Companies are adopting green marketing strategies as consumers are looking to purchase green products due to growing concerns for the environment. However, to gain market share, some firms opt to greenwash in advertisements. This is when claims regarding green performance outweigh the substantive truth. Underpinned by the attitude-behaviour-context theory, this study examines the relationship between greenwashing perceptions, green purchasing intentions and green advertising skepticism. In order to effectively collect the questionnaires from users, this study uses push technology as the medium for sending the questionnaires which yielded 247 respondents across Asia, Europe, and North America. The results show that green-washing perceptions significantly negatively affect green purchasing intentions and positively affect green advertising skepticism. Also, green advertising skepticism significantly negatively affect green purchasing intentions. These findings add theoretical value to the underexplored relationship between greenwashing perceptions and green consumer purchasing behaviours. It also provides substantive globalized evidence for companies showing that greenwashing in advertising has detrimental effects on product sales.

Keywords: Green marketing · Greenwashing perceptions · Green purchase intentions · Green advertising skepticism · Push technology

1 Introduction and Literature Review

Over the past 30 to 40 years there has been a growing concern towards the environment. Initially, this consideration came from developed western countries yet more recently the same thought process is proclaimed in developing nations due to the increased environmental damage caused by rapid industrialization. Governments and national bodies are imposing stricter laws to ensure sustainability of the planet. Being environmentally

D.-J. Deng et al. (Eds.): SGIoT 2022, LNICST 497, pp. 355–367, 2023.
https://doi.org/10.1007/978-3-031-31275-5_32

friendly truly has become a global issue. There is emphatic growing evidence in multiple sectors that showcase this change: government, energy, tourism, product packaging, clothing and slow fashion, organic food, architecture and green building design to name just a few [1]. Consumer's also care about the environment with environmental consideration and sustainability contribution along with personal and health benefits a key indication of their keenness to purchase green products [2, 3]. Indeed, early research shows consumers want to purchase environmentally friendly products [4]. As such, some companies have adapted towards green marketing to meet the changing needs of consumers by producing green products instead of traditional or conventional ones which may be more harmful to the environment [5]. Green products have been defined as having less environmental impact compared to traditional products in that they have the ability to be recycled or conserved and are environmentally-friendly as they do not harm the environment or deplore the planet of its natural resources [6].

1.1 Greenwashing

In light of this information some companies have seen the opportunity to implement green business strategies as a model revolved around talking instead of acting [7]. The overcommunication of environmental performance can be construed as greenwashing [8]. Indeed, if a consumer believes or suspects that an organization is promising more environmental benefits than they actually deliver, this application of green marketing can instead be regarded as greenwashing [9]. As the purpose of this study has a particular focus on products, greenwash is defined as when a company misleads a consumer regarding its environmental practices or environmental benefits of a service or product [10]. Precisely, if consumers believe that a company is fulfilling its social responsibility by engaging in environmental activities a consumer would be willing to purchase products from this company even if the price is higher than a traditional product [11]. As such, another definition and use-case for the application of greenwashing is that it can be strategically used to only reveal positive information about environmental performance and omit the negative information in an effort to build up a positive corporate image [12]. Ultimately, not all companies have the correct capabilities to partake in genuine green marketing strategies which allows firms to differentiate their products and seize new green markets via the increased green product demand and green purchasing intentions [13, 14] of consumers who are environmentally concerned [4, 5].

1.2 Green Purchasing Intentions

One definition of green purchasing intentions is the likelihood a consumer will buy a product based upon their environmental views towards that product or service or make purchases towards companies with a perceived reputation of engaging in environmentally friendly behaviours [15, 16]. Indeed, it has been suggested the consumers buy these products as a means to protect, or at least, not destroy the environment [17]. This is an important issue for research as there exists a research gap between the association of greenwashed products on green purchasing intentions; in particular, on the extent to which consumers are willing to buy these services or products [16, 18]. Indeed, it has been suggested the consumers buy these products as a means to protect, or at least, not destroy the environment [17].This is an important issue for research as there exists a research gap between the association of greenwashed products on green purchasing intentions; in particular, on the extent to which consumers are willing to buy these services or products [16, 18].

1.3 Green Advertising Skepticism

Due to the evidence showcasing the large number of corporations engaging in green-washing and their reasons for doing so, it is only natural that there has been a growing consumer skepticism towards companies. Skepticism in its most general form is the inclination or tendency of a person to doubt or distrust others [19]. This concept has been researched in the fields of philosophy, politics, psychology and sociology [20, 21]. Whereas business settings research have generally focused on skepticism in general advertising [22], corporate social responsibility [23], cause-related marketing [24] and green advertising [25].

Indeed, as greenwash continues to grow alongside the growth in demand for green products, consumers are paying more attention to it [14]. Studies conducted by GFK (2013) and Eurobarometer (2009) found that 39% and 48% of consumers did not trust the environmental claims of products. A big factor of this growing skepticism has come from the consumer desire to ensure they do not feel an opportune advantage has been taken of them and that the products they purchase are genuinely contributing to the wellbeing of the environment [26, 27].

1.4 Reasons for Study

This study looks at consumers on the global level with a primary focus on North American, European, and Asian markets. As such, this paper can offer generalized results on global green purchasing behaviours and understandings of perceived ability to identify greenwashed adverts. Overall, the findings of this study are expected to contribute to green marketing as a whole, particularly in the backpack product industry, aiding companies and consumers alike in understanding causes and consequences of green purchasing intentions in greenwashed situations.

2 Hypothesis Formulation and Research Framework

2.1 Theoretical Support

The research framework is illustrated in Fig. 1. This paper chose to underpin its theoretical explanations of behaviour using the attitude-behaviour-context (ABC) theory [28]. The theory operates by taking a means-end approach effect where a person behaves according to the gains they expect from that behaviour [29]. The framework has been useful in explaining how attitudes result in certain behaviors. In particular, past studies have shown the relationships between greenwashing perceptions or green skepticism and green purchasing intentions [3, 30]. Attitude is at the center of attempts to predict behaviour and attempt to explain it [31]and is understood as the evaluative rating of

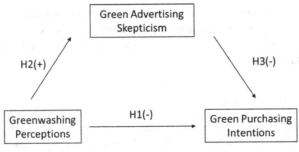

Fig. 1. Research model

an object, which consists of beliefs, perceptions and the evaluation of outcomes [28]. However, attitude alone does not guarantee a behaviour, as behaviours are dependent on contextual factors such as availability, costs, societal trends and personal relationships [29].

2.2 Greenwashing Perception and Green Purchasing Intention

Greenwash occurs when a company misleads a consumer regarding its environmental practices or environmental benefits of a service or product [10]. Greenwashing perception is consumers' ability to identify greenwashing [32]. When a consumer recognizes a companies' increased communication regarding the environment which is coupled with an inaction to support those claims, they are discouraged from purchasing the companies products [32].

In consumer sectors, up-to-date research has shown a significant indirect negative relationship between greenwashing perception and green purchasing intention [4, 33] as well as a significant direct negative relationship [26, 30, 34]. As such, this research hypothesizes:

H1: Greenwashing perception has a significant negative impact on green purchase intention.

2.3 Greenwashing Perception and Green Advertising Skepticism

Green skepticism is when a consumer doubts or distrusts the environmental performance or benefits of a green product [22, 35]. Evidence shows that green skepticism can arise from products being mislabeled, misinterpreted, misrepresented, or questionably certified - which are all forms of greenwashing. They all showed a significant positive relationship, meaning that greenwashing perception leads to green advertising skepticism in consumers [1, 26]. As such, it is hypothesized:

H2: Greenwashing perception has a significant positive relationship on green advertising skepticism.

2.4   Green Advertising Skepticism and Green Purchasing Intention

Green advertising skepticism can be understood as consumers' cynicism towards misleading or exaggerated claims found in green advertisements [36, 37]. This can be understood as a negative cognitive component of attitude towards green product advertising [35, 38]. When a consumer doubts the environmental quality of a product they evaluate them less favourably compared to when they have no such doubt [5]. Goh and Balaji [3] found that green skepticism significantly negatively impacts green purchasing intentions and that this is supported by the mediating effects of environmental concern and subjective environmental knowledge. As such, it is hypothesized:

H3: Green advertising skepticism has a significant negative relationship on green purchasing intentions.

3   Methodology and Measurements

3.1   Data Collection and the Sample

This research paper used the questionnaire survey method to test its hypotheses. Questionnaire is delivered to phone users using push technology. As major studies in the industry before it, consumer-level was the unit of analysis [4, 30]. A question was asked to assess if the respondent had any prior experience buying green products in the past. If yes, further questions were asked to determine the extent of green purchasing habits. Questions from the survey were derived from established previous research. Ultimately, a closed-ended questionnaire consisting of demographic data (gender, age, ethnicity, education background, occupation, income per month and green purchasing habits) as well as three latent constructs (green advertising skepticism, greenwashing perception, green purchasing intention). All questionnaire items were offered on a 5-point Likert-scale ranging 1 to 5; "strongly disagree" to "strongly agree" and two statement questions offered on a "yes" or "no" answer format.

3.1.1   Introduction of Push Technology

To effectively describe how the respondents responded and to clearly understand the development process, the system environment diagram is shown in Fig. 2. The publisher first developed the preliminary questionnaire based on reference articles and specialists confirmed its feasibility before uploading the questionnaire questions to the database for storage (Green Block). Respondents received and filled out the questionnaire (Red Block), and the results were sent to the data center for downloading and subsequent data analysis by the researcher (Yellow Block).

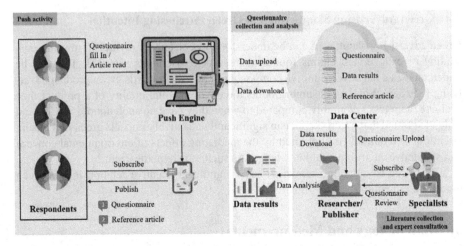

Fig. 2. System environment Framework (Color figure online)

3.1.2 The Screenshot of Delivered Content Using Push Technology

As shown in Fig. 3, the system transmits relevant information, including (a) Greenwash articles and related news, (b) questionnaire description, and (c) this survey, through push technology. Respondents subscribe to the system beforehand, and when the system receives new content, it immediately pushes the new content to respondents, and they can view the relevant information.

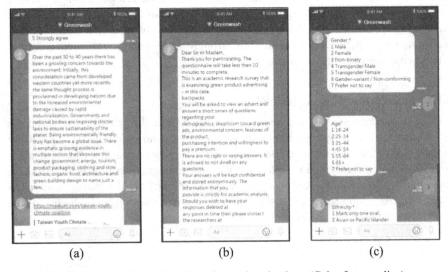

Fig. 3. Content of questionnaire using push technology (Color figure online)

3.2 Measurement of Variables

3.2.1 Green Purchasing Habits

The following section was used to establish green purchasing habits from a demographic perspective. This is not a direct variable. If the answer to question (1) was "no", they proceeded directly to the next section of the survey. If the answer to question (1) was "yes", they proceeded to answer four more questions. (1) I have purchased a green product before; (2) I have purchased a green, sustainable, or environmentally friendly backpack before; (3) I frequently buy products which are considered environmentally friendly; (4) I only exclusively purchase green products compared to traditional products; and (5) I inform myself about a product's environmental impact before purchasing it.

3.2.2 Greenwashing Perception

Greenwash is defined as "the act of misleading consumers regarding the environmental practices of a company or the environmental benefits of a product or service" [10]. Five questions are used to measure greenwashing perception. (1) This product misleads with words in its environmental features; (2) this product misleads with visuals or graphics in its environmental features; (3) this product possesses a green claim that is vague or seemingly un-provable; (4) this product overstates or exaggerates how its green functionality actually is; and (5) this product leaves out or masks important information, making the green claim sound better than it is.

3.2.3 Green Advertising Skepticism

Green advertising skepticism is defined as the consumers' cynicism towards misleading or exaggerated green advertising and its claims [36, 37] as well as the negative cognitive component of consumers' attitude toward green products and consumers' tendency not to believe the environmental claims made in advertising [38, 35]. Survey adapted from Wei, Kou, and Lee [39]. (1) Most green claims in advertising are intended to mislead rather than to inform consumers; (2) I do not believe most green claims made in advertising; and (3) I believe green claims in advertising are exaggerated; and (4) Consumers are better off without green advertisements.

3.2.4 Green Purchasing Intention

Green purchasing intention is defined as the likelihood to buy a product or service from a company based upon their reputation for being environmentally friendly [15, 16]. The survey statements were adapted from by Zhang et al. [30], in turn adapted from Abdul-Muhmin [40]and Goh and Balaji [3]. (1) I will purchase this backpack from this company because of its environmental concern; (2) I am willing to buy other backpack products from this company because of its environmental performance; and (3) I am happy to purchase any of the company's backpack products because they are environmentally friendly.

3.2.5 Control Variables

Demographic frequencies are shown in Table 1. Gender was measured and divided into four groups. Age was measured and divided into seven groups. Education was measured and divided into five groups. Income was measured and divided into five groups. Occupation was measured and divided into five groups. Income was measured and divided into seven groups. Green product purchasing behaviours were also measured and divided as a binary dummy variable. Demographic frequencies can be seen in Table 1.

Table 1. Demographics.

Gender	N	%
Male	149	60.3
Female	94	38.1
Gender-variant	1	0.4
Prefer not to say	3	1.2
Age		
18–24	59	23.9
25–34	121	49
35–44	33	13.4
45–54	15	6.1
55–64	8	3.2
65+	10	4
Prefer not to say	1	0.4
Education		
High school	23	9.3
Bachelor	133	53.8
Master	78	31.6
Doctorate	8	3.2
Prefer not to say	5	2
Occupation		
Student	51	20.6
Unemployed	15	6.1
Self-employed	37	15
Employed	133	53.8

(continued)

Table 1. (*continued*)

Gender	N	%
Retired	11	4.5
Income		
Under $20,000 NTD	38	15.4
$20,001–$45,000 NTD	37	15
$45,001–$75,000 NTD	46	18.6
$75,001–$100,000 NTD	46	18.6
$100,001–$150,000 NTD	14	5.7
$150,001 + NTD	34	13.8
Prefer not to say	32	13
Purchased a green product before		
No	58	23.5
Yes	189	76.5

4 Results

4.1 Reliability and Validity

This study examines the reliability of the constructs by examining Cronbach's alpha coefficients. As shown in Table 2, the Cronbach's alpha coefficient of green advertising skepticism, greenwashing perception, and green purchasing intentions are 0.781, 0.870, and 0.865 respectively. They all exceed the minimum level of 0.7, which indicates acceptable reliability and internal consistency.

The factor loading of each variable is above the recommended 0.6 threshold, showing acceptable structure validity of the measurements. To assess the discriminant validity the measurement of Average Variance Extracted (AVE) is used. As shown in Table 2, the square root of all construct's AVEs are higher than the correlations among all the constructs which shows the acceptance of the discriminant validity of the measurement. Additionally, the AVEs of green advertising skepticism, greenwashing perception and green purchasing intentions are 0.553, 0.606, 0.687, respectively. They all exceed the minimum level of 0.5, which indicates that the convergent validity of the measurement is acceptable.

Table 2. Validity.

Constructs	Items	Loadings	AVE	CR	Cronbach's Alpha	SQRT AVE
Green Advertising Skepticism	GAS1	0.8093	0.553	0.829	0.781	0.91
	GAS2	0.8216				

(*continued*)

Table 2. (*continued*)

Constructs	Items	Loadings	AVE	CR	Cronbach's Alpha	SQRT AVE
	GAS3	0.7683				
	GAS4	0.5409				
Greenwashing Perceptions	GWP1	0.8211	0.606	0.885	0.870	0.94
	GWP2	0.7874				
	GWP3	0.7750				
	GWP4	0.7832				
	GWP5	0.7228				
Green Purchasing Intentions	GPI1	0.8116	0.687	0.868	0.865	0.93
	GPI2	0.8445				
	GPI3	0.8300				

4.2 Correlation Analysis

The means, standard deviations and correlation matrix are calculated which can be seen in Table 3. The data suggests that greenwashing perception is significantly negatively correlated with green purchasing intentions ($p < 0.01$). Green advertising skepticism is significantly positively correlated with greenwashing perception ($p < 0.01$) and significantly negatively correlated with green purchasing intentions ($p < 0.01$).

Table 3. Descriptive statistics and correlation analysis

No.	Variables	Mean	SD	1	2	3
		Correlations				
1	Green Advertising Skepticism	2.98	0.80	1		
2	Greenwashing Perception	3.18	0.88	.48**	1	
3	Green Purchasing Intention	2.85	0.93	−23**	−38**	1
Note:	** Correlation is significant at the 0.01 level (2-tailed) * Correlation is significant at the 0.05 level (2-tailed)					

4.3 Hypothesis Testing

Initially, multiple linear regression was used to assess the research question. Tests were conducted to evaluate the prediction of the dependent variable, green purchasing intentions, from the independent variables, greenwashing perceptions, and green advertising skepticism. The path of greenwashing perception toward green purchasing intentions was negatively significant (B = -0.396, t (236) = -6.57, p < 0.01, R^2 = 0.212). The path of greenwashing perception on green advertising skepticism is positively significant (B = 0.463, t (236) = 7.924, p < 0.01, R^2 = 0.259). The path of green advertising skepticism towards green purchasing intentions was negatively significant (B = -0.235, t (236) = -3.731, p < 0.01, R^2 = 0.119) (Table 4).

Table 4. Outcome of hypotheses.

Hypotheses	Results
H1: Greenwashing perception has a significant negative impact on green purchase intention	Supported
H2: Greenwashing perception has a significant positive relationship on green advertising skepticism	Supported
H3: Green advertising skepticism has a significant negative relationship on green purchasing intentions	Supported

5 Conclusion

Although past research has shown that higher greenwashing perceptions lead to lower green purchasing intentions, there has been limited research incorporating green advertising skepticism in an effort to explain this relationship. This research has generated the following findings regarding overall green purchasing intentions and green advertising skepticism in the contexts of greenwashing.

First, we have extended evidence that greenwashing perceptions significantly directly negatively affect green purchasing intentions [26, 30]. In other terms, the more a consumer is able to perceive a product as greenwashed, the less likely they are to purchase it. This is important as it suggests that a consumer who can identify a greenwashed product knows that it is not as beneficial to the environment as is claimed, and therefore chooses to forgo purchasing the, potentially harmful, product. It shows that consumers care about the green quality of the products they purchase.

Second, we found that the more a consumer perceives greenwashing the more skeptical they are towards green advertising. These findings concur with previous research and add more value to a scarcely explored relationship [26, 3]. This suggests that a consumer who is highly skeptical of green advertisements is less likely to have strong purchasing intentions for that green product.

The findings from the direct relationship between green advertising skepticism and green purchasing intentions suggest that higher skepticism results in lower green purchase intentions. As such, it is in a company's best interest to avoid increasing green skepticism towards it's adverts as it reduces product judgements, but also to its brand/organization. This can be achieved by implementing believable and truthful green adverts and not participating in greenwashing activities, such as any of the seven greenwashing sins. Indeed, consumers are becoming more aware of greenwashing as the demand for green products grows which has naturally increased their skepticism and intent to pay attention to foul marketing strategies [14]. Here, it is important to acknowledge that skepticism is not a permanent state and opinions and attitudes can be changed when provided with clear and convincing evidence [35]. Therefore, we recommend that a company disclose all the relevant information pertaining to environmental performance at all marketing interaction steps the consumer experiences (e.g., manufacturing, product packaging, shipping and be clear on their ecommerce website) in order to reach a truthful green position. In sum, the recommendations here should help managers reduce consumer green advertising skepticism on current products and impede further green advertising skepticism on future products.

References

1. Leonidou, C.N., Skarmeas, D.: Gray shades of green: causes and consequences of green skepticism. J. Bus. Ethics **144**(2), 401–415 (2015). https://doi.org/10.1007/s10551-015-2829-4
2. Chen, Y.-S.: The driver of green innovation and green image – green core competence. J. Bus. Ethics **81**(3), 531–543 (2008)
3. Goh, S.K., Balaji, M.S.: Linking green skepticism to green purchase behavior. J. Clean. Prod. **131**, 629–638 (2016)
4. Chen, Y.-S., Chang, C.-H.: greenwash and green trust: the mediation effects of green consumer confusion and green perceived risk. J. Bus. Ethics **114**(3), 489–500 (2013)
5. Chang, C.-H.: The influence of corporate environmental ethics on competitive advantage: the mediation role of green innovation. J. Bus. Ethics **104**(3), 361–370 (2011)
6. Kim, M., Jang, Y.-C., Lee, S.: Application of delphi-AHP methods to select the priorities of WEEE for recycling in a waste management decision-making tool. J. Environ. Manage. **128**, 941–948 (2013)
7. Guo, R., Tao, L., Li, C.B., Wang, T.: A path analysis of greenwashing in a trust crisis among Chinese energy companies: the role of brand legitimacy and brand loyalty. J. Bus. Ethics **140**(3), 523–536 (2015). https://doi.org/10.1007/s10551-015-2672-7
8. Delmas, M.A., Burbano, V.C.: The drivers of greenwashing. Calif. Manage. Rev. **54**(1), 64–87 (2011)
9. Dahl, R.: Green washing: Do you know what you're buying? (1552–9924 (Electronic))
10. Parguel, B., Benoît-Moreau, F., Larceneux, F.: How sustainability ratings might deter 'greenwashing': a closer look at ethical corporate communication. J. Bus. Ethics **102**(1), 15–28 (2011)
11. Grimmer, M., Bingham, T.: Company environmental performance and consumer purchase intentions. J. Bus. Res. **66**(10), 1945–1953 (2013)
12. Lyon, T.P., Maxwell, J.W.: Greenwash: corporate environmental disclosure under threat of audit. J. Econ. Manage. Strategy **20**(1), 3–41 (2011)
13. Chen, Y.S., Chang, C.H.: Enhance green purchase intentions. Manage. Decis. **50**(3), 502–520 (2012)
14. Horiuchi, R., Schuchard, R., Shea, L., Townsend, S.: Understanding and preventing greenwash: A business guide Futerra Sustainability Communications London (2009)
15. Netemeyer, R.G., Maxham, J.G., Pullig, C.: Conflicts in the work-family interface: links to job stress, customer service employee performance, and customer purchase intent. J. Mark. **69**(2), 130–143 (2005)
16. Newton, J.D., et al.: Environmental concern and environmental purchase intentions: the mediating role of learning strategy. J. Bus. Res. **68**(9), 1974–1981 (2015)

17. Roe, B., et al.: US consumers' willingness to pay for green electricity. Energy Policy **29**(11), 917–925 (2001)
18. Lyon, T.P., Montgomery, A.W.: The means and end of greenwash. Organ. Environ. **28**(2), 223–249 (2015)
19. Obermiller, C., Spangenberg, E.R.: Development of a scale to measure consumer skepticism toward advertising. J. Consum. Psychol. **7**(2), 159–186 (1998)
20. Rosen, G.: Skepticism about moral responsibility. Philos. Perspect. **18**, 295–313 (2004)
21. Taber, C.S., Lodge, M.: Motivated skepticism in the evaluation of political beliefs. Am. J. Polit. Sci. **50**(3), 755–769 (2006)
22. Obermiller, C., Spangenberg, E., MacLachlan, D.L.: Ad skepticism: the consequences of disbelief. J. Advert. **34**(3), 7–17 (2005)
23. Kim, Y.J., Lee, W.-N.: Overcoming consumer skepticism in cause-related marketing: the effects of corporate social responsibility and donation size claim objectivity. J. Promot. Manage. **15**(4), 465–483 (2009)
24. Vlachos, P.A., et al.: Containing cause-related marketing skepticism: a comparison across donation frame types. Corp. Reput. Rev. **19**(1), 4–21 (2016)
25. do Paço, A.M.F., Reis, R.: Factors Affecting Skepticism toward Green Advertising. J. Advertising, **41**(4), 147–155 2012
26. Nguyen, T.T., et al.: Greenwash and green purchase intention: the mediating role of green skepticism. Sustainability **11**(9), 2653 (2019)
27. Pomering, A., Johnson, L.W.: Advertising corporate social responsibility initiatives to communicate corporate image. Corp. Commun. Int. J. **14**(4), 420–439 (2009)
28. Guagnano, G.A., Stern, P.C., Dietz, T.: Influences on attitude-behavior relationships: a natural experiment with curbside recycling. Environ. Behav. **27**(5), 699–718 (1995)
29. Feldmann, C., Hamm, U.: Consumers' perceptions and preferences for local food: A review. Food Qual. Prefer. **40**, 152–164 (2015)
30. Zhang, L., et al.: The influence of greenwashing perception on green purchasing intentions: the mediating role of green word-of-mouth and moderating role of green concern. J. Clean. Prod. **187**, 740–750 (2018)
31. Ajzen, I.: Attitudes, personality, and behavior. Attitudes, personality, and behavior. 1988, Homewood, IL, US: Dorsey Press. xiv, 175-xiv, 175
32. Paul, J., Modi, A., Patel, J.: Predicting green product consumption using theory of planned behavior and reasoned action. J. Retail. Consum. Serv. **29**, 123–134 (2016)
33. Akturan, U.: How does greenwashing affect green branding equity and purchase intention? an empirical research. Mark. Intell. Plan. **36**(7), 809–824 (2018)
34. Tarabieh, S.: The impact of greenwash practices over green purchase intention: the mediating effects of green confusion, green perceived risk, and green trust. Manage. Sci. Lett. **11**, 451–464 (2020)
35. Mohr, L.A., EroĞLu, D., Ellen, P.S.: The Development and testing of a measure of skepticism toward environmental claims in marketers' communications. J. Consum. Aff. **32**(1), 30–55 (1998)
36. Ríos, F., et al.: Improving attitudes toward brands with environmental associations: an experimental approach. J. Consum. Mark. **23**, 26 (2006)
37. Vermeir, I., Verbeke, W.: Sustainable food consumption: exploring the consumer "attitude – behavioral intention" gap. J. Agric. Environ. Ethics **19**(2), 169–194 (2006)
38. Manuel, E., Youn, S., Yoon, D.: Functional matching effect in CRM: moderating roles of perceived message quality and skepticism. J. Mark. Commun. **20**(6), 397–418 (2014)
39. Wei, C.-F., et al.: Toward sustainable livelihoods: investigating the drivers of purchase behavior for green products. Bus. Strateg. Environ. **26**(5), 626–639 (2017)
40. Abdul-Muhmin, A.G.: Explaining consumers' willingness to be environmentally friendly. Int. J. Consum. Stud. **31**(3), 237–247 (2007)

A Real-Time Streaming Application for License Plate Recognition Using OpenALPR

Hsi-Jen Chen[1], Halim Fathoni[2,3], Zheng-Yao Wang[1], Kai-Yu Lien[1], and Chao-Tung Yang[1,4](✉)

[1] Department of Computer Science, Tunghai University, Taichung, Taiwan
{huangcy,ctyang}@thu.edu.tw
[2] Department Industrial Engineering and Enterprise Information, Tunghai University, Taichung, Taiwan (R.O.C.)
fathoni@polinela.ac.id, D07330701@thu.edu.tw
[3] Department Ekonomi dan Bisnis, Politeknik Negeri Lampung, Bandar Lampung, Indonesia
[4] Research Center for Smart Sustainable Circular Economy, Tunghai University, Taichung, Taiwan

Abstract. Image recognition has been widely used in many places in our life. For license plate recognition, it can replace the manual inspection and registration of vehicles in the parking lot to complete automation, and it can also facilitate the management of the place to track the entry and exit of vehicles. In this implementation, we use OpenALPR and Tesseract to realize the basis of image recognition, use Python to connect the real-time image of the camera at the entrance of Tunghai University, and connect the database to compare the license plate and build a webpage to display it, so as to help the school traffic security personnel to be able to It is more convenient to judge whether the current vehicle entering the campus is a qualified vehicle, and to solve the traffic jam at the school gate during peak hours.

Keywords: License plate recognition · Image recognition · OpenALPR · Tesseract · Real-time streaming

1 Introduction

1.1 Research Background and Motivation

Image recognition is a very important part in the field of artificial intelligence applications, especially the use of artificial intelligence and machine learning in cooperative processing. Image recognition is actually quite widely used, from basic handwritten text recognition, object recognition, face recognition, even automated image description and driverless cars are applications that integrate deep learning and image recognition. In addition, applications in this area are bound to be widely used in the future, replacing human visual judgment with software, and even surpassing human beings. This is indispensable foundation for future technology.

© ICST Institute for Computer Sciences, Social Informatics and Telecommunications Engineering 2023
Published by Springer Nature Switzerland AG 2023. All Rights Reserved
D.-J. Deng et al. (Eds.): SGIoT 2022, LNICST 497, pp. 368–381, 2023.
https://doi.org/10.1007/978-3-031-31275-5_33

With the advancement of network transmission technology, the application of the Internet is no longer limited to the transmission of text or pictures. The maturity of the interactive multimedia network combining sound and video is an inevitable trend. A large amount of multimedia information is rapidly developed on the Internet by a new transmission technology called "streaming technology". In addition, compared to the traditional multimedia information stored on the Internet, it must be downloaded to the local computer before it can be played. The streaming technology allows the client to download a small amount of data in advance to start playing, saving a lot of waiting time; another advantage of the streaming technology is the use of the client buffer memory, so that the data does not need to be physically stored, directly It is read and played from the buffer memory and discarded, which effectively saves the local disk storage space. Based on the vigorous development of the two, we decided to combine the two [1] as the implementation goal.

1.2 Research Purposes

The license plate recognition system has been used in many places to control the entry and exit of vehicles, but schools still use manual methods to do this work, so I hope this implementation will help schools to complete their homework in a more efficient way. In this article, the license plate recognition application will be implemented, and the recognition rate is expected to reach the system on the market, so that the implementation results have commercial value.

1.3 Area of Research

This topic uses the existing open source suite OpenALPR as the main license plate recognition suite, and uses the Tesseract optical character recognition engine to train the model to improve the recognition accuracy, and integrates this system with real-time streaming, web pages, and databases to make a set a complete license plate recognition system that can be practically applied in daily life. Figure 1 shows the structure of the research process.

2 Related Literature Review

2.1 OpenALPR

OpenALPR is an automatic license plate recognition library written in C++. The software is distributed in commercial and open source versions. OpenALPR uses OpenCV and Tesseract OCR library. It can run as a command-line utility, standalone library, or as a background process. The software also integrates with video management systems such as Milestone XProtect.

2.2 RTSP

Live Streaming Protocol is a network application protocol designed for use by entertainment and communications systems to control streaming media servers. This protocol is used to establish and control media dialogue between terminals. Figure 2 shows the operational architecture of RTSP.

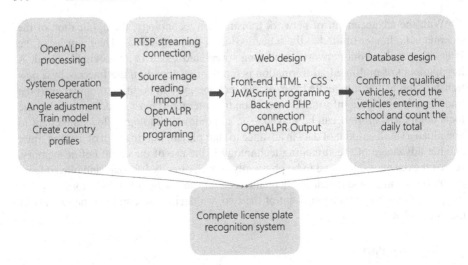

Fig. 1. Research Process Architecture Diagram.

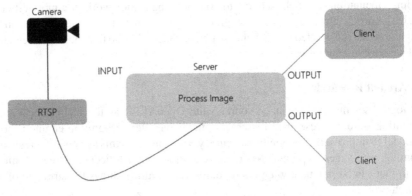

Fig. 2. RTSP Architecture Diagram.

2.3 Image Recognition

The visual image detection technology is to input the image into the analysis instrument for image analysis, especially widely used in the image monitoring system.

2.3.1 OpenCV

OpenCV is a cross-platform computer vision library for developing real-time image processing, computer vision and pattern recognition programs. Figure 3 shows the operation architecture of OpenCV.

2.4 OCR

Optical character recognition refers to the process of analyzing and identifying image files of text data to obtain text and layout information. Input has different storage formats and different compression methods for different image formats. Currently, there are OpenCV, CxImage, etc.

2.4.1 Tesseract

Tesseract is an OCR engine that supports multiple operating systems and is considered one of the most accurate open source OCR engines. Figure 4 shows the Tesseract architecture diagram.

Fig. 3. OpenCV Architecture Diagram.   **Fig. 4.** Tesseract Architecture Diagram.

3 Thematic Research and Development

3.1 Overall Development Process

The system architecture is shown in Fig. 5. Our overall production process and software setup are carried out on Ubuntu, using the monitor stream at the gate of Tunghai University as the identification object, and the license plate identification using the open source software OpenALPR for development, and then establishing a database to store the license plates The relevant information is compared with the identification result, and finally a webpage is created to display the identification result. Figure 6 shows the operation flow chart of the whole system.

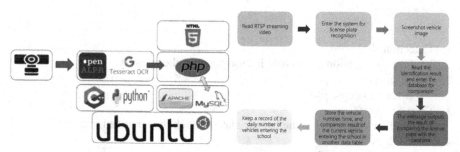

Fig. 5. System Architecture Diagram.   **Fig. 6.** Flow Chart of the Whole System Operation.

3.2 Research Methods

We use OpenALPR for license plate recognition. OpenALPR is a license plate recognition system written in C++. In the system, images are detected, binarized, character analysis, license plate edge search, license plate correction, and character cutting. The results are imported into Tesseract OCR for identification. The overall operation process of OpenALPR is shown in Fig. 7.

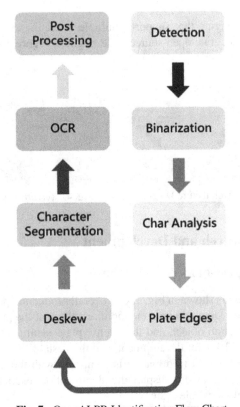

Fig. 7. OpenALPR Identification Flow Chart.

1. Detection
   Find the location of possible license plates in the imagery
2. Binarization
   Binarize license plate
3. Char Analysis
   Find the characters in the license plate through the binarized image
4. Plate Edges
   Find the border of the license plate
5. Deskew
   Re-output the size and orientation based on the license plate frame found

6. Character Segmentation
   Split out each character in the license plate
7. OCR
   Identify each character and output possible results and confidence
8. Post Processing
   Build a list of high-probability license plates based on the output of OCR

3.2.1 Dentification Research

During the development process, we first studied some operating instructions of the OpenALPR system and the parts that allow us to perform recognition optimization, and then we began to study some problems of image recognition. Test how to make the system output the highest accuracy and highest confidence after identification. In order to adjust the content of the system to suit our physical environment, we make many adjustments, the first is to adjust the angle, OpenALPR almost completely detects images that have not been adjusted at all angles. There are not any license plates, so we must first adjust a good angle and input the parameters into OpenALPR. After this step, most of the license plates can be recognized. Then, in order to improve the detection, we have to change the license plate format to Taiwan's data [2, 3], but since there is no Taiwan license plate format data in OpenALPR, we create the Taiwan license plate data by ourselves, let the system recognize the license plate better. After the completion, it is found that there is still a problem that has not been solved. Using the ready-made model to identify, the number 3 of the license plate is easily recognized as 5, and the new license plate is the most serious. Therefore, we trained the local license plate model [4], collect about 200 Taiwan license plates (as shown in Fig. 8), make the license plate binary and segment each character [5], and then compare the license plate set we trained with the Internet Open source license plate set integration, using train-ocr to train Taiwan's.traineddata, the test results can be as accurate as 99% in a good environment.

3.2.2 Implement Integration

When establishing a streaming connection, because we are using an open source version, we cannot directly import RTSP live streaming images into OpenALPR for identification. Therefore, we have studied some ways to deal with this problem, and finally found the most efficient and delay. The lowest method, after the above research and implementation, we can achieve low latency and high accuracy. In addition, a website is also established to display the results of license plate recognition. It is produced through HTML, CSS, JAVAScript, PHP, and Apache. The real-time streaming image of the gate will be output on the webpage. When a vehicle enters and undergoes license plate recognition, the recognition result can be displayed. A pop-up window at the top of a webpage.

3.3 Instructions

In the following, we will introduce the method of making a complete license plate recognition system to improve the accuracy rate and the integration of other systems in detail, which are mainly divided into training model, angle adjustment, country establishment, license plate format, license plate output, real-time streaming connection, production Websites, build databases.

3.3.1   Train the Model

OpenALPR uses Tesseract as OCR, and the way we make the model of Tesseract is to use Train-OCR. First, each license plate collected is binarized (as shown in Fig. 9), and each character is divided and definition, and finally integrate all the segmented image files into a large.tif image file (as shown in Fig. 10), and train the image file and box file to Train-OCR to get the training result the.traineddata file.

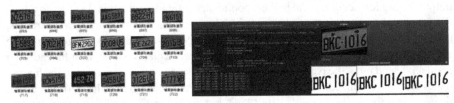

Fig. 8. Crop the Collected Vehicle Photos into Pure License Plates.

Fig. 9. Define the Characters in the License Plate.

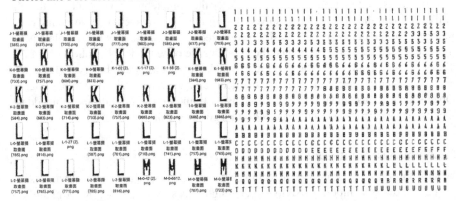

Fig. 10. Characters are Cut and Integrated into a.tif Image File.

3.3.2   Angle Adjustment

OpenALPR provides an instruction to adjust the angle. After inputting the image of the field to be adjusted (as shown in Fig. 11), you can use the pop-up window interface to make adjustments. After adjustment, parameters can be generated (as shown in Fig. 12). After entering the corresponding file and re-make, it can automatically adjust the image of the imported image recognized by the system. In our test, it can greatly improve the detection degree of the license plate compared with the original image.

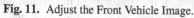

Fig. 11. Adjust the Front Vehicle Image.   **Fig. 12.** Adjusted Vehicle Image.

3.3.3 The Establishment of National

In the current version of OpenALPR, license plate information is provided for the United States, the European Union, Singapore and other countries. By default, the system will use the national data of the United States for license plate recognition, but if you want to improve license plate detection, you can use your own However, there is currently no national data for Taiwan [6]. The function of the national data is that after the license plate recognition system reads the image, it will identify the length and width of the license plate, the length and width of the license plate characters, the px of the license plate, and the characters of the license plate. px, the combination of characters and lengths in the license plate, etc., if it does not conform to the set national format, even if there is a license plate in the image, the system will still judge that there is no license plate. The output format conforms to the license plate of Taiwan, which can save the system from outputting some wrong outputs. At the same time, it can also identify the license plate in the most appropriate position, and it will not waste resources to calculate some images when the state is very bad as soon as the license plate is scanned.

3.3.4 License Plate Format

Each country's license plate has a different format. In Taiwan, we have the first two characters in English, the last four in numbers, and the first three in English and the last four in Chinese, and so on. So we established In order to obtain the license plate format from Taiwan, the recognition result must conform to the content in our document (as shown in Fig. 13), and the result will be output.

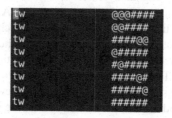

Fig. 13. Set Taiwanese Self-use (Rental) Passenger Car License Plate Style.

3.3.5 License Plate Output

We use Python to output the result of license plate recognition. The reason for this part is that each frame will output the result of license plate recognition once when recognizing dynamic images, Or sometimes it may be because the angle of the car is too oblique when it first enters the recognition area or when it finally leaves the recognition area, resulting in different outputs. Therefore, we compare the recognition output of the previous license plate with the output of the next license plate recognition. If the similarity between the previous output and the next output is more than 0.7, it will be regarded as the same car, and only the license plate with the highest confidence after recognition will be output., if the similarity of the license plate before and after the comparison is below 0.7, it will be regarded as a different car, and the license plate of the next car will be output and entered into the confidence comparison of the next car.

3.3.6 Live Streaming Connection

Because we are using the OpenALPR open source version, the RTSP signal cannot be directly identified to the system. To connect OpenALPR to the real-time image, the RTSP signal needs to be converted into MJPEG using FFmpeg and FFserver before it can be read by OpenALPR. However, in our test results, we found that this method will have a delay of more than ten seconds, so later we switched to using Python to read our OpenALPR suite. Using this method, we can directly let the open source version of OpenALPR receive RTSP signals. License plate recognition, the delay time is also greatly reduced.

3.3.7 Web Production

We use the front-end three Musketeers HTML, CSS, JavaScript to make the front-end of the web page, and the back-end uses PHP, and connects JavaScript and PHP through AJAX, so that the recognized license plate results are transmitted from the back-end to the front-end, We use the webpage to display the real-time video streaming screen. After the vehicle is identified by the license plate recognition system, the result of the identification of the license plate will be displayed in the floating window at the top of the webpage (Fig. 14), the light signal is connected to the database after license plate recognition to determine whether the vehicle is a qualified vehicle that has applied for admission to the school. The control of the light signal is set by using the return value of the database. When the recognized vehicle is a school vehicle. The database will return TRUE when it does not match, and it will return FALSE if it does not match. By using Python to capture the returned value, control the change of the light number. The light number is connected to the database after the license plate recognition to determine whether the vehicle has applied for admission to the school. For qualified vehicles, the green light will be on if the license plate matches, and the red light will be displayed when the license plate does not match. However, after the school traffic security personnel tested and used it, they believed that the output of the font color is more intuitive. Therefore, we will remove the light and change it to the desired interface of the traffic security team. In this way, traffic security personnel can more quickly and easily determine whether a vehicle needs to be intercepted.

Fig. 14. The Old Version Webpage Shows the Output Screen.

3.3.8 Build a Database

We use MySQL to build a database, and put in the license plate numbers that are qualified to be registered in the school. In addition, the license plate information entering the campus on the day and the number of vehicles entering the campus each day, including the time and identification results, will be recorded, which can facilitate management personnel to check the situation of vehicles entering the campus.

4 Implementation Results

4.1 Implementation Notes

In the implementation of this project, the monitor screen at the gate of Tunghai University is used as the subject of the implementation, and OpenALPR is used as the license plate recognition system to identify the vehicles entering the gate, and the output is compared with the license plate data in the database to verify the result. Output on the web. Authorized personnel are not limited to specific devices when using, as long as the device has Internet access, users can view the results of image recognition through the web at any place and at any time.

4.2 Implementation Display and Identification Data

After we used the gate of Tunghai University to test through real-time video streaming and pre-recorded videos at various times throughout the day, 261 of the 275 vehicles tested could be correctly identified [7], and about three of the remaining erroneous parts were identified by a few characters. Most of them are not recognized due to the high speed of the car, so almost all of them can be accurately recognized when using our system at a speed of about 20 km per hour [8, 9]. Below we provide some pictures of the test results. Figure 15 shows the background output of the OpenALPR system. Figure 16 shows the identification results displayed on the web page. Figure 17 shows the identification output at night.

4.2.1 License Plate Recognition System Background Interface

We use Python to import the OpenALPR package we made, connect the real-time video stream at the gate of Tunghai University, and use Python to judge whether it is the same car and select the license plate with the highest confidence for the result of license plate recognition. The output will be displayed on the terminal.

Fig. 15. Implementation Demonstration 1—Background Terminal Output Screen.

4.2.2 Display Styles on Web Pages

The actual webpage screen is as follows. After the vehicle enters and is identified by the system, it will take a screenshot of the current screen, and use a pop-up window at the top of the webpage to display the license plate identification result. If the result of the comparison with the database is that the school vehicle font will be displayed in black font, otherwise it will be displayed in red font.

4.2.3 Night Test

Many license plate recognition systems on the market need to install a strong light on the license plate at night because of the brightness problem. We have also suggested installing it at the school gate, but the traffic security team is afraid that the light will interfere with the driver and cannot install it for safety reasons., at the beginning, our system could not successfully identify without a training model, so we improved by increasing the training set. After testing, the correct vehicle number can be recognized at night, even when there is a locomotive, pedestrian interference or from behind the vehicle.

4.2.4 School Vehicle Record

If the traffic security personnel want to inquire about the information of the vehicles entering the school, they can click the "RECORD" button at the top of the webpage to

Fig. 16. Implementation Demonstration 2—The Actual Web Page Displays the Output Screen.

Fig. 17. Implementation Demonstration 3—Night Recognition.

view the database (as shown in Fig. 18), which stores all the recognized license plates, entry time and whether it is a school vehicle. In order to prevent the database from becoming too numerous, the content of the database will be refreshed every day. If you want to view a vehicle, you can also use the search box above. Entering the car number can only display the information of the car (as shown in Fig. 19), allowing managers to quickly make inquiries. In addition, you can also click the "COUNT" button at the top of the web page to record the statistics of vehicles entering the school every day (as shown in Fig. 20). When organizing activities, it is convenient for schools to estimate the number of vehicles in the school in advance for scheduling and adjustment of personnel or vehicles.

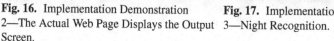

車牌	時間	結果
TDT5861	2022-10-7-00-12	0
AXY6123	2022-10-7-00-12	0
BLP8162	2022-10-7-00-13	0
TDQ0132	2022-10-7-00-13	0
TDT5860	2022-10-7-00-20	0
CP7581	2022-10-7-00-28	0
BHW5671	2022-10-7-00-29	0
AT6016	2022-10-7-00-33	0
ATW6016	2022-10-7-00-33	0

Fig. 18. Implementation Demonstration 4 - Viewing the Information of the Vehicle Entering the School through the Website.

車牌	時間	結果
BLP8162	2022-10-7-00-13	0

Fig. 19. Implementation Demonstration 5—Searching for Information on Enrollment of Specified Vehicles.

DATE	COUN
2022-5-9	1314
2022-5-10	1346
2022-5-11	1431
2022-5-12	1374
2022-5-13	1476
2022-5-14	843
2022-5-15	1163
2022-5-16	1130

Fig. 20. Implementation Demonstration 6—Daily Entry Vehicle Statistics.

5 Conclusion

5.1 In Conclusion

The result of the implementation is the combination of license plate recognition and live streaming. The license plate recognition rate can reach a very high recognition rate in both day and night, and the recognition time is nearly instant, achieving low latency. The light output on the webpage will judge whether the vehicle currently entering the campus is a qualified vehicle according to the license plate information in the database. The result is indicated by different colored lights, green qualified vehicles, red unqualified vehicles, intuitive and easy to understand, convenient for authorization personnel use. And establish another table to count the vehicles entering the school, make the application of the whole license plate recognition system more complete, reduce a lot of manual inspection time and save human resources at the same time, and bring relief solutions to traffic jams during peak hours.

5.2 Features of This System

There are some differences between this license plate recognition system and the license plate recognition system of the general parking lot. Generally, the parking lot only needs to store the vehicle information in the database after the vehicle enters. Our database has a list of approved vehicles that can enter. And when the vehicle enters, the information of the vehicle is stored in another table for record; in the identification part, the vehicle needs to be stationary when the identification is performed in the general parking lot, and ours can be identified when the vehicle is moving; the camera installed in the general parking lot The distance between the location and the license plate is also very close. At night, there is strong light near the license plate to increase the detection degree. However, the environment we made does not allow us to have this condition, but we can also make a good accuracy rate.

Acknowledgement. This research was supported in part by the National Science and Technology Council (NSTC), Taiwan R.O.C. grants numbers 111-2622-E-029-003, 111-2811-E-029-001, 111-2621-M-029-004, and 110-2221-E-029-020-MY3.

References

1. Desai, G.G., Bartakke, P.P.: Real-time implementation of Indian license plate recognition system. In: 2018 IEEE Punecon. College of Engineering, Pune (2018)

2. Handrik, M., Handriková, J., Vaško, M.: Parallel image signal processing in a distributed car plate recognition system. In: 2020 New Trends in Signal Processing (NTSP), University of Žilina (2020)

3. Prabhu, B.S., Kalambur, S., Sitaram, D.: Recognition of Indian license plate number from live stream videos. In: 2017 International Conference on Advances in Computing, Communications and Informatics (ICACCI), pp. 2359–2365, PES University (2017)

4. Tjandra, L.O., Nugroho, S., Utomo, D.: Electronic road pricing system prototype. In: 2016 International Seminar on Application for Technology of Information and Communication (ISemantic), pp. 126–129, Satya Wacana Christian University (2016)

5. Khurat, A., Siriphun, N., Saingthong, J., Sriwiphasathit, J.: An open-source based automatic car detection system using IoT. In: 2019 16th International Joint Conference on Computer Science and Software Engineering (JCSSE), pp. 283–288, Mahidol University (2019)

6. Lin, N.H., Aung, Y.L., Khaing, W.K.: Automatic vehicle license plate recognition system for smart transportation. In: 2018 IEEE International Conference on Internet of Things and Intelligence System (IOTAIS), Yangon Technological University, Singapore University of Technology and Design (2018)

7. Bui, V., Bui, M.: A truly smart airport parking solution. In: 2019 IEEE Asia-Pacific Conference on Computer Science and Data Engineering (CSDE), Southern Cross University, Royal Melbourne Institute of Technology (2019)

8. Hidayatno, A., Nurhediyanto, E., Syafei, W.A.: Implementation of OpenALPR for detecting vehicle license plate in smart toll gate. In: 2021 8th International Conference on Information Technology, Computer and Electrical Engineering (ICITACEE), Diponegoro University (2021)

9. Mahankali, S., Kabbin, S.V., Nidagundi, S., Srinath, R.: Identification of illegal garbage dumping with video analytics. In: 2018 International Conference on Advances in Computing, Communications and Informatics (ICACCI), Bengaluru, India (2018)

Author Index

© ICST Institute for Computer Sciences, Social Informatics and Telecommunications Engineering 2023
Published by Springer Nature Switzerland AG 2023. All Rights Reserved
D.-J. Deng et al. (Eds.): SGIoT 2022, LNICST 497, pp. 383–384, 2023.
https://doi.org/10.1007/978-3-031-31275-5

Printed in the United States
by Baker & Taylor Publisher Services